DEATH VALLEY IN '49

A California Legacy Book

Santa Clara University and Heyday Books are pleased to publish the California Legacy series, vibrant and relevant writings drawn from California's past and present.

Santa Clara University—founded in 1851 on the site of the eighth of California's original 21 missions—is the oldest institution of higher learning in the state. A Jesuit institution, it is particularly aware of its contribution to California's cultural heritage and its responsibility to preserve and celebrate that heritage.

Heyday Books, founded in 1974, specializes in critically acclaimed books on California literature, history, natural history, and ethnic studies.

Books in the California Legacy series appear as anthologies, single author collections, reprints of important books, and original works. Taken together, these volumes bring readers a new perspective on California's cultural life, a perspective that honors diversity and finds great pleasure in the eloquence of human expression.

Series editor: Terry Beers
Publisher: Malcolm Margolin
Advisory committee: Stephen Becker, William Deverell, Peter Facione, Charles Faulhaber, David Fine, Steven Gilbar, Dana Gioia, Ron Hansen, Gerald Haslam, Robert Hass, Jack Hicks, Timothy Hodson, James Houston, Jeanne Wakatsuki Houston, Maxine Hong Kingston, Frank LaPena, Ursula K. Le Guin, Jeff Lustig, Tillie Olsen, Ishmael Reed, Alan Rosenus, Robert Senkewicz, Gary Snyder, Kevin Starr, Richard Walker, Alice Waters, Jennifer Watts, Al Young.

Thanks to the English Department at Santa Clara University and to Regis McKenna for their support of the California Legacy series.

DEATH VALLEY
IN '49 ⌒

WILLIAM LEWIS MANLY

EDITED BY LEROY AND JEAN JOHNSON
FOREWORD BY PATRICIA NELSON LIMERICK

SANTA CLARA UNIVERSITY, SANTA CLARA, CALIFORNIA
HEYDAY BOOKS, BERKELEY, CALIFORNIA

Library of Congress Cataloging-in-Publication Data

Manly, William Lewis, b. 1820.
  Death Valley in '49 / William Lewis Manly ; edited by LeRoy and Jean Johnson ; foreword by Patricia Limerick.
      p. cm. — (A California legacy book)
Originally published: San Jose, Calif. : Pacific Tree and Vine Co., 1894.
  ISBN 1-890771-47-3 (pbk.)
  1. Manly, William Lewis, b. 1820. 2. Death Valley (Calif. and Nev.)—History. 3. California—Gold discoveries. 4. Overland journeys to the Pacific. 5. Pioneers—California—Biography. 6. California—Biography. I. Johnson, LeRoy, 1937- II. Johnson, Jean, 1937- III. Title. IV. Series.
  F868.D2 M283 2001
  979.4'87—dc21
                                            2001005528

Cover art courtesy of Circa:Art
Cover/interior design: Rebecca LeGates
Printing and binding: Publishers Press, Salt Lake City, UT

Orders, inquiries, and correspondence should be addressed to:
      Heyday Books
      P. O. Box 9145, Berkeley, CA 94709
      (510) 549-3564, Fax (510) 549-1889
      www.heydaybooks.com

Printed in the United States of America

10 9 8 7 6 5 4 3 2 1

CONTENTS

The Price of Gold: Remembering William Lewis Manly

TRAVELING FOR PERSONAL IMPROVEMENT

IMAGINE THIS SCENARIO: a rich person tells me that he believes, as I do, that reading the right books could help Americans reconsider our habit of putting the self first and consuming the lion's share of the world's resources. After having become rich from some of America's bad habits, this man has undergone a kind of Augustinian conversion and now plans to distribute free copies of a book to people who are waiting to board airplanes. The philanthropist's theory is that today's frequent flight delays and cancellations offer him a fine entrée to an audience looking for a way to pass the time, an opportunity that will be squandered if people turn to the usual offerings of airport bookstores; as they sit in the waiting area or on the tarmac, passengers might as well be widening the range of their souls.

Miraculously, the philanthropist is going to let me choose the book.

And so it comes to pass that every airplane holds twenty or thirty people reading William Lewis Manly's *Death Valley in '49*. The flight attendants are the first to see the results. Impatience and crabbiness die down as passengers consider the extraordinary amount of time that cross-country travel once required. An hour's delay seems a minor affliction when you are reading about people walking step by step, day after day, through Death Valley. But the flight attendants are even more struck by the newly generous behavior of their passengers. With the examples of William Lewis Manly and John Rogers so much on their minds, passengers rise instantly to help elderly and disabled people into their seats; they discover who among them is traveling to a sickbed or funeral, and they offer comfort and consolation; they help beleaguered mothers distract and entertain their shrieking toddlers and babies. And then the trend moves out from the airports to highways, city streets, office buildings, and neighborhoods. "What would William Lewis Manly do in this situation?" becomes the question everyone asks herself or himself. The results brighten the world.

Journey through Consequences

Hearing the news of California gold, William Lewis Manly and his friend Asabel Bennett decided to leave Wisconsin in search of their fortunes in the mines. Bennett took his wife and three children. Confusion over the place of departure separated Manly from his friends for a time; he ended up traveling across the Plains with a group of men that included a hardy fellow named John Rogers. Mistreated by the man who employed them as drivers, these men attempted to travel by boat down the Green River, hoping it would take them to California. They were actually on their way to the Grand Canyon. Advice from an Indian leader saved them from a likely death.

Against the odds, Manly and the Bennetts reunited near Salt Lake. Facing the difficult decision of how to get to California when the season was late and snow was likely in the Sierra Nevada, the party joined a group that had hired an experienced Mormon traveler to take them on a snow-free route to southern California. A few days later, a rebellion against the authority of the Mormon leader took place, and one group split off to take an unexplored "shortcut" across the desert. Manly stuck with the Bennetts and their friends, the Arcane family, in this choice.

How would they find their route? Where would they find water? Would Manly, a skilled hunter, be able to find game to feed them? How far would they have to travel before they came to the Mexican settlements in southern California? Would the oxen be able to haul the women and children over difficult terrain in wagons, or would they have to walk? In the winter of 1849, there were plenty of questions, and every one of them lacked an answer.

The situation was desperate from the start. Tempted to travel alone and save himself, Manly had to decide, and decide again, to risk death by starvation, thirst, exposure, or exhaustion by putting loyalty first and sticking by the Bennett and Arcane families. As the situation grew even grimmer, Bennett devised a plan: Manly and Rogers would find a way out of Death Valley, travel ahead to the Mexican settlements, get supplies, and return to rescue the families. On a journey made more agonizing by its unexpectedly long duration and Manly's affliction with a lame knee, Manly and Rogers traveled through Death Valley, across the mountains, into coastal California, and back.

Though they had answers to their questions when Manly and Rogers returned for them, the party still faced a long and draining walk, with the children riding uncomfortably in pockets hung on one incredibly tough ox. Manly now acted, in the most literal sense, to give courage, persuading deeply discouraged people to fight pain and despair and to keep moving.

It is hard to imagine that coastal California has ever looked more beautiful than it did to the Bennetts, the Arcanes, Manly, and Rogers in the early winter of 1850. The Mexicans were kind and hospitable, and survival was no longer a matter of doubt. While the word "lucky" hardly seems to apply to these hard-pressed overland travelers, the fact that they were crossing the desert in winter, and in an unusually wet winter at that, was very lucky indeed. They had experienced a prolonged encounter with the presence of death, and then they had been permitted to walk away from that presence. But what should they do next?

In Death Valley, there was nothing of value for gold to buy. Manly writes, "A hoard of twenty-dollar gold pieces could now stand before us the whole day long with no temptation to touch a single coin, for its very weight would drag us nearer death." On one occasion, when the children "were crying for water and there was not a drop to give them," the adults "reproached themselves as being the cause of all this trouble. For the love of gold they had left homes where hunger had never come...." And yet the magnet that drew them to California was the gold rush. Once they were safe in southern California, Manly began planning to move on to the mines. In a particularly memorable line from the book, he declares, "I said to myself that the only way now to keep me from getting to the gold mines was to kill me." It is a strange and unsettling reading experience to watch this group of people shift back to the material drives and ambitions of their times.

"For heaven's sake," an impatient reader might exclaim at this point. "After what these people went through, at the very least they deserved to make some money. What would you have expected them to do? Found a socialist sect and devote their lives to critiquing the profit motive?"

If only they had.

These men had gambled their own lives, and the lives of women and children, on the prospect of sudden riches. Who in America was better suited to question the lust for wealth that so many people took (and take) so thoroughly for granted? But then again, who in America had better reason to try to store their searing memories in the past and move into a bright and hopeful future?

MEMORIALS BY ACTION

I have a suggestion to make to the descendants of these noble pioneers: that to perpetuate the memory of their fathers, and do reverence to their good and noble deeds in the history of this grand state, there should be erected upon the highest mountaintop a memorial building, wherein may be inscribed the names and histories of the brave pioneers, so they may never be blotted out.

WILLIAM LEWIS MANLY

To our great benefit, William Lewis Manly had little talent or ability for forgetting. Memories haunted him, resisting any exorcism. In truth, he does not seem to have fled memory. He kept a diary during the trip to California and, drawing on that journal, wrote a long letter—some three hundred pages—to his parents. When their house burned, that manuscript was lost. As an older man, he wrote a serialized narrative of the trip for a local Santa Clara Valley periodical. Then, helped by an editor, he wrote and published *Death Valley in '49*.

Does the existence of this editor or ghostwriter reduce the value of this book or compromise its authenticity? Readers can answer the question in a variety of ways. My own conviction is that many patterns of phrasing in this text carry the tone and quality of Manly's own voice. Any novelist in the business of creating people could rest contented with the "characterization" that this individual's voice offers readers. A person with a strong sense of obligation to others, a man proud of his physical capabilities but willing to admit his frailties, an individual with a sometimes skeptical but usually forgiving view of human nature, and a figure whose equanimity and even sense of humor held up under the most trying of tests: however much another writer shaped some passages, *Death Valley in '49* still gives us a remarkably direct encounter with the mind and experience of a distinctive individual.

The words in which Manly described his ordeals of choice are treasures in our cultural inheritance, no matter what route they took to the printed page. Each time Manly traveled ahead in the desert, climbed a mountain, and assessed the prospect ahead, his loyalty was put to the test. "Prospects now seemed so hopeless," one passage reads, "that I heartily wished I was not in duty bound to stand by the women and small children." Without dependents, he could "pick up my knapsack and gun and go off," travel fast and save himself. But saving his own life would come at too high a price: "I felt I should be morally guilty of murder." Tracing this "dark line of thought" repeatedly, Manly "always felt better when I got around to the determination, as I always did, to stand by my friends."

As moving as these declarations are, Manly can nonetheless make twenty-first century readers flinch and squirm on occasion. Like many New Englanders of his time, he did not like slavery, but he did not show much recognition or respect for the full equality of African Americans. He enjoyed his trip on a steamer to St. Louis, accepting the service of "polite and well-dressed darkies," raising no questions on the status of their freedom. His gratitude to the Mexicans who gave him and his friends refuge in southern California was genuine and lasting, but then there is the tale of how he secured his mining claim. A man named Williams "went to a dry gulch where a Spaniard was working and told him that all of California, now that the war was over, belonged to Americans and he must leave. Williams had his gun in his hand and war might follow, so Mr. Spaniard left and his claim was presented to Bennett and myself." Manly, in other words, sometimes exceeds our standards for admirable human behavior, and he sometimes swoops below them.

In appraising this book as a trustworthy historical document, we must face this limitation: the story of the Death Valley ordeal refuses capture in words, regardless of the writer's literary skill or honesty. Words like "suffering," "despair," "grief," "loyalty," and "persistence" are shapeless generalities wrapped loosely around sharp and angular events and feelings. We are not going to get the "full story" of this historical episode, and there is some real mercy in that limitation. "It is but fair to tell the reader," Manly says, "that the hardest and worst of it has never been told nor will it ever be." Yet, even with the necessary omissions and elisions, this remains a book that is hard to put aside and forget.

When you finish reading *Death Valley in '49,* you may feel as if you should find someone in need and offer your help. Do it. The greatest tribute we can pay to the author of this book is to take the example of his heroism to heart, and to action. He reminds us what mercy, courage, and self-sacrifice mean in down-to-earth practice. With Manly as our predecessor, we are invited to replace indifference with commitment, narrow self-interest with connection and community. Our acts of nobility are unlikely to equal his in duration and intensity, but that, thank heavens, is not the point. Read *Death Valley in '49,* and sign up as a volunteer for Meals on Wheels or Habitat for Humanity. You could tutor a child, teach an adult to read, act as an advocate for a crime victim, or provide company to a dying person. In place of a marble memorial with a plaque that few would read, dedicate this action to the memory of William Lewis Manly and his repeated choice for loyalty in 1849. And the next time someone tells you that America lacks real heroes, introduce them to this book.

Patricia Nelson Limerick
August 2001

WILLIAM LEWIS MANLY WAS ABOUT SEVENTY YEARS old in 1890 when he started to write *Death Valley in '49*, but this book is not merely an old man's recollections of a journey taken in his youth; it is an account much enriched by his return trips to the Death Valley area and by conversations with contemporaries who had also made the trek across the forbidding deserts of the American Southwest.

By 1890 Manly had written three accounts of his heroic trek: he had kept a diary during the trip, he had written a three-hundred-page letter about it to his parents, and he had penned a serialized version, thirty-eight monthly columns, titled "From Vermont to California" for *The Santa Clara Valley,* a horticultural magazine. He had also dictated a brief version to a newspaperman, in which he was credited with naming Death Valley. The diary and long letter are gone, but most of his very important serialized account is extant.

After deciding to edit and compile these articles in *Death Valley in '49,* Manly began a lively correspondence with other forty-niners, to refresh his memory and to glean more information for the book. (These conversations were later collected by Arthur Woodward in *The Jayhawkers' Oath and Other Sketches.*) At this point, Manly apparently felt he needed help compiling his book. In a letter to John Colton on April 4, 1894, he wrote, "I had to have one assistant because I am not able to do such work & have it grammatical," and the introduction to Chapter XIV says, "The following was dictated to the editor of this book." Although the original edition of *Death Valley in '49* does not give the name of the editor, Lillie M. Kirkgaard (head of the Fine Arts and California Department of the Pasadena Public Library for many years) stated in a letter to Lawrence Clark Powell dated June 10, 1871, that Miss Helen E. Harley had "written" the book for Manly when she was seventeen years old. Miss Harley's father, an editor for a northern California newspaper, had tutored his daughter·in journalism. It must have been a fascinating and daunting task for the young editor. In her letter to Powell, Mrs. Kirkgaard wrote that Miss Harley had told her that Manly often "came with

scribbled notes on grease-spotted paper bags and would sometimes break
into uncontrolled weeping during his reminiscences." Miss Harley occasionally got the facts wrong and sometimes embellished the text. In the endnotes
we have pointed out some of these additions and many of the factual dis-
crepancies that can be attributed to Miss Harley.

In a letter to T. S. Palmer, an entomologist who went to Death Valley
in 1891 on a government survey, Manly said he had drawn four maps "from
memory after many years have passed by." We call them the Walker map (now
housed at Death Valley National Park Museum), the Jayhawker map and the
Palmer map (both in the Huntington Library), and the Williams map (at the
Newberry Library in Chicago). We think Manly drew the Palmer map so his
editor would have a visual reference to help her understand his narrative.
When Carl I. Wheat published it in the third volume of *Mapping the Trans-
mississippi West,* he commented that it was "crude, lacking in scale, [and]
strangely oriented." This is certainly true; considerable explanation is
required in order to read the map. Manly drew it on a 39 cm x 50 cm sheet
of paper with Salt Lake City in the upper right-hand corner and the San
Francisceto [sic] Rancho at the bottom center of the map. The top 40 percent (20 cm, the portion from Salt Lake to the latitude of Beatty, Nevada) is
correctly oriented, with north to the top of the map. But the next 30 percent (14 cm) is 90 degrees off, with the northward orientation pointing to
the west (to the left side of map). This section covers the area from Beaty to
Indian Wells Spring at the base of the Sierra Nevada. The next 20 percent
(11 cm) is correctly oriented, but the bottom 10 percent (5 cm, the portion
from Acton, near San Gabriel Pass, to the rancho near Saugus) is again 90
degrees off (north pointing west to the left side of the map). Thus, when reading the middle and the bottom of the map, it must be rotated 90 degrees
clockwise. It seems Manly was more interested in recording the landmarks of
his travels on a single sheet of paper than in drawing a proper map. Helen
Harley apparently used this map to help orient the reader to the geography
of the story, but in doing so she unwittingly transferred the map's directional
errors to the book. To facilitate the reader's understanding, we have omitted
the incorrect directions and put the correct directions in brackets in the text.

There is one more element of *Death Valley in '49* that has hindered
readers' experience of Manly's account. As journalist, publisher, and promoter
Charles F. Lummis wrote when he reviewed Manly's book for *The Land of
Sunshine* in 1897, it was "one of the most interesting books of the season"
but was "printed by 'blacksmiths' who have disfigured its every page with
misspellings and letters upside down....Pity it is that a narrative of so much

worth historically should have fallen to the tough mercies of (let us hope) the most incompetent printers in California."

We have retained the original text with the following exceptions: the upside-down and broken letters have been corrected, inconsistencies in capitalization and spelling have been made uniform, and the punctuation has been modified to facilitate comprehension; obvious errors have been corrected silently, and some words that were apparently left out of the original edition have been inserted in brackets; and, as mentioned above, directions have been adjusted to reflect the reality of Manly's travels and to correct the peculiarities of the Palmer map. Extensive annotations can be found in the notes at the end of the book. We hope that these adjustments and additions will allow readers to appreciate, unimpaired, a unique and thrilling account of the forty-niner experience.

LeRoy and Jean Johnson

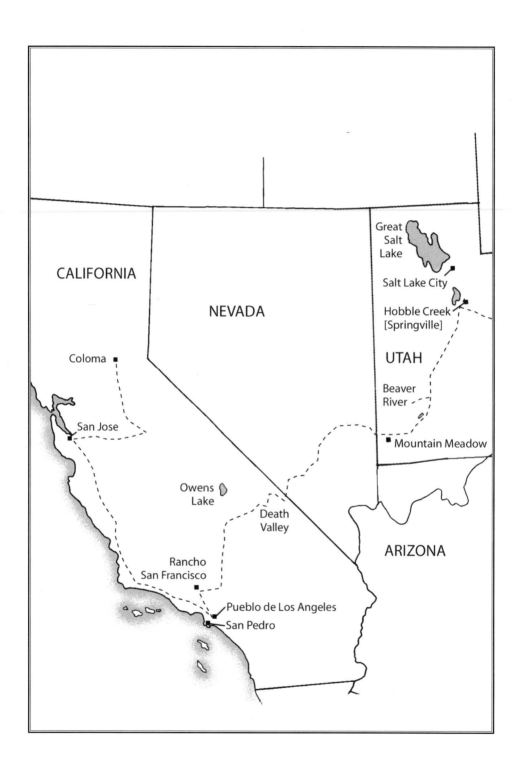

CALIFORNIA

NEVADA

Great
Salt
Lake

Salt Lake City

Hobble Creek
[Springville]

UTAH

Beaver
River

Coloma

San Jose

Owens
Lake

Death
Valley

Mountain Meadow

ARIZONA

Rancho
San Francisco

Pueblo de Los Angeles

San Pedro

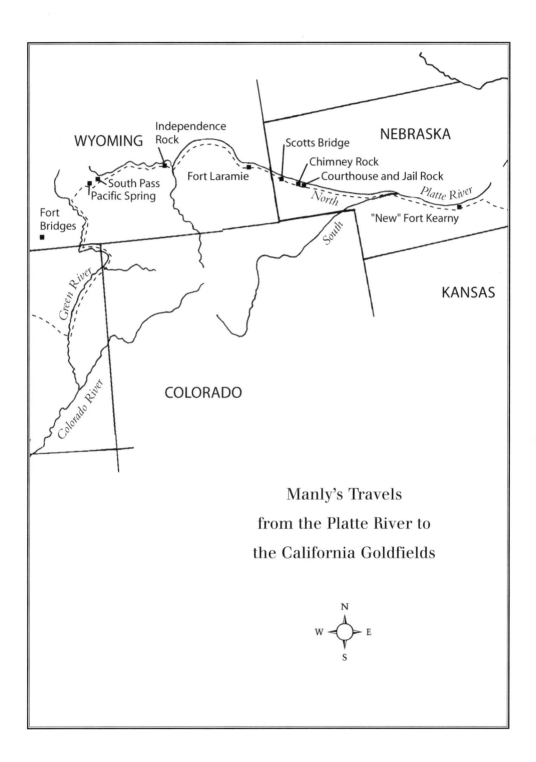

WYOMING

Independence
Rock

NEBRASKA

South Pass
Pacific Spring

Fort Laramie

Scotts Bridge

Chimney Rock

Courthouse and Jail Rock

North

Platte River

Fort
Bridges

"New" Fort Kearny

South

Green River

KANSAS

Colorado River

COLORADO

Manly's Travels
from the Platte River to
the California Goldfields

N

W — E

S

William Lewis Manly. Courtesy of the Bancroft Library,
University of California, Berkeley

Early Life in Vermont

ST. ALBANS, VERMONT, IS NEAR THE EASTERN SHORE of Lake Champlain, and only a short distance south of "five-and-forty north degrees,"[1] which separates the United States from Canada, and some sixty or seventy miles from the great St. Lawrence River and the city of Montreal. Near here it was, on April 6, 1820, I was born—so the record says[2]—and from this point with wondering eyes of childhood I looked across the waters of the narrow lake to the slopes of the Adirondack Mountains in New York, green as the hills of my own Green Mountain State.

The parents of my father were English people and lived near Hartford, Connecticut, where he was born. While still a little boy he came with his parents to Vermont. My mother's maiden name was Phoebe Calkins, born near St. Albans of Welsh parents, and, being left an orphan while yet in very tender years, she was given away to be reared by people who provided food and clothes, but permitted her to grow up to womanhood without knowing how to read or write. After her marriage[3] she learned to do both and acquired the rudiments of an education.

Grandfather and his boys, four in all, fairly carved a farm out of the big forest that covered the cold, rocky hills. Giant work it was for them in such heavy timber—pine, hemlock, maple, beech, and birch—the clearing of a single acre being a man's work for a year. The place where the maples were thickest was reserved for a sugar grove, and from it was made all of the sweet material they needed, and some besides. Economy of the very strictest kind had to be used in every direction. Main strength and muscle were the only things dispensed in plenty. The crops raised consisted of a small flint corn, rye, oats, potatoes, and turnips. Three cows, ten or twelve sheep, a few pigs, and a yoke of strong oxen comprised the livestock; horses—they had none for many years. A great oxcart was the only wheeled vehicle on the place, and this, in winter, gave place to a heavy sled, the runners cut from a tree having a natural crook and roughly but strongly made.

In summer there were plenty of strawberries, raspberries, whortleber-ries,[4] and blackberries growing wild, but all the cultivated fruit was apples. As these ripened, many were peeled by hand, cut in quarters, strung on long strings of twine, and dried before the kitchen fire for winter use. They had a way of burying up some of the best keepers in the ground, and opening the apple hole was quite an event of early spring.

The children were taught to work as soon as large enough. I remem-ber they furnished me with a little wooden fork to spread the heavy swath of grass my father cut with easy swings of the scythe, and when it was dry and being loaded on the great oxcart, I followed closely with a rake, gather-ing every scattering spear. The barn was built so that every animal was housed comfortably in winter, and the house was such as all settlers built, not considered handsome, but capable of being made very warm in winter, and the great piles of hardwood in the yard, enough to last as fuel for a year, not only helped to clear the land but kept us comfortable. Mother and the girls washed, carded, spun, and wove the wool from our own sheep into good, strong cloth. Flax was also raised, and I remember how they pulled it, rotted it by spreading [it] on the green meadow, then broke and dressed it, and then the women made linen cloth of various degrees of fineness, quality, and beauty.[5] Thus, by the labor of both men and women, we were clothed. If an extra fine Sunday dress was desired, part of the yarn was colored and from this they managed to get up a very nice plaid goods for the purpose.

In clearing the land the hemlock bark[6] was peeled and traded off at the tannery for leather, or used to pay for tanning and dressing the hide of an ox or cow which they managed to fatten and kill about every year. [Shoes] for the family were either made by a neighboring shoemaker, or by a traveling one who went from house to house, making up a supply for the family—whipping the cat, they called it then. They paid him in something or other produced upon the farm, and no money was asked or expected.

Wood was one thing plenty, and the fireplace was made large enough to take in sticks four feet long or more, for the more they could burn the better, to get it out of the way. In an outhouse,[7] also provided with a fireplace and chimney, they made shingles during the long winter evenings, the shav-ings making plenty of fire and light by which to work. The shingles sold for about a dollar a thousand. Just beside the fireplace in the house was a large brick oven where mother baked great loaves of bread, big pots of pork and beans, mince pies and loaf cake, [and] a big turkey or a young pig on grand occasions. Many of the dishes used were of tin or pewter; the milk pans were of earthenware, but most things about the house in the line of furniture were of domestic manufacture.

The store bills were very light. A little tea for father and mother, a few spices and odd luxuries were about all, and they were paid for with surplus eggs. My father and my uncle had a sawmill, and in winter they hauled logs to it, and could sell timber for eight dollars per thousand feet.

The school was taught in winter by a man named Bowen, who managed forty scholars and considered sixteen dollars a month, boarding himself, was pretty fair pay. In summer some smart girl would teach the small scholars and board round among the families.

When the proper time came, the property holder would send off to the collector an itemized list of all his property, and at another the taxes fell due. A farmer who would value his property at two thousand or three thousand dollars would find he had to pay about six or seven dollars. All the money in use then seemed to be silver, and not very much of that. The whole plan seemed to be to have every family and farm self-supporting as far as possible. I have heard of a note being given, payable in a good cow to be delivered at a certain time—say October 1st—and on that day it would pass from house to house in payment of a debt, and at night only the last man in the list would have a cow more than his neighbor. Yet those were the days of real independence, after all. Every man worked hard from early youth to a good old age. There were no millionaires, no tramps, and the poorhouse had only a few inmates.

I have very pleasant recollections of the neighborhood cider mill. There were two rollers formed of logs carefully rounded and four or five feet long, set closely together in an upright position in a rough frame, a long crooked sweep coming from one of them to which a horse was hitched and [which it pulled] round and round. One roller had mortises in it, and projecting wooden teeth on the other fitted into these, so that as they both slowly turned together, the apples were crushed. A huge box of coarse slats, notched and locked together at the corners, held a vast pile of the crushed apples while clean rye straw was added to strain the flowing juice and keep the cheese[8] from spreading too much; then the ponderous screw [pressed the cheese] and [out flowed] streams of delicious cider. Sucking cider through a long rye straw inserted in the bunghole of a barrel was just the best of fun, and cider taken that way [was] "awful" good while it was new and sweet.

The winter ashes, made from burning so much fuel and gathered from the brush heaps and log heaps, were carefully saved and traded with the potash men for potash or sold for a small price. Nearly everyone went barefooted in summer and in winter wore heavy leather moccasins made by the Canadian French who lived nearby.

CHAPTER II

The Western Fever

ABOUT 1828 PEOPLE BEGAN TO TALK ABOUT THE FAR WEST. Ohio was the place we heard most about, and the most we knew was that it was a long way off and [there was] no way to get there except over a long and tedious road, with oxen or horses and a cart or wagon. More than one got the western fever, as they called it, my uncle James Webster and my father among the rest, when they heard some traveler tell about the fine country he had seen; so they sold their farms and decided to go to Ohio. Uncle James was to go ahead, in the fall of 1829, and get a farm to rent if he could, and Father and his family were to come on the next spring.

Uncle fitted out with two good horses and a wagon; goods were packed in a large box made to fit, and under the wagon seat was the commissary chest for food and bedding for daily use, all snugly arranged. Father had, shortly before, bought a fine Morgan mare and a light wagon which served as a family carriage, having wooden axles and a seat arranged on wooden springs, and they finally decided they would let me take the horse and wagon and go on with Uncle, and Father and Mother would come by water, either by way of the St. Lawrence River and the lakes or by way of the new canal recently built, which would take them as far as Buffalo.

So they loaded up the little wagon with some of the mentioned things and articles in the house, among which I remember a fine brass kettle, considered almost indispensable in housekeeping. There was a good lot of bedding and blankets, and a quilt nicely folded was placed on the spring seat as a cushion.

As may be imagined I was the object of a great deal of attention about this time, for a boy not yet ten years old just setting out into a region almost unknown was a little unusual. When I was ready they all gathered round to say good-bye and my good mother seemed most concerned. She said, "Now you must be a good boy till we come in the spring. Mind Uncle and Aunt and take good care of the horse, and remember us. May God protect you." She embraced me and kissed me and held me till she was exhausted. Then they lifted me up into the spring seat, put the lines in my hand and handed me my little whip with a leather strip for a lash. Just at the last moment Father handed me a purse containing about a dollar, all in copper cents—pennies we called them then. Uncle had started on—they had kept me so long—but I started up and they all followed me along the road for a mile or so before we finally separated and they turned back. They waved hats and handkerchiefs till out of sight as they returned, and I wondered if we should ever meet again.

I was up with uncle very soon and we rolled down through St. Albans and took our road southerly along in sight of Lake Champlain. Uncle and Aunt often looked back to talk to me, "See what a nice cornfield!" or "What nice apples on those trees," seeming to think they must do all they could to cheer me up, [so] that I might not think too much of the playmates and home I was leaving behind.

I had never driven very far before, but I found the horse knew more than I did how to get around the big stones and stumps that were found in the road, so that as long as I held the lines and the whip in hand I was an excellent driver.

We had made plans and preparations to board ourselves on the journey. We always stopped at the farmhouses overnight, and they were so hospitable that they gave us all we wanted free. Our supper was generally of bread and milk, the latter always furnished gratuitously, and I do not recollect that we were ever turned away from any house where we asked shelter. There were no hotels, or taverns as they called them, outside of the towns.

In due time we reached Whitehall, at the head of Lake Champlain, and the big box in Uncle's wagon proved so heavy over the muddy roads that he put it in a canal boat to be sent on to Cleveland, and we found it much easier after this for there were too many mud holes, stumps and stones, and log bridges for so heavy a load as he had. Our road many times after this led along near the canal, the Champlain or the Erie, and I had a chance to see something of the canal boys' life. The boy who drove the horses that drew the packet boat was a well-dressed fellow and always rode at a full trot or a gallop, but the freight driver was generally ragged and barefoot, and walked when it was too cold to ride, threw stones or clubs at his team, and cursed and abused the packet boy who passed, as long as he was in hearing. Reared as I had been, I thought it was a pretty wicked part of the world we were coming to.

We passed one village of low, cheap houses near the canal. The men about were very vulgar and talked rough and loud, nearly everyone with a pipe and poorly dressed, loafing around the saloon, apparently the worse for whisky. The children were barefooted, bareheaded, and scantily dressed, and it seemed awfully dirty about the doors of the shanties. Pigs, ducks, and geese were at the very door, and the women I saw wore dresses that did not come down very near the mud, and big brogan shoes, and their talk was saucy and different from what I had ever heard women use before. They told me they were Irish people—the first I had ever seen.

It was along here somewhere that I lost my little whip and to get another one made sad inroads into the little purse of pennies my father gave me. We traveled slowly on day after day. There was no use to hurry, for we could not do it. The roads were muddy, the log ways very rough, and the only way was to take a moderate gait and keep it. We never traveled on Sunday. One Saturday evening my uncle secured the privilege of staying at a well-to-do farmer's house until Monday. We had our own food and bedding, but were glad to get some privileges in the kitchen and some fresh milk or vegetables. After all had taken supper that night they all sat down and made themselves quiet with their books, and the children were as still as mice till an early bed time when all retired. When Sunday evening came the women got out their work—their sewing and their knitting—and the children romped and played and made as much noise as they could, seeming as anxious to break the Sabbath as they had been to have a pious Saturday night. I had never seen that way before and asked my uncle, who said he guessed they were Seventh Day Baptists.

After many days of travel, which became to me quite monotonous, we came to Cleveland, on Lake Erie, and here my uncle found his box of goods, loaded it into the wagon again, and traveled on through rain and mud, making very slow headway, for two or three days after. When we stopped at a four-corners[1] in Medina County they told us we were only twenty-one miles from Cleveland. Here was a small town consisting of a hotel, store, church, schoolhouse, and blacksmith shop, and as it was getting cold and bad, Uncle decided to go no farther now, and rented a room for himself and Aunt, and found a place for me to lodge with Daniel Stevens's boy close by. We got good stables for our horses.

I went to the district school here, and studied reading, spelling, and Colburn's mental arithmetic, which I mastered. It began very easy, "How many thumbs on your right hand?" "How many on your left?" "How many altogether?" but it grew harder further on.[2]

Uncle took employment at anything he could find to do. Chopping was his principal occupation. When the snow began to go off he looked around for a farm to rent for us and [for] Father to live on when he came, but he found none such as he needed. He now got a letter from Father telling him that he had good news from a friend named Cornish, who said that good land nearly clear of timber could be bought of the government in Michigan Territory, some sixty or seventy miles beyond Detroit, and this being an opportunity to get what land they needed with their small capital, they would start for that place as soon as the waterways were thawed out, probably in April.[3]

We then gave up the idea of staying here and prepared to go to Michigan as soon as the frost was out of the ground. Starting, we reached Huron River to find it swollen and out of its bank, giving us much trouble to get across, the road along the bottomlands being partly covered with logs and rails, but once across we were in the town, and when we inquired about the road around to Detroit, they said the country was all a swamp and thirty miles wide and, in spring, impassable. They called it the Maumee or Black Swamp. We were advised to go by water. When a steamboat came up the river bound for Detroit we put our wagons and horses on board and camped on the lower deck ourselves. We had our own food and were very comfortable, and glad to have escaped the great mud hole.

CHAPTER III

At Detroit and Westward

WE ARRIVED IN DETROIT SAFELY, and a few minutes answered to land our wagons and goods, when we rolled outward in a westerly direction. We found very muddy roads, stumps, and log bridges plenty, making our rate of travel very slow. When out upon our road about thirty miles, near Ypsilanti,[1] the thick forest we had been passing through grew thinner, and the trees soon dwindled down into what they called oak openings, and the road became more sandy. When we reached McCracken's Tavern we began to inquire for Ebenezer Manley and family, and were soon directed to a large house nearby, where he was stopping for a time.

We drove up to the door and they all came out to see who the new-comers were. Mother saw me first and ran to the wagon and pulled me off and hugged and kissed me over and over again, while the tears ran down her cheeks. Then she would hold me off at arm's length, and look me in the eye and say, "I am so glad to have you again," and then she embraced me again and again. "You are our little man," said she, "you have come over this long road, and brought us our good horse and our little wagon." My sister Polly,[2] two years older than I, stood patiently by, and when Mother turned to speak to Uncle and Aunt, she locked arms with me and took me away with her. We had never been separated before in all our lives, and we had loved each other as good children should who have been brought up [on] good and moral principles. We loved each other and our home and respected our good father and mother, who had made it so happy for us.

We all sat down by the side of the house and talked pretty fast, telling our experience on our long journey by land and water, and when the sun went down we were called to supper and went hand in hand to surround the bountiful table as a family again. During the conversation at supper Father said to me, "Lewis, I have bought you a smoothbore rifle, suitable for either ball or shot." This, I thought, was good enough for anyone, and I thanked him heartily. We spent the greater part of the night in talking over our adventures since we left Vermont, and sleep was forgotten by young and old.

Next morning Father and Uncle took the horse and little wagon and went out in search of government land. They found an old acquaintance in Jackson County and government land all around him and, searching till they found the section corner, they found the number of the lots they wanted to locate on, two hundred acres in all. They then went to the Detroit land office and secured the pieces they had chosen.[3]

Father now bought a yoke of oxen, a wagon, and a cow, and as soon as we could get loaded up, our little emigrant train started west to our future home, where we arrived safely in a few days and secured a house to live in about a mile away from our land. We now worked with a will and built two log houses and also hired ten acres broken, which was done with three or four yoke of oxen and a strong plow. The trees were scattered over the ground, and some small brush and old limbs and logs, which we cleared away as we plowed. Our houses went up very fast—all rough oak logs, with oak puncheons[4] or hewed planks for a floor, and oak shakes for a roof, all of our own make. The shakes were held down upon the roof by heavy poles, for we had no nails, the door of split stuff hung with wooden hinges, and the fireplace of stone laid up with the logs, and from the loft floor upward the chimney was built of split stuff plastered heavily with mud. We had a small four-paned window in the house. We then built a log barn for our oxen, cow, and horse and got pigs, sheep, and chickens as fast as a chance offered.

As fast as possible we fenced in the cultivated land, Father and Uncle splitting out the rails, while a younger brother and myself, by each getting hold of an end of one of them, managed to lay up a fence four rails high, all we small men could do. Thus working on, we had a pretty well cultivated farm in the course of two or three years, on which we produced wheat, corn, and potatoes, and had an excellent garden. We found plenty of wild cranberries and whortleberries, which we dried for winter use. The lakes were full of good fish, black bass and pickerel, and the woods had deer, turkeys, pheasants, pigeons, and other things, and I became quite an expert in the capture of small game for the table with my new gun. Father and Uncle would occasionally kill a deer, and the Indians came along and sold venison at times.

One fall after work was done and preparations were made for the winter, Father said to me, "Now Lewis, I want you to hunt every day—come home nights—but keep on till you kill a deer." So with his permission I started with my gun on my shoulder and with feelings of considerable pride. Before night I startled two deer in a brushy place, and they leaped high over the oak bushes in the most affrighted way. I brought my gun to my shoulder and fired at the bounding animal when in most plain sight. Loading then quickly, I hurried up the trail as fast as I could and soon came to my deer, dead, with a bullet hole in its head. I was really surprised myself, for I had fired so hastily at the almost flying animal that it was little more than a random shot. As the deer was not very heavy, I dressed it and packed it home myself, about as proud a boy as the state of Michigan contained. I really began to think I was a capital hunter, though I afterward knew it was a bit of good luck and not a bit of skill about it.

It was some time after this before I made another lucky shot. Father would once in a while ask me, "Well, can't you kill us another deer?" I told him that when I had crawled a long time toward a sleeping deer, I got so trembly that I could not hit an ox in short range. "Oh," said he, "you got the buck fever—don't be so timid—they won't attack you." But after a while this fever wore off, and I got so steady that I could hit anything I could get in reach of.

We were now quite contented and happy. Father could plainly show us the difference between this country and Vermont and the advantages we had here. There the land was poor and stony and the winters terribly severe. Here there were no stones to plow over, and the land was otherwise easy to till. We could raise almost anything, and have nice wheat bread to eat, far superior to the "rye-and-Indian" we used to have. The nice white bread was good enough to eat without butter, and in comparison this country seemed a real paradise.

The supply of clothing we brought with us had lasted until now— more than two years—and we had sowed some flax and raised sheep so that we began to get material of our own raising, from which to manufacture some more. Mother and Sister spun some nice yarn, both woolen and linen, and Father had a loom made on which Mother wove it up into cloth, and we were soon dressed up in brand-new clothes again. Domestic economy of this kind was as necessary here as it was in Vermont, and we knew well how to practice it.

About this time the emigrants began to come in very fast, and every piece of government land anywhere about was taken. So much land was plowed, and so much vegetable matter turned under and decaying, that there came a regular epidemic of fever and ague and bilious fever, and a large majority of the people were sick.[4] At our house Father was the first one attacked, and when the fever was at its height he was quite out of his head and talked and acted like a crazy man. We had never seen anyone so sick before, and we thought he must surely die, but when the doctor came he said, "Don't be alarmed. It is only 'fever 'n' ague,' and no one was ever known to die of that." Others of us were sick too, and most of the neighbors, and it made us all feel rather sorrowful. The doctor's medicines consisted of calomel, jalap and quinine,[5] all used pretty freely, by some with benefit, and by others to no visible purpose, for they had to suffer until the cold weather came and froze the disease out. At one time I was the only one that remained well, and I had to nurse and cook, besides all the outdoor work that fell to me.

My sister married a man nearby with a good farm and moved there with him, a mile or two away. When she went away I lost my real bosom companion and felt very lonesome, but I went to see her once in a while, and that was pretty often, I think. There was not much going on as a general thing. Some little neighborhood society and news was about all. There was, however, one incident which occurred in 1837 [that] I never shall forget and which I will relate in the next chapter.

CHAPTER IV

The Lost Filley Boy

ABOUT TWO MILES WEST [OF] FATHER'S FARM in Jackson County, Michigan, lived Ami Filley, who moved here from Connecticut and settled about two and a half miles from the town of Jackson, then a small village with plenty of stumps and mud holes in its streets. Many of the roads leading thereto had been paved with tamarack poles, making what is now known as corduroy roads. The country was still new and the farmhouses far between.

Mr. Filley secured government land in the oak openings and settled there with his wife and two or three children, the oldest of which was a boy named Willie. The children were getting old enough to go to school, but there being none, Mr. Filley hired one of the neighbor's daughters to come to his house and teach the children there, so they might be prepared for usefulness in life or ready to proceed further with their education—to college, perhaps, in some future day.

The young woman he engaged lived about a mile [and] a half away— Miss Mary Mount—and she came over and began her duties as private school ma'am, not a very difficult task in those days. One day after she had been teaching some time, Miss Mount desired to go to her father's on a visit, and as she would pass a huckleberry swamp on the way, she took a small pail to fill with berries as she went, and by consent of Willie's mother, the little boy went with her for company. Reaching the berries she began to pick, and the little boy found this dull business, got tired and homesick, and wanted to go home. They were about a mile from Mr. Filley's and, as there was a pretty good foot trail over which they had come, the young woman took the boy to it and, turning him toward home, told him to follow it carefully and he would soon see his mother. She then filled her pail with berries, went on to her own home, and remained there till nearly sundown, when she set out to return to Mr. Filley's, reaching there yet in the early twilight. Not seeing Willie, she inquired for him and was told that he had not returned, and that they supposed he was safe with her. She then hastily related how it happened that he had started back toward home, and that she supposed he had safely arrived.

Mr. Filley then started back on the trail, keeping close watch on each side of the way, for he expected he would soon come across Master Willie fast asleep. He called his name every few rods but got no answer, nor could he discover him, and so returned home again, still calling and searching, but no boy was discovered. Then he built a large fire and put lighted candles in all the windows, then took his lantern and went out in the woods calling and looking for the boy. Sometimes he thought he heard him, but on going where the sound came from, nothing could be found. So he looked and called all night, along the trail and all about the woods, with no success. Mr. Mount's home was situated not far from the shore of Fitch's Lake, and the trail went along the margin, and in some places the ground was quite a boggy marsh, and the trail had been fixed up to make it passably good walking.

Next day the neighbors were notified and asked to assist, and although they were in the midst of wheat harvest, a great many laid down the cradle[1] and rake and went out to help search. On the third day the whole county became excited and quite an army of searchers turned out, coming from the whole country miles around.

Mr. Filley was much excited and quite worn out and beside himself with fatigue and loss of sleep. He could not eat. Yielding to entreaty he would sit at the table, and suddenly rise up, saying he heard Willie calling, and go out to search for the supposed voice, but it was all fruitless, and the whole people were sorry indeed for the poor father and mother.

The people then formed a plan for a thorough search. They were to form in a line so near each other that they could touch hands and were to march thus, turning out for nothing except impassable lakes, and thus we marched, fairly sweeping the county in search of a sign. I was with this party and we marched south and kept close watch for a bit of clothing, a footprint or even bones, or anything which would indicate that he had been destroyed by some wild animal. Thus we marched all day with no success, and the next went north in the same careful manner, but with no better result. Most of the people now abandoned the search, but some of the neighbors kept it up for a long time.

Some expressed themselves quite strongly that Miss Mount knew where the boy was, saying that she might have had some trouble with him and, in seeking to correct him, had accidentally killed him and then hidden the body away—perhaps in the deep mire of the swamp or in the muddy waters on the margin of the lake. Search was made with this idea foremost, but nothing was discovered. Rain now set in, and the grain, from neglect, grew in the head as it stood, and many a settler ate poor bread all winter in consequence of his neighborly kindness in the midst of harvest. The bread would not rise, and to make it into pancakes was the best way it could be used.

Still no tidings ever came of the lost boy. Many things were whispered about Mr. Mount's dishonesty of character and there were many suspicions about him, but no real facts could be shown to account for the boy. The neighbors said he never worked like the rest of them, and that his patch of cultivated land was altogether too small to support his family, a wife and two daughters, grown. He was a very smooth and affable talker, and had lots of acquaintances. A few years afterwards Mr. Mount was convicted of a crime which sent him to the Jackson State Prison,[2] where he died before his term expired. I visited the Filley family in 1870, and from them heard the facts anew and that no trace of the lost boy had ever been discovered.

CHAPTER V

Rather Catch Chipmunks in the Rocky Mountains than Live in Michigan

THE SECOND YEAR OF SICKNESS I WAS AFFECTED with the rest, though it was not generally so bad as the first year. I suffered a great deal and felt so miserable that I began to think I had rather live on the top of the Rocky Mountains and catch chipmunks for a living than to live here and be sick, and I began to have very serious thoughts of trying some other country. In the winter of 1839 and 1840 I went to a neighboring school for three months, where I studied reading, writing, and spelling, getting as far as Rule of Three in Daboll's arithmetic.[1] When school was out I chopped and split rails for William Hanna till I had paid my winter's board. After this, myself and a young man named Orrin Henry, with whom I had become acquainted, worked awhile scoring timber to be used in building the Michigan Central Railroad, which had just then begun to be built. They laid down the ties first (sometimes a mudsill under them) and then put down four-by-eight wooden rails with strips of band iron half an inch thick spiked on top. I scored the timber and Henry used the broadaxe after me. It was pretty hard work and the hours as long as we could see, our wages being thirteen dollars per month, half cash.

In thinking over our prospect it seemed more and more as if I had better look out for my own fortune in some other place. The farm was pretty small for all of us. There were three brothers[2] younger than I, and only two hundred acres in the whole, and as they were growing up to be men, it seemed as if it would be best for me, the oldest, to start out first and see what could be done to make my own living. I talked to Father and Mother about my plans, and they did not seriously object, but gave me some good advice, which I remember to this day: "Weigh well everything you do; shun bad company; be honest and deal fair; be truthful and never fear when you know you are right." But, said he, "Our little peach trees will bear this year, and if you go away you must come back and help us eat them; they will be the first we ever raised or ever saw." I could not promise.

Henry and I drew our pay for our work. I had five dollars in cash and the rest in pay from the company's store. We purchased three nice whitewood boards, eighteen inches wide, from which we made us a boat and a good-sized chest, which we filled with provisions and some clothing and quilts. This, with our guns and ammunition, composed the cargo of our boat. When all was ready, we put the boat on a wagon and were to haul it to the river some eight miles away for embarkation. After getting the wagon loaded, Father said to me, "Now my son, you are starting out in life alone, no one to watch or look after you. You will have to depend upon yourself in all things. You have a wide, wide world to operate in—you will meet all kinds of people and you must not expect to find them all honest or true friends. You are limited in money, and all I can do for you in that way is to let you have what ready money I have." He handed me three dollars as he spoke, which, added to my own, gave me seven dollars as my money capital with which to start out into the world among perfect strangers, and no acquaintances in prospect, on our western course.

When ready to start, Mother and sister Polly came out to see us off and to give us their best wishes, hoping we would have good health and find pleasant paths to follow. Mother said to me, "You must be a good boy, honest and law-abiding. Remember our advice and honor us, for we have striven to make you a good and honest man, and you must follow our teachings, and your conscience will be clear. Do nothing to be ashamed of; be industrious, and you have no fear of punishment." We were given a great many "Good-byes" and "God bless yous" as, with hands, hats, and handkerchiefs, they waved us off as far as we could see them. In the course of an hour or so we were at the water's edge, and on a beautiful morning in early spring of 1840 we found ourselves floating down the Grand River below Jackson.

The stream ran west, that we knew, and it was west we thought we wanted to go, so all things suited us. The stream was small with tall timber on both sides, and so many trees had fallen into the river that our navigation was at times seriously obstructed. When night came we hauled our boat on shore, turned it partly over so as to shelter us, built a fire in front, and made a bed on a loose board which we carried in the bottom of the boat. We talked till pretty late and then lay down to sleep, but for my part my eyes would not stay shut, and I lay till break of day and the little birds began to sing faintly.

I thought of many things that night which seemed so long. I had left a good, dear home, where I had good, warm meals and a soft and comfortable bed. Here I had reposed on a board with a very hard pillow and none too many blankets, and I turned from side to side on my hard bed, to which I had gone with all my clothes on. It seemed the beginning of another chapter in my pioneer life and a rather tough experience. I arose, kindled a big fire, and sat looking at the glowing coals in still further meditation.

Neither of us felt very gleeful as we got our breakfast and made an early start down the river again. Neither of us talked very much, and no doubt my companion had similar thoughts to mine, and wondered what was before us. But I think that as a pair we were at that moment pretty lonesome. Henry had rested better than I but probably felt no less keenly the separation from our homes and friends. We saw plenty of squirrels and pigeons on the trees which overhung the river, and we shot and picked up as many as we thought we could use for food. When we fired our guns the echoes rolled up and down the river for miles, making the feeling of loneliness still more keen as the sound died faintly away. We floated along generally very quietly. We could see the fish dart under our boat from their feeding places along the bank, and now and then some tall crane would spread his broad wings to get out of our way.

We saw no houses for several days and seldom went on shore. The forest was all hardwood, such as oak, ash, walnut, maple, elm, and beech. Farther down we occasionally passed the house of some pioneer hunter or trapper, with a small patch cleared. At one of these a big, green boy came down to the bank to see who we were. We said "How d'you do," to him and, getting no response, Henry asked him how far it was to Michigan, at which a look of supreme disgust came over his features as he replied, "'Tain't no far at all."

The stream grew wider as we advanced along its downward course, for smaller streams came pouring in to swell its tide. The banks were still covered with heavy timber and in some places with quite thick undergrowth. One day we saw a black bear in the river washing himself, but he went ashore before we were near enough to get a sure shot at him. Many deer tracks were seen along the shore, but as we saw very few of the animals themselves, they were probably night visitors.

One day we overtook some canoes containing Indians: men, women and children. They were poling their craft around in all directions, spearing fish. They caught many large mullet and then went on shore and made camp, and the red ladies began scaling the fish. As soon as their lords and masters had unloaded the canoes, a party started out with four of the boats, two men in a boat, to try their luck again. They ranged all abreast, and moved slowly down the stream in the still, deep water, continually beating the surface with their spear handles, till they came to a place so shallow that they could see the bottom easily, when they suddenly turned the canoe's head upstream, and while one held the craft steady by sticking his spear handle down on the bottom, the other stood erect, with a foot on either gunwale so he could see whatever came down on either side. Soon the big fish would try to pass, but Mr. Indian had too sharp an eye to let him escape unobserved, and when he came within his reach he would turn his spear and throw it like a dart, seldom missing his aim. The poor fish would struggle desperately, but soon came to the surface, when he would be drawn in and knocked in the head with a tomahawk to quiet him, then the spear was cut out and the process repeated. We watched them about an hour, and during that time some one of the boats was continually hauling in a fish. They were sturgeon and very large. This was the first time we had ever seen the Indian's way of catching fish and it was a new way of getting grub for us. When the canoes had full loads they paddled up toward their camp, and we drifted on again.

When we came to Grand Rapids we had to go on shore and tow our boat carefully along over the many rocks to prevent accident. Here was a small, cheap looking town. On the west bank of the river a waterwheel was driving a drill, boring for salt, it seemed through solid rock.[3] Up to this time the current was slow and its course through a dense forest. We occasionally saw an Indian gliding around in his canoe, but no houses or clearings. Occasionally we saw some pine logs which had been floated down some of the streams of the north. One of these small rivers they called the Looking Glass, and [it] seemed to be the largest of them.

Passing on we began to see some pine timber and realized that we were near the mouth of the river where it emptied into Lake Michigan. There were some steam sawmills here, not then in operation, and some houses for the mill hands to live in when they were at work. This prospective city was called Grand Haven. There was one schooner in the river loaded with lumber, ready to sail for the west side of the lake as soon as the wind should change and become favorable, and we engaged passage for a dollar and a half each. While waiting for the wind we visited the woods in search of game, but found none. All the surface of the soil was clear lake sand, and some quite large pine and hemlock trees were half buried in it. We were not pleased with this place for it looked as if folks must get their grub from somewhere else or live on fish.

Next morning we were off early, as the wind had changed, but the lake was very rough and a heavy, choppy sea was running. Before we were halfway across the lake nearly all were seasick, passengers and sailors. The poor fellow at the helm stuck to his post, casting up his accounts at the same time, putting on an air of terrible misery.

This, I thought, was pretty hard usage for a landlubber like myself who had never been on such rough water before. The effect of this seasickness was to cure me of a slight fever and ague, and in fact the cure was so thorough that I have never had it since. As we neared the western shore a few houses could be seen, and the captain said it was Southport.[4] As there was no wharf our schooner put out into the lake again for an hour or so and then ran back again, lying off and on in this manner all night. In the morning it was quite calm and we went on shore in the schooner's yawl, landing on a sandy beach. We left our chest of clothes and other things in a warehouse and shouldered our packs and guns for a march across what seemed an endless prairie stretching to the west. We had spent all our lives thus far in a country where all the clearing had to be made with an axe, and such a broad field was to us an entirely new feature. We laid our course westward and tramped on. The houses were very far apart, and we tried at every one of them for a chance to work, but could get none, not even if we would work for our board. The people all seemed to be new settlers, and very poor, compelled to do their own work until a better day could be reached. The coarse meals we got were very reasonable, generally only ten cents, but sometimes a little more.

As we traveled westward the prairies seemed smaller, with now and then some oak openings between. Some of the farms seemed to be three or four years old, and what had been laid out as towns consisted of from three to six houses, small and cheap, with plenty of vacant lots. The soil looked rich, as though it might be very productive. We passed several small lakes that had nice fish in them and plenty of ducks on the surface.

Walking began to get pretty tiresome. Great blisters would come on our feet, and, tender as they were, it was a great relief to take off our boots and go barefoot for a while when the ground was favorable. We crossed a wide prairie and came down to the Rock River where there were a few houses on the east side but no signs of habitation on the west bank. We crossed the river in a canoe and then walked seven miles before we came to a house where we stayed all night and inquired for work. None was to be had and so we tramped on again. The next day we met a real live Yankee with a one-horse wagon, peddling tinware in regular eastern style. We inquired of him about the road and prospects, and he gave us an encouraging idea—said all was good. He told us where to stop the next night at a small town called Sugar Creek. It had but a few houses and was being built up as a mining town, for some lead ore had been found there. There were as many Irish as English miners here, a rough class of people. We put up at the house where we had been directed, a low log cabin, rough and dirty, kept by Bridget & Co. Supper was had after dark and the light on the table was just the right one for the place, a saucer of grease, with a rag in it lighted and burning at the edge of the saucer. It at least served to make the darkness apparent and to prevent the dirt being visible. We had potatoes, beans, and tea, and probably dirt too, if we could have seen it. When the meal was nearly done Bridget brought in and deposited on each plate a good thick pancake as a dessert. It smelled pretty good, but when I drew my knife across it to cut it in two, all the center was uncooked batter, which ran out upon my plate, and spoiled my supper.

We went to bed and soon found it had other occupants beside ourselves which, if they were small, were lively and spoiled our sleeping. We left before breakfast, and a few miles out on the prairie we came to a house occupied by a woman and one child, and we were told we could have breakfast if we could wait to have it cooked. Everything looked cheap but cheery, and after waiting a little while outside we were called in to eat. The meal consisted of corn bread, bacon, potatoes, and coffee. It was well cooked and looked better than things did at Bridget's. I enjoyed all but the coffee, which had a rich brown color, but when I sipped it there was such a bitter taste I surely thought there must be quinine in it, and it made me shiver. I tried two or three times to drink but it was too much for me and I left it. We shouldered our loads and went on again. I asked Henry what kind of a drink it was. "Coffee," said he, but I had never seen any that tasted like that and never knew my father to buy any such coffee as that.

We labored along and in time came to another small place called Hamilton's Diggings,[5] where some lead mines were being worked. We stopped at a long, low log house with a porch the entire length, and called for bread and milk, which was soon set before us. The lady was washing and the man was playing with a child on the porch. The little thing was trying to walk; the man would swear terribly at it—not in an angry way, but in a sort of careless, blasphemous style that was terribly shocking. I thought of the child being reared in the midst of such bad language and reflected on the kind of people we were meeting in this faraway place. They seemed more wicked and profane the farther west we walked. I had always lived in a more moral and temperate atmosphere, and I was learning more of some things in the world than I had ever known before. I had little to say and much to see and listen to and my early precepts were not forgotten. No work was to be had here and we set out across the prairie toward Mineral Point,[6] twenty miles away. When within four miles of that place we stopped at the house of Daniel Parkinson, a fine looking two-story building, and after the meal was over Mr. Henry hired out to him for sixteen dollars per month, and went to work that day. I heard of a job of cutting cordwood six miles away and went after it, for our money was getting very scarce, but when I reached the place I found a man had been there half an hour before and secured the job. The proprietor, Mr. Crow, gave me my dinner, which I accepted with many thanks, for it saved my coin to pay for the next meal. I now went to Mineral Point and searched the town over for work. My purse contained thirty-five cents only and I slept in an unoccupied outhouse without supper. I bought crackers and dried beef for ten cents in the morning and made my first meal since the day before, [and] felt pretty low-spirited. I then went to Vivian's smelting furnace where they bought lead ore, smelted it, and [ran] it into pigs of about seventy pounds each. He said he had a job for me if I could do it. The furnace was propelled by water and they had a small buzz saw for cutting four-foot wood into blocks about a foot long. These blocks they wanted split up in pieces about an inch square to mix in with charcoal in smelting ore. He said he would board me with the other men and give me a dollar and a quarter a cord for splitting the wood. I felt awfully poor, and a stranger, and this was a beginning for me at any rate, so I went to work with a will and never lost a minute of daylight till I had split up all the wood and filled his woodhouse completely up. The board was very coarse—bacon, potatoes, and bread—a man cook, and bread mixed up with salt and water. The old log house where we lodged was well infested with troublesome insects which worked nights at any rate, whether they rested days or not, and the beds had a mild odor of polecat.[7] The house was long, low, and without windows. In one end was a fireplace, and there were two tiers of bunks on each side, supplied with straw only. In the space between the bunks was a stationary table, with stools for seats. I was the only American who boarded there and I could not well become very familiar with the boarders.

The country was rolling, and there were many beautiful brooks and clear springs of water, with fertile soil. The Cornish miners were in the majority and governed the locality politically. My health was excellent, and so long as I had my gun and ammunition I could kill game enough to live on, for prairie chickens and deer could be easily killed, and meat alone would sustain life, so I had no special fears of starvation. I was now paid off, and went back to see my companion, Mr. Henry. I did not hear of any more work, so I concluded I would start back toward my old home in Michigan and shouldered my bundle and gun, turning my face eastward for a long tramp across the prairie. I knew I had a long tramp before me, but I thought best to head that way, for my capital was only ten dollars, and I might be compelled to walk the whole distance. I walked till about noon and then sat down in the shade of a tree to rest, for this was June and pretty warm. I was now alone in a big territory, thinly settled, and thought of my father's home, the well-set table, all happy and well-fed at any rate, and here was my venture, a sort of forlorn hope. Prospects were surely very gloomy for me here away out west in Wisconsin Territory,[8] without a relative, friend, or acquaintance to call upon, and very small means to travel two hundred and fifty miles of lonely road—perhaps all the way on foot. There were no laborers required, hardly any money in sight, and no chance for business. I knew it would be a safe course to proceed toward home, for I had no fear of starving, the weather was warm, and I could easily walk home long before winter should come again. Still the outlook was not very pleasing to one in my circumstances.

I chose a route which led me some distance north of the one we traveled when we came west, but it was about the same. [In] every house was a new settler, and hardly one who had yet produced anything to live upon. In due time I came to the Rock River, and the only house in sight was upon the east bank. I could see a boat over there and so I called for it, and a young girl came over with a canoe for me. I took a paddle and helped her hold the boat against the current, and we made the landing safely. I paid her ten cents for ferriage and went on again. The country was now level, with burr-oak openings.[9] Near sundown I came to a small prairie of about five hundred acres surrounded by scattering burr-oak timber, with not a hill in sight, and it seemed to me to be the most beautiful spot on earth. This I found to belong to a man named Meachem, who had an octagon concrete house built on one side of the opening. The house had a hollow column in the center, and the roof was so constructed that all the rainwater went down this central column into a cistern below for house use. The stairs wound around this central column, and the whole affair was quite different from the most of settlers' houses. I stayed here all night, had supper and breakfast, and paid my bill of thirty-five cents. He had no work for me so I went on again. I crossed Heart Prairie, passed through a strip of woods, and [came] out at Round Prairie. It was level as a floor with a slight rise in one corner, and on it were five or six settlers. Here fortune favored me, for here I found a man whom I knew, who once lived in Michigan, and was one of our neighbors there for some time. His name was Nelson Cornish. I rested here a few days and made a bargain to work for him two or three days every week for my board as long as I wished to stay. As I got acquainted I found some work to do and many of my leisure hours I spent in the woods with my gun, killing some deer, some of the meat of which I sold. In haying and harvest I got some work at fifty cents to one dollar per day, and as I had no clothes to buy, I spent no money, saving up about fifty dollars by fall. I then got a letter from Henry saying that I could get work with him for the winter, and I thought I would go back there again.

Before thinking of going west again, I had to go to Southport on the lake and get our clothes we had left in our box when we passed in the spring. So I started one morning at break of day, with a long cane in each hand to help me along, for I had nothing to carry, not even wearing a coat. This was a new road, thinly settled, [with] a few log houses [being built]. I got a bowl of bread and milk at noon and then hurried on again. The last twenty miles was clear prairie, and houses were very far apart, but little more thickly settled as I neared Lake Michigan. I arrived at the town just after dark and went to a tavern and inquired about the things. I was told that the warehouse had been broken into and robbed, and the proprietor had fled for parts unknown. This robbed me of all my good clothes, and I could now go back as lightly loaded as when I came. I found I had walked sixty miles[10] in that one day, and also found myself very stiff and sore, so that I did not start back next day, and I took three days for the return trip—a very unprofitable journey.

I was now ready to go west, and coming across a pet deer which I had tamed, I knew if I left it, it would wander away with the first wild ones that came along, and so I killed it and made my friends a present of some venison. I chose a still newer route this time, [so] that I could see all that was possible of this big territory when I could do it so easily. I was always a great admirer of Nature and things which remained as they were created, and to the extent of my observation, I thought this the most beautiful and perfect country I had seen between Vermont and the Mississippi River. The country was nearly level, the land rich, the prairies small with oak openings surrounding them, very little marshland, and streams of clear water. Rock River was the largest of these, running south. Next west was Sugar River, then the Picatonica. Through the mining region the country was rolling and abundantly watered with babbling brooks and health-giving springs.

In point of health it seemed to me to be far better than Michigan. In Mr. Henry's letter to me he had said that he had taken a timber claim in Kentuck Grove, and had all the four-foot wood engaged to cut at thirty-seven cents a cord. He said we could board ourselves and save a little money and that in the spring he would go back to Michigan with me. This had decided me to go back to Mineral Point. I stopped a week or two with a man named Webb, hunting with him, and sold game enough to bring me in some six or seven dollars, and then resumed my journey.

On my way I found a log house ten miles from a neighbor just before I got to the Picatonica River. It belonged to a Mr. Shook, who, with his wife and three children, lived on the edge of a small prairie and had a good crop of corn. He invited me to stay with him a few days, and as I was tired I accepted his offer and we went out together and brought in a deer. We had plenty of corn bread, venison, and coffee, and lived well. After a few days he wanted to kill a steer, and he led it to a proper place while I shot it in the head. We had no way to hang it up so he rolled the intestines out, and I sat down with my side against the steer and helped him to pull the tallow off.

It was now getting nearly dark, and while he was splitting the back-bone with an axe, it slipped in his greasy hands and, glancing, cut a gash in my leg six inches above the knee. I was now laid up for two or three weeks, but was well cared for at his house. Before I could resume my journey, snow had fallen to the depth of about six inches, which made it rather unpleasant walking, but in a few days I reached Mr. Henry's camp in Kentuck Grove, when, after comparing notes, we both began swinging our axes and piling up cordwood, [and] cooking potatoes, bread, bacon, coffee, and flapjacks ourselves, which we enjoyed with a relish.

I now went to work for Peter Parkinson, who paid me thirteen dollars per month, and I remained with him till spring. While with him a very sad affliction came to him in the loss of his wife. He was presented by her with his first heir, and during her illness she was cared for by her mother, Mrs. Cullany, who had come to live with them during the winter. When the little babe was two or three weeks old, the mother was feeling in such good spirits that she was left alone a little while, as Mrs. Cullany was attending to some duties which called her elsewhere. When she returned she was surprised to see that both Mrs. Parkinson and the babe were gone. Everyone turned out to search for her. I ran to the smokehouse, the barn, the stable in quick order and, not finding her, a search was made for tracks, and we soon discovered that she had passed over a few steps leading over a fence and down an incline toward the springhouse, and there, fallen face downward on the floor of the house, which was covered only a few inches deep with water, lay the unfortunate woman and her child, both dead. This was doubly distressing to Mr. Parkinson and saddened the whole community. Both were buried in one grave, not far from the house, and a more impressive funeral I never beheld.

I now worked awhile again with Mr. Henry and we sold our wood to Bill Park, a collier, who made and sold charcoal to the smelters of lead ore.

When the ice was gone in the streams, Henry and I shouldered our guns and bundles, and made our way to Milwaukee, where we arrived in the course of a few days. The town was small and cheaply built and had no wharf, so that when the steamboat came we had to go out to it in a small boat. The stream which came in here was too shallow for the steamer to enter. When near the lower end of the lake, we stopped at an island to take on food and several cords of white birch wood. The next stopping place was at Michilimackinac, afterward called Mackinaw.[11] Here was a short wharf, and a little way back a hill, which seemed to me to be a thousand feet high, on which a fort had been built. On the wharf was a mixed lot of people—Americans, Canadians, Irish, Indians, squaws, and papooses. I saw there some of the most beautiful fish I had ever seen. They would weigh twenty pounds or more and had bright red and yellow spots all over them. They called them trout, and they were beauties, really. At the shore nearby, the Indians were loading a large, white birch bark canoe, putting their luggage along the middle lengthways, and the papooses on top. One man took a stern seat to steer, and four or five more had seats along the gunwale as paddlers, and as they moved away, their strokes were as even and regular as the motions of an engine, and their crafts danced as lightly on the water as an eggshell. They were starting for the Michigan shore some eight or ten miles away. This was the first birch bark canoe I had ever seen and [it] was a great curiosity in my eyes.

We crossed Lake Huron during the night, and [went] through its outlet, so shallow that the wheels stirred up the mud from the bottom; then through Lake St. Clair,[12] and landed safely at Detroit next day. Here we took the cars on the Michigan Central Railroad, and on our way westward stopped at the very place where we had worked, helping to build the road, a year or more before. After getting off the train, a walk of two and one-half miles brought me to my father's house, where I had a right royal welcome, and the questions they asked me about the wild country I had traveled over—how it looked and how I got along—were numbered by the thousand.

I remained at home until fall, getting some work to do by which I saved some money, but in August was attacked with bilious fever, which held me down for several weeks; but nursed by a tender and loving mother with untiring care, I recovered quite slowly but surely. I felt that I had been close to death, and that this country was not to be compared to Wisconsin, with its clear and bubbling springs of health-giving water. Feeling thus, I determined to go back there again.

CHAPTER VI

Hunting and Trapping in the Woods

WITH THE IDEA OF RETURNING TO WISCONSIN I made plans for my movements. I purchased a good outfit of steel traps of several kinds and sizes, thirty or forty in all [and] made me a pine chest with a false bottom to separate the traps from my clothing when it was packed in traveling order, the clothes at the top. My former experience had taught me not to expect to get work there during winter, but I was pretty sure something could be earned by trapping and hunting at this season, and in summer I was pretty sure of something to do. I had about forty dollars to travel on this time and quite a stock of experience. The second parting from home was not so hard as the first one. I went to Huron,[1] took the steamer to Chicago, then a small, cheaply built town with rough sidewalks and terribly muddy streets, and the people seemed pretty rough, for sailors and lake captains were numerous, and knockdowns quite frequent. The country for a long way west of town seemed a low, wet marsh or prairie.

Finding a man going west with a wagon and two horses without a load, I hired him to take me and my baggage to my friend Nelson Cornish, at Round Prairie. They were glad to see me, and as I had not yet got strong from my fever, they persuaded me to stay awhile with them and take some medicine, for he was a sort of a doctor. I think he must have given me a dose of calomel, for I had a terribly sore mouth and could not eat anything for two or three weeks. As soon as I was able to travel I had myself and chest taken to the stage station on the line from the lake to Mineral Point. I think this place was called Geneva. On the stage I got along pretty fast, and part of the time on a new road. The first place of note was Madison, the capital of the territory, situated on a block of land nearly surrounded by four lakes, all plainly seen from the big house. Further on at the Blue Mounds I left the stage, putting my chest in the landlord's keeping till I should come or send for it.

I walked about ten miles to the house of a friend named A. Bennett, who was a hunter and lived on the bank of the Picatonica River with his wife and two children. I had to take many a rest on the way, for I was very weak.

[After] resting the first few days, Mrs. Bennett's father, Mr. J. P. Dilly, took us out about six miles and left us to hunt and camp for a few days. We were quite successful and killed five nice, fat deer, which we dressed and took to Mineral Point, selling them rapidly to the Cornish miners for twenty-five cents a quarter for the meat. We followed this business till about January first. When the game began to get poor, we hung up our guns for a while. I had a little money left yet. The only money in circulation was American silver and British sovereigns. They would not sell lead ore for paper money nor on credit. During the spring I used my traps successfully, so that I saved something over board and expenses.

In summer I worked in the mines with Edwin Buck of Bucksport, Maine, but only found lead ore enough to pay our expenses in getting it. Next winter I chopped wood for thirty-five cents per cord and boarded myself. This was poor business, poorer than hunting. In summer I found work at various things, but in the fall Mr. Buck and myself concluded that as we were both hunters and trappers, we would go northward toward Lake Superior on a hunting expedition and perhaps remain all winter. We replenished our outfit and engaged Mr. Bennett to take us well up into the north country. We crossed the Wisconsin River near Muscoda, went then to Prairie du Chien,[2] where we found a large, stone fur-trading house owned by Mr. Brisbois, a Frenchman, from whom we obtained some information of the country farther on. He assured us there was no danger from the Indians if we let them alone and treated them fairly.

We bought fifty pounds of flour for each of us and then started up the divide between the Wisconsin and Mississippi Rivers. On one side flowed the Bad [Axe] River, and on the other the Kickapoo. We traveled on this divide about three days, when Mr. Bennett became afraid to go any farther, as he had to return alone and the Indians might capture him before he could get back to the settlement. We camped early one night and went out hunting to get some game for him. I killed a large, black bear and Mr. Bennett took what he wanted of it, including the skin, and started back next morning.

We now cached our things in various places, scattering them well. Some went in hollow logs, and some under heaps of brush or other places, where the Indians could not find them. We then built a small cabin about six by eight feet in size and four feet high, in shape like an upside-down "V." We were not thoroughly pleased with this location and started out to explore the country to the north of us, for we had an idea that it would be better hunting there.

The first day we started north we killed a bear and filled our stomachs with the fat, sweet meat. The next night we killed another bear after a little struggling. The dog made him climb a tree and we shot at him; he would fall to the ground as if dead but would be on his feet again in an instant, when, after the dog had fastened to his ham, he would climb the tree again. In the third trial he lay in the fork and had a good chance to look square at his tormentor. I shot him in the head, and as he lay perfectly still, Buck said, "Now you have done it—we can't get him." But in a moment he began to struggle, and soon came down, lifeless.

Here we camped on the edge of the pine forest, ate all the fat bear meat we could, and in the morning took separate routes, agreeing to meet again a mile or so farther up a small brook. I soon saw a small bear walking on a log and shot him dead. His mate got away, but I set my dog on him and he soon had to climb a tree. When I came up to where the dog was barking, I saw Mr. Bear and fired a ball in him that brought him down. Just then I heard Mr. Buck shoot close by, and I went to him and found he had killed another and larger bear. We stayed here another night, dressed our game, and sank the meat in the brook[3] and fastened it down, thinking we might want to get some of it another time.

We were so well pleased with this hunting ground that we took the bearskins and went back to camp. When we got there our clothes were pretty well saturated with bear's oil, and we jokingly said it must have soaked through our bodies, we had eaten so much bear meat. I began to feel quite sick, and had a bad headache. I felt as if something must be done, but we had no medicine. Mr. Buck went down by the creek and dug some roots he called Indian physic, then steeped them until the infusion seemed as black as molasses, and, when cool, told me to take a swallow every fifteen minutes for an hour, then half as much for another hour as long as I could keep it down. I followed directions and vomited freely and for a long time, but felt better afterward, and soon got well.[4] It reminded me some of the feelings I had when I was seasick on Lake Michigan.

It may be interesting to describe how we were dressed to enter on this winter campaign. We wore moccasins of our own make. I had a buckskin jumper, and leggins that came up to my hips. On my head a drab hat that fitted close and had a rim about two inches wide. In fair weather I went bareheaded, Indian fashion. I carried a tomahawk which I had made. The blade was two inches wide and three inches long—the poll[5] two inches long and about as large round as a dime; handle, eighteen or twenty inches long with a knob on the end so it would not easily slip from the hand. Oiled patches for our rifle, balls on a string, a firing wire, a charger to measure the powder, and a small piece of leather with four nipples on it for caps—all on my breast, so that I could load very rapidly. My bed was a comfort I made myself, a little larger than usual. I lay down on one side of the bed and, with my gun close to me, turned the blanket over me. When out of camp I never left my gun out of my reach. We had to be real Indians in custom and actions in order to be considered their equals. We got our food in the same way they did, and so they had nothing to ask us for. They considered themselves the real kings of the forest.

We now determined to move camp, which proved quite a job, as we had to pack everything on our backs, which we did for ten or fifteen miles to the bank of a small stream where there were three pine trees, the only ones to be found in many miles. We made us a canoe of one of them.[6] While we were making the canoe three Indians came along, and after they had eaten some of our good venison, they left us. These were the first we had seen, and we began to be more cautious and keep everything well hid away from camp and make them think we were as poor as they were, so they might not be tempted to molest us.

We soon had the canoe done and loaded, and embarked on the brook downstream. We found it rather difficult work, but the stream grew larger and we got along very well. We came to one place where otter signs seemed fresh, and stopped to set a trap for them. Our dog sat on the bank and watched the operation, and when we started on we could not get him to ride or follow. Soon we heard him cry and went back to find he had the trap on his forefoot. To get it off we had to put a forked stick over his neck and hold him down, he was so excited over his mishap. When he was released he left at full speed and was never seen by us after.

When we got well into the pine woods we camped and cached our traps and provisions on an island, and made our camp further down the stream and some little distance from the shore. We soon found this was very near a logging camp, and as no one had been living there for a year, we moved camp down there and occupied one of the empty cabins. We began to set deadfall traps in long lines in many different directions, blazing the trees so we could find them if the snow came on. West of this about ten miles, where we had killed some deer earlier, we made a cabin shaped like an upside-down "V" and made deadfalls many miles around to catch fishes, foxes, mink, and raccoons. We made weekly journeys to the places and generally stayed about two nights.

One day, when going over my trap lines, I came to a trap which I had set where I had killed a deer, and saw by the snow that an eagle had been caught in the trap and had broken the chain and gone away. I followed on the trail he made and soon found him. He tried to fly but the trap was too heavy, and he could only go slowly and a little way. I fired and put a ball in him and he fell and rolled under a large log on the hillside. As I took the trap off I saw an Indian coming down the hill and brought my gun to bear on him. He stopped suddenly and made signs not to shoot, and I let him come up. He made signs that he wanted the feathers of the bird, which I told him to take, and then he wanted to know where we slept. I pointed out the way and made him go ahead of me there, for I did not want him behind me. At camp he made signs for something to eat, but when I showed him meat he shook his head. However, he took a leg of deer and started on, I following at a good distance till satisfied that he would not come back.

We had not taken pains to keep track of the day of the week or month; the rising and setting of the sun and the changes of the moon were all the almanacs we had. Then snow came about a foot deep, and some days were so cold we could not leave our campfire at all. As no Indians appeared we were quite successful and kept our bundle of furs in a hollow standing tree some distance from camp, and when we went that way we never stopped or left any sign that we had a deposit there.

Some time after it was all frozen up solid, some men with two yoke of oxen came up to cut and put logs in the river to raft down when the ice went out. With them came a shingle weaver,[7] with a pony and a small sled, and some Indians also. We now had to take up all of our steel traps, and rob all our deadfalls and quit business generally—even then they got some of our traps before we could get them gathered in. We were now comparatively idle.

Until these loggers came we did not know exactly where we were situated, but they told us we were on the Lemonai River, a branch of the Wisconsin, and that we could get out by going west till we found the Mississippi River and then home. We hired the shingle man with his pony to take us to Black River, farther north, which we reached in three days, and found a sawmill there in charge of a keeper. Up the river farther we found another mill, looked after by Sam Ferguson. Both mills were frozen up. The Indians had been here all winter. They come from Lake Superior when the swamps freeze up there, to hunt deer till the weather gets warm, then they returned to the lake to fish.

Of course the presence of the Indians made game scarce, but the mill men told us if we would go up farther into the marten country, they thought we would do well. We therefore made us a hand sled, put some provisions and traps on board, and started up the river on the ice. As we went the snow grew deeper and we had to cut hemlock boughs for a bed on top of the snow. It took about a half a cord of wood to last us all night, and it was a trouble to cut holes in the ice to water, for it was more than two feet thick. Our fire, kindled on the snow, would be two or three feet below on the ground by morning. This country was heavily timbered with cedar or spruce and apparently very level.

One day we saw two otters coming toward us on the ice. We shot one, but as the other gun missed fire, the other one escaped, for I could not overtake it in the woods. We kept on up the river till we began to hear the Indians' guns, and then we camped and did not fire a gun for two days, for we were afraid we might be discovered and robbed, and we knew we could not stay long after our grub was gone. All the game we could catch was the marten or sable, which the Indians called *waubusash*. The males were snuff color and the females much darker. Mink were scarce, and the beaver, living in the riverbank, could not be got at till the ice went out in the spring.

We now began to make marten traps or deadfalls, and set them for this small game. There were many cedar and tamarack swamps—indeed that was the principal feature—but there were some ridges a little higher where some small pines and beech grew. Now, our camp was one place where there was no large timber caused by the stream being dammed by the beaver. Here were some of the real Russian balsam trees, the most beautiful in shape I had ever seen. They were very dark green, the boughs very thick, and the tree in shape like an inverted top. Our lines of traps led for miles in every direction, marked by blazed trees. We made a trap of two poles and chips which we split from the trees. These were set in the snow and covered with brush. We sometimes found a porcupine in the top of a pine tree. The only signs of his presence were the chips he made in gnawing the bark for food. They never came down to the ground as we saw. They were about all the game that was good to eat. I would kill one, skin it, and drag the carcass after me all day as I set traps, cutting off bits for bait and cooking the rest for ourselves to eat.

We tried to eat the marten but it was pretty musky, and it was only by putting on plenty of salt and pepper that we managed to eat them. We would be really forced to do it if we remained here. We secured a good many of these little fellows, which have about the best fur that is found in America.

We were here about three weeks, and our provisions giving out and the ice becoming tender in the swamp were two pretty strong reasons for our getting out, so we shouldered our packs of fur and our guns and, getting our course from a pocket compass, we started out. As we pushed on we came to some old windfalls that were troublesome to get through. The dense timber seemed to be six feet deep, and we would sometimes climb over and sometimes crawl under, the fallen trees were so thickly mixed and tangled.

Mr. Buck got so completely tired that he threw away his traps. We reached our starting place at O'Neil's sawmill after many days of the hardest work, and nearly starved, for we had seen no game on our trip. We found our traps and furs all safe here, and as this stream was one of the tributaries of the Mississippi, we decided to make us a boat and float down toward that noted stream. We secured four good boards and built the boat in which we started down the river, setting traps and moving at our leisure. We found plenty of fine ducks, two bee trees, and caught some catfish with a hook and line we got at the mill. We also caught some otter, and, on a little branch of the river, killed two bears, the skin of one of them weighing five pounds.[8] We met a keelboat being poled up the river and, with the last cent of money we possessed, bought a little flour of them.

About the first of May we reached Prairie du Chien. Here we were met with some surprise, for Mr. Brisbois said he had heard we were killed or lost. He showed us through his warehouses and pointed out to us the many bales of different kinds of furs he had on hand. He told us we were the best fur handlers he had seen, and paid us two hundred dollars in American gold for what we had. We then stored our traps in the garret of one of his warehouses, which was of stone, two stories and an attic, as we thought of making another trip to this country if all went well.

We now entered our skiff again and went on down the great river till we came to a place nearly opposite Mineral Point, when we gave our boat to a poor settler and, with guns and bundles on our backs, took a straight shot for home on foot. The second day about dark we came to the edge of the town and were seen by a lot of boys, who eyed us closely and with much curiosity, for we were dressed in our trapping suits. They followed us, and as we went along, the crowd increased so that when we got to Crum Lloyd's tavern, the door was full of boys' heads looking at us as if we were a circus. Here we were heartily welcomed, and everybody was glad to see us, as they were about to start a company to go in search of their reported murdered friends. It seems a missionary got lost on his way to Prairie La Crosse and had come across our deserted cabin, and when he came in he reported us as no doubt murdered.

I invested all of my hundred dollars in buying eighty acres of good government land. This was the first hundred dollars I ever had and I felt very proud to be a landowner.[9] I felt a little more like a man now than I had ever felt before, for the money was hard earned and all mine.

CHAPTER VII

Nothing Will Cure it But California

MR. BUCK AND MYSELF CONCLUDED WE WOULD TRY our luck at lead mining for the summer and purchased some mining tools for the purpose. We camped out and dug holes around all summer, getting just about enough to pay our expenses—not a very encouraging venture, for we had lived in a tent and had picked and shoveled and blasted and twisted a windlass hard enough to have earned a good bit of money.

In the fall we concluded to try another trapping tour, and set out for Prairie du Chien. We knew it was a poor place to spend money up in the woods, and when we got our money it was all in a lump and seemed to amount to something. Mr. Brisbois said that the prospects were very poor indeed, for the price of fur was very low and no prospect of a better market. So we left our traps still in storage at his place and went back again. This was in 1847, and before spring the war was being pushed in Mexico.[1] I tried to enlist for this service, but there were so many ahead of me I could not get a chance.

I still worked in the settlement and made a living, but had no chance to improve my land. The next winter I lived with Mr. A. Bennett, hunted deer and sold them at Mineral Point, and in this way made and saved a few dollars.

There had been from time to time rumors of a better country to the west of us and a sort of a pioneer [fever], or western fever, would break out among the people occasionally. Thus in 1845 I had a slight touch of the disease on account of the stories they told us about Oregon. It was reported that the government would give a man a good farm if he would go and settle and make some specified improvement. They said it was in a territory of rich soil, with plenty of timber, fish, and game, and some Indians, just to give a little spice of adventure to the whole thing. The climate was very mild in winter, as they reported, and I concluded it would suit me exactly. I began at once to think about an outfit and a journey, and I found that it would take me at least two years to get ready. A trip to California was not thought of in those days, for it did not belong to the United States.

In the winter of 1848-49 news began to come that there was gold in California,[2] but [that was] not generally believed till it came through a U.S. officer, and then, as the people were used to mines and mining, a regular gold fever spread as if by swift contagion. Mr. Bennett was aroused and sold his farm, and I felt a change in my Oregon desires and had dreams at night of digging up the yellow dust. Nothing would cure us then but a trip, and that was quickly decided on.

As it would be some weeks yet before grass would start, I concluded to haul my canoe and a few traps over to a branch of the Wisconsin and make my way to Prairie du Chien, do a little trapping, [and] get me an Indian pony on which to ride to California. There were no ponies to be had at Mineral Point. Getting a ride up the river on a passing steamboat, I reached Prairie La Crosse,[3] where the only house was that of a Dutch trader, from whom I bought a Winnebago pony which he had wintered on a little brushy island, and I thought if he could winter on brush and rushes he must be tough enough to take me across the plains. He cost me thirty dollars, and I found him to be a poor, lazy little fellow. However, I thought that when he got some good grass and a little fat on his ribs he might have more life, and so I hitched a rope to him and drove him ahead down the river. When I came to the Bad Axe River I found it swimming full, but had no trouble in crossing, as the pony was as good as a dog in the water.

Before leaving Bennett's I had my gun altered over to a pill lock[4] and secured ammunition to last for two years. I had tanned some nice buckskin and had a good outfit of clothes made of it, or rather cut and made it myself. Where I crossed the Bad Axe was the battleground where General Dodge fought the Winnebago Indians.[5] At Prairie du Chien I found a letter from Mr. Bennett, saying that the grass was so backward he would not start up for two or three weeks, and I had better come back and start with them; but as the letter bore no date I could only guess at the exact time. I had intended to strike directly west from here to Council Bluffs and meet them there, but now thought perhaps I had better go back to Mineral Point and start out with them there, or follow on rapidly after them if by any chance they had already started.

On my way back I found the Kickapoo River too high to ford, so I pulled some basswood bark and made a raft of a couple of logs on which to carry my gun and blanket; starting the pony across I followed after. He swam across quickly, but did not seem to like it on the other side, so before I got across, back he came again, not paying the least attention to my scolding. I went back with the raft, which drifted a good way downstream, and caught the rascal and started him over again, but when I got halfway across he jumped and played the same joke on me again. I began to think of the old puzzle of the story of the man with the fox, the goose, and a peck of corn, but I solved it by making a basswood rope to which I tied a stone and [which I] threw across, then sending the pony over with the other end.[6] He stayed this time, and after three days of swimming streams and pretty hard travel [I] reached Mineral Point, to find Bennett had been gone two weeks and had taken my outfit with him as we first planned.

I was a little troubled, but set out light loaded for Dubuque, crossed the river there and then [traveled] alone across Iowa, over wet and muddy roads, till I fell in with some wagons west of the Des Moines River. They were from Milwaukee, owned by a Mr. Blodgett, and I camped with them a few nights, till we got to the Missouri River.

I rushed ahead the last day or two and got there before them. There were a few California wagons here and some campers, so I put my pony out to grass and looked around. I waded across the low bottom to a strip of dry land next to the river, where there were a post office, store, and a few cabins. I looked first for a letter, but there was none. Then I began to look over the cards in the trading places and saloons, and read the names written on the logs of the houses, and everywhere I thought there might be a trace of the friends I sought. No one had seen or knew them. After looking half a day, I waded back again to the pony—pretty blue. I thought first I would go back and wait another year, but there was a small train near where I left the pony, and it was not considered very safe to go beyond there except with a pretty good train. I sat down in camp and turned the matter over in my mind, and talked with Charles Dallas of Lynn, Iowa, who owned the train. Bennett had my outfit and gun, while I had his light gun, a small light tent, a frying pan, a tin cup, one woolen shirt, and the clothes on my back. Having no money to get another outfit, I about concluded to turn back when Dallas said that if I would drive one of his teams through, he would board me, and I could turn my pony in with his loose horses. I thought it over, and finally put my things in the wagon and took the ox whip to go on. Dallas intended to get provisions here, but could not, so we went down to St. Jo,[7] following the river near the bluff. We camped near town and walked in, finding a small train on the main emigrant road to the west. My team was one yoke of oxen and one yoke of cows. I knew how to drive, but had a little trouble with the strange animals till they found I was kind to them, and then they were all right.

This was in a slave state, and here I saw the first negro auction.[8] One side of the street had a platform such as we build for a political speaker. The auctioneer mounted this with a black boy about eighteen years old, and after he had told all his good qualities and had the boy stand up bold and straight, he called for bids, and they started him at five hundred dollars. He rattled away as if he were selling a steer, and when Mr. Rubideaux,[9] the founder of St. Jo, bid eight hundred dollars, he went no higher and the boy was sold. With my New England notions it made quite an impression on me.

Here Dallas got his supplies, and when the flour and bacon were loaded up the ferryman wanted fifty dollars to take the train across. This Mr. Dallas thought too high and went back up the river a day's drive, where he got across for thirty dollars. From this crossing we went across the country without much of a road till we struck the road from St. Jo, and were soon on the Platte bottom.

We found some fine strawberries at one of the camps across the country. We found some hills, but now the country was all one vast prairie, not a tree in sight till we reached the Platte, there some cottonwood and willow. At the first camp on the Platte I rolled up in my blanket under the wagon and thought more than I slept, but I was in for it and [there was] no other way but to go on. I had heard that there were two forts, new Fort Kearny[10] and Fort Laramie,[11] on the south side of the river, which we must pass before we reached the South Pass of the Rocky Mountains, and beyond there, there would be no place to buy medicine or food. Our little train of five wagons, ten men, one woman, and three children would not be a formidable force against the Indians if they were disposed to molest us, and it looked to me very hazardous, and that a larger train would be more safe, for government troops were seldom molested on their marches.

If I should not please Mr. Dallas and get turned off with only my gun and pony I should be in a pretty bad shape, but I decided to keep right on and take the chances on the savages, who would get only my hair and my gun as my contribution to them if they should be hostile. I must confess, however, that the trail ahead did not look either straight or bright to me, but I hoped it might be better than I thought. So I yoked my oxen and cows to the wagon and drove on. All the other teams had two drivers each, who took turns, and thus had every other day off for hunting if they chose, but I had to carry the whip every day and leave my gun in the wagon.

When we crossed Salt Creek the banks were high and we had to tie a strong rope to the wagons and, with a few turns around a post, lower them down easily, while we had to double the teams to get them up the other side.

Night came on before half the wagons were over, and though it did not rain, the water rose before morning so it was ten feet deep. We made a boat of one of the wagon beds and had a regular ferry, and when they pulled the wagons over they sank below the surface but came out all right. We came to a Pawnee village on the Platte, a collection of mud huts, oval in shape, and an entrance low down to crawl in at. A ground owl and some prairie dogs were in one of them, and we suspected they might be winter quarters for the Indians.

Dallas and his family rode in the two-horse wagon. Dick Field was cook, and the rest of us drove the oxen. We put out a small guard at night to watch for Indians and keep the stock together so there might be no delay in searching for them. When several miles from Fort Kearny, I think on July 3rd, we camped near the river where there was a slough and much cottonwood and willow. Just after sundown a horse came galloping from the west and went in with our horses that were feeding a little farther down. In the morning two soldiers came from the fort, inquiring after the stray horse, but Dallas said he had seen none, and they did not hunt around among the willows for the lost animal. Probably it would be the easiest way to report back to the fort, "Indians got him." When we hitched up in the morning he put the horse on the off side of his own, and when near the fort, he went ahead on foot and entertained the officers while the men drove by, and the horse was not discovered. I did not like this much, for if we were discovered, we might be roughly handled, and perhaps the property of the innocent even confiscated. Really my New England ideas of honesty were somewhat shocked.

Reaching the South Platte, it took us all day to ford the sandy stream, as we had first to sound out a good crossing by wading through ourselves, and when we started our teams across we dared not stop a moment, for fear the wagons would sink deep into the quicksand. We had no mishaps in crossing, and when well camped on the other side a solitary buffalo made his appearance about two hundred yards away and all hands started after him, some on foot. The horsemen soon got ahead of him, but he did not seem inclined to get out of their way, so they opened fire on him. He still kept his feet and they went nearer; Mr. Rogers, being on a horse with a blind bridle, got near enough to fire his Colt's revolver at him, when he turned, and the horse, being unable to see the animal quick enough to get out of the way, suffered the force of a sudden attack of the old fellow's horns, and came out with a gash in his thigh six inches long, while Rogers went on a flying expedition over the horse's head and did some lively scrambling when he reached the ground. The rest [of] them worried him along for about half a mile, and finally, after about forty shots, he lay down but held his head up defiantly, receiving shot after shot with an angry shake, till a side shot laid him out. This game gave us plenty of meat which, though tough, was a pleasant change from bacon. I took no part in this battle except as an observer. On examination it was found that the balls had been, many of them, stopped by the matted hair about the old fellow's head, and none of them had reached the skull.

A few days after this we were stopped entirely by a herd of buffaloes crossing our road.[12] They came up from the river and were moving south. The smaller animals seemed to be in the lead, and the rear was brought up by the old cows and the shaggy, burly bulls. All were moving at a smart trot, with tongues hanging out, and seemed to take no notice of us, though we stood within a hundred yards of them. We had to stand by our teams and stock to prevent a stampede, for they all seemed to have a great wonder and something of fear at their relatives of the plains. After this we often saw large droves of them in the distance. Sometimes we could see what in the distance seemed a great patch of brush, but by watching closely we could see it was a great drove of these animals. Those who had leisure to go up to the bluffs often reported large droves in sight. Antelopes were also seen, but these occupied the higher ground, and it was very hard to get near enough to them to shoot successfully. Still we managed to get a good deal of game which was very acceptable as food.

One prominent landmark along the route was what they called Courthouse Rock, standing to the south from the trail and much resembling an immense square building, standing high above surrounding country.[13] The farther we went on, the more plentiful became the large game, and also wolves and prairie dogs, the first of which seemed to follow the buffaloes closely.

About this time we met an odd looking train going east, consisting of five or six Mormons from Salt Lake, all mounted on small Spanish mules. They were dressed in buckskin and moccasins, with long spurs jingling at their heels, the rowels fully four inches long, and each one carried a gun, a pistol, and a big knife. They were rough-looking fellows with long, matted hair, long beards, old slouch hats, and a generally backwoods-getup air in every way. They had an extra pack mule, but the baggage and provisions were very light. I had heard much about the Mormons, both at Nauvoo and Salt Lake, and some way or other I could not separate the idea of horse thieves from this party, and I am sure I would not like to meet them if I had a desirable mule that they wanted, or any money, or a good-looking wife. We talked with them half an hour or so and then moved on.

We occasionally passed by a grave along the road, and often a small headboard would state that the poor unfortunate had died of cholera.[14] Many of these had been torn open by wolves and the blanket encircling the corpse partly pulled away. Our route led a few miles north of Chimney Rock,[15] standing on an elevated point like a tall column, so perfect and regular on all sides, that from our point it looked as if it might be the work of stonecutters. Some of the party went to see it and reported there was no way to ascend it, and that as far as a man could reach, the rocks were inscribed with the names of visitors and travelers who passed that way.

At Scott's Bluffs,[16] the bluffs came close to the river, so there was considerable hill climbing to get along, the road in other places finding ample room in the bottom. Here we found a large camp of the Sioux Indians on the bank of a ravine, on both sides of which were some large cottonwood trees. Away up in the large limbs, platforms had been made of poles, on which were laid the bodies of their dead, wrapped in blankets and fastened down to the platform by a sort of a network of smaller poles tightly lashed so that they could not be dragged away or disturbed by wild animals. This seemed a strange sort of cemetery, but when we saw the desecrated earth-made graves, we felt that perhaps this was the best way, even if it was a savage custom.

These Indians were fair-sized men, and pretty good-looking for red men. Some of our men went over to their camp, and some of their youths came down to ours, and when we started on they seemed quite proud that they had learned a little of the English language, but the extent of their knowledge seemed to be a little learned of the ox drivers, for they would swing their hands at the cattle and cry out, "Whoa! haw, g—d d—n." Whether they knew what was meant, I have my doubts. They seemed pretty well provided for and begged very little, as they are apt to do when they are hard pressed.

We saw also some bands of Pawnee Indians on the move across the prairies. They would hitch a long, light pole on each side of a pony, with the ends dragging behind on the ground, and on a little platform at the hind end the children sat and were dragged along.[17]

As we passed on beyond Scott's Bluff the game began to be perceptibly scarcer, and what we did find was back from the traveled road, from which it had apparently been driven by the passing hunters.

In time we reached Fort Laramie,[18] a trading post, where there were some Indian lodges, and we noticed that some of the occupants had lighter complexions than any of the other Indians we had seen. They had cords of dried buffalo meat, and we purchased some. It was very fat, but was so perfectly cured that the clear tallow tasted as sweet as a nut. I thought it was the best dried meat I had ever tasted, but perhaps a good appetite had something to do with it.

As we passed Fort Laramie we fell in company with some U.S. soldiers who were going to Fort Hall[19] and thence to Oregon. We considered them pretty safe to travel with and kept with them for some time, though their rate of travel was less than ours. Among them were some Mormons, employed as teamsters and in other ways, and they told us there were some Missourians on the road who would never live to see California. There had been some contests between the Missourians and the Mormons, and I felt rather glad that none of us hailed from Pike County.

We turned into what they called the Black Hills,[20] leaving the Platte to the north of us. The first night on this road we had the hardest rain I ever experienced and the only one of any account on our journey. Our camp was on a level piece of ground on the bank of a dry creek, which soon became a very wet creek indeed, for by morning it was one hundred yards wide and absolutely impassible. It went down, however, as quickly as it rose, and by ten o'clock it was so low that we easily crossed and went on our way. We crossed one stream where there were great drifts or piles of hail which had been brought down by a heavy storm from higher up the hills. At one place we found some rounded boulders from six to eight inches in diameter which were partly hollow, and broken open were found to contain most beautiful crystals of quartz, clear as purest ice. The inside was certainly very pretty, and it was a mystery how it came there. I have since learned that such stones are found at many points, and that they are called geodes.

We came out at the river again at the mouth of Deer Creek,[21] and as there was some pretty good coal there quite easy to get,[22] we made camp one day to try to tighten our wagon tires, John Rogers acting as blacksmith. This was my first chance to reconnoiter, and so I took my gun and went up the creek, a wide, treeless bottom. In the ravines on the south side were beautiful groves of small fir trees and some thick brush, wild rosebushes I think. I found here a good many heads and horns of elk, and I could not decide whether they had been killed in winter during the deep snow or had starved to death.

There was a ferry here to cross the river and go up along [the] north side. Mr. Dallas bought the whole outfit for a small sum and when we were safely over he took with him such ropes as he wanted and tied the boat to the bank. The road on this side was very sandy and led over and among some rolling hills. In talking with the men of the U.S. troops in whose company we still were, I gathered much information concerning our road farther west.

They said we were entirely too late to get through to California, on account of crossing the Sierra Nevada mountains, which they said would be covered with snow by November or even earlier, and that we would be compelled to winter at Salt Lake. Some of the drivers overheard Mr. Dallas telling his family the same thing, and that if he should winter at Salt Lake, he would discharge his drivers as soon as he arrived, as he could not afford to board them all winter.

This was bad news for me, for I had known of the history of them [the Mormons] at Nauvoo and in Missouri, and the prospect of being thrown among them with no money to buy bread was a very sorry prospect for me. From all I could learn we could not get a chance to work, even for our board there, and the other drivers shared my fears and disappointment. In this dilemma we called a council, and invited the gentleman in to have an understanding. He came and our spokesman stated the case to him, and our fears, and asked him what he had to say to us about it. He flew quite angry at us, and talked some and swore a great deal more, and the burden of his speech was, "This train belongs to me and I propose to do with it just as I have a mind to, and I don't care a d—n what you fellows do or say. I am not going to board you fellows all winter for nothing, and when we get to Salt Lake you can go where you please, for I shall not want you any longer." We talked a little to him and, under the circumstances, to talk was about all we could do. He gave us no satisfaction and left us, apparently much offended that we had any care for ourselves.

Then we had some talk among ourselves, at the time and from day to day as we moved along. We began to think that the only way to get along at all in Salt Lake would be to turn Mormons, and none of us had any belief or desire that way, and [we] could not make up our minds to stop our journey and lose so much time, and if we were not very favored travelers our lot might be cast among the sinners for all time.

We were now on the Sweetwater River, and began to see the snow on the Rocky Mountains ahead of us, another reminder that there was a winter coming and only a little more than half our journey was done. We did not feel very happy over it, and yet we had to laugh once in a while at some of the funny things that would happen.

The government party we were with had among them a German mule driver who had a deal of trouble with his team, but who had a very little knowledge of the English language. When the officers tried to instruct him a little he seemed to get out of patience and would say something very like "*Sacramento.*" We did not know exactly what this meant. We had heard there

41

was a river of that name or something very near like that; and then again some said that was the Dutch for swearing. If this latter was the truth then he was a very profane mule driver when he got mad.

The captain of the company had a very nice looking lady with him, and they carried a fine wall tent, which they occupied when they went into camp. The company cook served their meals to them in the privacy of their tent, and they seemed to enjoy themselves very nicely. Everybody thought the captain was very lucky to have such an accomplished companion journey along quietly to the gold fields at government expense.

There seemed to be just a little jealousy between the captain and the lieutenant, and one day I saw them both standing in angry attitude before the captain's quarters, both mounted, with their carbines lying across their saddles before them. They had some pretty sharp, hot words, and it looked as if they both were pretty nearly warmed up to the shooting point. Once the lieutenant moved his right hand a little, and the captain was quick to see it, shouting, "Let your gun alone or I will make a hole through you," at the same time grasping his own and pointing it straight at the other officer. During all this time the captain's lady stood in the tent door, and when she saw her favorite had the drop on the lieutenant she clapped her delicate little hands in a gleeful manner, "Just look at the captain! Ain't he spunky?" And then she laughed long and loud to see her lord show so much military courage. She seemed more pleased at the affair than anyone else. I don't know exactly what the others thought, but I never could believe that the lady and the captain were ever married.

The lieutenant was no coward, but probably thinking that prudence was the better part of valor, refrained from handling his gun, and the two soon rode away in opposite directions.

We passed a lone rock standing in the river bottom on the Sweetwater, which they named Independence Rock.[23] It was covered with the names of thousands of people who had gone by on that road. Some were pretty neatly chiseled in, some very rudely scrawled, and some put on with paint. I spent all the time I could hunting Mr. Bennett's name, but I could not find it anywhere. To have found his name, and thus to know that he had safely passed this point, would have been a little reassuring in those rather doubtful days. Some had named the date of their passing, and some of them were probably pretty near the gold fields at this time.

All along in this section we found alkali water near the road, some very strong and dangerous for man or beast to use. We traveled on up the Sweetwater for some time, and at last came to a place where the road left the river, and we had a long, hard hill to pull up. When we reached the top of this we were in the South Pass[24] of the Rocky Mountains, the backbone of the American continent. To the north of us were some very high peaks white with snow, and to the south were some lower hills and valleys. The summit of the mountains [here][25] was not quite as imposing as I expected, but it was the summit, and we were soon surely moving down the western side, for at Pacific Springs[26] the water ran to the westward, toward the Pacific coast. The next day we came to the nearly dry bed of the river—the Big Sandy. The country round about seemed volcanic, with no timber, but plenty of sagebrush, in which we were able to shoot an occasional sage hen. The riverbed itself was nothing but sand, and where there was water enough to wet it, it was very miry and hard traveling over it. There are two streams, the Big Sandy and Little Sandy, both tributaries to Green River, which we soon reached and crossed.

It was a remarkably clear and rapid stream and was now low enough to ford. One of the government teams set out to make the crossing at a point where it looked shallow enough, but before the lead mules reached the opposite shore, they lost their footing and were forced to swim. Of course the wagon stopped and the team swung round and tangled up in a bad shape. They were unhitched and the wagon pulled back, [but] the load was somewhat dampened, for the water came into the wagon box about a foot. We camped here and laid by one day, having thus quite a little chance to look around.

When we came to the first water that flowed toward the Pacific coast at Pacific Springs, we drivers had quite a little talk about a new scheme. We put a great many "ifs" together and they amounted to about this: if this stream were large enough; if we had a boat; if we knew the way; if there were no falls or bad places; if we had plenty of provisions; if we were bold enough [to] set out on such a trip, etc., we might come out at some point or other on the Pacific Ocean. And now when we came to the first of the "ifs," a stream large enough to float a small boat, we began to think more strongly about the other "ifs."

In the course of our rambles we actually did run across the second "if" in the shape of a small ferryboat filled up with sand upon a bar, and it did not take very long to dig it out and put it into shape to use, for it was just large enough to hold one wagon at a time. Our military escort intended to leave us at this point, as their route now bore off to the north of ours. I had a long talk with the surgeon, who seemed well informed about the country, and asked him about the prospects. He did not give the Mormons a very good name. He said to me, "If you go to Salt Lake City, do not let them know you are from Missouri, for I tell you that many of those from that state will never see California. You know they were driven from Missouri, and will get revenge if they can." Both the surgeon and the captain said the stream came out on the Pacific coast and that we had no obstacles except cataracts, which they had heard were pretty bad. I then went to Dallas and told him what we proposed doing, and to our surprise he did not offer any objections, and offered me sixty dollars for my pony.[27] He said he would sell us some flour and bacon for provisions also.

We helped them in crossing the river, which was somewhat difficult, being swift with boulders in the bottom, but we got all safely over and then made the trade we had spoken of. Mr. Dallas paid me for my pony and we took what flour and bacon he would let go. He gave us some ropes for head and stern lines to our boat and a couple of axes, and we laid these and our provisions in a pile by the roadside. Six of us then gave up our whips. Mr. S. McMahon, a driver, hesitated for some time, but being pressed by Dallas for a decision, at last threw down his whip and said, "I will go with the boys." This left Dallas with only one driver, but he took a whip himself, and with the aid of the children and his wife, who drove the two-horse wagon, they got along very well. I paid for such provisions as we had taken, as the rest of the fellows had almost no money.

So we parted company, the little train slowly moving on its way westward—our military captain, the soldier boys, and the gay young lady taking the route to Oregon—and we sitting on the bank of the river whose waters flowed to the great Pacific. Each company wished the other good luck, we took a few long breaths and then set to work in earnest to carry out our plans.

CHAPTER VIII

Floating Down the River

ABOUT THE FIRST THING WE DID WAS TO ORGANIZE and select a captain, and, very much against my wishes, I was chosen to this important position. Six of us had guns of some sort; Richard Field, Dallas's cook, was not armed at all. We had one regular axe and a large camp hatchet, which was about the same as an axe, and several very small hatchets owned by the men. All our worldly goods were piled up on the bank, and we were alone.

An examination of the old ferryboat showed it to be in pretty good condition, the sand with which it had been filled keeping it very perfectly. We found two oars in the sand under the boat, and hooked up some poles to assist us in navigation. Our cordage was rather scant but the best we could get and all we could muster. The boat was about twelve feet long and six or seven feet wide, not a very well-proportioned craft, but having the ability to carry a pretty good load. We swung it up to the bank and loaded up our goods and then ourselves. It was not a heavy load for the craft, and it looked as if we were taking the most sensible way to get to the Pacific, and almost wondered that everybody was so blind as not to see it as we did.

This party was composed of W. L. Manly, M. S. McMahon, Charles and Joseph Hazelrig, Richard Field, Alfred Walton, and John Rogers. We untied the ropes, gave the boat a push, and commenced to move down the river with ease and comfort, feeling much happier than we would had we been going toward Salt Lake with the prospect of wintering there.

At the mouth of Ham's Fork[1] we passed a camp of Indians, but we kept close to the opposite shore to avoid being boarded by them. They beckoned very gently for us to come ashore, but I acted as if I did not understand them, and gave them the go-by.

As we were floating down the rapid stream it became more and more a rapid, roaring river, and the bed contained many dangerous rocks that were difficult to shun. Each of us had a setting pole, and we ranged ourselves along the sides of the boat and tried to keep ourselves clear from the rocks and dangers. The water was not very deep and made such a dashing noise as the current rushed among the rocks that one had to talk pretty loud to be heard. As we were gliding along quite swiftly, I set my pole on the bottom and gave the boat a sudden push to avoid a boulder, when the pole stuck in the crevice between two rocks, and instead of losing the pole by the sudden jerk I gave, I was the one who was very suddenly yanked from the boat by the spring of the pole and landed in the middle of the river. I struck pretty squarely on my back, and so got thoroughly wet, but swam for shore amid the shouts of the boys, who waved their hats and hurrahed for the captain when they saw he was not hurt. I told them that was nothing, as we were on our way to California by water anyway, and such things must be expected.

The next day after this I went on shore and sighted a couple of antelope, one of which I shot, which gave us good grub, and good appetites we already had. As near as we could estimate we floated about thirty miles a day, which beat the pace of tired oxen considerably. In one place there was a fringe of thick willows along the bank, and a little farther back a perpendicular bluff, while between the two was a strip of fine green grass. As we were passing this we scared up a band of elk in this grass meadow, and they all took a run down the river like a band of horses. One of them turned up a small ravine with walls so steep he could not get out, so we posted a guard at the entrance, and three of us went up the cañon after him, and after the others had each fired a shot, I fired the third and brought him down. This was about the finest piece of Rocky Mountain beef that one could see. We took the carcass on board and floated on again.

Thus far we had a very pleasant time, each taking his turn in working the boat while the others rested or slept. About the fifth day, when we were floating along in very gently running water, I had laid down to take a rest and a little sleep. The mountains here on both sides of the river were not very steep, but ran gradually for a mile or so. While I was sleeping, the boat came around a small angle in the stream, and all at once there seemed to be a higher, steeper range of mountains right across the valley. The boys thought the river was coming to a rather sudden end and hastily awoke me, and for the life of me I could not say they were not right, for there was no way in sight for it to go to. I remembered while looking over a map the military men had,[2] I found a place named Brown's Hole, and I told the boss I guessed we were elected to go on foot to California after all, for I did not propose to follow the river down any sort of hole into any mountain. We were floating directly toward a perpendicular cliff, and I could not see any hole anywhere, nor any other place where it could go. Just as we were within a stone's throw of the cliff, the river turned sharply to the right and went behind a high point of the mountain that seemed to stand squarely on edge. This was really an immense crack or crevice, certainly two thousand feet deep and perhaps much more, and seemed much wider at the bottom than it did at the top, two thousand feet or more above our heads. Each wall seemed to lean in toward the water as it rose.

We were now for some time between two rocky walls, between which the river ran very rapidly, and we often had to get out and work our boat over the rocks, sometimes lifting it off when it caught. Fortunately we had a good towline, and one would take this and follow along the edge when it was so he could walk. The mountains seemed to get higher and higher on both sides as we advanced, and in places we could see quite a number of trees overhanging the river, and away up on the rocks we could see the wild mountain sheep looking down at us. They were so high that they seemed a mile away, and consequently safe enough. This was their home and they seemed very independent, as if they dared us fellows to come and see them. There was an old cottonwood on [the] bank with marks of an axe on it, but this was all the sign we saw that anyone had ever been here before us. We got no game while passing through this deep cañon and began to feel the need of some fresh provisions very sorely.

We passed many deep, dark cañons coming into the main stream, and at one place, where the rock hung a little over the river and had a smooth wall, I climbed up above the high-water mark, which we could clearly see, and with a mixture of gunpowder and grease for paint, and a bit of cloth tied to a stick for a brush, I painted in fair-sized letters on the rock, CAPT. W. L. MANLY, U.S.A. We did not know whether we were within the bounds of the United States or not, and we put on all the majesty we could under the circumstances. I don't think the sun ever shone down to the bottom of the cañon, for the sides were literally sky-high, for the sky, and a very small portion of that, was all we could see.

Just before night we came to a place where some huge rocks as large as cabins had fallen down from the mountain, completely filling up the riverbed and making it completely impassible for our boat. We unloaded it, and while the boys held the stern line, I took off my clothes and pushed the boat out into the torrent which ran around the rocks, letting them pay the line out slowly till it was just right. Then I sang out to "let go" and away it dashed. I grasped the bowline, and at the first chance jumped overboard and got to shore, where I held the boat and brought it in below the obstructions. There was some deep water below the rocks, and we went into camp. While some loaded the boat, others with a hook and line caught some good fish, which resembled mackerel.

While I was looking up toward the mountaintop, and along down the rocky wall, I saw a smooth place about fifty feet above where the great rocks had broken out, and there, painted in large black, letters, were the words ASHLEY, 1824.[3] This was the first real evidence we had of the presence of a white man in this wild place, and from this record it seems that twenty-five years before some venturesome man had here inscribed his name. I have since heard there were some persons in St. Louis of this name, and of some circumstances which may link them with this early traveler.

When we came to look around we found that another big rock blocked the channel three hundred yards below, and the water rushed around it with a terrible swirl. So we unloaded the boat again and made the attempt to get around it as we did the other rocks. We tried to get across the river but failed. We now, all but one, got on the great rock with our poles, and the one man was to ease the boat down with the rope as far as he could, then let go, and we would stop it with our poles and push it out into the stream and let it go over, but the current was so strong that when the boat struck the rock we could not stop it, and the gunwale next to us rose, and the other went down, so that in a second the boat stood edgewise in the water and the bottom tight against the big rock, and the strong current pinned it there so tight that we could no more move it than we could move the rock itself.

This seemed a very sudden ending to our voyage, and there were some very rapid thoughts as to whether we would not [be] safer among the Mormons than out in this wild country, afoot and alone. Our boat was surely lost beyond hope, and something must be done. I saw two pine trees, about two feet through, growing on a level place just below, and I said to them that we must decide between going afoot and making some canoes out of these pine trees. Canoes were decided on, and we never let the axes rest, night or day, till we had them completed. While my working shift was off, I took an hour or two for a little hunting, and on a low divide partly grown over with small pines and juniper I found signs, old and new, of many elk, and so concluded the country was well stocked with noble game. The two canoes, when completed, were about fifteen feet long and two feet wide, and we lashed them together for greater security. When we tried them we found they were too small to carry our load and us, and we landed half a mile below, where there were two other pine trees—white pine—about two feet through, and much taller than the ones we had used. We set at work making a large canoe of these. I had to direct the work, for I was the only one who had ever done such work. We worked night and day at these canoes, keeping a big fire at night and changing off to keep the axes busy. This canoe we made twenty-five or thirty feet long, and when completed they made me captain of it and into it loaded the most valuable things, such as provisions, ammunition, and cooking utensils. I had to take the lead, for I was the only skillful canoeist in the party. We agreed upon signals to give when danger was seen or game in sight and, leading off with my big canoe, we set sail again and went flying downstream.

This rapid rate soon brought us out of the high mountains and into a narrow valley where the stream became more moderate in its speed and we floated along easily enough. In a little while after we struck this slack water, as we were rounding a point, I saw on a sand bar in the river five or six elk, standing and looking at us with much curiosity. I signaled for those behind to go to shore, while I did the same, and two or three of us took our guns and went carefully down along the bank, the thick brush hiding us from them, till we were in fair range, [and] then, selecting our game, we fired on them. A fine doe fell on the opposite bank, and a magnificent buck which Rogers and I selected went below and crossed the river on our side. We followed him down along the bank, which was here a flat meadow with thick bunches of willows, and soon came pretty near to Mr. Elk, who started off on a high and lofty trot. As he passed an opening in the bushes I put a ball through his head and he fell. He was a monster. Rogers, who was a butcher, said he would weigh five hundred or six hundred pounds. The horns were fully six feet long, and by placing the horns on the ground, point downwards, one could walk under the skull between them.[4] We packed the meat to our canoes, and stayed up all night cutting the meat in strips and drying it, to reduce bulk and preserve it, and it made the finest kind of food, fit for an epicure.

Starting on again, the river lost more and more of its rapidity as it came out into a still wider valley and became quite sluggish. We picked red berries that grew on bushes that overhung the water. They were sour and might have been high cranberries. One day I killed an otter and afterward, hearing a wild goose on shore, I went for the game and killed it on a small pond on which there were also some mallard ducks. I killed two of these. When I fired, the ones not killed did not fly away, but rather swam toward me. I suppose they never before had seen a man or heard the report of a gun. On the shore around the place I saw a small bear track, but I did not have time to look for his bearship and left, with the game already killed, and passed on down through this beautiful valley.

We saw one place where a large band of horses had crossed, and as the men with them must have had a raft, we were pretty sure that the men in charge of them were white men. Another day we passed the mouth of a swollen stream which came in from the west side. The water was thick with mud, and the fish, about a foot long, came to the top, with their noses out of water. We tried to catch some, but could not hold them. One night we camped on an island, and I took my gun and went over toward the west side, where I killed a deer. The boys, hearing me shoot, came out, guns in hand, thinking I might need help, and I was very glad of their assistance. To make our flour go as far as possible we ate very freely of meat and, having excellent appetites, it disappeared very fast.

It took us two or three days to pass this beautiful valley, and then we began to get into a rougher country again, the cañons deeper and the water more tumultuous. McMahon and I had the lead always, in the big canoe. The mountains seemed to change into bare rocks and get higher and higher as we floated along. After the first day of this, the river became so full of boulders that many times the only way we could do was to unload the canoes and haul them over, load up and go ahead, only to repeat the same tactics in a very short time again. At one place where the river was more than usually obstructed, we found a deserted camp, a skiff, and some heavy cooking utensils, with a notice posted up on an alder tree saying that they had found the river route impracticable, and being satisfied that the river was so full of rocks and boulders that it could not be safely navigated, they had abandoned the undertaking and were about to start overland to make their way to Salt Lake. I took down the names of the parties at the time in my diary, which has since been burned, but have now forgotten them entirely. They were all strangers to me. They had left such heavy articles as could not be carried on foot. This notice rather disconcerted us, but we thought we had better keep on and see for ourselves, so we did not follow them, but kept on down the rocky river. We found generally more boulders than water, and the downgrade of the riverbed was heavy.

Some alders and willows grew upon the bank, and up quite high on the mountains we could see a little timber. Some days we did not go more than four or five miles, and that was serious work, loading and unloading our canoes, and packing them over the boulders, with only small streams of water curling around between them. We went barefooted most of the time, for we were more than half of the time in the water, which roared and dashed so loud that we could hardly hear each other speak. We kept getting more and more venturesome and skillful, and managed to run some very dangerous rapids in safety.

On the high peaks above our heads we could see the Rocky Mountain sheep looking defiantly at us from their mountain fastnesses, so far away they looked no larger than jackrabbits. They were too far off to try to shoot at, and we had no time to try to steal up any nearer, for at the rate we were making, food would be the one thing needful, for we were consuming it very fast. Sometimes we could ride a little ways, and then would come the rough-and-tumble with the rocks again.

One afternoon we came to a sudden turn in the river, more than a right angle, and just below, a fall of two feet or more. This I ran in safety, as did the rest who followed, and we cheered at our pluck and skill. Just after this the river swung back the other way at a right angle or more, and I quickly saw there was danger below and signaled them to go on shore at once, and lead the canoes over the dangerous rapids. I ran my own canoe near shore and got by the rapid safely, waiting for the others to come also. They did not obey my signals but thought to run the rapid the same as I did. The channel here was straight for two hundred yards, without a boulder in it, but the stream was so swift that it caused great, rolling waves in the center, of a kind I have never seen anywhere else. The boys were not skillful enough to navigate this stream, and the suction drew them to the center, where the great waves rolled them over and over, bottom side up and every way. The occupants of our canoe let go and swam to shore. Fields had always been afraid of water and had worn a life preserver every day since we left the wagons. He threw up his hands and splashed and kicked at a terrible rate, for he could not swim, and at last made solid ground. One of the canoes came down into the eddy below, where it lodged close to the shore, bottom up. Alfred Walton in the other canoe could not swim, but held on to the gunwale with a death grip, and it went on down through the rapids. Sometimes we could see the man and sometimes not, and he and the canoe took turns in disappearing. Walton had very black hair, and as he clung fast to his canoe his black head looked like a crow on the end of a log. Sometimes he would be under so long that we thought he must be lost, when up he would come again, still clinging manfully.

McMahon and I threw everything out of the big canoe and pushed out after him. I told McMahon to kneel down so I could see over him to keep the craft off the rocks, and by changing his paddle from side to side as ordered, he enabled me to make quick moves and avoid being dashed to pieces. We fairly flew, the boys said, but I stood up in the stern and kept it clear of danger till we ran into a clear piece of river and overtook Walton clinging to the overturned boat; McMahon seized the boat and I paddled all to shore, but Walton was nearly dead and could hardly keep his grasp on the canoe. We took him to a sandy place and worked over him and warmed him in the sun till he came to life again, then built a fire and laid him up near to it to get dry and warm. If the canoe had gone on twenty yards farther with him before we caught it, he would have gone into another long rapid and been drowned. We left Walton by the fire and, crossing the river in the slack water, went up to where the other boys were standing, wet and sorry looking, saying that all was gone and lost. Rogers put his hand in his pocket and pulled out three half dollars and said sadly, "Boys, this is all I am worth in the world." All the clothes he had were a pair of overalls and a shirt. If he had been possessed of a thousand in gold he would have been no richer, for there was no one to buy from and nothing to buy. I said to them, "Boys, we can't help what has happened; we'll do the best we can. Right your canoe, get the water out, and we'll go down and see how Walton is." They did as I told them, and lo and behold, when the canoe rolled right side up, there were their clothes and blankets, safe and sound. These light things had floated in the canoe and were safe. We now tried, by joining hands, to reach out far enough to recover some of the guns, but by feeling with their feet they found the bottom smooth as glass and the property all swept on below, no one knew where. The current was so powerful that no one could stand in it where it came up above his knees. The eddy which enabled us to save the first canoe with the bedding and clothes was caused by a great boulder as large as a house which had fallen from above and partly blocked the stream. Everything that would sink was lost.

We all got into the two canoes and went down to Walton, where we camped and stayed all night for Walton's benefit. While we were waiting I took my gun and tried to climb up high enough to see how much longer this horrible cañon was going to last, but after many attempts, I could not get high enough to see in any direction. The mountain was all bare rocks in terraces, but it was impossible to climb from one to the other, and the benches were all filled with broken rocks that had fallen from above.

By the time I got back to camp, Walton was dry and warm and could talk. He said he felt better, and pretty good over his rescue. When he was going under the water, it seemed sometimes as if he never would come to the top again, but he held on and eventually came out all right. He never knew how he got to shore, he was so nearly dead when rescued.

The next morning Walton was so well we started on. We were now very poorly armed. My rifle and McMahon's shotgun were all the arms we had for seven of us, and we could make but a poor defense if attacked by man or beast, to say nothing of providing ourselves with food. The mountains on each side were very bare of timber, those on the east side particularly so, and very high and barren. Toward night—we were floating along in a piece of slack water—the river below made a short turn around a high and rocky point almost perpendicular from the water. There was a terrace along the side of this point about fifty feet up, and the bench grew narrower as it approached the river. As I was coming down quite close under this bank I saw three mountain sheep on the bench above and, motioning to the boys, I ran on shore and, with my gun in hand, crept down toward them, keeping a small pine tree between myself and the sheep. There were some cedar bushes on the point, and the pines grew about halfway up the bank. I got in as good a range as possible and fired at one of them, which staggered around and fell down to the bottom of the cliff. I loaded and took the next largest one, which came down the same way. The third one tried to escape by going down the bend and then creeping up a crevice, but it could not get away and turned back, cautiously, which gave me time to load again and put a ball through it. I hit it a little too far back for instant death, but I followed it up and found it down and helpless, and soon secured it. I hauled this one down the mountain, and the other boys had the two others secure by this time. McMahon was so elated at my success that he said, "Manly, if I could shoot as you do I would never want any better business." And the other fellows said they guessed we were having better luck with one gun than with six, so we had a merry time after all. These animals were of a bluish color, with hair much finer than deer, and resembled a goat more than a sheep. These three were all females and their horns were quite straight, not curved like the big males. We cut the meat from the bones and broke them up, making a fine soup which tasted pretty good. They were in pretty good order, and the meat like very good mutton.

We kept pushing on down the river. The rapids were still dangerous in many places, but not so frequent nor so bad as the part we had gone over, and we could see that the river gradually grew smoother as we progressed.

After a day or two we began to get out of the cañons, but the mountains and hills on each side were barren and of a pale yellow cast, with no chance for us to climb up and take a look to see if there were any chances for us farther along. We had now been obliged to follow the cañon for many miles, for the only way to get out was to get out endwise, climbing the banks being utterly out of the question. But these mountains soon came to an end, and there were some cottonwood and willows on the bank of the river, which was now so smooth we could ride along without the continual loading and unloading we had been forced to practice for so long. We had begun to get a little desperate at the lack of game, but the new valley, which grew wider all the time, gave us hope again, [even] if it was quite barren everywhere except back of the willow trees.

We were floating along very silently one day, for none of us felt very much in the mood for talking, when we heard a distant sound which we thought was very much like the firing of a gun. We kept still, and in a short time a similar sound was heard, plainer and evidently some ways down the stream. Again and again we heard it, and decided that it must be a gunshot, and yet we were puzzled to know how it could be. We were pretty sure there were no white people ahead of us, and we did not suppose the Indians in this far-off land had any firearms. It might be barely possible that we were coming now to some wagon train taking a southern course, for we had never heard that there were any settlements in this direction and the barren country would preclude any such thing, as we viewed it now. If it was a hostile band we could not do much with a rifle and a shotgun toward defending ourselves or taking the aggressive. Some of the boys spoke of our scalps ornamenting a spear handle and indulged in such like cheerful talk, which comforted us wonderfully.

Finally we concluded we did not come out into that wild country to be afraid of a few gunshots and determined to put on a bold front, fight if we had to, run away if we could not do any better, and take our chances on getting scalped or roasted. Just then we came in sight of three Indian lodges just a little back from the river, and now we knew for certain who had the guns. McMahon and I were in the lead as usual, and it was only a moment before one of the Indians appeared, gun in hand, and made motions for us to come on shore. A cottonwood tree lay nearly across the river, and I had gone so far that I had to go around it and land below, but the other boys behind were afraid to do otherwise than to land right there, as the Indian kept his gun lying across his arm. I ran our canoe below to a patch of willows, where we landed and crawled through the brush till we came in sight of the other boys, where we [then] stood and waited a moment to see how they fared and whether our red men were friends or enemies. There were no suspicious movements on their part, so we came out and walked right up to them. There was some little talk, but I am sure we did not understand one another's language, so we made motions and they made motions, and we got along better. We went with them down to the tepee, and there we heard the first word that was at all like English and that was "Mormonee," with a sort of questioning tone. Pretty soon one said "buffalo," and then we concluded they were on a big hunt of some sort. They took us into their lodges and showed us blankets, knives, and guns, and then, with a suggestive motion, said all was "Mormonee," by which we understood they had got them from the Mormons. The Indian in the back part of the lodge looked very pleasant and his countenance showed a good deal of intelligence for a man of the mountains. I now told the boys that we were in a position where we were dependent on someone, and that I had seen enough to convince me that these Indians were perfectly friendly with the Mormons, and that for our own benefit we had better pass ourselves off for Mormons also. So we put our right hand to our breast and said "Mormonee," with a cheerful countenance, and that act conveyed to them the belief that we were chosen disciples of the great and only Brigham and we became friends at once, as all acknowledged. The fine-looking Indian who sat as king in the lodge now, by motions and a word or two, made himself known as Chief Walker, and when I knew this I took great pains to cultivate his acquaintance.[5]

I was quite familiar with the sign language used by all the Indians, and found I could get along pretty well in making him understand and knowing what he said. I asked him first how many "sleeps" or days it was from there to "Mormonee." In answer he put out his left hand and then put two fingers of his right astride of it, making both go up and down with the same motion of a man riding a horse. Then he shut his eyes and laid his head on his hand three times, by which I understood that a man could ride to the Mormon settlement in three sleeps or four days. He then wanted to know where we were going, and I made signs that we were wishing to go toward the setting sun and to the big water, and I said "California." The country off to the west of us now seemed an open, barren plain, which grew wider as it extended west. The mountains on the north side seemed to get lower and smaller as they extended west, but on the south or east side they were all high and rough. It seemed as if we could see one hundred miles down the river and, up to the time we met the Indians, we thought we had got through all our troublesome navigation and could now sail on, quietly and safely, to the great Pacific Ocean and land of gold.

When I told Chief Walker this he seemed very much astonished, as if wondering why we were going down the river when we wanted to get west across the country. I asked him how many sleeps it was to the big water, and he shook his head, pointed out across the country and then to the river and shook his head again; by which I understood that water was scarce, out the way he pointed. He then led me down to a smooth sandbar on the river and then, with a crooked stick, began to make a map in the sand. First he made a long crooked mark, ten feet long or so, and pointing to the river to let me know that the mark in the sand was made to represent it. He then made a straight mark across near the north end of the stream, and showed the other streams which came into the Green River which I saw at once was exactly correct. Then he laid some small stones on each side of the cross mark, and making a small hoop of a willow twig, he rolled it in the mark he had made across the river, then flourished his stick as if he were driving oxen. Thus he represented the emigrant road. He traced the branches off to the north where the soldiers had gone, and the road to California, which the emigrants took, all of which we could see was correct. Then he began to describe the river down which we had come. A short distance below the road he put some small stones on each side of the river to represent mountains. He then put down his hands, one on each side of the crooked mark, and then raised them up again saying "e-e-e-e-e-e" as he raised them, to say that the mountains there were very high. Then he traced down the stream to a place below where we made our canoes; then he placed the stone back from the river farther, to show that there was a valley there; then he drew them in close again farther down, and piled them up again two or three tiers high; then placing both fists on them he raised them higher than the top of his head, saying "e-e-e-e-e-e" and looking still higher and shaking his head as if to say "Awful bad cañon"; and thus he went on describing the river till we understood that we were near the place where we now were, and then pointed to his tepee, showing that I understood him all right. It was all correct, as I very well knew, and assured me that he knew all about the country.

I became much interested in my newfound friend and had him continue his map down the river. He showed two streams coming in on the east side and then he began piling up stones on each side of the river and then got longer ones and piled them higher and higher yet. Then he stood with one foot on each side of his river and put his hands on the stones and then raised them as high as he could, making a continued "e-e-e-e-e-e" as long as his breath would last, pointed to the canoe and made signs with his hands how it would roll and pitch in the rapids and finally capsize and throw us all out. He then made signs of death to show us that it was a fatal place. I understood perfectly plain from this that below the valley where we now were was a terrible cañon, much higher than any we had passed, and the rapids were not navigable with safety. Then Chief Walker shook his head more than once and looked very sober, and said "Indiano," and reaching for his bow and arrows, he drew the bow back to its utmost length and put the arrow close to my breast, showing how I would get shot. Then he would draw his hand across his throat and shut his eyes as if in death to make us understand that this was a hostile country before us, as well as rough and dangerous.

I now had a description of the country ahead and believed it to be reliable. As soon as I could, conveniently, after this, I had a council with the boys, who had looked on in silence while I was holding the silent confab with the chief. I told them where we were and what chances there were of getting to California by this route, and that for my part I had as soon be killed by Mormons as by savage Indians, and that I believed the best way for us to do was to make the best of our way to Salt Lake. "Now," I said, "those of you who agree with me can follow—and I hope all will."

McMahon said that we could not understand a word the old Indian said, and as to following his trails, I don't believe a word of it, and it don't seem right.

He said he had a map of the country, and it looked just as safe to him to go on down the river as to go wandering across a dry and desolate country which we knew nothing of. I said to McMahon, "I know this sign language pretty well. It is used by almost all the Indians and is just as plain and certain to me as my talk is to you. Chief Walker and his forefathers were born here and know the country as well as you know your father's farm, and for my part, I think I shall take one of his trails and go to Salt Lake and take the chances that way. I have no objections to you going some other way if you wish to and think it is best." McMahon and Fields concluded they would not follow me any farther.

I then went to Chief Walker and had him point out the trail to "Mormonee" as well as he could. He told me where to enter the mountains leading north, and when we got partway he told me we would come to an Indian camp, when I must follow some horse tracks newly made; he made me know this by using his hands like horses' forefeet, and pointed the way.

Some of the young men motioned for me to come out and shoot at a mark with them, and as I saw it would please them, I did so and took good care to beat them every time too. Then they wanted to swap *(narawaup)* guns with me, which I declined doing. After this the chief came to me and wanted me to go and hunt buffalo with them. I told him I had no horse, and then he went and had a nice gray one brought up and told me I could ride him if I would go. He took his bow and arrow and showed me how he could shoot an arrow straight through a buffalo just back of his short ribs and that the arrow would go clear through and come out on the other side without touching a bone. Those fellows were in fine spirit, on a big hunt, and when Walker pointed out his route to me he swung his hand around to Salt Lake.

57

They all spoke the word buffalo quite plainly. I took his strong bow and found I could hardly pull it halfway out, but I have no doubt he could do as he said he could. I hardly knew how to refuse going with him. I asked him how long it would be before he would get around his long circuit and get to Salt Lake, to which he replied by pulverizing some leaves in his hands and scattering them in the air to represent snow, which would fall by the time he got to "Mormonee." I shivered as he said this and by his actions I saw that I understood him right.

I told him I could not go with him, for the other boys would depend on me to get them something to eat, and I put my finger into my open mouth to tell him this. I think if I had been alone I should have accepted his offer and should have had a good time. I gave them to understand that we would swap *(narawaup)* with them for some horses, so he brought up a pair of nice two-year-old colts for us. I offered him some money for them; he did not want that, but would take clothing of almost any kind. We let them have some that we could get along without, and someone let Walker have a coat. He put it on, and being more warmly dressed than ever before, the sweat ran down his face in streams. We let them have some needles and thread and some odd notions we had to spare. We saw that Walker had some three or four head of cattle with him which he could kill if they did not secure game at the time they expected.

McMahon and Field still persisted they would not go with us, and so we divided our little stock of flour and dried meat with them as fairly as possible and decided we would try the trail. When our plans were settled we felt in pretty good spirits again, and one of the boys got up a sort of corn-stalk fiddle which made a squeaking noise, and in a little while there was a sort of mixed American and Indian dance going on in which the squaws joined in and we had a pretty jolly time till quite late at night. We were well pleased that these wild folks had proved themselves to be true friends to us.

The morning we were to start, I told the boys a dream I had in which I had seen that the course we had decided on was the correct one, but McMahon and Field thought we were foolish and said they had rather take the chances of going with the Indians, or going on down the river. He seemed to place great stress on the fact that he could not understand the Indians.

Said he, "This Indian may be all right, and maybe he will lead us all into a dreadful trap. They are treacherous and revengeful, and for some merely fancied wrong done by us, or by someone else of whom we have no control or knowledge, they may take our scalps, wipe us out of existence, and no one will ever know what became of us. Now, this map of mine don't show any bad places on this river, and I believe we can get down easily enough, and get to California sometime. Field and I cannot make up our minds so easily as you fellows. I believe your chances are very poor."

The boys now had our few things loaded on the two colts, for they had fully decided to go with me, and I was not in the least put back by McMahon's dire forebodings. We shook hands with quivering lips as we each hoped the other would meet good luck and find enough to eat, and all such sort of friendly talk, and then with my little party on the one side and McMahon and Field, whom we were to leave behind, on the other, we bowed to each other with bared heads, and then we started out of the little young cottonwoods into the broad plain that seemed to get wider and wider as we went west.

The mountains on the northern side grew smaller and less steep as we went west, and on the other hand reached down the river as far as we could see. The plain itself was black and barren and for a hundred miles, at least, ahead of us, it seemed to have no end. Walker had explained to us that we must follow some horse tracks and enter a cañon some miles to the northwest. He had made his hands work like horses' feet, placing then near the ground as if following a trail. We were not much more than a mile away when, on looking back, we saw Chief Walker coming towards us on a horse at full speed and motioning for us to stop. This we did, though some of the boys said we would surely be marched back and scalped. But it was not for that he came. He had been watching us and saw that we had failed to notice the tracks of the horses he told us about, so he rode after us, and now took us off some little distance to the right, got off his horse and showed us the faint horse tracks which we were to follow and said "Mormonee." He pointed out to us the exact cañon we were to enter when we reached the hills and said after three "sleeps" we would find an Indian camp on top of the mountain. He then bade us good-bye again and galloped back to his own camp.

We now resumed our journey, keeping watch of the tracks more closely, and as we came near the spurs of the mountain which projected out into the barren valley we crossed several well-marked trails running along the foothills, at right angles to our own. This we afterwards learned was the regular trail from Santa Fé to Los Angeles.[6] At some big rocks farther on we camped for the night and found water in some pools or holes in the flat rocks which held the rain.

Reading people of today, who know so well the geography of the American continent, may need to stop and think that in 1849 the whole region west of the Missouri River was very little known. The only men venturesome enough to dare to travel over it were hunters and trappers who, by a wild life, had been used to all the privations of such a journey and [were] shrewd as the Indians themselves in the mysterious ways of the trail and the chase. Even these fellows had only investigated certain portions best suited to their purpose.

The Indians here have the reputation of being bloodthirsty savages who took delight in murder and torture, but here, in the very midst of this wild and desolate country we found a chief and his tribe, Walker and his followers, who were as humane and kind to white people as could be expected of anyone. I have often wondered at the knowledge of this man respecting the country, of which he was able to make us a good map in the sand, point out to us the impassable cañon, locate the hostile Indians, and many points which were not accurately known by our own explorers for many years afterward. He undoubtedly saved our little band from a watery grave, for without his advice we [would have] gone on and on, far into the great Colorado cañon, from which escape would have been impossible and securing food another impossibility, while destruction by hostile Indians was among the strong probabilities of the case. So in a threefold way I have for these more than forty years credited the lives of myself and comrades to the thoughtful interest and humane consideration of old Chief Walker.

In another pool or pond near the one where we were camped, I shot a small duck. Big sage was plenty here for fuel and we had duck for supper. Our party consisted of five men and two small ponies only two years old, with a stock of provisions very small including what the old chief had given us. We started on in the morning, following our faint trail till we came to the cañon we had in view, and up this we turned as we had been directed, finding in the bottom a little running stream. Timber began to appear as we ascended, and grass also. There were signs of deer and grouse but we had no time to stop to hunt, for I had the only gun and while I hunted the others must lie idly by. We reached the summit at a low pass, and just above, on the north side of the higher mountains, were considerable banks of snow. Following the chief's instructions, we left the trail and followed some horse tracks over rolling hills, high on the mountainside. We found the Indian camp exactly as the chief had described, consisting of two or three lodges. The men were all absent hunting, but the women were gathering and baking some sort of root which looked like a carrot. They made a pile of several bushels and covered it with earth, then made a fire, treating the pile same as a charcoal burner does his pit of coal. When sufficiently cooked they beat them up and made the material into small cakes, which were dried in the sun. The dried cakes were as black as coal and intended for winter use. These roots before roasting were unfit for food, as they contained a sort of acrid juice that would make the tongue smart and very sore, but there was a very good, rich taste when cooked. The women pointed to our horses and said "Walker," so we knew they were aware that we got them of him, and might have taken us for horse thieves for aught I know. As it was not yet night when we came to the camp, we passed on and camped on a clear mountain brook where grew some pine trees. After a little, some of the Indians belonging to the camp we had passed came in, bringing some venison, for which we traded by giving them some needles and a few other trinkets. I beat these fellows shooting at a mark, and then they wanted to trade guns, which I declined. This piece of meat helped us along considerably with our provisions, for game was very scarce and only some sage hens had come across our trail. One day I scared a hawk off the ground, and we took the sage hen he had caught and was eating, and made some soup of it.

After being on this trail six or seven days, we began to think of killing one of our colts for food, for we had put ourselves on two meals a day and the work was very hard, so that hunger was all the time increasing. We thought this was a pretty long road for Walker to ride over in three sleeps as he said he could, and we began also to think there might be some mistake somewhere, although it had otherwise turned out just as he said. On the eighth day our horse tracks came out into a large trail which was on a downgrade leading in a northward direction. On the ninth day we came into a large valley, and near night came in sight of a few covered wagons, a part of a train that intended going on a little later over the southern route to Los Angeles but were waiting for the weather to get a little cooler, for a large part of the route was over almost barren deserts. We were very glad to find these wagons, for they seemed to have plenty of food and the bountiful supper they treated us to was the very thing we needed. We camped here and told them of the hardships we had passed through. They had hired a guide, each wagon paying him ten dollars for his service.[7] Our little party talked over the situation among ourselves and concluded that as we were good walkers, we must allow ourselves to be used in any way so that we had grub, and concluded as many of us as possible would try to get some service to do for our board and walk along with the party. John Rogers had a dollar and a half and I had thirty dollars, which was all the money we had in our camp. We found out we were about sixty miles south of Salt Lake City. Some of the boys next day arranged to work for their board, and the others would be taken along if they would furnish themselves with flour and bacon. This part of the proposition fell to me and two others, and so Hazelrig and I took the two colts and started for the city, where they told us we could get all we needed with our little purse of money. We reached Hobble Creek[8] before night, near Salt Lake where there was a Mormon fort, and [where there] were also a number of wagons belonging to some prospecting train. There seemed to be no men about and we were looking about among the wagons for someone to inquire of, when a woman came to the front of the last wagon and looked out at us, and to my surprise it was Mrs. Bennett, wife of the man I had been trying to overtake ever since my start on this long trip. Bennett had my entire outfit with him on this trip and was all the time wondering whether I would ever catch up with them. We stayed till the men came in with their cattle towards night, and Bennett was glad enough to see me, I assure you. We had a good, substantial supper and then sat around the campfire nearly all night telling of our experience since leaving Wisconsin. I had missed Bennett at the Missouri River. I knew of no place where people crossed the river except Council Bluff; here I had searched faithfully, finding no trace of him, but it seems they had crossed farther up at a place called Kanesville, a Mormon crossing, and followed up the Platte River on the north side.[9] Their only bad luck had been to lose a fine black horse which was staked out, and when a herd of buffaloes came along he broke his rope and followed after them. He was looked for with other horses, but never found and doubtless became a prize for some enterprising Mr. Lo who was fortunate enough to capture him.[10] Hazelrig and I told of our experience on the south side of the Platte; why we went down Green River; what a rough time we had; how we were stopped by the Indians and how we had come across from the river, arriving the day before, and were now on our way to Salt Lake to get some flour and bacon so we could go on with the train when it started, as they had offered to haul our grub for our service if we could carry ourselves on foot.

Mr. Bennett would not hear of my going on to Salt Lake City, for he said there must be provisions enough in the party, and in the morning we were able to buy flour and bacon of John Philips of Mineral Point, Wisconsin, and of William Philips, his brother. I think we got a hundred pounds of flour and a quantity of bacon and some other things. I had some money which I had received for my horse sold to Dallas, but as the others had none I paid for it all, and told Hazelrig to take the ponies and go back to camp with a share of the provisions and do the best he could. I had now my own gun and ammunition, with some clothing and other items which I had prepared in Wisconsin before I started after my Winnebago pony, and I felt I ought to share the money I had with the other boys to help them as best I could. I felt that I was pretty well fixed and had nothing to fear.

Mr. Bennett told me much of the trip on the north side of the Platte. He said they had some cholera, of which a few people died, and related how the outer if not the inner nature of the men changed as they left civilization, law, and the courts behind them. Some who had been raised together and lived together all their lives without discord or trouble, who were considered model men at home and just the right people to be connected with in such an expedition, seemed to change their character entirely out on these wild wastes. When anything excited their displeasure, their blood boiled over, and only the interference of older and wiser heads on many occasions prevented bloodshed. Some dissolved the solemn contract they had made to travel together systematically and in order and to stand by, even unto death, and when they reached the upper Platte, the journey only half over, talked of going back, or splitting up the outfit and joining others they had taken a fancy to. Some who could not agree upon a just division of a joint outfit, thinking one party was trying to cheat, would not yield but would cut their wagons in two lengthwise just for spite so that no carts could be made and the whole vehicle spoiled for both parties. The ugly disagreements were many and the cloven foot was shown in many ways. Guns were often drawn and pointed, but someone would generally interfere and prevent bloodshed. Others were honest and law-abiding to the last degree beyond law and churches, and would act as harmoniously as at home, obeying their chosen captain in the smallest particular without any grumbling or dissension, doing to everyone as they would be done by. These were the pride of the train. The trains were most of them organized, and all along the river bottom one was hardly ever out of sight of some of the wagons, all going west. Buffalo and antelope were plenty and in great droves, followed always by wolves great and small, who were on the lookout for crippled or dead animals with which to fill their hungry stomachs. Buffalo meat was plenty and much enjoyed while passing this section of the road, and this opportunity of replenishing enabled the stock to last them over more desolate regions where game was scarce.

After Bennett had told his stories, and I had related more of our own close escapes, I began to ask him why he went this way, which seemed to be very circuitous and much longer than the way they had first intended to go. He said that it was too late in the season to go the straight road safely, for there were yet seven hundred miles of bad country to cross, and doing the best they could it would be at the commencement of the rainy season before the Sierra Nevada mountains could be reached, and in those mountains there was often a snowfall of twenty feet or more, and anyone caught in it would surely perish. If they tried to winter at the base of the mountains it was a long way to get provisions, and no assurance of wild game, and this course was considered very hazardous for anyone to undertake. This they had learned after consulting mountaineers and others who knew about the regions, and as there was nothing doing among the Latter Day Saints to give employment to anyone, it was decided best to keep moving and go the southern route by way of Los Angeles. No wagons were reported as ever getting through that way, but a trail had been traveled through that barren desert country for perhaps a hundred years, and the same could be easily broadened into a wagon road.

After days of argument and campfire talks, this southern route was agreed upon, and Captain Hunt was chosen as guide. Captain Hunt was a Mormon, and had more than one wife, but he had convinced them that he knew something about the road.[11] Each agreed to give him ten dollars to pilot the train to San Bernardino, where the Mormon Church had bought a Spanish grant of land, and no doubt they [the Church members] thought a wagon road to that place would benefit them greatly, and probably gave much encouragement for the parties to travel this way.[12] It was undoubtedly safer than the northern mountain route at this season of the year. It seemed at least to be a new venture for westbound emigrant trains—at least as to ultimate success, for we had no knowledge of any that had gone through safely.

Some western people remembered the history of the Mormons in Illinois and Missouri and their doings there [and] feared somewhat for their own safety now that they were so completely under their power, for they knew the Mormons to be revengeful, and it was considered very unsafe for any traveler to acknowledge he was from Missouri. Many a one who had been born there and lived there all his life would promptly claim some other state as his native place. I heard one Mormon say that there were some Missourians on the plains that would never reach California. "They used us bad," said he, and his face took on a really murderous look.

These Mormons at Salt Lake were situated as if on an island in the sea, and no enemy could reach any adjoining state or territory if Brigham Young's band of destroying angels were only warned to look after them.[13]

At a late hour that night we lay down to sleep, and morning came clear and bright. After breakfast Mr. Bennett said to me, "Now Lewis, I want you to go with me; I have two wagons and two drivers and four yoke of good oxen and plenty of provisions. I have your outfit yet, your gun and ammunition and your two good hickory shirts which are just in time for your present needs. You need not do any work. You just look around and kill what game you can for us, and this will help as much as anything you can do." I was, of course, glad to accept this offer, and thanks to Mr. Bennett's kind care of my outfit, was better fixed than any of the other boys.

We inquired around among the other wagons as to their supply of flour and bacon, and succeeded in getting flour from Mr. Philips and bacon from some of the others, as much as we supposed the other boys would need, which I paid for, and when this was loaded on the two colts, Hazelrig started back alone to the boys in camp. As I was so well provided for, I gave him all my money, for they might need some and I did not.

The wagons which composed the intended train were very much scattered about, having moved out from Salt Lake at pleasure, and it was said to be too early to make the start on the southern route, for the weather on the hot, barren desert was said to grow cooler a little later in the season, and it was only at this cool season that the southwest part of the desert could be crossed in safety. The scattering members of the train began to congregate, and Captain Hunt said it was necessary to have some sort of system about the move, and that before they moved they must organize and adopt rules and laws which must be obeyed. He said they must move like an army, and that he was to be a dictator in all things, except that, in case of necessity, a majority of the train could rule otherwise. It was thought best to get together and try a march out one day, then go in camp and organize.

This they did, and at the camp there were gathered one hundred and seven wagons, a big drove of horses and cattle, perhaps five hundred in all. The train was divided into seven divisions and each division was to elect its own captain. Division No. 1 should lead the march the first day, and their men should take charge of the stock and deliver them to the wagons in the morning, and then No. 1 should take the rear with No. 2 in the lead to break the road. The rear division would not turn a wheel before ten o'clock the next day, and it would be about that time at night before they were in camp and unyoked. The numbers of animals cleaned out the feed for a mile or two each side of the camp and a general meeting was called for the organization of the whole. Mr. L. Granger got up so he could look over the audience, and proceeded to explain the plan and to read a preamble and resolutions which had been prepared as the basis for government. I remember that it began thus, "This organization shall be known and designated as the Sand Walking Company, and shall consist of seven divisions, etc." detailing the manner of marching as we have recited.[14] Captain J. Hunt was chosen commander and guide, and his orders must be obeyed. All possible trouble that we could imagine might come was provided against in our written agreement, and all promised to live up to it.

CHAPTER IX

Off in Fine Style

WE MOVED OFF IN GOOD STYLE FROM THIS CAMP. After a day or two and before we reached what is called Little Salt Lake, an attempt was made to make a shortcut, to save distance. The train only went on this cutoff a day or two when Captain Hunt came back from the front and said they had better turn back to the old trail again, which all did.[1] This was a bad move, the train much broken [up] and not easy to get into regular working order again. We were now approaching what they called the Rim of the Basin. Within the basin the water all ran to the north or toward Great Salt Lake, but when we crossed the rim, all was toward the Colorado River, through which it reached the Pacific Ocean. About this time we were overtaken by another train commanded by Captain Smith.[2] They had a map with them made by one Williams of Salt Lake, a mountaineer who was represented to know all the routes through all the mountains of Utah,[3] and this map showed a way to turn off from the southern route, not far from the divide which separated the waters of the basin from those which flowed toward the Colorado, and pass over the mountains, coming out in what they called Tulare Valley, much nearer [the goldfields] than by Los Angeles.

This map was quite frequently exhibited and the matter freely discussed in camp; indeed speeches were made in the interest of the cutoff route which was to be so much shorter. A clergyman, the Reverend J. W. Brier, was very enthusiastic about this matter and discussed learnedly and plausibly about it.[4] The more the matter was talked about, the more there were who were converted to the belief that the short road would be the best. The map showed every camp on the road and showed where there was water and grass, and as to obstacles to the wagons, it was thought they could easily be overcome. A general meeting was called, for better consideration of the question. Captain Hunt said, "You all know I was hired to go by way of Los Angeles, but if you all wish to go and follow Smith I will go also. But if even one wagon decides to go the original route, I shall feel bound to go with that wagon."

A great many were anxious to get the opinion of Captain Hunt on the feasibility of the new route, for he was a mountain man and could probably give us some good advice. He finally consented to talk of it, and said he really knew no more than the others about this particular route, but he very much doubted if a white man ever went over it, and that he did not consider it at all safe for those who had wives and children in their company to take the unknown road. Young men who had no family could possibly get through and save time, even if the road was not as good as [the] Los Angeles road. But said he, "If you decide to follow Smith I will go with you, even if the road leads to hell."

On the route from near Salt Lake to this point we found the country to grow more barren as we progressed. The grass was thinner, and sagebrush took the place of timber. Our road took us in sight of Sevier Lake and also, while going through the low hills, passed Little Salt Lake, which was almost dry, with a beach around it almost as white as snow. It might have had a little more the dignity of a lake in wet weather, but it was a rather dry affair as we saw it.

At one point on this route we came into a long, narrow valley, well-covered with sagebrush, and before we had gone very far we discovered that this was a great place for long-eared rabbits—we would call them jackrabbits now. Everyone who had a gun put it into service on this occasion, and there was much popping and shooting on every side. Great clouds of smoke rolled up as the hunters advanced and the rabbits ran in every direction to get away. Many ran right among the horses, and under the feet of the cattle and under the wagons, so that the teamsters even killed some with a whip. At the end of the valley we went into camp, and on counting up the game found we had over five hundred, or about one for every person in camp. This gave us a feast of fresh meat not often found.

It was on this trip that one of Mr. Bennett's ox drivers was taken with a serious bowel difficulty, and for many days we thought he would die, but he eventually recovered. His name was Silas Helmer.

It was really a serious moment when the front of the train reached the Smith trail.[5] Team after team turned to the right, while now and then one would keep straight ahead as was at first intended. Captain Hunt came over to the larger party after the division was made, and wished them all a hearty farewell and a pleasant, happy journey. My friend Bennett, whose fortune I shared, was among the seceders who followed the Smith party.[6] This point, when our paths diverged, was very near the place afterward made notorious as Mountain Meadows, where the famous massacre took place under the direction of the Mormon generals.[7] Our route from here up to the mountain was a very pleasant one, steadily upgrade, over rolling hills, with wood, water, and grass in plenty. We came at last to what seemed the summit of a great mountain, about three days' journey on the new trail. Juniper trees grew about in bunches, and my experience with this timber taught me that we were on elevated ground.[8]

Immediately in front of us was a cañon, impassible for wagons, and down into this the trail descended. Men could go, horses and mules, perhaps, but wagons could no longer follow that trail, and we proposed to camp while explorers were sent out to search a pass across this steep and rocky cañon. Wood and bunchgrass were plenty, but water was a long way down the trail and had to be packed up to the camp. Two days passed, and the parties sent out began to come in, all reporting no way to go farther with the wagons. Some said the trail on the west side of the cañon could be ascended on foot by both men and mules, but that it would take years to make it fit for wheels.

The enthusiasm about the Smith cutoff had begun to die and now the talk began of going back to follow Hunt. On the third morning a lone traveler with a small wagon and one yoke of oxen died. He seemed to be on this journey to seek to regain his health. He was from Kentucky, but I have forgotten his name. Some were very active about his wagon, and some thought too much attention was paid to a stranger. He was decently buried by the men of the company.[9]

This very morning a Mr. Rynierson called the attention of the crowd and made some remarks upon the situation. He said, "My family is near and dear to me. I can see by the growth of the timber that we are in a very elevated place. This is now the 7th of November, it being the 4th at the time of our turning off on this trail. We are evidently in a country where snow is liable to fall at any time in the winter season, and if we were to remain here and be caught in a severe storm we should all probably perish. I, for one, feel in duty bound to seek a safer way than this. I shall hitch up my oxen and return at once to the old trail. Boys [to his teamsters], get the cattle and we'll return."[10] This was decisive, and Mr. Rynierson would tarry no longer. Many others now proceeded to get ready and follow, and as Mr. Rynierson drove out of camp, quite a respectable train fell in behind him. As fast as the hunters came in and reported no road available, they also yoked up their oxen and rolled out. Some waited awhile for companions yet in the fields, and all were about ready to move, when a party came in with news that the pass was found and no trouble could be seen ahead. About twenty-seven wagons remained when this news came, and as their proprietors had brought good news they agreed to travel on westward and not go back to the old trail.

Mr. Bennett had gone only a short distance out when he had the misfortune to break the axle of his wagon, and he then went back to camp and took an axle out of the dead man's wagon, and by night had it fitted into his own. He had to stay until morning, and there were still a few others who were late in getting a start, who camped there also. Among these were J. B. Arcane, wife and child; two Earhart brothers and sons, and some two or three other wagons.[11]

When all was ready we followed the others who had gone ahead. The route led at first directly to the north and a pass was said to be in that direction. Of the Green River party, only Rogers and myself remained with this train. After the wagons straightened out nicely, a meeting was called to organize, so as to travel systematically. A feeling was very manifest that those without any families did not care to bind themselves to stand by and assist those who had wives and children in their party, and there was considerable debate which resulted in all the family wagons being left out of the arrangements.

A party who called themselves the Jayhawkers passed us, and we followed along in the rear, over rolling hills covered with juniper timber and small grassy valleys between where there was plenty of water, and went well, for those before us had broken out the road so we could roll along very pleasantly.[12]

At the organization Jim Martin was chosen captain. Those who were rejected were Reverend J. W. Brier and his family, J. B. Arcane and family, and Mr. A. Bennett and family. Mr. Brier would not stay put out, but forced himself in, and said he was going with the rest, and so he did. But the other families remained behind. I attended the meeting and heard what was said, but Mr. Bennett was my friend and had been faithful to me and my property when he knew not where I was, and so I decided to stand by him and his wife at all hazards.

As I had no team to drive I took every opportunity to climb the mountains along the route, reaching the highest elevations even if they were several miles from the trail. I sometimes remained out all night. I took Mr. Arcane's field glass with me and was thus able to see all there was of the country. I soon became satisfied that going north was not taking us in the direction we ought to go. I frequently told them so, but they still persisted in following on. I went to the leaders and told them we were going back toward Salt Lake again, not making any headway toward California. They insisted they were following the directions of Williams, the mountaineer, and they had not yet got as far north as he indicated. I told them, and Mr. Bennett and others, that we must either turn west or retrace our steps and get back into the regular Los Angeles road again. In the morning we held another consultation and decided to turn west here and leave the track we had been following.

Off we turned at nearly right angles to our former course, to the west now, over a piece of tableland that gave us little trouble in breaking our own road. When we camped, the oxen seemed very fond of a white weed that was very plenty, and some borrowed a good deal of trouble thinking that perhaps it might be poison. I learned afterwards that this plant was the nutritious white sage, which cattle eat freely with good results. We now crossed a low range and a small creek running south, and here were also some springs. Some corn had been grown here by the Indians. Pillars of sandstone, fifteen feet high and very slim, were round about in several places and looked strange enough.[13] The next piece of tableland sloped to the east, and among the sage grew also a bunchgrass a foot high, which had seeds like broomcorn seeds. The Indians had gathered the grass, and made it in piles of one hundred pounds or so, and used it for food, as I found by examining their camps.

One day I climbed a high mountain where some pine grew, in order to get a view of the country. As I neared its base I came to a flat rock, perhaps fifty feet square. I heard some pounding noise as I came near, but whatever it was, it ceased on my approach. There were many signs of the rock being used as a camp, such as pine burrs,[14] bones of various kinds of animals, and other remains of food which lay everywhere about and on the rock. Near the center was a small, oblong stone fitted into a hole. I took it out and found it covered a fine well of water about three feet deep and thus protected against any small animal being drowned in it. I went on up the mountain and from the top I saw that the land west of us looked more and more barren.

The second night the brave Jayhawkers who had been so firm in going north hove in sight in our rear. They had at last concluded to accept my advice and had come over our road quite rapidly.[15] We all camped together that night, and next morning they took the lead again. After crossing a small range, they came to a basin which seemed to have no outlet and was very barren. Some of the boys in advance of the teams had passed over this elevation and were going quite rapidly over the almost level plain which sloped into the basin, when they saw among the bunches of sagebrush behind them a small party of Indians following their road, not very far off, but still out of bow and arrow range. The boys were suddenly able to take much longer steps than usual and a little more rapidly too, and [started] swinging round toward the teams as soon as possible, for they already had some fears that an arrow might be sticking in their backs in an unpleasantly short space of time, for the Indians were good travelers. When they came in sight of the wagons, the Indians vanished as quickly as if they had gone into a hole, with no sign remaining, except a small dog which greatly resembled a prairie wolf and kept a safe distance away. No one could imagine where the fellows went so suddenly.

We drove to the west side of this basin and camped near the foot of a low mountain. The cattle were driven down into the basin where there was some grass, but at camp we had only the water in our kegs.

Some of the boys climbed the mountain on the north but found no springs. Coming down a cañon they found some rainwater in a basin in the rocks and all took a good drink. Lew West lay down and swallowed all he could and then told the boys to kill him, for he never would feel so good again. They finished the pool—it was so small—before they left it. In going on down the cañon, they saw an Indian dodge behind some big rocks, and searching, they found him in a cave as still as a dead man. They pulled him out and made him go with them, and tried every way to find out from him where they were and where Owen's Lake was, as they had been told the lake was on their route. But he proved to be no wiser than a man of mud, and they led him along to camp, put a red flannel shirt on him to cover his nakedness, and made him sleep between two white men so he could not get away easily. In the morning they were more successful, and he showed us a small ravine four miles away which had water in it, enough for our use, and we moved up and camped there, while the boys and the Indian started over a barren, rocky mountain and, when over on the western slope, they were led to a water hole on a steep, rocky cliff where no one but an Indian would ever think of looking for water. They took out their cups and had a good drink all around, then offered the Indian some, but he disdained the civilized way and, laying down his bow and arrows, took a long drink directly out of the pool. He was so long in getting a good supply that the boys almost forgot him as they were gazing over the distant mountain and discussing prospects till, attracted by a slight noise, they looked and saw Mr. Indian going down over the cliffs after the fashion of a mountain sheep, and in a few bounds he was out of sight. They could not have killed him if they had tried, the move so sudden and unlooked for. They had expected the fellow to show them the way to Owen's Lake, but now their guide was gone, and left nothing to remember him by except his bow and arrows. So they returned to their wagons not much wiser than before.

All kinds of game were now very scarce and so seldom seen that the men got tired of carrying their guns and grew fearless of enemies. A heavy rifle was indeed burdensome over so long a road when there was no frequent use for it. The party kept rolling along as fast as possible but the mountains and valleys grew more barren and water more scarce all the time. When found, the water would be in holes at the outlet of some cañon, or in little pools which had filled up with rain that had fallen on the higher ground. Not a drop of rain had fallen on us since we started on this cutoff, and every night was clear and warm. The elevated parts of the country seemed to be isolated buttes with no running streams between them, but instead dry lakes with a smooth clay bed, very light in color, and so hard that the track of an ox could not be seen on its glittering surface. At a distance those clay beds looked like water shining in the sun and were generally about three times as far as anyone would judge—the air was so clear. This mirage, or resemblance to water, was so perfect as often to deceive us, almost to our ruin on one or two occasions.

I took Arcane's field glass and took pains to ascend all the high buttes within a day's walk of the road, and this enabled me to get a good survey of the country north and west. I would sometimes be gone two or three days with no luggage but my canteen and gun. I was very cautious in regard to Indians, and tried to keep on the safe side of surprises. I would build a fire about dark and then travel on till I came to a small washed place and lie down and stay till morning, so if Mr. Indian did come to my fire he would not find anyone to kill. One day I was going up a wide ravine leading to the summit, and before I reached the highest part I saw a smoky curl up before me. I took a side ravine and went cautiously, bowed down pretty low so no one could see me, and when near the top of the ridge and [within] about one hundred yards of the fire I ventured to raise slowly up and take a look to see how many there were in camp. I could see but two and as I looked across the ravine an Indian woman seemed looking at me also, but I was so low she could only see the top of my head, and I sank down again out of sight. I crawled farther up so as to get a better view, and when I straightened up again she got a full view of me. She instantly caught her infant off its little pallet, made of a small piece of thin wood covered with a rabbit skin and, putting the baby under one arm and giving a smart jerk to a small girl that was crying to the top of her voice, she bounded off and fairly flew up the gentle slope toward the summit, the girl following after very close. The woman's long black hair stood out as she rushed along, looking over her shoulder every instant as if she expected to be slain. The mother flying with her children, untrammeled with any of the arts of fashion, was the best natural picture I ever looked upon, and wild in the extreme. No living artist could do justice to the scene as the lady of the desert, her little daughter, and her babe passed over the summit out of sight. I followed, but when I reached the highest summit, no living person could be seen. I looked the country over with my glass. The region to the north was black, rocky, and very mountainous. I looked some time and then concluded I had better not go any farther that way, for I might be waylaid and filled with arrows at some unsuspected moment. We saw Indian signs almost every day, but as none of them ever came to our camp, it was safe to say they were not friendly. I now turned back and examined the Indian woman's camp. She had only fire enough to make a smoke. Her conical shaped basket, left behind, contained a few poor arrows and some cactus leaves from which the spines had been burned, and there lay the little pallet where the baby was sleeping. It was a bare looking kitchen for hungry folks.

I now went to the top of a high butte and scanned the country very carefully, especially to the west and north, and found it very barren. There were no trees, no fertile valleys, nor anything green. Away to the west some mountains stood out clear and plain, their summits covered white with snow. This, I decided, was our objective point. Very little snow could be seen elsewhere, and between me and the snowy mountains lay a low, black, rocky range, and a wide, level plain that had no signs of water, as I had learned them in our trip thus far across the country. The black range seemed to run nearly north and south, and to the north and northwest the country looked volcanic, black, and desolate.

As I looked and thought, I believed that we were much farther from a fertile region then most of our party had any idea of. Such of them as had read Frémont's travels, and most of them going to California had fortified themselves before starting by reading Frémont, said that the mountains were near California and were fertile from their very summits down to the sea, but that to the east of the mountains it was a desert region for hundreds of miles.[16] As I explained it to them, and so they soon saw for themselves, they believed that the snowy range ahead of us was the last range to cross before we entered the long-sought California, and it seemed not far off, and [the] prospect quite encouraging.

Our road had been winding around among the buttes, which looked like the Indian baskets turned upside down on the great barren plain. What water we found was in small pools in the washout places near the foothills at the edge of the valley, probably running down the ravines after some storm. There were dry lake beds scattered around over the plain, but it did not seem as if there had ever been volume of water enough lately to force itself out so far into the plain as these lakes were. All the lakes appeared about the same, the bed white and glistening in the sun, which made it very hard for the eyes, and so that a man in passing over it made no visible track. It looked as if it, one time, might have been a smooth bed of plastic mortar and had hardened in the sun. It looked as if there must have been water there sometime, but we had not seen a drop, or a single cloud; every day was clear and sunny and very warm, and at night no stars forgot to shine.

Our oxen began to look bad, for they had poor food. Grass had been very scarce, and now when we unyoked them and turned them out, they did not care to look around much for something to eat. They moved slowly and cropped disdainfully the dry scattering shrubs and bunches of grass from six inches to a foot high. Spending many nights and days on such dry food and without water they suffered fearfully, and though fat and sleek when we started from Salt Lake, they now looked gaunt and poor and dragged themselves slowly along, poor faithful servants of mankind. No one knew how long before we might have to kill some of them to get food to save our own lives.

We now traveled several days down the bed of a broad ravine which led to a southwest direction. There seemed to be a continuous range of mountains on the south, but to the north was the level plain with scattered buttes, and what we had all along called dry lakes, for up to this time we had seen no water in any of them. I had carried my rifle with me every day since we took this route, and though I was an experienced hunter, a professional one if there be such a thing, I had killed only one rabbit, and where no game lived I got as hungry as other folks.

Our line soon brought us in sight of a high butte which stood apparently about twenty miles south of our route, and I determined to visit and climb it to get a better view of things ahead. I walked steadily all day and reached the summit about dusk. I wandered around among the big rocks and found a projecting cliff where I would be protected from enemies, wind, or storm, and here I made my camp. While the light lasted I gathered a small stock of fuel which consisted of a stunted growth of sage and other small shrubs, dry but not dead, and with this I built a little fire Indian fashion and sat down close to it. Here was a good chance for undisturbed meditation, and somehow I could not get around doing a little meditating as I added a new bit of fuel now and then to the small fire burning at my side. I thought it looked dark and troublesome before us. I took a stone for a pillow with my hat on it for a cushion, and lying down close under the shelving rock, I went to sleep, for I was very tired. I woke soon from being cold, for the butte was pretty high, and so I busied myself the remainder of the night in adding little sticks to the fire, which gave me some warmth, and thus in solitude I spent the night. I was glad enough to see the day break over the eastern mountains, and light tip the vast, barren country I could see on every hand around me. When the sun was fairly up I took a good survey of the situation, and it seemed as if pretty near all creation was in sight. North and west was a level plain, fully one hundred miles wide it seemed, and from anything I could see it would not afford a traveler a single drink in the whole distance or give a poor ox many mouthfuls of grass. On the western edge it was bounded by a low, black, and rocky range extending nearly north and south for a long distance and no pass through it which I could see, and beyond this range still another one apparently parallel to it. In a due west course from me was the high peak we had been looking at for a month, and [the] lowest place was on the north side, which we had named Martin's Pass and had been try-ing so long to reach.[17] This high peak, covered with snow, glistened in the morning sun, and as the air was clear from clouds or fog, and no dust or haze to obscure the view, it seemed very near.

I had learned by experience that objects a day's walk distant seemed close by in such a light and that when clear, lakes appeared only a little dis-tance in our front: we might search and search and never find them. We had to learn how to look for water in this peculiar way. In my Wisconsin travel I had learned that when I struck a ravine I must go down to look for living water, but here we must invariably travel upward, for the water was only found in the high mountains.

Prospects now seemed to me so hopeless that I heartily wished I was not in duty bound to stand by the women and small children who could never reach a land of bread without assistance. If I was in the position that some of them were who had only themselves to look after, I could pick up my knapsack and gun and go off, feeling I had no dependent ones to leave behind. But as it was, I felt I should be morally guilty of murder if I should forsake Mr. Bennett's wife and children and the family of Mr. Arcane with whom I had been thus far associated. It was a dark line of thought, but I always felt better when I got around to the determination, as I always did, to stand by my friends, their wives, and children, let come what might.

I could see with my glass the train of wagons moving slowly over the plain toward what looked to me like a large lake. I made a guess of the point they would reach by night, and then took a straight course for it all day long in steady travel. It was some time after dark, and I was still a quarter of a mile from the campfires, when in the bed of a cañon I stepped into some mud, which was a sign of water. I poked around in the dark for a while and soon found a little pool of it, and having been without a drop of it for two days, I lay down and took a hasty drink. It did not seem to be very clear or clean, but it was certainly wet, which was the main thing just then. The next morning I went to the pond of water, and found the oxen had been watered there. They stirred up the mud a good deal and had drank off about all the clean part, which seemed to refresh them very much. I found the people in the camp on the edge of the lake I had seen from the mountain, and fortunately it contained about a quarter of an inch of water. They had dug some holes here, which filled up, and they were using this water in the camp.

The ambitious mountain climbers of our party had, by this time, abandoned that sort of work, and I was left alone to look about and try to ascertain the character of the road they were to follow. It was a great deal to do to look out for food for the oxen and for water for the camp, and besides all this, it was plain there were Indians about, even if we did not see them. There were many signs, and I had to be always on the lookout to outgeneral[18] them. When the people found I was in camp this night they came around to our wagons to know what I had seen and found, and what the prospects were ahead. Above all they wanted to know how far it was, in my opinion, to the end of our journey. I listened to all their inquiries and told them plainly what I had seen, and what I thought of the prospect. I did not like telling the whole truth about it, for fear it might dampen their spirits, but being pressed for an opinion, I told them in plain words that it would at least be another month before their journey would be ended. They seemed to think I ought to be pretty good authority, and if I was not mistaken, the oxen would get very poor and provisions very scarce before we could pull through so long. I was up at daybreak and found Mr. Bennett sitting by the fire. About the first thing he said [was], "Lewis, if you please, I don't want you hereafter to express your views so openly and emphatically as you did last night about our prospects. Last night when I went to bed I found Sarah (his wife) crying, and when pressed for the cause, she said she had heard your remarks on the situation, and that if Lewis said so it must be correct, for he knows more about it than all of you. She felt that she and the children must starve."

In the morning, [the] Jayhawkers and others of the train that were not considered strictly of our own party yoked up and started due west across the level plain which I had predicted as having no water, and I really thought they would never live to get across to the western border. Mr. Culverwell and Mr. Fish stayed with us, making another wagon in our train. We talked about the matter carefully. I did not think it possible to get across that plain in less than four or six days, and I did not believe there was a drop of water on the route. To the south of us was a mountain that now had considerable snow upon its summit and some small pine trees also.[19] Doubtless we could find plenty of water at the base, but being due south, it was quite off our course. The prospects for reaching water were so much better in that way that we finally decided to go there rather than follow the Jayhawkers on their desolate tramp over the dry plain.

So we turned up a cañon leading toward the mountain and had a pretty heavy upgrade and a rough bed for a road. Partway up we came to a high cliff and in its face were niches or cavities as large as a barrel or larger, and in some of them we found balls of a glistening substance looking something like pieces of variegated candy stuck together. The balls were as large as small pumpkins. It was evidently food of some sort, and we found it sweet but sickish, and those who were so hungry as to break up one of the balls and divide it among the others, making a good meal of it, were a little troubled with nausea afterwards.[20] I considered it bad policy to rob the Indians of any of their food, for they must be pretty smart people to live in this desolate country and find enough to keep them alive, and I was pretty sure we might count them as hostiles, as they never came near our camp. Like other Indians, they were probably revengeful and might seek to have revenge on us for the injury. We considered it prudent to keep careful watch for them, so they might not surprise us with a volley of arrows.

The second night we camped near the head of the cañon we had been following, but thus far there had been no water, and only some stunted sagebrush for the oxen, which they did not like and only ate when near the point of starvation. They stood around the camp looking as sorry as oxen can. During the night a stray and crazy looking cloud passed over us and left its moisture on the mountain in the shape of a coat of snow several inches deep. When daylight came the oxen crowded around the wagons, shivering with cold and licking up the snow to quench their thirst. We took pattern after them and melted snow to get water for ourselves.

By the looks of our cattle it did not seem as if they could pull much, and light loads were advisable on this upgrade. Mr. Bennett was a carpenter and had brought along some good tools in his wagon. These he reluctantly unloaded, and almost everything else except bedding and provisions, and leaving them upon the ground, we rolled up the hills slowly, with loads as light as possible.

Rogers and I went ahead with our guns to look out the way and find a good camping place. After a few miles we got out of the snow and out upon an incline, and in the bright clear morning air, the foot of the snowy part of the mountain seemed nearby, and we were sure we could reach it before night. From here no guide was needed and Rogers and I, with our guns and canteens, hurried on as fast as possible. When a camp was found we were to raise a signal smoke to tell them where it was. We were here, as before, badly deceived as to the distance, and we marched steadily and swiftly till nearly night before we reached the foot of the mountain.

Here was a flat place in a tableland and on it a low brush hut with a small smoke nearby, which we could plainly see as we were in the shade of the mountain, and that place lighted up by the nearly setting sun. We looked carefully and satisfied ourselves there was but one hut, and consequently but few people could be expected. We approached carefully and cautiously, making a circuit around so as to get between the hut and the hill in case the occupants should retreat in that direction. It was a long time before we could see any entrance to this wickiup, but we found it at last and approached directly in front, very cautiously indeed. We could see no one, and thought perhaps they were in ambush for us, but hardly probable, as we had kept closely out of sight. We consulted a moment and concluded to make an advance and if possible capture someone who could tell us about the country, as we felt we were completely lost. When within thirty yards, a man poked his head out of a doorway and drew it back again quick as a flash. We kept out our guns at full cock and ready for use, and [I] told Rogers to look out for arrows, for they would come now if ever. But they did not pull a bow on us, and the red man, almost naked, came out and beckoned for us to come on, which we did.

We tried to talk with the fellow in the sign language, but he could understand about as much as an oyster. I made a little basin in the ground and filled it with water from our canteens to represent a lake, then pointed in an inquiring way west and north, made signs of ducks and geese flying and squawking, but I did not seem to be able to get an idea into his head of what we wanted. I got thoroughly provoked at him and may have shown some signs of anger. During all this time a child or two in the hut squalled terribly, fearing, I suppose, they would all be murdered. We might have lost our scalps under some circumstances, but we appeared to be fully the strongest party and had no fear, for the Indian had no weapon about him and we had both guns and knives. The poor fellow was shivering with cold, and with signs of friendship we fired off one of the guns, which waked him up a little, and he pointed to the gun and said "Walker," probably meaning the same good Chief Walker who had so fortunately stopped us in our journey down Green River. I understood from the Indian that he was not friendly to Walker, but to show that he was all right with us, he went into the hut and brought out a handful of corn for us to eat. By the aid of a warm spring near-by they had raised some corn here, and the dry stalks were standing around.[21]

As we were about to leave I told him we would come back next day and bring him some clothes if we could find any to spare, and then we shouldered our guns and went back toward the wagons, looking over our shoulders occasionally to see if we were followed. We walked fast down the hill and reached the camp about dark, to find it a most unhappy one indeed. Mrs. Bennett and Mrs. Arcane were in heartrending distress. The four children were crying for water but there was not a drop to give them, and none could be reached before sometime next day. The mothers were nearly crazy, for they expected the children would choke with thirst and die in their arms, and would rather perish themselves than suffer the agony of seeing their little ones gasp and slowly die. They reproached themselves as being the cause of all this trouble. For the love of gold they had left homes where hunger had never come, and often in sleep dreamed of the bounteous tables of their old homes, only to be woefully disappointed in the morning. There was great gladness when John Rogers and I appeared in the camp and gave the mothers full canteens of water for themselves and little ones, and there were tears of joy and thankfulness upon their cheeks as they blessed us over and over again.

The oxen fared very hard. The ground was made up of broken stone, and all that grew was a dry and stunted brush not more than six inches high of which the poor animals took an occasional dainty bite and seemed hardly able to drag along.

It was only seven or eight miles to the warm spring, and all felt better to know for a certainty that we would soon be safe again. We started early—even the women walked—so as to favor the poor oxen all we could. When within two miles of the water, some of the oxen lay down and refused to rise again, so we had to leave them and a wagon, while the rest pushed on and reached the spring soon after noon. We took water and went back to the oxen left behind, and gave them some to drink. They were somewhat rested and got up, and we tried to drive them in without the wagons, but they were not inclined to travel without the yoke, so we put it on them and hitched to the wagon again. The yoke and the wagon seemed to brace them up a good deal, and they went along thus much better than when alone and scattered about with nothing to lean upon.

The warm spring was quite large and ran a hundred yards or more before the water sank down into the dry and thirsty desert. The dry cornstalks of last year's crop, some small willows, sagebrush, weeds, and grass suited our animals very well, and they ate better than for a long time, and we thought it best to remain two or three days to give them a chance to get rest. The Indian we left here the evening before had gone and left nothing behind but a chunk of crystallized rock salt. He seemed to be afraid of his friends.

The range we had been traveling nearly parallel with seemed to come to an end here where this snow peak stood, and immediately north and south of this peak there seemed to be a lower pass. The continuous range north was too low to hold snow. In the morning I concluded to go to the summit of that pass and with my glass have an extensive view. Two other boys started with me, and as we moved along the snow line we saw tracks of our runaway Indian in the snow, passing over a low ridge. As we went on uphill our boys began to fall behind, and long before night I could see nothing of them. The ground was quite soft, and I saw many tracks of Indians, which put me on my guard. I reached the summit, and as the shade of its mountain began to make it a little dark, I built a fire of sagebrush, ate my grub, and when it was fairly dark, renewed the fire and passed on a mile, where in a small ravine with banks two feet high I lay down sheltered from the wind and slept till morning. I did this to beat the Indian in his own cunning.

Next morning I reached the summit about nine o'clock and had the grandest view I ever saw. I could see north and south almost forever. The surrounding region seemed lower, but much of it black, mountainous, and barren. On the west the snow peak shut out the view in that direction. To the south the mountains seemed to descend for more than twenty miles, and near the base, perhaps ten miles away, were several smokes, apparently from campfires, and as I could see no animals or camp wagons anywhere, I presumed them to be Indians. A few miles to the north and east of where I stood, and somewhat higher, was the roughest piece of ground I ever saw. It stood in sharp peaks and was of many colors, some of them so red that the mountain looked red-hot. I imagined it to be a true volcanic point and had never been so near one before, and [it was] the most wonderful picture of grand desolation one could ever see.

Toward the north I could see the desert the Jayhawkers and their comrades had undertaken to cross, and if their journey was as troublesome as ours and very much longer, they might by this time be all dead of thirst. I remained on this summit an hour or so, bringing my glass to bear on all points within my view and scanning closely for everything that might help us or prove an obstacle to our progress. The more I looked, the more I satisfied myself that we were yet a long way from California, and the serious question of our ever living to get there presented itself to me as I tramped along down the grade to camp. I put down at least another month of heavy, weary travel before we could hope to make the land of gold, and our stock of strength and provisions were both pretty small for so great a tax upon them. I thought so little about anything else that the Indians might have captured me easily, for I jogged along without a thought of them. I thought of the bounteous stock of bread and beans upon my father's table, to say nothing about all the other good things, and here was I, the oldest son, away out in the center of the Great American Desert, with an empty stomach and a dry and parched throat, and clothes fast wearing out with constant wear. And perhaps I had not yet seen the worst of it. I might be forced to see men, and the women and children of our party, choke and die, powerless to help them. It was a darker, gloomier day than I had ever known could be, and alone I wept aloud, for I believed I could see the future, and the results were bitter to contemplate. I hope no reader of this history may ever be placed in a position to be thus tried, for I am not ashamed to say that I have a weak point to show under such circumstances. It is not in my power to tell how much I suffered in my lonely trips, lasting sometimes days and nights, that I might give the best advice to those of my party. I believed that I could escape at any time myself, but all must be brought through or perish, and with all I knew I must not discourage the others. I could tell them the truth, but I must keep my worst apprehensions to myself lest they lose heart and hope and faith needlessly.

I reached the camp on the third day, where I found the boys who went partway with me and whom I had outwalked. I related to the whole camp what I had seen, and when all was told, it appeared that the route from the mountains westerly was the only route that could be taken. They told me of a discovery they had made of a pile of squashes probably raised upon the place, and sufficient in number so that every person could have one. I did not approve of this, for we had no title to this produce and might be depriving the rightful owner of the means of life. I told them not only was it wrong to rob them of their food, but they could easily revenge themselves on us by shooting our cattle, or scalp us, by gathering a company of their own people together. They [the campers] had no experience with red men and were slow to see the results I spoke of as possible.

During my absence an ox had been killed, for some were nearly out of provisions, and flesh was the only means to prevent starvation. The meat was distributed amongst the entire camp, with the understanding that when it became necessary to kill another, it should be divided in the same way. Some one of the wagons would have to be left for lack of animals to draw it. Our animals were so poor that one would not last long as food. No fat could be found on the entire carcass, and the marrow of the great bones was a thick liquid, streaked with blood, resembling corruption.

Our road led us around the base of the mountain. There were many large rocks in our way, some as large as houses, but we wound around among them in a very crooked way and managed to get along. The feet of the oxen became so sore that we made moccasins for them from the hide of the ox that was killed, and with this protection they got along very well. Our train now consisted of seven wagons. Bennett had two; Arcane, two; the Earhart brothers, one; Culverwell, Fish and others, one; and there was one other, the owners of which I have forgotten. The second night we had a fair camp with water and pretty fair grass and brush for the oxen. We were not very far from the snow line, and this had some effect on the country.

When Bennett retired that night he put on a camp kettle of the fresh beef and so arranged the fire that it would cook slowly and be done by daylight for breakfast. After an hour or so Mr. Bennett went out to replenish the fire and see how the cooking was coming on, and when he went to put more water in the kettle, he found that, to his disappointment, most of the meat was gone. I was rolled up in my blanket under his wagon, and awoke when he came to the fire, and saw him stand and look around as if to fasten the crime on the right party if possible, but soon he came to me and in a whisper said, "Did you see anyone around the fire after we went to bed?" I assured him I did not, and then he told me someone had taken his meat. "Do you think," said he "that anyone is so near out of food as to be starving? I know the meat is poor, and whoever took it must be nearly starving." After a whispered conversation we went to bed, but we both rose at daylight and, as we sat by the fire, kept watch of those who got up and came around. We thought we knew the right man but were not sure and could not imagine what might happen if stealing grub should begin and continue. It is a sort of unwritten law that in parties such as ours, he who steals provisions forfeits his life. We knew we must keep watch, and if the offense was repeated, the guilty one might be compelled to suffer. Bennett watched closely, and for a few days, I kept closely with the wagons for fear there might be trouble. It was really the most critical point in our experience. After three or four days all hope of detecting the criminal had passed and all danger was over [and we were] out of any difficulty.

One night we had a fair camp, as we were close to the base of the snow butte, and found a hole of clear, or what seemed to be living, water. There were a few minnows in it, not much more than an inch long. This was among a big pile of rocks, and around these the oxen found some grass.[22]

There now appeared to be a pass away to the south, as a sort of outlet to the great plain which lay to the north of us. But immediately west and across the desert waste, extending to the foot of a low, black range of mountains—through which there seemed to be no pass—the distant snowy peak lay still farther on, with Martin's Pass over it, still a long way off though we had been steering toward it for a month. Now, as we were compelled to go west, this impassable barrier was in our way, and if no pass could be found in it, we would be compelled to go south and make no progress in a westerly direction.

Our trail was now descending to the bottom of what seemed to be the narrowest part of the plain, the same one the Jayhawkers had started across, further north, ten days before. When we reached the lowest part of this valley we came to a running stream, and as dead grass could be seen in the bed where the water ran very slowly, I concluded it only had water in it after hard rains in the mountains, perhaps a hundred miles to the north. This water was not pure; it had a bitter taste, and no doubt in dry weather was a rank poison. Those who partook of it were affected about as if they had taken a big dose of salts.[23]

A short distance above this we found the trail of the Jayhawkers going west, and thus we knew they had got safely across the great plain and then turned southward. I hurried along their trail for several miles and looked the country over with [the] field glass, becoming fully satisfied we should find no water till we reached the summit of the next range, and then, fearing the party had not taken the precaution to bring along some water, I went back to them and found they had none. I told them they would not see a drop for the next forty miles, and they unloaded the lightest wagon and drove back with everything they had which would hold water, to get a good supply.

I turned back again on the Jayhawkers' road, and followed it so rapidly that well toward night I was pretty near the summit, where a pass through this rocky range had been found, and on this mountain not a tree, a shrub, or spear of grass could be found—desolation beyond conception. I carried my gun along every day but, for the want of a chance to kill any game, a single load would remain in my gun for a month. Very seldom a rabbit could be seen, but not a bird of any kind, not even a hawk, buzzard, or crow, made their appearance here.

When near the steep part of the mountain, I found a dead ox the Jayhawkers had left. As no camp could be made here, for lack of water and grass, the meat could not be saved. I found the body of the animal badly shrunken, but in condition, as far as putrefaction was concerned, as perfect as when alive. A big gash had been cut in the ham clear to the bone, and the sun had dried the flesh in this. I was so awful hungry that I took my sheath knife and cut a big steak, which I devoured as I walked along, without cooking or salt. Some may say they would starve before eating such meat, but if they have ever experienced hunger till it begins to draw down the life itself, they will find the impulse of self-preservation something not to be controlled by mere reason. It is an instinct that takes possession of one in spite of himself.

I went down a narrow, dark cañon high on both sides, and perpendicular, and quite so in many places. In one of the perpendicular portions it seemed to be a variegated clay formation, and a little water seeped down its face. Here the Indians had made a clay bowl and fastened it to the wall so that it would collect and retain about a quart of water, and I had a good drink of water, the first one since leaving the running stream.[24] Near here I stayed all night, for fear of Indians, who, I firmly believe, would have taken my scalp had a good opportunity offered. I slept without a fire, and my supply of meat just obtained drove hunger away.

In the morning I started down the cañon, which descended rapidly and had a bed of sharp, volcanic, broken rock. I could sometimes see an Indian track and kept a sharp lookout at every turn, for fear of revenge on account of the store of squashes which had been taken. I felt I was in constant danger, but could do nothing else but go on and keep eyes open, trusting to circumstances to get out of any sudden emergency that might arise.

As I recollect, this was Christmas day, and about dusk I came upon the camp of one man with his wife and family, the Reverend J. W. Brier, Mrs. Brier, and two sons.[25] I inquired for others of his party and he told me they were somewhere ahead. When I arrived at his camp I found the reverend gentleman very coolly delivering a lecture to his boys on education. It seemed very strange to me to hear a solemn discourse on the benefits of early education when, it seemed to me, starvation was staring us all in the face, and the barren desolation all around gave small promise of the need of any education higher than the natural impulses of nature. None of us knew exactly where we were, nor when the journey would be ended, nor when substantial relief would come. Provisions were wasting away, and some had been reduced to the last alternative of subsisting on the oxen alone. I slept by the fire that night, without a blanket, as I had done on many nights before, and after they hitched up and drove on in the morning, I searched the camp carefully, finding some bacon rinds they had thrown away. As I chewed these and could taste the rich grease they contained, I thought they were the sweetest morsels I ever tasted.

Here on the north side of the cañon were some rolling hills and some small weak springs, the water of which, when gathered together, made a small stream which ran a few yards down the cañon before it lost itself in the rocks and sand.[26] On the side there stood what seemed to be one-half of a butte, with the perpendicular face toward the cañon. Away on the summit of the butte I saw an Indian, so far away he looked no taller than my finger, and when he went out of sight I knew pretty well he was the very fellow who grew the squashes. I thought it might be he, at any rate.

I now turned back to meet the teams and found them seven or eight miles up the cañon, and although it was a downgrade, the oxen were barely able to walk slowly with their loads, which were light, as [the] wagons were almost empty except [for] the women and children. When night came on it seemed to be cloudy, and we could hear the cries of the wild geese passing east. We regarded this as a very good sign and no doubt Owen's Lake, which we expected to pass on this route, was not very far off.[27] Around in those small hills and damp places was some coarse grass and other growths, but those who had gone before devoured the best, so our oxen had a hard time to get anything to eat.

Next morning I shouldered my gun and followed down the cañon, keeping the wagon road, and when half a mile down, at the sink of the sickly stream, I killed a wild goose. This had undoubtedly been attracted here the night before by the light of our campfire. When I got near the lower end of the cañon, there was a cliff on the north or right-hand side, which was perpendicular or perhaps a little overhanging, and at the base a cave which had the appearance of being continuously occupied by Indians. As I went on down I saw a very strange looking track upon the ground. There were handprints and footprints as if a human being had crawled upon all fours. As this track reached the valley where the sand had been clean swept by the wind, the tracks became more plain, and the sand had been blown into small hills not over three or four feet high. I followed the track till it led to the top of one of these small hills, where a small well-like hole had been dug, and in this excavation was a kind of Indian mummy curled up like a dog. He was not dead, for I could see him move as he breathed, but his skin looked very much like the surface of a well-dried venison ham. I should think by his looks he must be two hundred or three hundred years old—indeed he might be Adam's brother and not look any older than he did. He was evidently crippled. A climate which would preserve for many days or weeks the carcass of an ox so that an eatable round steak could be cut from it might perhaps preserve a live man for a longer period than would be believed.

I took a good long look at the wild creature, and during all the time he never moved a muscle, though he must have known someone was in the well looking down at him. He was probably practicing one of the directions for a successful political career: looking wise and saying nothing. At any rate he was not going to let his talk get him into any trouble. He probably had a friend around somewhere who supplied his wants. I now left him and went farther out into the lowest part of the valley. I could look to the north for fifty miles and it seemed to rise gradually in that direction. To the south the view was equally extended, and down that way a lake could be seen. The valley was here quite narrow, and the lofty snowcapped peak we had tried so hard to reach for the past two months now stood before me.[28] Its east side was almost perpendicular and seemed to reach the sky, and the snow was drifting over it, while here the day sun was shining uncomfortably hot. I believe this mountain was really miles from its base to its summit, and that nothing could climb it on the eastern side except a bird, and the only bird I had seen for two months was the goose I shot. I looked every day for some sort of game but had not seen any.

As I reached the lower part of the valley I walked over what seemed to be boulders of various sizes, and as I stepped from one to another, the tops were covered with dirt, and they grew larger as I went along. I could see behind them, and they looked clear like ice, but on closer inspection proved to be immense blocks of rock salt, while the water which stood at their bases was the strongest brine. After this discovery I took my way back to the road made by the Jayhawkers and found it quite level, but sandy. Following this I came to a campfire soon after dark at which E. Doty and mess were camped. As I was better acquainted [with them than with Reverend Brier,] I camped with them. They said the water there was brackish and I soon found out the same thing for myself.[29] It was a poor camp; no grass, poor water, and scattered, bitter sagebrush for food for the cattle. It would not do to wait long here, and so they hurried on.

I inquired of them about Martin's Pass, as they were now quite near it, and they said it was no pass at all, only the mountain was a little lower than the one holding the snow. No wagon could get over it, and the party had made up their minds to go on foot, and were actually burning their wagons as fuel with which to dry the meat of some of the oxen which they had killed.[30] They selected those which were weakest and least likely to stand the journey, and by drying it the food was much concentrated. They were to divide the provisions equally and it was agreed [that] thereafter everyone must look out for himself and not expect any help from anyone. If he used up his own provisions, he had no right to expect anyone else to divide with him. Rice, tea, and coffee were measured out by the spoonful, and the small amount of flour and bacon which remained was divided out as evenly as possible. Everything was to be left behind but blankets and provisions, for the men were too weak to carry heavy packs, and the oxen could not be relied on as beasts of burden, and it was thought best not to load them so as to needlessly break them down.

When these fellows started out they were full of spirit, and the frolic and fun along the Platte River was something worth laughing at, but now they were very melancholy and talked in the lowest kind of low spirits. One fellow said he knew this was the Creator's dumping place, where he had left the worthless dregs after making a world, and the devil had scraped these together a little. Another said this must be the very place where Lot's wife was turned into a pillar of salt, and the pillar [had] been broken up and spread around the country.[31] He said if a man was to die he would never decay, on account of the salt. Thus the talk went on, and it seemed as if there were not bad words enough in the language to properly express their contempt and bad opinion of such a country as this. They treated me to some of their meat, a little better than mine, and before daylight in the morning I was headed back on the trail to report the bad news I had learned of the Jayhawkers.

About noon I met two of our camp companions with packs on their backs, following the wagon trail, and we stopped and had a short talk. They were oldish men perhaps fifty years old, one a Mr. Fish of Indiana and another named Gould. They said they could perhaps do as well on foot as to follow the slow ox teams, but when I told them what those ahead of them were doing, and how they must go, they did not seem to be entirely satisfied, as what they had on their backs would need to be replenished, and no such chance could be expected. They had an idea that the end of the journey was not as far off as I predicted. Mr. Fish had a long, nicely made whiplash wound around his waist, and when I asked him why he carried such a useless thing which he could not eat, he said perhaps he could trade it off for something to eat. After we had set on a sand hill and talked for a while, we rose and shook each other by the hand and bade each other good-bye with quivering lips. There was with me a sort of impression I could not repel that I should never see the middle-aged men again.

As my road was now out and away from the mountains and level, I had no fear of being surprised by enemies, so walked on with eyes downcast, thinking over the situation, and wondering what would be the final outcome. If I were alone, with no one to expect me to help them, I would be out before any other man, but with women and children in the party, to go and leave them would be to pile everlasting infamy on my head. The thought almost made me crazy, but I thought it would be better to stay and die with them, bravely struggling to escape, than to forsake them in their weakness.

It was almost night before I reached our camp, and sitting around our little fire I told, in the most easy way I could, the unfavorable news of the party in advance. They seemed to look to me as a guide and adviser, I presume because I took such pains to inform myself on every point, and my judgment was accepted with very little opposing opinion—they moved as I thought best. During my absence from camp for the two days, the Indians had shot arrows into three of our oxen, and one still had an arrow in his side forward of the hip, which was a dangerous place. To be sure and save him for ourselves, we killed him. Some were a little afraid to eat the meat, thinking perhaps the arrow might be poisoned, but I agreed that they wanted meat themselves and would not do that. I told them if they got a shot themselves it would very likely be a poisoned arrow and they must take the most instant measures to cut it out before it went into the blood. So we ventured to dry the meat and take it with us.

Now I said to the whole camp, "You can see how you have displeased the red men, taking their little squashes, and when we get into a place that suits them for that purpose, they may meet us with a superior force and massacre us, not only for revenge but to get our oxen and clothing." I told them we must ever be on guard against a surprise, as the chances were greatly against us.

We pulled the arrows out of the other oxen, and they seemed to sustain no great injury from the wounds. The little, faint stream where we camped has since been named as Furnace Creek and is still known as such. It was named in 1862 by some prospectors who built what was called an air furnace (on a small scale) to reduce some ore found nearby, which they supposed to contain silver. But I believe it turned out to be lead and too far from transportation to be available.[32]

CHAPTER X

A Long, Narrow Valley

BENNETT AND ARCANE NOW CONCLUDED NOT TO WAIT for me to go ahead and explore out a way for them to follow, as I had done for a long time, but to go ahead, as it was evidently the best way to turn south and make our own road and find the water and passes all for ourselves. So they hitched up and rolled down the cañon and out into the valley and then turned due south. We had not gone long on this course before we saw that we must cross the valley and get over to the west side. To do this we must cross through some water, and for fear the ground might be miry, I went to a sand hill nearby and got a mesquite stick about three feet long with which to sound out our way. I rolled up my pants, pulled off my moccasins, and waded in, having the teams stand still till I could find out whether it was safe for them to follow or not by ascertaining the depth of the water and the character of the bottom.

The water was very clear and the bottom seemed uneven, there being some deep holes. Striking my stick on the bottom it seemed solid as a rock, and breaking off a small projecting point I found it to be solid rock salt. As the teams rolled along they scarcely roiled the water. It looked to me as if the whole valley, which might be a hundred miles long, might have been a solid bed of rock salt. Before we reached this water there were many solid blocks of salt lying around, covered with a little dirt on the top.[1]

The second night we found a good spring of fresh water coming out from the bottom of the snow peak almost over our heads. The small flow from it spread out over the sand and sank in a very short distance and there was some quite good grass growing around.[2]

This was a temporary relief, but brought us face to face with stronger difficulties and a more hopeless outlook. There was no possible way to cross this high, steep range of mountains anywhere to the north, and the Jayhawkers had abandoned their wagons and burned them, and we could no longer follow on the trail they made. It seemed that there was no other alternative but for us to keep along the edge of the mountain to the south and search for another pass. Some who had read Frémont's travels said that the range immediately west of us must be the one he described, on the west side of which was a beautiful country of rich soil and having plenty of cattle and horses, and containing some settlers, but on the east all was barren, dry, rocky, sandy desert as far as could be seen. We knew this eastern side answered well the description and believed that this was really the range[3] described, or at least it was close by.

We had to look over the matter very carefully and consider all the conditions and circumstances of the case. We could see the mountains were lower to the south, but they held no snow and seemed only barren rocks piled up in lofty peaks and, as we looked, it seemed the most godforsaken country in the world.

We had been in the region long enough to know the higher mountains contained [the] most water, and that the valleys had bad water or none at all, so that while the lower altitudes to the south gave some promise of easier crossing, [they] gave us no promise of water or grass, without which we must certainly perish. In a certain sense we were lost. The clear nights and days furnished us with the means of telling the points of [the] compass as the sun rose and set, but not a sign of life in nature's wide domain had been seen for a month or more. A vest-pocketful of powder and shot would last a good hunter till he starved to death, for there was not a living thing to shoot, great or small.

We talked over our present position pretty freely, and everyone was asked to speak his unbiased mind, for we knew not who might be right or who might be wrong, and someone might make a suggestion of the utmost value. We all felt pretty much downhearted. Our civilized provisions were getting so scarce that all must be saved for the women and children, and the men must get along some way on ox meat alone. It was decided not a scrap of anything that would sustain life must go to waste. The blood, hide, and intestines were all prepared in some way for food. This meeting lasted till late at night. If some of them had lost their minds I should not have been surprised, for hunger swallows all other feelings. A man in a starving condition is a savage. He may be as blood[thirsty] and selfish as a wild beast, as docile and gentle as a lamb, or as wild and crazy as a terrified animal, devoid of affection, reason, or thought of justice. We were none of us as bad as this, and yet there was a strange look in the eyes of some of us sometimes, as I saw by looking round, and as others no doubt realized, for I saw them making mysterious glances even in my direction.

Morning came and all were silent. The dim prospect of the future seemed to check every tongue. When one left a water hole he went away as if in doubt whether he would ever enjoy the pleasure of another drop. Every camp was sad beyond description, and no one can guide the pen to make it tell the tale as it seemed to us. When our morning meal of soup and meat was finished, Bennett's two teamsters and the two of Arcane's concluded their chances of life were better if they could take some provisions and strike out on foot, and so they were given what they could carry, and they arranged their packs and bade us a sorrowful good-bye, hoping to meet again on the Pacific coast. There were genuine tears shed at the parting, and I believe neither party ever expected to see each other in this life again.

Bennett's two men were named Silas Helmer and S. S. or C. C. Abbott, but I have forgotten the names of Arcane's men. Mr. Abbott was from New York, a harness maker by trade, and he took his circular cutting knife with him, saying it was light to carry and the weapon he should need. One of them had a gun. They took the trail taken by the Jayhawkers. All the provisions they could carry besides their blankets could not last them to exceed ten days, and I well knew they could hardly get off the desert in that time. Mr. Abbott was a man I loved fondly. He was good company in camp, and happy and sociable. He had shown no despondency at any time until the night of the last meeting and the morning of the parting. His chances seemed to me to be much poorer than my own, but I hardly think he realized it. When in bed I could not keep my thoughts back from the old home I had left, where good water and a bountiful spread were always ready at the proper hour. I know I dreamed of taking a draft of cool, sweet water from a full pitcher and then woke up with my mouth and throat as dry as dust. The good home left behind was a favorite theme about the campfire, and many a one told of the dream pictures, natural as life, that came to him of the happy eastern home with comfort and happiness surrounding it, even if wealth was lacking. The home of the poorest man on earth was preferable to this place. Wealth was of no value here. A hoard of twenty-dollar gold pieces could now stand before us the whole day long with no temptation to touch a single coin, for its very weight would drag us nearer death. We could purchase nothing with it and we would have cared no more for it as a thing of value than we did the desert sands. We would have given much more for some of the snow which we could see drifting over the peak of the great snow mountains over our heads like a dusty cloud.[4]

Deeming it best to spare the strength as much as possible, I threw away everything I could, retaining only my glass, some ammunition, sheath knife and tin cup. No unnecessary burden could be put on any man or beast, lest he lie down under it, never to rise again. Life and strength were sought to be husbanded in every possible way.

Leaving this camp where the water was appreciated, we went over a road for perhaps eight miles and came to the mouth of a rocky cañon leading up west to the summit of the range.[5] This cañon was too rough for wagons to pass over. Out in the valley near its mouth was a mound about four feet high, and in the top of this a little well[6] that held about a pailful of water that was quite strong of sulfur. When stirred it would look quite black. About the mouth of the well was a wire grass that seemed to prevent it caving in. It seems the drifting sand had slowly built this little mound about the little well of water in a curious way. We spent the night here and kept a man at the well all night to keep the water dipped out as fast as it flowed, in order to get enough for ourselves and cattle. The oxen drank this water better than they did the brackish water of the former camp.

The plain was thinly scattered with sagebrush, and up near the base of the mountain some greasewood grew in little bunches like currant bushes.

The men with wagons decided they would take this cañon[7] and follow it up to try to get over the range, and not wait for me to go ahead and explore, as they said it took too much time, and the provisions, consisting now of only ox meat, were getting more precarious every day. To help them all I could, and if possible to be forewarned a little of danger, I shouldered my gun and pushed on ahead as fast as I could. The bottom was of sharp, broken rock, which would be very hard for the feet of the oxen, although we had rawhide moccasins for them for some time and this was the kind of footgear I wore myself. I walked on as rapidly as I could, and after a time came to where the cañon spread out into a kind of basin enclosed on all sides but the entrance, with a wall of high steep rock, possible to ascend on foot but which would apparently bar the further progress of the wagons, and I turned back utterly disappointed.[8] I got on an elevation where I could look over the country east and south, and it looked as if there was not a drop of water in its whole extent, and there was no snow on the dark mountains that stretched away to the southward, and it seemed to me as if difficulties beset me on every hand. I hurried back down the cañon, but it was nearly dark before I met the wagons. By a mishap I fell and broke the stock of my gun, over which I was very sorry, for it was an excellent one, the best I ever owned. I carried it in two pieces to the camp and told them the way was barred, at which they could hardly endure their disappointment. They turned in the morning, as the cattle had nothing to eat here and no water, and not much of any food since leaving the spring. They looked terribly bad, and the rough road coming up had nearly finished them. They were yoked up and the wagons turned about for the return. They went better downhill, but it was not long before one of Bennett's oxen lay down and could not be persuaded to rise again. This was no place to tarry in the hot sun, so the ox was killed and the carcass distributed among the wagons. So little draft was required that the remaining oxen took the wagon down. When within two or three miles of the water hole, one of Arcane's oxen also failed and lay down, so they turned him out, and when he had rested a little he came on again for a while, but soon lay down again.

Arcane took a bucket of water back from camp, and after drinking it and resting awhile, the ox was driven down to the spring.[9]

This night we had another meeting to decide upon our course and determine what to do. At this meeting no one was wiser than another, for no one had explored the country and knew what to expect. The questions that now arose were, "How long can we endure this work in this situation?" "How long will our oxen be able to endure the great hardship on the small nourishment they receive?" "How long can we provide ourselves with food?"

We had a few small pieces of dry bread. This was kept for the children, giving them a little now and then. Our only food was in the flesh of the oxen, and when they failed to carry themselves along we must begin to starve. It began to look as if the chances of leaving our bones to bleach upon the desert were the most prominent ones.

One thing was certain: we must move somewhere at once. If we stay here we can live as long as the oxen do, and no longer, and if we go on, it is uncertain where to go to get a better place. We had guns and ammunition, to be sure, but of late we had seen no living creature in this desert wild. Finally Mr. Bennett spoke and said, "Now I will make you a proposition. I propose that we select two of our youngest, strongest men and ask them to take some food and go ahead on foot to try to seek a settlement and food, and we will go back to the good spring[10] we have just left and wait for their return. It will surely not take them more than ten days for the trip, and when they get back we shall know all about the road and its character and how long it will take us to travel it. They can secure some other kind of food that will make us feel better, and when the oxen have rested a little at the spring, we can get out with our wagons and animals and be safe. I think this is the best and safest way. Now what do you all say?"

After a little discussion all seemed to agree that this was the best, and now it remained to find the men to go. No one offered to accept the position of advance messengers. Finally Mr. Bennett said he knew one man well enough to know that he would come back if he lived, and he was sure he would push his way through. "I will take Lewis (myself) if he will consent to go." I consented, though I knew it was a hazardous journey, exposed to all sorts of things—Indians, climate, and probable lack of water—but I thought I would do it and would not refuse. John Rogers, a large, strong, Tennessee man, was then chosen as the other one, and he consented also.

Now preparations began. Mr. Arcane killed the ox which had so nearly failed, and all the men went to drying and preparing meat. Others made us some new moccasins out of rawhide, and the women made us each a knapsack.

Our meat was closely packed, and one can form an idea how poor our cattle were from the fact that John and I actually packed seven-eighths of all the flesh of an ox into our knapsacks and carried it away. They put in a couple of spoonfuls of rice and about as much tea. This seemed like robbery of the children, but the good women said that in case of sickness even that little bit might save our lives. I wore no coat or vest but took half of a light blanket, while Rogers wore a thin summer coat and took no blanket. We each had a small tin cup and a small camp kettle holding a quart. Bennett had me take his seven-shooter rifle, and Rogers had a good double-barreled shotgun. We each had a sheath knife, and our hats were small-brimmed, drab affairs fitting close to the head and not very conspicuous to an enemy, as we might rise up from behind a hill into possible views. We tried on our packs and fitted the straps a little so they would carry easy. They collected all the money there was in camp and gave it to us. Mr. Arcane had about thirty dollars and others threw in small amounts from forty cents upward. We received all sorts of advice. Captain Culverwell was an old seafaring man and was going to tell us how to find our way back, but Mr. Bennett told the captain that he had known Lewis as a hunter for many years, and that if he went over a place in the daytime he could find his way back at night every time. Others cautioned us about the Indians and told us how to manage. Others told us not to get caught in deep snow which we might find on the mountains.

This advice we received in all the kindness in which it was given, and then we bade them all good-bye. Some turned away, too much affected to approach us, and others shook our hands with deep feeling, grasping them firmly, and heartily hoping we would be successful and be able to pilot them out of this dreary place into a better land. Everyone felt that a little food to make a change from the poor dried meat would be acceptable. Mr. and Mrs. Bennett and J. B. Arcane and wife were the last to remain when the others had turned away. They had most faith in the plan and felt deeply. Mrs.

Bennett was the last, and she asked God to bless us and bring some food to her starving children.

We were so much affected that we could not speak and silently turned away and took our course again up the cañon we had descended the night before.

After a while we looked back, and when they saw us turn around, all the hats and bonnets waved us a final parting.

Those left in the camp were Asabel Bennett and Sarah, his wife, with three children, George, Melissa, and Martha; J. B. Arcane and wife, with son Charles. The youngest children were not more than two years old.[11] There were also the two Earhart brothers and a grown son, and Captain Culverwell, and some others I cannot recall; eleven grown people in all, besides a Mr. Wade, his wife, and three children, who did not mingle with our party but usually camped a little distance off, followed our trail, but seemed to shun company.[12] We soon passed round a bend of the cañon and then walked on in silence.

We both of us meditated some over the homes of our fathers but took new courage in view of the importance of our mission and passed on as fast as we could.

By night we were far up the mountain, near the perpendicular rough peak, and far above us on a slope we could see some bunches of grass and sagebrush. We went to this and found some small water holes. No water ran from them, they were so small. Here we stayed all night. It did not seem very far to the snowy peak to the north of us.[13] Just where we were seemed the lowest pass, for to the south were higher peaks and the rocks looked as if they were too steep to be got over.

Through this gap came a cold breeze, and we had to look round to get a sheltered place in which to sleep. We lay down close together, spoon fashion, and made the little blanket do as cover for the both of us. In the morning we filled our canteens, which we had made by binding two powder cans together with strips of cloth, and started for the summit nearby.[14] From this was the grandest sight we ever beheld. Looking east we could see the country we had been crawling over since November 4th. "Just look at the cursed country we have come over!" said Rogers as he pointed over it. To the north was the biggest mountain [range][15] we ever saw, peaks on peaks and towering far above our heads, and covered with snow which was apparently everlasting.

This mountain [range] seemed to have very few trees on it, and in extent, as it reached away to the [northwest], seemed interminable. South was a nearly level plain, and to the [south] I thought I could dimly see a range of mountains that held a little snow upon their summits, but on the main range to the south there was none. It seemed to me the dim, snowy mountains must be as far as two hundred miles away, but of course I could not judge accurately. After looking at this grand but worthless landscape long enough to take in its principal features, we asked each other what we supposed the people we left behind would think to see mountains so far ahead. We knew that they had an idea that the coast range[16] was not very far ahead, but we saw at once to go over all these mountains and return within the limits of fifteen days, which had been agreed upon between us, would probably be impossible, but we must try as best we could, so down the rocky steep we clambered and hurried on our way.[17] In places the way was so steep that we had to help each other down, and the hard work made us perspire freely so that water was a prime necessity. In one place near here, we found a little water and filled our canteens besides drinking a good present supply. There were two low, black, rocky ranges directly ahead of us which we must cross.[18]

When partway down the mountain, a valley or depression opened up in that direction up which it seemed as if we could look a hundred miles.[19] Nearby and a short distance north was a lake of water, and when we reached the valley, we crossed a clear stream of water flowing slowly toward the lake.

Being in need of water, we rushed eagerly to it and prepared to take a big drink, but the tempting fluid was as salty as brine and made our thirst all the more intolerable. Nothing grew on the bank of this stream[20] and the bed was of hard clay which glistened in the sun.

We now began the ascent of the next ridge, keeping a westerly course, and walked as fast as we could up the rough mountainside. We crossed the head of a cañon near the summit about dark, and here we found a trail which, from indications, we knew to be that of the Jayhawkers, who had evidently been forced to the southward of the course they intended to take. They had camped here and had dug holes in the sand in search of water, but had found none.[21]

We stayed all night here and dug around in some other places in the bottom of the cañon, in the hope to have better luck than they did, but we got no water anywhere.

We seemed almost perishing for want of water, the hard exercise made us perspire so freely. In the morning we started on, and near the summit we came to the dead body of Mr. Fish, laying in the hot sun, as there was no material near here with which his friends could cover the remains. This Mr. Fish was the man who left camp some two weeks before in company with another and who carried the long whiplash wound about his body in hope he could somewhere be able to trade it for bread. No doubt in this very place where he breathed his last, his bones still lie.

As we came in sight of the next valley, we could see a lake of water some distance south of our western course.[22]

We had followed the Jayhawkers' trail thus far, but as we found no water in small holes in the rocks, as we were likely to do when we were the first to pass, we decided to take a new route in the hope to find a little water in this way, for we had no hope of finding it in any other. This valley we now crossed seemed to come to an end about ten miles to the north of us. To the south it widened out, enclosing the lake spoken of. This valley was very sandy and hard to walk over. When about halfway across, we saw some ox tracks leading toward the lake, and in the hope we might find the water drinkable, we turned off at right angles to our course and went that way also. Long before we reached the water of the lake, the bottom became a thin, slimy mud which was very hard on our moccasins. When we reached the water we found it to be of a wine color, and so strongly alkaline as to feel slippery to the touch and under our feet.[23]

This side trip had cost us much exertion and made us feel more thirsty than ever.

We turned now west again, making for a cañon up which we passed in the hope we should at some turn find a little basin of rainwater in some rock.[24] We traveled in it miles and miles, and our mouths became so dry we had to put a bullet or a small smooth stone in and chew it and turn it around with the tongue to induce a flow of saliva. If we saw a spear of green grass on the north side of a rock, it was quickly pulled and eaten to obtain the little moisture it contained.

Thus we traveled along for hours, never speaking, for we found it much better for our thirst to keep our mouths closed as much as possible and prevent the evaporation. The dry air of that region took up water as a sponge does. We passed the summit of this [range] without finding any water, and on our way down the western side we came to a flat place where there was an Indian hut made of small brush. We now thought there surely must be some water near, and we began a thorough search. The great snow mountain did not seem far off, but to the south and southwest a level or inclined plain extended for a long distance.[25] Our thirst began to be something terrible to endure, and in the warm weather and hard walking we had secured only two drinks since leaving camp.

We were so sure that there must be water near here that we laid our knapsacks down by the little hut and looked around in every possible place we could think of. Soon it got dark, and then we made a little fire as a guide and looked again. Soon the moon arose and helped us some, and we shouted frequently to each other so as not to get lost.

We were so nearly worn out that we tried to eat a little meat, but after chewing a long time, the mouth would not moisten it enough so we could swallow, and we had to reject it. It seemed as if we were going to die with plenty of food in our hand, because we could not eat it.

We tried to sleep but could not, but after a little rest we noticed a bright star two hours above the horizon, and from the course of the moon we saw the star must be pretty truly west of us. We talked a little, and the burden of it was a fear that we could not endure the terrible thirst a while longer. The thought of the women and children waiting for our return made us feel more desperate than if we were the only ones concerned. We thought we could fight to the death over a water hole if we could only secure a little of the precious fluid. No one who has never felt the extreme of thirst can imagine the distress, the despair, which it brings. I can find no words, no way to express it so others can understand.

The moon gave us so much light that we decided we would start on our course and get as far as we could before the hot sun came out, and so we went on slowly and carefully in the partial darkness, the only hope left to us being that our strength would hold out till we could get to the shining snow on the great mountain before us. We reached the foot of the range we were descending about sunrise.[26] There was here a wide wash from the snow mountain,[27] down which some water had sometime run after a big storm and had divided into little rivulets only reaching out a little way before they had sunk into the sand.

We had no idea we could now find any water till we at least got very near the snow, and as the best way to reach it, we turned up the wash, although the course was nearly to the north. The course was up a gentle grade and seemed quite sandy and not easy to travel.[28] It looked as if there was an all-day walk before us, and it was quite a question if we could live long enough to make the distance. There were quite strong indications that the water had run here not so very long ago, and we could trace the course of the little streams round among little sandy islands. A little stunted brush grew here, but it was so brittle that the stems would break as easy as an icicle.

In order to not miss a possible bit of water, we separated and agreed upon a general course, and that if either one found water he should fire his gun as a signal. After about a mile or so had been gone over, I heard Rogers' gun and went in his direction. He had found a little ice that had frozen under the clear sky. It was not thicker than window glass. After putting a piece in our mouths we gathered all we could and put it into the little quart camp kettle to melt. We gathered just a kettle full, besides what we ate as we were gathering, and kindled a little fire and melted it.

I can but think how providential it was that we started in the night, for in an hour after the sun had risen, that little sheet of ice would have melted and the water sunk into the sand. Having quenched our thirst, we could now eat, and found that we were nearly starved also. In making this meal we used up all our little store of water, but we felt refreshed and our lives renewed so that we had better courage to go on.[29]

We now took our course [southwest], again taking a beeline for a bluff[30] that lay a little to the south of the big snow mountain. On and on we walked till the dark shadow of the great mountain in the setting sun was thrown about us, and still we did not seem more than halfway to the bluff before us.

All the way had been uphill and very tiresome walking. There was considerable small brush scattered about, here and there, over this steeply inclined plain.

We were still several miles from the base of this largest of the mountains and we could now see that it extended [north] for many miles. The buttes to the south were low, black, and barren, and to the [southwest] as far as we could see, there were no mountains with any snow. As the sun got further down we could see a small smoke curling up near the base of the mountain, and we thought it must be some signal made by the Indians, as we had often seen them signal in that way, but we stopped and talked the matter over, and as we were yet a long way from the bluff which had been our objective point, we concluded we would investigate the smoke signal a little closer. So we set off toward it in the dusk and darkness, and when within about a mile, we found we were in a track that had been somewhat beaten. Feeling with my fingers, I was quite sure I could distinguish ox tracks, and then was quite sure that we had overtaken the Jayhawkers, or at least were on their trail. And then I thought perhaps they had fallen among the Indians, who now might be feasting on their oxen, and it became necessary to use great caution in approaching the little smoke.

We took a circuitous route and soon saw that the persons were on a little bench above us, and we kept very cautious and quiet, listening for any sounds that might tell us who they were.

If they were Indians we should probably hear some of their dogs, but we heard none, and kept creeping closer and closer, till we were within fifty yards, without hearing a sound to give us any idea of who they were.

We decided to get our guns at full cock and then hail the camp, feeling that we had a little the advantage of position. We hailed and were answered in English. "Don't shoot," said we, and they assured us they had no idea of such a thing, and asked us to come in. We found here, to our surprise, Ed Doty, Tom Shannon, L. D. Stevens, and others whom I do not recollect, the real Jayhawkers. They gave us some fresh meat for supper, and near the camp were some water holes that answered well for camp purposes.[31]

Here an ox had given out, and they had stopped long enough to dry the meat, while the others had gone on a day ahead.

Coming around the mountain from the north was quite a well-defined trail leading to the [south], and they said they were satisfied someone lived at the end of it, and they were going to follow it if it led to Mexico or anywhere else. They said that Mr. Brier and his family were still on behind, and alone. Everyone must look out for himself here, and we could not do much for another in any way.

We inquired of them about the trail over which they had come, and where they had found water, and we told them of our experience in this respect. We then related how our train could not go over the mountains with wagons, how they had returned to the best spring, and that we [had] started to go through to the settlements to obtain relief while they waited for our return. We explained to them how they must perish without assistance. If we failed to get through, they could probably live as long as the oxen lasted and would then perish of starvation. We told them how nearly we came to the point of perishing that very morning, of thirst, and how we were saved by finding a little patch of ice in an unexpected place, and were thus enabled to come on another day's travel.

These men were not as cheerful as they used to be and their situation and prospects constantly occupied their minds. They said to us that if the present trail bore away from the mountain and crossed the level plain, that there were some of them who could not possibly get along safely to the other side. Some were completely discouraged, and some were completely out of provisions and dependent on those who had either provisions or oxen yet on hand. An ox was frequently killed, they said, and no part of it was wasted. At a camp where there was no water, for stewing, a piece or hide would be prepared for eating by singeing off the hair and then roasting in the fire. The small intestines were drawn through the fingers to clean them, and these when roasted made very fair food.

They said they had been without water for four or five days at a time and came near starving to death, for it was impossible to swallow food when one became so thirsty. They described the pangs of hunger as something terrible and not to be described. They were willing to give us any information we desired, and we anxiously received all we could, for on our return we desired, to take the best possible route, and we thus had the experience of two parties instead of one. They told us about the deaths of Mr. Fish and Mr. Isham, and where we would find their bodies if we went over their trail.[32]

In the morning we shouldered our packs again and took the trail leading to the [south], and by night we had overtaken the advance party of the Jayhawkers, camped in a cañon[33] where there was a little water, barely sufficient for their use. We inquired why they did not take the trail leading more directly west at the forks,[34] and they said they feared it would lead them into deep snow which would be impassible. They said they considered the trail they had taken as altogether the safest one.

We met Bennett and Arcane's teamsters, and as we expected, they were already out of grub and no way to get anymore. When the party killed an ox they had humbly begged for some of the poorest parts, and thus far were alive. They came to us and very pitifully told us they were entirely out, and although an ox had been killed that day, they had not been able to get a mouthful. We divided up our meat and gave them some, although we did not know how long it would be before we would ourselves be in the same situation.

Thus far we had not seen anything to shoot, big or little, although we kept a sharp lookout.

The whole camp was silent, and all seemed to realize their situation. Before them was a level plain which had the appearance of being so broad as to take five or six days to cross. Judging by the look from the top of the mountain as we came over, there was little to hope for in the way of water. We thought it over very seriously. All the water we could carry would be our canteens full, perhaps two drinks apiece, and the poor meat had so little nourishment that we were weak and unable to endure what we once could.

We were alone, Rogers and I, in interest at any rate, even if there were other men about. For the time it really seemed as if there was very little hope for us, and I have often repeated the following lines as very closely describing my own feelings at that time.

> Oh hands, whose loving, gentle grasp I loosed
> When first this weary journey was begun,
> If I could feel your touch as once I could
> How gladly would I wish my work undone
>   HARRIET KEYNON

During the evening, I had a talk with Captain Asa Haines, in which he said he left a good home in Illinois where he had everything he could wish to eat, and every necessary comfort, and even some to spare, and now he felt so nearly worn out that he had many doubts whether he could live to reach the mountains on the other side. He was so deeply impressed that he made me promise to let his wife and family know how I found him and how he died, for he felt sure he would never see the California mines. I said I might not get through myself, but he thought we were so young and strong that we would struggle through. He said if he could only be home once more he would be content to stay. This was the general tenor of the conversation. There was no mirth, no jokes, and everyone seemed to feel that he was very near the end of his life, and such a death as stood before them—choking, starving in a desert—was the most dreary outlook I ever saw.

This camp of trouble, of forlorn hope, on the edge of a desert stretching out before us like a small sea, with no hope for relief except at the end of a struggle which seemed almost hopeless, is more than any pen can paint, or at all describe. The writer had tried it often. Picture to yourself, dear reader, the situation, and let your own imagination do the rest. It can never come up to the reality.

In the morning, as Rogers and I were about to start, several of the oldest men came to us with their addresses and wished us to forward them to their families if we ever got within the reach of mails. These men shed tears, and we did also as we parted. We turned silently away and again took up our march.

As we went down the cañon we came to one place where it was so narrow that a man or a poor ox could barely squeeze through between the rocks, and in a few miles more reached the open, level plain. When three or four miles out on the trail and not far from the hills, we came to a bunch of quite tall willows. The center of the bunch had been cut out and the branches woven in so as to make a sort of corral. In the center of this was a spring of good water and some good grass growing around.[35] This was pretty good evidence that someone had been here before. We took a good drink and filled our canteens anew, for we did not expect to get another drink for two or three days at least.

We took the trail again and hurried on, as the good water made us feel quite fresh. After a few miles we began to find the bones of animals, some badly decayed and some well preserved. All the heads were those of horses, and it puzzled us to know where they came from.[36] As we passed along we noticed the trail was on a slight upgrade and somewhat crooked. If we stepped off from it, the foot sank in about two inches in dirt finer than the finest flour.[37] The bones were scattered all along, sometimes the bones of several animals together. Was it the long drive, poison water, or what? It was evident they had not been killed but had dropped along the way.

It was a dreary trail at best, and these evidences of death did not help to brighten it in the least. We wondered often where it led to and what new things would be our experience. After walking fast all day, we came to quite an elevation, where we could stand and look in all directions. The low, black range where we left the Jayhawkers was in sight, and this spur[38] of the great snowy mountains extended a long way to the [east] and seemed to get lower and lower, finally ending in low, rocky buttes a hundred miles away. Some may think this distance very far to see, but those who have ever seen the clear atmosphere of that region will bear me out in these magnificent distances. Generally a mountain or other object seen at a distance would be three or four times as far off as one would judge at first sight, so deceptive are appearances there. The broad [east] end of the great mountain which we first saw the next morning after we left the wagons was now plain in sight, peak after peak extending away to the [west], all of them white with snow.[39] Standing thus out in the plain we could see the breadth of the mountain [south] and [north], and it seemed as though it must have been nearly a hundred miles. The south end was very abrupt and sank as one into a great plain in which we stood, twenty miles from the mountain's base.[40]

To the [southwest] we could see a clay lake, or at least that was what we called it, and a line of low hills seemed to be an extension of the mountain in a direction swinging around to the south to enclose this thirsty, barren plain before us, which was bounded by mountains or hills on these sides. To the [east] this range seemed to get higher, and we could see some snow-capped mountains to the [east] of our [southerly] course. The low mountains as those seen in the [southwest] direction are the same place now crossed by the Southern Pacific Railroad and known as the Tehachapi Pass, the noted loop in which the railroad crosses itself, being on the west slope and Fort Tejon being on the same range a little further south, where the Sierra Nevada mountains and the Coast Range join. The first mountain bearing snow south of our course was probably what is known as Wilson's Peak,[41] and the high mountains still farther [east], the San Bernardino Mountains. There were no names there known to us, nor did we know anything of the topography of the country except that we supposed a range of mountains was all that separated us from California.

We were yet in the desert, and if we kept our due [south][42] course, we must cross some of the snow before us which, if steep, gave us some doubts whether we could get through or not.

We did not know exactly what the people left behind would do if we were gone longer than we intended, but if they started on, it was quite plain to us they would be lost, and as seven days had already passed, we were in serious trouble for fear we could not complete the trip in the time allotted to us. We surveyed the plain and mountains to learn its situation and then started on, following our trail. As we went on we seemed to be coming to lower ground, and near our road stood a tree of a kind we had not seen before. The trunk was about six or eight inches through and six or eight feet high, with arms at the top quite as large as the body, and at the end of the arms a bunch of long, stiff, bayonet-shaped leaves.[43]

It was a brave little tree to live in such a barren country. As we walked on, these trees were more plenty, and some were much larger than the first. As we came to the lowest part of the valley, there seemed to be little, faint waterways running around little clouds of stunted shrubs, but there was no sign that very much water ever ran in them. We thought that these were the outlet of the big, sandy lake, which might get full of water and overflow through these channels after some great storm.

As this low ground was quite wide, we lost our trail in crossing it, and we separated as we went along, looking to find it again till nearly dark, when we looked for a camping place. Fortunately we found a little pond of rain-water, and some of our strange trees that were dead gave us good material for a fire, so that we were very comfortable indeed, having both drink and fire.

Starting on again, our course was now ascending slightly, and we came across more and more of the trees, and larger ones than at first. We saw some that seemed to have broken down with their own weight. The bayonet-shaped leaves seemed to fall off when old and the stalk looked so much like an old overgrown cabbage stump that we named them "cabbage trees," but afterward learned they were a species of yucca. We were much worried at losing our trail and felt that it would be quite unsafe to try to cross the mountain without finding it again, so we separated, Rogers going [south-west], and I [southeast], agreeing to swing round so as to meet again about noon, but when we met, neither of us had found a trail, and we were still about ten miles from the foothills. Rogers said he had heard some of the people say that the trail leading from Salt Lake to Los Angeles crossed such a mountain in a low pass with very high mountains on each side, and he sup-posed that the high mountain to the [southeast] must be the one where the trail crossed. But as this would take us fully fifty miles [east] of our course as we supposed it was, we hesitated about going there and concluded we would try the lowest place in the mountain first, and if we failed we could then go and try Rogers' route, more to the [east].[44]

So we pushed on, still keeping a distance apart to look out for the trail, and before night, in the rolling hills, we saw here and there faint traces of it which grew plainer as we went along, and about sundown we reached some water holes and some old skulls of oxen lying around the ground, showing that it had at some previous time been a camping ground.[45] We found some good, large sagebrush which made a pretty good fire, and if we could have had a little fresh meat to roast, we thought we were in a good position for supper. But that poor meat was pretty dry food. However, it kept us alive, and we curled up together and slept, for the night was cool, and we had to make the little blanket do its best. We thought we ought to find a little game, but we had not seen any to shoot since we started.

In the morning the trail led us toward the snow, and as we went along, a brave old crow surprised us by lighting on a bush near the trail, and we surprised him by killing him with a charge of shot. "Here's your fresh meat," said Rogers as he put it into his knapsack to cook for supper and marched on. As we approached the summit we could see, on the high mountains south of us, some trees, and when we came near the highest part of our road there were some juniper trees near it, which was very encouraging.[46] We crossed over several miles of hard snow, but it moistened up our moccasins and made them soft and uncomfortable. After we had turned down the [southern] slope, we killed a small hawk. "Here's your meat," said I, as the poor, thin fellow was stowed away for future grub, to cook with the crow.

When we got out of the snow we had lost the trail again, but the hills on the sides were covered with large brush, and on a higher part of the mountain [to the] south were some big trees, and we began to think the country would change for the better pretty soon. We followed down the ravine for many miles, and when this came out into a larger one, we were greatly pleased at the prospect, for down the latter came a beautiful little running brook of clear, pure water, singing as it danced over the stones a happy song, and telling us to drink and drink again, and you may be sure we did drink, for it had been months and months since we had had such water, pure, sweet, free from the terrible alkali and stagnant taste that had been in almost every drop we had seen.[47] Rogers leveled his shotgun at some birds and killed a beautiful one with a topknot on his head and colors bright all down his neck. It was a California quail. We said birds always lived where human beings did, and we had great hopes born to us of a better land. I told John that if the folks were only there, now I could kill game enough for them.

We dressed our three birds and got them boiling in the camp kettle, and while they were cooking, talked over the outlook, which was so flattering that our tongues got loose and we rattled away in strange contrast to the ominous silence of a week ago. While eating our stew of crow and hawk, we could see willows, alders, and big sagebrush around, and we had noticed what seemed to be cottonwoods farther down the cañon and green trees on the slope of the mountain. We were sure we were on the edge of the promised land and were quite lighthearted, till we began to tell of plans to get the good people out who were waiting for us beside the little spring in the desert. We talked of going back at once, but our meat was too near gone, and we must take them something to encourage them a little and make them strong for the fearful trip. As to these birds—the quail was as superb a morsel as ever a man did eat; the hawk was pretty fair and quite good eating; but that abominable crow! His flesh was about as black as his feathers and full of tough and bony sinews. We concluded we did not want any more of that kind of bird, and ever since that day, when I have heard people talk of "eating crow" as a bitter pill, I think I know all about it from experience.

There seemed to be no other way for us but to push on in the morning and try to obtain some relief for the poor women and children and then get back to them as fast as ever we could, so we shouldered our packs and went on down the cañon as fast as we could. We came soon to evergreen oaks and tall cottonwoods, and the creek bottom widened out to two hundred yards. There were trees on the south side and the brush kept getting larger and larger. There was a trail down this cañon but, as it passed under fallen trees, we knew it could not have been the same one we had been following on the other side of the summit, and when we discovered a bear track in a soft place, we knew very well it was not a trail intended for human beings, and we might be ordered out almost any moment.

On the high, bold, grassy point about four hundred yards [away], we saw two horses that held their heads aloft and gave a snort, then galloped away out of sight. About ten o'clock I felt a sudden pain in my left knee, keen and sharp, and as we went along it kept growing worse. I had to stop often to rest, and it was quite plain that if this increased or continued I was sure enough disabled, and would be kept from helping those whom we had left. Nerved with the idea we must get help to them, and that right soon, I hobbled along as well as I could, but soon had to say to Rogers that he had better go on ahead and get help and let me come on as best I could, for every moment of delay was a danger of death to our party who trusted us to get them help. Rogers refused to do this. He said he would stay with me and see me out, and that he could not do much alone, and had better sit till I got better. So we worked along through a tangled brush, being many times compelled to wade the stream to get along, and this made our moccasins soft and very uncomfortable to wear. I endured the pain all day, and we must have advanced quite a little distance in spite of my lameness, but I was glad when night came and we camped in the dark, brushy cañon, having a big fire which made me quite comfortable all night though it was quite cold and we had to keep close together so as to use the blanket. I felt a little better in the morning, and after eating some of our poor dried meat, which was about as poor as crow—and I don't know but a little worse—we continued on our way.

The tangle got worse and worse as we descended, and at times we walked in the bed of the stream in order to make more headway, but my lameness increased and we had to go very slow indeed. About noon we came to what looked like an excavation, a hole four feet square or more, it looked to be, and on the dirt thrown out some cottonwood trees had grown, and one of the largest of these had been cut down sometime before. This was the first sign of white men we had seen and it was evidently an attempt at mining, no one knows how long ago.[48] It encouraged us at any rate, and we pushed on through brush and briers, tangles of wild rosebushes and bushes of every sort, till all of a sudden we came out into an open, sandy valley, well covered with sagebrush and perhaps a hundred yards wide, probably more.

The hills on the south side had on them some oak trees and grassy spots, but the north side was thickly covered with brush. Our beautiful little brook that had kept us company soon sank into the dry sand out of sight, and we moved rather slowly along. Every little while we spoke of the chances of wagons ever getting through the road we had come, and the hope that my lameness might not continue to retard our progress in getting back to the place of our starting, [so] that the poor waiting people might begin to get out of the terrible country they were in and enjoy, as we had done, the beautiful running stream of this side of the mountain. If I did not get better, the chances were that they would perish, for they never could come through alone, as the distance had proved much greater than we had anticipated, and long, dry stretches of the desert were more than they would be prepared for. As it was, we feared greatly that we had consumed so much time [that] they would get impatient and start out and be lost.

I continued to hobble along down the barren valley as well as I could, and here and there some tracks of animals were discovered, but we could not make out whether they were those of domestic cattle or elk. Soon, on the side of a hill, rather high up, a pack of prairie wolves were snarling around the carcass of some dead animal, and this was regarded as another sign that more and better meat could be found, for these animals only live where some sort of game can be found, and they knew better than we that it was not for their health to go into the barren desert.

Before us now was a spur from the hills that reached nearly across our little valley and shut out further sight in that direction, and when we came to it, we climbed up over it to shorten the distance.[49] When the summit was reached, a most pleasing sight filled our sick hearts with a most indescribable joy. I shall never have the ability to adequately describe the beauty of the scene as it appeared to us, and so long as I live, that landscape will be impressed upon the canvas of my memory as the most cheering in the world. There before us was a beautiful meadow of a thousand acres, green as a thick carpet of grass could make it, and shaded with oaks, wide-branching and symmetrical, equal to those of an old English park, while all over the low mountains that bordered it on the south and over the broad acres of luxuriant grass was a herd of cattle numbering many hundreds, if not thousands. They were of all colors, shades, and sizes. Some were calmly lying down in happy rumination, others rapidly cropping the sweet grass, while the gay calves worked off their superfluous life and spirit in vigorous exercise or drew rich nourishment in the abundant mother's milk. All seemed happy and content, and such a scene of abundance and rich plenty and comfort bursting thus upon our eyes, which for months had seen only the desolation and sadness of the desert, was like getting a glimpse of paradise, and tears of joy ran down our faces. If ever a poor mortal escapes from this world where so many trials come and joys of a happy heaven are opened up to him, the change cannot be much more than this which was suddenly opened to us on that bright day, which was either one of the very last of December 1849 or the first of January 1850. I am inclined to think it was the very day of the new year, but the accuracy of the calendar was among the least of our troubles. If it was, as I believe, the beginning of the year, it was certainly a most auspicious one and one of the most hopeful of my life.[50]

"And now if the others were only here" was the burden of our thought, and a serious awakening from the dream of beauty and rich plenty spread out before us. This ringstraked and speckled herd might be descended directly from Jacob's famous herd, blessed of the Lord, and while we could not keep our thoughts from some sad doubts as to the fate of those whom we had left behind, we tried to be generally hopeful and courageous and brightened up our steps to prepare for a relief and return to the hot, dry plain beyond the mountains where they were awaiting us, no doubt with much tribulation.

I now thought of myself and my failing knee, and we sat down under the shade of an oak to rest, and after a little, better feeling seemed to come. Down by a deep gully cut by the rains, a yearling steer was feeding, and I took the rifle and crawled down near him and put first one ball through him and then another before he fell dead on the other side of the wash, when we sprang with all the agility of a deer. We quickly got some good meat and had it roasted and eaten almost quicker than can be told. We hardly realized how near starved we were till we had plenty before us again. We ate till we were satisfied for once, and for the first time in many long, dreary weeks. We kindled a fire and commenced drying the meat, one sleeping while the other kept the fire, changing off every few hours. What a rest it was! One who has never been nearly worn out, starved down nearly to the point of death, can never know what it is to rest in comfort. No one can tell. It was like a dream, a sweet, restful dream where troubles would drown themselves in sleep. How we felt the strength come back to us with that food and the long draughts of pure, clear water.

The miserable dried meat in our knapsacks was put away and this splendid jerked beef put in its place. The wolves came to our camp and howled dreadful disappointment at not getting a meal. Rogers wanted me to shoot the miserable howlers, but I let them have their concert out and thought going without their breakfast must be punishment enough for them. As our moccasins were worn out, we carefully prepared some sinews from the steer and made new footgear from the green hide, which placed us in shape for two or three weeks' walking.

The morning was clear and pleasant. We had our knapsacks filled with good food we had prepared and were enjoying the cool breeze which came up the valley when we heard faintly the bark of a dog, or at least we thought we did. If this were true, there must be someone living not very far away, and we felt better. I was still very lame and as we started along, the walking seemed to make it worse again, so that it was all I could do to follow John on the trail down the valley. As we went along, a man and woman passed us some distance on the left, and they did not seem to notice us, though we were in plain sight. They were curiously dressed. The woman had no hoops nor shoes, and a shawl wound about her neck, and one end thrown over her head was a substitute bonnet. The man had sandals on his feet, with white cotton pants, a calico shirt, and a wide-rimmed, comical, snuff-colored hat.

We at once put them down as Spaniards, or then, descendants of Mexico, and if what we had read about them in books was true, we were in a set of land pirates and bloodthirsty men whom we might have occasion to be aware of. We had never heard a word of Spanish spoken, except perhaps a word or two upon the plains which some fellow knew, and how we could make ourselves known and explain who we were was a puzzle to us.

Difficulties began to arise in our minds, now we were in an apparent land of plenty, but in spite of all, we went along as fast as my lame knee would permit me to do. A house on higher ground soon appeared in sight. It was low, of one story with a flat roof, gray in color, and of a different style of architecture from any we had ever seen before.[51] There was no fence around it, and no animals or wagons in sight nor person to be seen. As we walked up the hill toward it, I told John our moccasins made of green hide would betray us as having recently killed an animal, and as these people might be the owners and detain us by having us arrested for the crime, this would be especially bad for us just now. We determined to face the people and let the fact of our close necessities be a sufficient excuse for us, if we could make them understand our circumstances.

As we came near the house no person was seen, but a mule tied to a post told us there was someone about, and a man soon made an appearance, dressed about [the] same style as the one we had passed a short time before. As we came near we saluted him, bidding him good morning, and he in turn touched his hat politely, saying something in reply which we were not able to understand. I showed him that I was lame and, taking out some money, pointed to the mule, but he only shook his head and said something I could not comprehend. Rogers now began looking around the house, which was built of sun-dried bricks about one by two feet in size, and one end was used [as] a storehouse. As he looked in, a man came to him and wanted a black, patent leather belt which Rogers wore, having a watchpocket attached to it. He offered a quart or more of coarse cornmeal, and Rogers made the trade.

We tried to inquire where we were or where ought [we] to go, but could get no satisfactory answer from the man, although when we spoke "San Francisco," he pointed to the north. This was not very satisfactory to us and we seemed as badly lost as ever, and where or which way to go we did not seem very successful in finding out. So we concluded to go on a little way at least, and I hobbled off in the direction he pointed, which was down the hill and past a small, poorly fenced field which was sometimes cultivated, and across the stream which followed down the valley. Passing on a mile or two, we stopped on a big patch of sand to rest.

I told Rogers I did not think this course would lead us to anyplace in a month, and just now a delay was ruinous to us and to those who were waiting for us, and it would not do for us to go off to the north to find a settlement. While I was expressing my opinion on matters and things, Rogers had wet up a part of his meal with water and put it to bake on the cover of his camp kettle. There was a fair-sized cake for each of us, and it was the first bread of any kind we had eaten for months, being a very acceptable change from an exclusively meat diet. Looking up the valley we could see a cloud of dust, thick and high, and soon several men on horseback who came at a rushing gallop. I told Rogers they were after us, and believed them to be a murderous set who might make trouble for us. I hastily buried our little store of money in the sand, telling him that if they got us, they would not get our money. Putting our guns across our laps in an easy position, we had them cocked and ready for business, and our knives where we could get them handy, and awaited their arrival.

They came on with a rush until within a short distance and halted for consultation just across the creek, after which one of them advanced toward us, and as he came near us, we could see he was a white man who wished us good evening in our own language. We answered him rather cooly, still sitting in the sand, and he no doubt saw that we were a little suspicious of the crowd. He asked us where we were from, and we told him our circumstances and condition and that we would like to secure some means of relief for the people we had left in the desert, but our means were very limited and we wanted to do the best we could. He said we were about five hundred miles from San Francisco, not far from one hundred miles from the coast, and thirty miles from Los Angeles. We were much afraid we would not be able to get anything here, but he told us to go across the valley to a large live oak tree which he pointed out and said we would find an American there, and we should wait there till morning. He said he would go back and stay at the house we had passed and would do what he could to assist us to go to Los Angeles, where we could get some supplies. Then he rode away, and as we talked it over we saw no way but to follow the directions of our newfound friend.

It seemed now that my lameness had indeed been a blessing. If I had been able to walk we would now have been well on toward the seashore, where we could have found no such friend as this who had appeared to us. The way seemed clearer to us, but the time for our return was almost up and there was no way of getting back in fifteen days as we had agreed upon, so there was great danger to our people yet.[52] It seemed very likely to take us twenty-four or thirty days at best, and while they probably had oxen enough to provide them food for so long a time, they might take a notion to move on, which would be fatal.

At the big live oak tree we found an American camper who was on his way to the gold mines. He was going a new route and said the mines could be reached much quicker than by going up the coast by way of San Francisco. A new company with wagons was soon to start out to break the road, and when they crossed the east end of the valley he would follow them. I think this man's name was Springer. He had come by way of the Santa Fe route, and the people of Los Angeles had told him this route was an easy one, being often traveled by saddle horses, and if the company could make it possible for wagons, they could have all the cattle they wanted to kill along the road as their pay for doing the work. Our new friend lay down early, and as he saw we were scant in blankets, he brought some to us for our use, which were most thankfully received.

As soon as we were alone, Rogers mixed up some more of the meal, which we baked in our friend's frying pan, and we baked and ate and baked and ate again, for our appetites were ravenous, and the demand of our stomachs got the better of the judgment of our brains.

It was hard to find time to sleep, we were so full of the plans about the way—now we must manage to get relief for the people. We had many doubts if animals could ever come over the route we had come over. From deliberation we decided that by selecting a route with that idea in our minds, we could get mules and perhaps horses over the country. We perhaps could go more to the north and take the Jayhawkers' trail, but this would take us fully a hundred miles farther and four or five days longer, at the best, and every moment of delay was to be carefully avoided as a moment of danger to our friends.

Thus again, our sleep was troubled from another cause. Being so long unaccustomed to vegetable food, and helped on, no doubt, by our poor judgment in gauging the quantity of our food, we were attacked by severe pains in the stomach and bowels, from which we suffered intensely. We arose very early, and with a very light breakfast, for the sickness admonished us, we started back for the house we had first passed, at which our friend on horseback said he would spend the night, and where we were to meet him this morning. He said he could talk Spanish all right and would do all he could to help us.

Our suffering and trouble caused us to move very slowly, so that it was nine or ten o'clock before we reached the house, and we found they had two horses all ready for us to go to Los Angeles. There were no saddles for us, but we thought this would be a good way to cure my lameness. The people seemed to be friends to us in every way. We mounted, having our packs on our backs and our guns before us, and with a friendly parting to the people who did not go, all four of us started on a trip of thirty miles to the town of Los Angeles.

When we reached the foot of the mountain, which was very steep but not rocky, John and I dismounted and led our animals to the top, where we could see a long way west and south, and it looked supremely beautiful.[53] We could not help comparing it to the long, wide desert we had crossed, and John and myself said many times how we wished the folks were here to enjoy the pleasant sight, the beautiful, fertile picture.

There appeared to be one quite large house in sight, and not far off, which the man told us was the Mission of San Fernando, a Roman Catholic church and residence for priests and followers.[54] The downward slope of the mountain was as steep as the other side and larger, and John and I did not attempt to mount till we were well down on the level ground again, but the other two men rode up and down without any trouble. We would let our leaders get half a mile or so ahead of us and then mount and put our horses to a gallop till we overtook them again. We had walked so long that riding was very tiresome to us, and for comfort alone we would have preferred the way on foot, but we could get along a little faster, and the frequent dismounting kept us from becoming too lame from riding.

We passed the mission about noon or a little after, and a few miles beyond met a man on horseback who lived to the north about a hundred miles. His name was French and he had a cattle range at a place called Tejon (Tahone).[55] Our friends told him who we were, and what assistance we needed. Mr. French said he was well acquainted in Los Angeles and had been there some time, and that all the travelers who would take the coast route had gone. Those who had come by way of Salt Lake had got in from two to four weeks before, and a small train which had come the Santa Fe route was still upon the road. He said Los Angeles was so clear of emigrants that he did not think we could get any help there at the present time.

"Now," said Mr. French, "you boys can't talk Spanish and it is not very likely you will be able to get any help. Now I say, you boys turn back and go with me and I will give you the best I have, I will let you have a yoke of gentle oxen, or more if you need them, and plenty of beans, which are good food, for I live on them; besides this I can give an Indian guide to help you back. Will that do?" After a moment we said we doubted if oxen could be got over the road, and if they were fat now they would soon get poor, and perhaps not stand it as well as the oxen which had become used to that kind of life, and of those, they had in camp all they needed. We wanted to get something for the women and children to ride, for we knew they must abandon the wagons and could not walk so far over that dry, rough country. "Well," said Mr. French, "I will stop at the place you were this morning—I know them well—and they are good folks, and I am sure when I tell them what you want they will help you if they possibly can. This looks to me to be the most sensible course." After talking an hour, our two companions advised us that the proposition of Mr. French seemed the most reasonable one that appeared. But for us to go clear back to his range would take up so much valuable time that we were almost afraid of the delay, which might mean the destruction of our friends. French said he had a packsaddle with him, taking it home, and we could put it on one of our horses, and when we came back to Los Angeles, could leave it at a certain saloon or place he named and tell them it belonged to him and to keep it for him. I have forgotten the name of the man who kept the saloon. We agreed to this, and bidding our two companions farewell, we turned back again with Mr. French.

When night came we were again at the mission we had passed on the way down. We were kindly treated here, for I believe Mr. French told them about us. They sent an Indian to take our horses, and we sat down beside the great house. There were many smaller houses and quite a large piece of ground fenced in by an adobe wall. The roof of the buildings was like that of our own buildings, in having eaves on both sides, but the covering was of semicircular tiles made and burned like brick. Rows of these were placed close together, the hollow sides up, and then another course over the joints, placed with the round side up, which made a roof that was perfectly waterproof but must have been very heavy. These tiles were about two feet long. All the surroundings and general makeup of the place were new to us and very wonderful. They gave us good dried meat to eat and let us sleep in the big house on the floor, which was as hard as granite, and we turned over a great many times before daylight and were glad when morning came. We offered to pay them, but they would take nothing from us, and we left, leading our horses over the steep mountain and reaching the house again late in the day. They turned our horses loose and seemed disposed to be very friendly and disposed to do for us what they could.

We were very tired and sat down by the side of the house and rested, wondering how we would come out with our preparations. They were talking together, but we could not understand a word. A dark woman came out and gave each of us a piece of cooked squash. It seemed to have been roasted in the ashes and was very sweet and good. These were all signs of friendship and we were glad of the good feeling. We were given a place to sleep in the house, in a storeroom on a floor which was not soft. This was the second house we had slept in since leaving Wisconsin, and it seemed rather pent up to us.

In the morning we were shown a kind of mill like a coffee mill, and by putting in a handful of wheat from a pile and giving the mill a few turns, we were given to understand we should grind some flour for ourselves. We went to work with a will, but found it hard, slow work.

After a little, our dark woman came and gave us each a pancake and a piece of meat, also another piece of roasted squash, for our breakfast, and this, we thought, was the best meal we had ever eaten. The lady tried to talk to us but we could not understand the words, and I could convey ideas to her better by the sign language than any other way. She pointed out the way from which we came and wanted to know how many days' travel it might be away, and I answered by putting my hand to my head and closing my eyes, which was repeated as many times as there had been nights on our journey, at which she was much surprised that the folks were so far away. She then placed her hand upon her breast and then held it up, to ask how many women there were, and I answered her by holding up three fingers,[56] at which she shrugged her shoulders and shook her head. Then pointing to a child by her side, four or five years old, [she] in the same way asked how many children. I answered by holding up four fingers,[57] and she almost cried, opening her mouth in great surprise, and turned away.

I said to Rogers that she was a kind, well-meaning woman, and that Mr. French had no doubt told her something of our story. Aside from her dark complexion, her features reminded me of my mother, and at first sight of her I thought of the best woman on earth, my own far-off mother, who little knew the hardships we had endured. We went to work again at the mill and after a while the woman came again and tried to talk and to teach us some words of her own language. She placed her finger on me and said *hombre* and I took out my little book and wrote down *hombre* as meaning man, and in the same way she taught me that *mujer* was woman; *trigo,* wheat; *frijoles,* beans; *carne,* meat; *calabasa,* pumpkin; *caballo,* horse; *vaca,* cow; *muchacho,* boy; and several other words in this way.

I got hold of many words thus to study, so that if I ever came back I could talk a little and make myself understood as to some of the common objects and things of necessary use. Such friendly, human acts shown to us strangers were evidences of the kindest disposition. I shall never forget the kindness of those original Californians. When in Walker's camp[58] and finding he was friendly to Mormonism, we could claim that we were also Mormons, but the good people, though well-known Catholics, did not so much as mention the fact nor inquire whether we favored that sect or not. We were human beings in distress and we represented others who were worse even than we, and those kind acts and great goodwill were given freely because we were fellow human beings.

The provisions we prepared were a sack of small yellow beans; a small sack of wheat; a quantity of good dried meat; and some of the coarse, unbolted flour we had made at the mills. They showed us how to properly pack the horse, which was a kind of work we had not been used to, and we were soon ready for a start. I took what money we had and put it on a block, making signs for them to take what the things were worth. They took thirty dollars, and we were quite surprised to get two horses, provisions, packsaddles, and ropes, some of the latter made of rawhide and some of hair, so cheaply, but we afterward learned that the mares furnished were not considered of much value, and we had really paid a good, fair price for everything. To make it easy for us they had also fixed our knapsacks on the horses.

The good lady with the child came out with four oranges and, pointing to her own child and then to the east, put them in the pack, meaning we should carry them to the children. With a hearty good-bye from them and a polite lifting of our hats to them, we started on our return, down toward the gentle decline of the creek bottom, and then up the valley, the way we came. Toward night we came to a wagon road crossing the valley, and as we well knew we could not go up the tangled creekbed with horses, we took this road to the north, which took a dry ravine for its direction, and in which there was a pack trail, and this the wagons were following.[59] We kept on the trail for a few miles and overtook them in their camp and camped with them overnight. We told them we considered our outfit entirely too small for the purpose intended, which was to bring two women and four children out of the desert, but that being the best we could get, we were taking this help to them and hoped to save their lives. Our mission became well known, and one man offered to sell us a poor little one-eyed mule, its back all bare of covering from the effect of a great saddle sore that had very recently healed. He had picked it up somewhere in Arizona, where it had been turned out to die, but it seemed the beast had enough of the good Santa Ana stock in it to bring it through, and it had no notion of dying at the present time, though it was scarcely more than a good fair skeleton, even then. The beast became mine at the price of fifteen dollars, and the people expressed great sympathy with us and the dear friends we were going to try to save.

Another man offered a little snow-white mare as fat as butter for fifteen dollars, which I paid, though it took the last cent of money I had. This little beauty of a beast was broken to lead at halter, but had not been broken in any other way. Rogers said he would ride her where he could, and before she got to the wagons she would be as gentle as a lamb. He got a bridle and tried her at once, and then there was a scene of rearing, jumping, and kicking that would have made a good Buffalo Bill circus in these days. No use, the man could not be thrown off, and the crowd cheered and shouted to Rogers to "hold her level."

After some bucking and backing on the part of the mare, and a good deal of whipping and kicking on the part of the man, and a good many furious dashes in lively but very awkward ways, the little beast yielded the point and carried her load without further trouble.

The people gave us a good supper and breakfast, and one man came and presented us with twenty-five pounds of unbolted wheat flour. They were of great assistance to us in showing us how to pack and sack our load, which was not heavy and could be easily carried by our two animals which we had at first. However, we arranged a pack on the mule and this gave me a horse to ride and a mule to lead, while Rogers rode his milk-white steed and led the other horse. Thus we went along and, following the trail, soon reached the summit, from which we could see off to the east [and north] a wonderful distance, probably two hundred miles of the dry and barren desert of hill and desolate valley over which we had come.

The trail bearing still to the north from this point, we left and turned due east across the country and soon came to a beautiful lake of sweet, fresh water situated well up toward the top of the mountain. This lake is now called Elizabeth Lake.[60] Here we watered our animals and filled our canteens, then steered a little south of east among the cabbage trees, aiming to strike the rainwater hole where we had camped as we came over. We reached the water hole about noon and here found the Jayhawkers' trail, which we took. They had evidently followed us and passed down the same brushy cañon while we, having taken a circuitous route to the north, had gone around there.[61] Getting water here for ourselves and horses, we went back to the trail and pushed on as fast as the animals could walk, and as we now knew where we could get water, we kept on till after dark, one of us walking to keep the trail, and sometime in the night reached the willow corral I have spoken of before.[62] There was good water here, but the Jayhawkers' oxen had eaten all the grass that grew in the little moist place around, and our animals were short of feed. One of us agreed to stand guard the forepart of the night and the other later, so that we might not be surprised by Indians and lose our animals. I took the first watch and let the blaze of the fire go out so as not to attract attention, and as I sat by the dull coals and hot ashes I fell asleep. Rogers happened to wake and see the situation and arose and waked me again, saying that we must be more careful or the Indians would get our horses. You may be sure I kept awake the rest of my watch.

Next day we passed the water holes at the place where we had so stealthily crawled up to Doty's camp when coming out.[63] These holes held about two pails of water each, but no stream ran away from them. Our horses seemed to want water badly, for when they drank they put their heads in up to their eyes and drank ravenously.

Thirty miles from here to the next water, Doty had told us, and night overtook us before we could reach it, so a dry camp was made. Our horses began now to walk with drooping heads and slow, tired steps, so we divided the load among them all and walked ourselves. The water,[64] when reached, proved so salty the horses would not drink it, and as Doty had told us the most water was over the mountain ahead of us, we still followed their trail, which went up a very rocky cañon in which it was hard work for the horses to travel.[65] The horses were all very gentle now and needed some urging to make them go. Rogers' fat horse no longer tried to unseat its rider or its pack but seemed to be the most downhearted of the train. The little mule was the liveliest, sharpest-witted animal of the whole. She had probably traveled on the desert before and knew better how to get along. She had learned to crop every spear of grass she came to, and every bit of sagebrush that offered a green leaf was given a nip. She would sometimes leave the trail and go out to one side to get a little bunch of dry grass, and come back and take her place again as if she knew her duty. The other animals never tried to do this. The mule was evidently better versed in the art of getting a living than the horses.

Above the rough bed of the cañon, the bottom was gravelly and narrow, and the walls on each side nearly perpendicular. Our horses now poked slowly along, and as we passed the steep wall of the cañon, the white animal left the trail and walked with full force, head first, against the solid rock. She seemed to be blind, and though we went quickly to her and took off the load she carried, she had stopped breathing by the time we had it done. Not knowing how far it was to water, nor how soon some of our other horses might fall, we did not tarry, but pushed on as well as we could, finding no water. We reached the summit and turned down a ravine,[66] following the trail, and about dark came to the water they had told us about, a faint running stream which came out of a rocky ravine and sank almost immediately in the dry sand.[67] There was water enough for us, but no grass. It seemed as if the horses were not strong enough to carry a load, and as we wanted to get them through if possible, we concluded to bury the wheat and get it on our return. We dug a hole and lined it with fine sticks, then put in the little bag and covered it with dry brush and sand, making the surface as smooth as if it had never been touched, then made our bed on it. The whole work was done after dark so the deposit could not be seen by the red men, and we thought we had done it pretty carefully.

Next morning the little mule carried all the remaining load, the horses bearing only their saddles, and [they] seemed hardly strong enough for that. There were now seven or eight miles of clean, loose sand to go over, across a little valley which came to an end about ten miles north of us and extended south to the lake where we went for water on our outward journey and found it red alkali.[68] Near the eastern edge of the valley we turned aside to visit the grave of Mr. Isham, which they had told us of. They had covered his remains with their hands as best they could, piling up a little mound of sand over it. Our next camp was to be on the summit of the range just before us, and we passed the dead body of Mr. Fish we had seen before and went on a little to a level, sandy spot in the ravine, just large enough to sleep on. This whole range is a black mass [of] rocky pieces of earth, so barren that not a spear of grass can grow, and not a drop of water in any place. We tied our horses to rocks and there they stayed all night, for if turned loose there was not a mouthful of food for them to get.

In the morning an important question was to be decided, and that was whether we should continue to follow the Jayhawkers' trail which led far to the north to cross the mountain, which stood before us, a mass of piled-up rocks so steep that it seemed as if a dog could hardly climb it. Our wagons were nearly due east from this point over the range and not more than fifty miles away, while to go around to the north was fully a hundred miles and would take us four or five days to make. As we had already gone so long, we expected to meet them any day trying to get out, and if we went around we might miss them. They might have all been killed by Indians or they might have already gone. We had great fears on their account. If they had gone north they might have perished in the snow.

The range was before us, and we must get to the other side in some way. We could see the range for a hundred miles to the north and, along the base, some lakes of water that must be salt. To the south it got some lower, but very barren and ending in black, dry buttes. The horses must have food and water by night or we must leave them to die, and all things considered, it seemed to be the quickest way to camp to try and get up a rough looking cañon which was nearly opposite us on the other side.[69] So we loaded the mule and made our way down the rocky road to the ridge, and then left the Jayhawkers' trail, taking our course more south so as to get around a salt lake which lay directly before us. On our way we had to go close to a steep bluff and cross a piece of ground that looked like a well-dried mortar bed, hard and smooth as ice, and thus got around the head of a small stream of clear water, salty as brine. We now went directly to the mouth of the cañon we had decided to take and traveled up its gravelly bed. The horses now had to be urged along constantly to keep them moving, and they held their heads low down as they crept along, seemingly so discouraged that they would much rather lie down and rest forever than take another step. We knew they would do this soon in spite of all our urging if we could not get water for them. The cañon was rough enough where we entered it, and a heavy upgrade too, and this grew more and more difficult as we advanced, and the rough, yellowish, rocky walls closed in nearer and nearer together as we ascended.[70]

A perpendicular wall or, rather, rise in the rocks was approached, and there was a great difficulty to persuade the horses to take exertion to get up and over the small obstruction, but the little mule skipped over as nimbly as a well-fed goat and rather seemed to enjoy a little variety in the proceedings. After some coaxing and urging the horses took courage to try the extra step and succeeded all right, when we all moved on again, over a path that grew more and more narrow, more and more rocky underfoot at every moment. We wound around among and between the great rocks and had not advanced very far before another obstruction that would have been a fall of about three feet, had water been flowing in the cañon, opposed our way. A small pile of lone rocks enabled the mule to go over all right, and she went on looking for every spear of grass and smelling eagerly for water, but all our efforts were not enough to get the horses along another foot. It was getting nearly night, and every minute without water seemed an age. We had to leave the horses and go on. We had deemed them indispensable to us, or rather to the extrication of the women and children, and yet the hope came to us that the oxen might help some of them out as a last resort. We were sure the wagons must be abandoned, and such a thing as women riding on the backs of oxen we had never seen. Still, it occurred to us as not impossible, and although leaving the horses here was like deciding to abandon all for the feeble ones, we saw we must do it, and the new hope arose to sustain us for further effort. We removed the saddles and placed them on a rock, and after a few moments' hesitation, moments in which were crowded torrents of wild ideas and desperate thoughts that were enough to drive reason from its throne, we left the poor animals to their fate and moved along. Just as we were passing out of sight, the poor creatures neighed pitifully after us, and one who has never heard the last, despairing, pleading neigh of a horse left to die can form no idea of its almost human appeal. We both burst into tears, but it was no use to try to save them, we must run the danger of sacrificing ourselves and the little party we were trying so hard to save.

We found the little mule stopped by a still higher precipice or perpendicular rise of fully ten feet.[71] Our hearts sank within us and we said that we should return to our friends as we went away, with our knapsacks on our backs, and hope grew very small. The little mule was nipping some stray blades of grass, and as we came in sight she looked around to us and then up the steep rocks before her with such a knowing, intelligent look of confidence that it gave us new courage. It was a strange, wild place. The north wall of the cañon leaned far over the channel, overhanging considerably, while the south wall sloped back about the same, making the walls nearly parallel and like a huge crevice descending into the mountain from above in a sloping direction.

We decided to try to get the confident little mule over this obstruction. Gathering all the loose rocks we could, we piled them up against the south wall, beginning some distance below. Putting up all those in the bed of the stream and throwing down others from narrow shelves above, we built a sort of inclined plane along the walls, gradually rising till we were nearly as high as the crest of the fall. Here was a narrow shelf scarcely four inches wide and a space of from twelve to fifteen feet to cross to reach the level of the crest. It was all I could do to cross this space, and there was no foundation to enable us to widen it so as to make a path for an animal. It was [a] forlorn hope, but we made the most of it. We unpacked the mule and, getting all our ropes together, made a leading line of it. Then we loosened and threw down all the projecting points of rocks we could above the narrow shelf, and every piece that was likely to come loose in the shelf itself. We fastened the leading line to her, and with one above and one below, we thought we could help her to keep her balance and, if she did not make a misstep on that narrow way, she might get over safely. Without a moment's hesitation the brave animal tried the pass. Carefully and steadily she went along, selecting a place before putting down a foot and, when she came to the narrow ledge, leaned gently on the rope, never making a sudden start or jump, but cautiously as a cat moved slowly along. There was now no turning back for her. She must cross this narrow place over which I had to creep on hands and knees, or be dashed down fifty feet to a certain death.[72] When the worst place was reached, she stopped and hesitated, looking back as well as she could. I was ahead with the rope, and I called encouragingly to her and talked to her a little. Rogers wanted to get all ready, he said, and "holler" at her as loud as he could and frighten her across, but I thought the best way [was] to talk to her gently and let her move steadily.

I tell you, friends, it was a trying moment. It seemed to be weighed down with all the trials and hardships of many months. It seemed to be the time when helpless women and innocent children hung on the trembling balance between life and death. Our own lives we could save by going back, and sometimes it seemed as if we would perhaps save ourselves the additional sorrow of finding them all dead to do so at once. I was so nearly in despair that I could not help bursting in tears, and I was not ashamed of the weakness. Finally Rogers said, "Come, Lewis," and I gently pulled the rope, calling the little animal to make a trial. She smelled all around and looked over every inch of the strong ledge, then took one careful step after another over the dangerous place. Looking back I saw Rogers with a very large stone in his hand, ready to "holler" and perhaps kill the poor beast if she stopped. But she crept along, trusting to the rope to balance, till she was halfway across, then another step or two when, calculating the distance closely, she made a spring and landed on a smooth bit of sloping rock below that led up to the highest crest of the precipice, and safely climbed to the top, safe and sound above the falls. The mule had no shoes and it was wonderful how her little hoofs clung to the smooth rock. We felt relieved. We would push on and carry food to the people; we would get them through some way; there could be no more hopeless moment than the one just past, and we would save them all.

It was the work of a little while to transfer the load up the precipice and pack the mule again, when we proceeded. Around behind some rocks only a little distance beyond this place, we found a small willow bush and enough good water for a camp.[73] This was a strange cañon. The sun never shone down to the bottom in the fearful place where the little mule climbed up, and the rocks had a peculiar yellow color. In getting our provisions up the precipice, Rogers went below and fastened the rope while I pulled them up. Rogers wished many times we had the horses up safely where the mule was, but a dog could hardly cross the narrow path, and there was no hope. Poor brutes, they had been faithful servants, and we felt sorrowful enough at their terrible fate.

We had walked two days without water, and we were wonderfully refreshed as we found it here. The way up this cañon was very rough and the bed full of sharp, broken rocks in loose pieces which cut through the bottoms of our moccasins and left us with bare feet upon the acute points and edges. I took off one of my buckskin leggins and gave it to Rogers, and with the other one for myself, we fixed the moccasins with them as well as we could, which enabled us to go ahead, but I think if our feet had been shod with steel those sharp rocks would have cut through.

Starting early we made the summit about noon, and from here we could see the place where we found a water hole and camped the first night after we left the wagons.[74] Down the steep cañon we turned, the same one in which we had turned back with the wagons, and over the sharp, broken pieces of volcanic rock that formed our only footing, we hobbled along with sore and tender feet. We had to watch for the smoothest place for every step and then moved only with the greatest difficulty. The Indians could have caught us easily if they had been around, for we must keep our eyes on the ground constantly and stop if we looked up and around. But we at last got down and camped on [the] same spot where we had set out twenty-five days before to seek the settlements. Here was the same little water hole in the sand plain,[75] and the same strong sulfur water which we had to drink the day we left. The mule was turned loose dragging the same piece of rawhide she had attached to her when we purchased her, and she ranged and searched faithfully for food, finding little except the very scattering bunches of sagebrush. She was industrious and walked around rapidly, picking here and there, but at dark came into camp and lay down close to us to sleep.

There was no sign that anyone had been here during our absence, and if the people had gone to hunt a way out, they must either have followed the Jayhawkers' trail or some other one. We were much afraid that they might have fallen victims to the Indians. Remaining in camp so long, it was quite likely they had been discovered by them, and it was quite likely they had been murdered for the sake of the oxen and camp equipage. It might be that we should find the hostiles waiting for us when we reached the appointed camping place, and it was small show for two against a party. Our mule and her load would be a great capture for them. We talked a great deal and said a great many things at that campfire, for we knew we were in great danger, and we had many doubts about the safety of our people that would soon be decided, and whether for joy or sorrow we could not tell.

From this place, as we walked along, we had a wagon road to follow in soft sand, but not a sign of a human footstep could we see as we marched toward this, the camp of the last hope. We had the greatest fears the people had given up our return and started out for themselves and that we should follow on only to find them dead or dying. My pen fails me as I try to tell the feelings and thoughts of this trying hour. I can never hope to do so, but if the reader can place himself in my place, his imagination cannot form a picture that shall go beyond reality.

We were some seven or eight miles along the road when I stopped to fix my moccasin while Rogers went slowly along. The little mule went on ahead of both of us, searching all around for little bunches of dry grass, but always came back to the trail again and gave us no trouble. When I had started up again I saw Rogers ahead, leaning on his gun and waiting for me, apparently looking at something on the ground. As I came near enough to speak I asked what he had found and he said, "Here is Captain Culverwell, dead." He did not look much like a dead man. He lay upon his back with arms extended wide and his little canteen made of two powder flasks lying by his side.[76] This looked indeed as if some of our saddest forbodings were coming true. How many more bodies should we find? Or should we find the camp deserted, and never find a trace of the former occupants?

We marched toward camp like two Indians, silent and alert, looking out for dead bodies and live Indians, for really we more expected to find the camp devastated by those rascals than to find that it still contained our friends. To the east we could plainly see what seemed to be a large, salt lake with a bed that looked as if of the finest, whitest sand, but really a wonder of salt crystal. We put the dreary steps steadily one forward of another, the little mule the only unconcerned one of the party, ever looking for an odd blade of grass dried in the hot dry wind but yet retaining nourishment, which she preferred.

About noon we came in sight of the wagons, still a long way off, but in the clear air we could make them out and tell what they were without being able to see anything more. Half a mile was the distance between us and the camp before we could see very plainly, as they were in a little depression. We could see the covers had been taken off, and this was an ominous sort of circumstance to us, for we feared the depredations of the Indians in retaliation for the capture of their squashes. They had shot our oxen before we left and they [must] have slain them this time and the people too.

We surely left seven wagons. Now we could see only four and nowhere the sign of an ox.[77] They must have gone ahead with a small train and left these four standing, after dismantling them.

No signs of life were anywhere about, and the thought of our hard struggles between life and death to go out and return with the fruitless results that now seemed apparent was almost more than human heart could bear. When should we know their fate? When should we find their remains, and how learn of their sad history—if we ourselves should live to get back again to settlements and life? If ever two men were troubled, Rogers and I surely passed through the furnace.

We kept as low and as much out of sight as possible, trusting very much to the little mule that was ahead, for we felt sure she would detect danger in the air sooner than we, and we watched her closely to see how she acted. She slowly walked along, looking out for food, and we followed a little way behind, but still no decisive sign to settle the awful suspense in which we lived and suffered. We became more and more convinced that they had taken the trail of the Jayhawkers and we had missed them on the road, or they had perished before reaching the place where we turned from their trail.

One hundred yards now to the wagons and still no sign of life, no positive sign of death, though we looked carefully for both. We feared that perhaps there were Indians in ambush, and with nervous, irregular breathing we counseled what to do. Finally Rogers suggested that he had two charges in his shotgun and I seven in the Colt's rifle, and that I fire one of mine and await results before we ventured any nearer, and if there were any of the red devils there we could kill some of them before they got to us. And now, both closely watching the wagons, I fired the shot. Still as death and not a move for a moment, and then, as if by magic, a man came out from under a wagon and stood up, looking all around, for he did not see us. Then he threw up his arms high over his head and shouted, "The boys have come. The boys have come!" Then other bare heads appeared, and Mr. Bennett and wife and Mr. Arcane came toward us as fast as ever they could. The great suspense was over and our hearts were first in our mouths, and then the blood all went away and left us almost fainting as we stood and tried to step. Some were safe, perhaps all of those nearest us and the dark shadow of death that had hovered over us and cast what seemed a pall upon every thought and action was lifted and fell away, a heavy oppression gone. Bennett and Arcane caught us in their arms and embraced us with all their strength, and Mrs. Bennett, when she came, fell down on her knees and clung to me like a maniac in the great emotion that came to her, and not a word was spoken. If they had been strong enough, they would have carried us to camp upon their shoulders. As it was, they stopped two or three times and turned as if to speak, but there was too much feeling for words; convulsive weeping would choke the voice.

All were a little calmer soon, and Bennett soon found voice to say, "I know you have found some place, for you have a mule," and Mrs. Bennett, through her tears, looked staringly at us, as she could hardly believe our coming back was a reality, and then exclaimed, "Good boys! Oh, you have saved us all! God bless you forever! Such boys should never die!" It was some time before they could talk without weeping. Hope almost died within them, and now, when the first bright ray came, it almost turned reason from its throne. A brighter, happier look came to them than we had seen, and then they plied us with questions, the first of which was, "Where were you?"

We told them it must be two hundred and fifty miles yet to any part of California where we could live. Then came the question, "Can we take our wagons?" "You will have to walk" was our answer, for no wagons could go over that unbroken road that we had traveled. As rapidly and carefully as we could, we told them of our journey, and the long distance between the water holes; that we had lost no time and yet had been twenty-six days on the road; that for a long distance the country was about as dry and desolate as the region we had crossed east of this camp. We told them of the scarcity of grass, and all the reasons that had kept us so long away from them.

We inquired after the others whom we had left in camp when we went away, and we were told all they knew about them. Hardly were we gone before they began to talk about the state of affairs which existed. They said that as they had nothing to live on but their oxen, it would be certain death to wait here and eat them up, and that it would be much better to move on a little every day and get nearer and nearer the goal before the food failed. Bennett told them they would know surely about the way when the boys returned and, knowing the road, would know how to manage and what to expect and work for, and could get out successfully. But the general opinion of all but Mr. Bennett and Mr. Arcane and their families was, as expressed by one of them, "If those boys ever get out of this cussed hole, they are d—d fools if they ever come back to help anybody."

Some did not stay more than a week after we were gone, but took their oxen and blankets and started on. They could not be content to stay idly in camp with nothing to occupy their minds or bodies. They could see that an ox, when killed, would feed them only a few days, and that they could not live long on them, and it stood them in hand to get nearer the western shore, as the less distance, the more hope while the meat lasted. Bennett implored them to stay, as he was sure we would come back, and if the most of them deserted him, he would be exposed to the danger of the Indians with no hope of a successful resistance against them.

But the most seemed to think that to stay was to die, and it would be better to die trying to escape than to set idly down to perish. These men seemed to think their first duty was to save themselves and, if fortunate, help others afterward, so they packed their oxen and left in separate parties, the last some two weeks before. They said that Captain Culverwell went with the last party. I afterward learned that he could not keep up with them and turned to go back to the wagons again and perished, stretched out upon the sand as we saw him, dying all alone, with no one to transmit his last words to family or friends. Not a morsel to eat, and the little canteen by his side empty. A sad and lonely death indeed!

There was no end to the questions about the road we had to answer, for this was uppermost on their minds, and we tried to tell them and show them how we must get along on our return. We told them of the great snow mountains we had seen all to the north of our road, and how deep the snow appeared to be, and how far west it extended. We told them of the black and desolate ranges and buttes to the south, and of the great, dry plains in the same direction. We told them of the Jayhawkers' trail; of Fish's dead body; the salt lake and slippery alkali water to which we walked, only to turn away in disappointment; of the little sheets of ice which saved our lives; of Doty's camp and what we knew of those gone before; of the discouraged ones who gave us their names to send back to friends; of the hawk and crow diet; of my lameness; of the final coming out into a beautiful valley, in the midst of fat cattle and green meadows; and the trouble to get the help arranged on account of not knowing the language to tell the people what we needed. They were deeply impressed that my lameness had been a blessing in disguise, or we would have gone on to the coast and consumed more time than we did in walking slowly to favor the cripple knee. Our sad adventures and loss of the horses in returning was sorrowfully told, and we spoke of the provisions we had been able to bring on the little mule which had clambered over the rocks like a cat; that we had a little flour and beans, and some good dried meat with fat on it which we hoped would help to eke out the poorer fare and get them through at last. They were so full of compliments that we really began to think we had been brought into the world on purpose to assist someone, and the one who could forecast all things had directed us and all our ways so that we should save those people and bring them to a better part of God's footstool, where plenty might be enjoyed and the sorrows of the desert forgotten. It was midnight before we could get them all satisfied with their knowledge of our experience.

It was quite a treat to us to sleep again between good blankets, arranged by a woman's hand, and it was much better resting than the curled up, cramped position we had slept in while away, with only the poor protection of the half blanket for both of us, in nights that were pretty chilly.

We had plenty of water here, and there being no fear of the mule going astray, we turned her loose. As the party had seen no Indians during our absence we did not concern ourselves much about them. At breakfast we cautioned them about eating too much bread, remembering our own experience in that way.

They said they had about given up our coming back a week before and had set about getting ready to try to move on themselves. Bennett said he was satisfied that they never could have got through alone, after what we had told them of the route and its dangers. He said he knew now that not one of them would have lived if they had undertaken the journey alone without knowledge of the way.

They had taken off the covers of the wagons to make them into harnesses for the oxen so they could be used as pack animals. The strong cloth had been cut into narrow strips and well made into breast straps and breeching, for the cattle were so poor and their hide so loose, it was almost impossible to keep anything on their backs. They had emptied the feathers out of the beds to get the cloth to use and had tried to do everything that seemed best to do to get along without wagons. The oxen came up for water, and the mule with them. They looked better than when we left, but were still poor. They had rested for some time and might feel able to go along willingly for a few days at least. I was handy with the needle and helped them to complete the harness for the oxen, while Bennett and John went to the lake to get a supply of salt to take along, a most necessary article with our fresh meat. I looked around a little at our surroundings and could see the snow still drifting over the peak of the snowy mountain as we had seen it farther east, where we were ourselves under the burning sun. This was now pretty near February first,[78] or midwinter. The eastern side of this great mountain was too steep to be ascended, and no sign of a tree could be seen on the whole eastern slope. The range of mountains on the east side of this narrow valley was nearly all volcanic, barren in the extreme, and the roughest of all the mountains we had ever seen.[79] I had now looked pretty thoroughly and found it to be pretty nearly a hundred miles long, and this was the only camp I had seen where water could be had.

When Mrs. Bennett was ready to show me what to do on the cloth harness, we took a seat under the wagon, the only shady place,[80] and began work. The great mountain I have spoken of as the snow mountain has since been known as Telescope Peak, reported to be eleven thousand feet high.[81] It is in the range running north and south and has no other peak so high. Mrs. Bennett questioned me closely about the trip, and particularly if I had left anything out which I did not want her to know. She said she saw her chance to ride was very slim, and she spoke particularly of the children and that it was impossible for them to walk. She said little Martha had been very sick since we had been gone, and that for many days they had expected her to die. They had no medicine to relieve her and the best they could do was to select the best of the ox meat and make a little soup of it and feed her. They had watched her carefully for many days and nights, expecting they would have to part with her anytime and bury her little body in the sands. Sometimes it seemed as if her breath would stop, but they had never failed in their attentions and were at last rewarded by seeing her improve slowly, and even to relish a little food, so that if no relapse set in, they had hopes to bring her through. They brought the little one and showed her to me, and she seemed so different from what she was when we went away. Then she could run about camp, climb out and in the wagons, and move about so spry that she reminded one of a quail. Now she was strangely misshapen. Her limbs had lost all the flesh and seemed nothing but skin and bones, while her body had grown corpulent and distended, and her face had a starved, pinched, and suffering look with no healthy color in it.

She told me of their sufferings while we were gone and said she often dreamed she saw us suffering fearfully for water and lack of food and could only picture to herself as their own fate that they must leave the children by the trailside, dead, and one by one drop out themselves in the same way. She said she dreamed often of her old home, where bread was plenty, and then to awake to find her husband and children starving was a severe trial indeed, and the contrast terrible. She was anxious to get me to express an opinion as to whether I thought we could get the oxen down the falls where we had so much trouble.

I talked to her as encouragingly as I could, but she did not cheer up much and sobbed and wept over her work most all the time. It was not possible to encourage her much, the outlook seemed so dark. Mrs. Arcane sat under another wagon and said nothing, but she probably heard all we had to say, and did not look as if her hopes were any brighter.[82] Bennett and Rogers soon returned with a supply of salt and said the whole shore of the lake was a windrow of it that could be shoveled up in enormous quantities.

We now, in a counsel of the whole, talked over the matter and the way which seemed most promising. If we went by the Jayhawkers' trail, there was a week of solid travel to get over the range and back south again as far as a point directly opposite our camp, and this had taken us only three days to come over as we had come. The only obstacle in the way was the falls, and when we explained that there was some sand at the bottom of them, Bennett said he thought we could get them [the oxen] over without killing them, and that, [as] we knew exactly where the water was, this was the best trail to take. Arcane was quite of the same opinion, the saving of a week of hard and tiresome travel being in each case the deciding reason. They then explained to me what they had decided on doing if we had not come back. They had selected two oxen for the women to ride, one to carry water, and one to carry the four children. There were no saddles, but blankets enough to make a soft seat, and they proposed to put a band or belt around the animals for them to hold on by, and the blankets would be retained in place by the breast and breeching straps which we had made. They had found out that it was very difficult to keep a load of any kind upon an ox and had devised all this harness to meet the trouble.

Bennett had one old bridle ox called Old Crump, which had been selected to carry the children because she was slow and steady. "How in the world do you expect it to keep the children on?" said I. "Well," said Bennett, with a sort of comical air—about the first relief from the sad line of thought that had possessed us all—"we have taken two strong hickory shirts, turned the sleeves inside, sewed up the necks, then sewed the two shirts together by the tail, and when these are placed on the ox they will make two pockets for the youngest children, and we think the two others will be able to cling to his back with the help of a band around the body of the ox to which they can cling with their hands." Now, if Old Crump went steady and did not kick up and scatter things, he thought this plan would operate first-rate. Now, as to the mule, they proposed [that] as we knew how to pack the animal, we should use her to pack our provisions so they would go safe.

From a piece of hide yet remaining, John and I made ourselves some new moccasins and were all ready to try the trip over our old trail for now the third time, and the last, we hoped.

Mrs. Bennett and Mrs. Arcane had taken our advice and, in cooking, had not put too much of the flour or beans into the soup for the children, and they had gotten along nicely, and even began to smile a little with satisfaction after a full meal. They got along better than John and I did when we got hold of the first nutritions after our arrival on the other side.

We must leave everything here we could get along without. No clothing except that on our backs. Only a camp kettle in which to make soup, a tin cup for each one, and some knives and spoons which each happened to have. Each one had some sort of a canteen for water, which we must fill up at every opportunity, and we decided to carry a shovel along so we might bury the body of Captain Culverwell and shovel up a pile of sand at the falls to enable us to get the oxen over. Every ox had a cloth halter on his head so he might be led or tied up at night when we had a dry camp and they would most assuredly wander off if not secured. Old Crump was chosen to lead the train, and Rogers was to lead him. We had made an extra halter for this old fellow, and quite a long strip of bed ticking sewed into a strap to lead him by.

This packing business was a new idea, and a hard matter to get anything firmly fixed on their backs. We had made shoulder straps, hip straps, breast straps, and breeching as the correct idea for a harness. The only way we could fasten the band around the animals was for one to get on each side and pull it as tight as possible, then tie a knot, as we had no buckles or ring in our harness.

The loads of the oxen consisted of blankets and bedding and a small, light tent of their sheeting, about four by six feet in size. We rose early and worked hard till about the middle of the forenoon getting all things ready. They had been in a state of masterly inactivity so long in this one camp that they were anxious to leave it now forever. Only in progress was there hope, and this was our last and only chance. We must succeed or perish. We loaded the animals from the wagons, and some of the oxen seemed quite afraid at this new way of carrying loads. Old Crump was pretty steady, and so was the one with the two water kegs, one on each side, but the other oxen did not seem to think they needed any blankets on these warm days.

Mrs. Arcane was from a city and had fondly conveyed thus far some articles of finery, of considerable value and much prized. She could not be persuaded to leave them here to deck the red man's wife and have her go flirting over the mountains with, and as they had little weight, she concluded she would wear them, and this perhaps would preserve them. So she got out her best hat and trimmed it up with extra ribbon, leaving some with quite long ends to stream out behind. Arcane brought up his ox [called] Old Brigham, for he had been purchased at Salt Lake and named in honor of the great Mormon saint.

Mrs. Arcane also dressed her little boy Charlie up in his best suit of clothes, for she thought they might as well wear them out as throw them away. She made one think of a fairy in gay and flying apparel. In the same way, all selected their best and most serviceable garments, for it was not considered prudent to carry any load, and poor clothes were good enough to leave for Indians. We set it down as a principle that we must save ourselves all we could, for it would be a closely contested struggle with us and death, at the very best, and we wanted to get all the advantage for ourselves we could. As we were making the preparations, the women grew more hopeful, as it seemed as if something was really going to be accomplished.

Bennett and Arcane were emphatic in their belief and expressions that we would succeed. "I know it—don't you, Sally?" said Bennett very cheerfully but, after all, Mrs. Bennett could not answer quite as positively, but said, "I hope so." Mrs. Bennett's maiden name was Sarah Dilley, which I mention here as I may otherwise forget it afterward. She realized that hers was no easy place to ride, that they would have hard fare at best, and that it must be nearly or quite a month before they could reach a fertile spot on which to place their feet. One could easily see that the future looked quite a little dark to her, on account of her children, as [to] a mother [it] naturally would.

High overhead was the sun, and very warm indeed on that day in the forepart of February 1850 when the two children were put on Old Crump to see if he would let them ride. The two small children were placed in the pockets on each side, face outward, and they could stand or sit as they should choose. George and Melissa were placed on top and given hold of the strap that was to steady them in their place. I now led up Mrs. Bennett's ox, and Mr. Bennett helped his wife to mount the animal, on whose back as soft a seat as possible had been constructed. Mrs. Arcane in her ribbons, was now helped to her seat on the back of Old Brigham, and she carefully adjusted herself to position and arranged her dress and ornaments to suit, then took hold of the strap that served to hold on by, as there were no bridles on these two.

Rogers led the march with his ox; Bennett and I started the others along, and Arcane followed with Old Crump and the children. Bennett and Arcane took off their hats and bade the old camp good-bye. The whole procession moved, and we were once more going toward our journey's end, we hoped. The road was sandy and soft, the grade practically level, and everything went well for about four miles, when the pack on one of the oxen near the lead got loose and turned over to one side, which he no sooner saw thus out of position than he tried to get away from it by moving sidewise. Not getting clear of the objectionable load in this way, he tried to kick it off, and thus really got his foot in it, making matters worse instead of better. Then he began a regular waltz, and bawled at the top of his voice in terror. Rogers tried to catch him, but his own animal was so frisky that he could not hold him and do much else, and the spirit of fear soon began to be communicated to the others, and soon the whole train seemed to be taken crazy.

They would jump up high and then come down, sticking their forefeet as far as possible into the sand, after which, with elevated tails and terrible plunges, [they] would kick and thrash and run till the packs came off, when they stopped, apparently quite satisfied. Mrs. Bennett slipped off her ox as quick as she could, grabbed her baby from the pocket on Old Crump and,

Leaving Death Valley.—The Manly Party On The March After Leaving Their Wagons.

shouting to Melissa and George to jump, got her family into safe position in pretty short order. Arcane took his Charlie from the other pocket and laid him on the ground while he devoted his own attention to the animals. Mrs. Arcane's ox followed suit and waltzed around in the sand, bawled at every turn, fully as bad as any of the others, but Mrs. Arcane proved to be a good rider and hard to unseat, clingling desperately to her strap as she was tossed up and down and whirled about at a rate enough to make anyone dizzy. Her many fine ribbons flew out behind like the streamers from a masthead, and the many fancy fixin's she had donned fluttered in the air in gayest mockery. Eventually she was thrown, however, but without the least injury to herself, but somewhat disordered in raiment. When I saw Bennett, he was standing half bent over, laughing in almost hysterical convulsion at the entirely impromptu circus, which had so suddenly performed an act not on the pro-gram. Arcane was much pleased and laughed heartily when he saw no one was hurt. We did not think the cattle had so much life and so little sense as to waste their energies so uselessly. The little mule stepped out [to] one side and looked on in amazement, without disarranging any article of her load.

Mrs. Bennett, carrying her baby and walking around to keep out of the way, got very much exhausted and sat down on the sand, her face as red as if the blood were about to burst through the skin, and perspiring freely. We car-ried a blanket and spread [it] down for her while we gathered in the scat-tered baggage. Then the oxen were got together again and submitted to being loaded up again as quietly as if nothing had happened. Myself and the women had to mend the harnesses considerably, and Arcane and his ox went back for some water, while Rogers and Bennett took the shovel and went ahead about a mile to cover up the body of Captain Culverwell, for some of the party feared the cattle might be terrified at seeing it. All this took so much time that we had to make a camp of it right here.

We put the camp kettle on two stones, built a fire, put in some beans and dried meat cut very fine, which cooked till Arcane came with more water, which was added and thickened with a little of the unbolted flour, making a pretty good and nutritious soup which we all enjoyed. We had to secure the animals, for there was neither grass nor water for them, and we thought they might not be in so good spirits another day.

We had little trouble in packing up again in the morning and con-cluded to take a nearer route[83] to the summit, so as to more quickly reach the water holes where Rogers and I camped on our first trip over the country. This would be a hard, rocky road on its course leading up a small rocky cañon, hard on the feet of the oxen, so they had to be constantly urged on,

134

THE OXEN GET FRISKY.

as they seemed very tender footed. They showed no disposition to go on a spree again and, so far as keeping the loads on, behaved very well indeed. The women did not attempt to ride but followed on, close after Old Crump and the children, who required almost constant attention, for in their cramped position they made many cries and complaints. To think of it, two children cramped up in narrow pockets in which they could not turn around, jolted and pitched around over the rough road, made them objects of great suffering to themselves, and anxiety and labor on the part of the mothers.

Mrs. Bennett said she would carry her baby if she could, but her own body was so heavy for her strength that she could not do it. Bennett, Rogers, and myself hurried the oxen all we could, so that we could reach the water and let Bennett go back with some to meet the rest and refresh them for the end of the day's march, and he could take poor little Martha from the pocket and carry her in his arms, which would be a great relief to her. Arcane also took his child when he met them, throwing away his double-barreled gun, saying, "I have no use for you."

When the women reached camp we had blankets already spread down for them, on which they cast themselves, so tired as to be nearly dead. They were so tired and discouraged they were ready to die, for they felt they could not endure many days like this.

We told them this was the first day and they were not used to exercise, therefore more easily tired than after they became a little used to it. We told them not to be discouraged, for we knew every water hole, and all the road over which we would pilot them safely. They would not consent to try riding again after their circus experience, and Mrs. Arcane said her limbs ached so much she did not think she could even go on the next day. They had climbed over the rocks all day and were lame and sore, and truly thought they could not endure such another day. The trail had been more like stairs than a road in its steep ascent, and our camp was at a narrow pass in the range. The sky was clear and cloudless as it had been for so long, for thus far upon this route no rain had fallen, and only once a little snow that came to us like manna in the desert. For many days we had been obliged to go without water, both we and our cattle, and over the route we had come we had not seen any signs of a white man's presence older than our own. I have no doubt we were the first to cross the valley in this location, a visible sinkhole in the desert.

The women did not recover sufficient energy to remove their clothing but slept as they were and sat up and looked around with uncombed hair in the morning, perfect pictures of dejection. We let them rest as long as we could, for their swollen eyes and stiffened joints told how sadly unprepared they were to go forward at once. The sun came out early and made it comfortable, while a cool and tonic breeze came down from the great snow mountain, the very thing to brace them up after a thorough rest.

The slope to the east was soon met by a high ridge, and between this and the main mountain was a gentle slope scattered over with sagebrush and a few little stools of bunchgrass here and there between. This gave our oxen a little food, and by dipping out the water from the holes and letting them fill up again, we managed to get water for camp use and to give the animals nearly all they wanted.[84]

While waiting for the women, Bennett and Arcane wanted to go out and get a good view of the great snowy mountain I had told them so much about. The best point of view was near our camp, perhaps three or four hundred yards away,[85] and I went with them. This place where we now stood was lower than the mountains either north or south, but [which] were difficult to climb, and gave a good view in almost every direction and there, on the backbone of the ridge, we had a grand outlook, but some parts of it brought back doleful recollections. They said they had traveled in sight of that mountain for months and seen many strange formations, but never one like this, as developed from this point.[86] It [the Sierra Nevada] looked to be seventy-five miles to its base, and to the north and west there was a succession of snowy peaks that seemed to have no end. Bennett and Arcane said they never before supposed America contained mountains so grand with peaks that so nearly seemed to pierce the sky. Nothing except a bird could ever cross such steep ranges as that one.

West and south it seemed level, and low, dark, and barren buttes rose from the plain, but never high enough to carry snow, even at this season of the year. I pointed out to them the route we were to follow, noting the prominent points, and it could be traced for fully one hundred and twenty-five miles from the point on which we stood. This plain, with its barren ranges and buttes, is now known as the Mojave Desert. This part of the view they seemed to study over, as if to fix every point and water hole upon their memory. We turned to go to camp, but no one looked back on the country we had come over since we first made out the distant snow peak, now so near us, on November 4, 1849. The only butte in this direction that carried snow was the one where we captured the Indian and where the squashes were found.

The range next east of us across the low valley was barren to look upon as a naked, single rock. There were peaks of various heights and colors, yellow, blue, fiery red, and nearly black. It looked as if it might sometime have been the center of a mammoth furnace. I believe this range is known as the Coffin's Mountains.[87] It would be difficult to find earth enough in the whole of it to cover a coffin.

Just as we were ready to leave and return to camp, we took off our hats and then, overlooking the scene of so much trial, suffering, and death, spoke the thought uppermost, saying, "Good-bye, Death Valley!" Then [we] faced away and made our steps toward camp.[88] Ever after this, in speaking of this long and narrow valley over which we had crossed into its nearly central part, and on the edge of which the lone camp was made for so many days, it was called Death Valley.

Many accounts have been given to the world as to the origin of the name and by whom it was thus designated, but ours were the first visible footsteps, and we [were] the party which named it the saddest and most dreadful name that came to us first from its memories.

CHAPTER XI

Struggling Along

OUT OF DEATH VALLEY WE SURELY WERE. To Rogers and I, the case seemed hopeful, for we had confidence in the road and believed all would have power to weather difficulties, but the poor women—it is hard to say what complaints and sorrows were not theirs. They seemed to think they stood at death's door, and would about as soon enter as to take up a farther march over the black, desolate mountains and dry plains before them, which they considered only a dreary vestibule to the dark door after all. They even had an idea that the road was longer than we told them and they never could live to march so far over the sandy, rocky roads. The first day nearly satisfied them that it was no use to try. Rogers and I counted up the camps we ought to reach each day and in this way could pretty near convince them of [the] time that would be consumed in the trip. We encouraged them in every way we could, told them we had better get along a little every day and make ourselves a little nearer the promised land, and the very exercise would soon make them stronger and able to make a full day's march.

Rogers and I told them we felt in much better spirits now than we did when we set out alone, now that nothing but the arrows of an Indian could stop us. We said to them, "We are not going to leave you two ladies out here to die, for there is not a sign of a grave to put you in," and it was a pretty tough place to think of making one. We told them of the beautiful flowery hillsides over the other side and begged them to go over there to die, as it would be so much better and easier to perform the last sad rites there instead of here on the top of the dismal mountain. It seemed quite like a grim joke, but it produced a reaction that turned the tide of thoughts and brought more courage. We only laid out the march for this day as far as the falls and, after a little, prepared to move. The cattle seemed to have quit their foolishness, and they were loaded without trouble. The children fitted into the pockets better than usual, and the mothers with full canteens strapped across their shoulders picked out soft places on which to place their poor blistered feet at every step. They walked as if they were troubled with corns on every toe, and on their heels into the bargain, and each foot was so badly affected that they did not know on which one to limp. But still they moved, and we were once more on our way westward. They often stopped to rest, and Arcane waited for them with Old Crump, while they breathed and complained awhile and then passed on again.

The route was first along the foot of the high peak, over bare rocks, and we soon turned south somewhat so as to enter the cañon leading down to the falls.[1] The bottom of this was thick with broken rock, and the oxen limped and picked out soft places about as bad as the women did. A pair of moccasins would not last long in such rocks and we hoped to get out of them very soon. Rogers and I hurried along, assisting Arcane and his party as much as we could, while Bennett stayed behind and assisted the women as much as possible, taking their arms, and by this means they also reached camp, an hour behind the rest.

A kettle of hot, steaming soup, and blankets all spread out on which to rest, was the work Rogers and I had done to prepare for them, and they sank down on the beds completely exhausted. The children cried some but were soon pacified and were contented to lie still. A good supper of hot soup made them feel much better all around.

The first thing Bennett and Arcane did was to look round and see the situation at the falls, and see if the obstacle was enough to stop our progress, or if we must turn back and look for a better way. They were in some doubt about it, but concluded to try and get the animals over rather than to take the time to seek another pass, which might take a week of time. We men all went down to the foot of the fall and threw out all the large rocks, then piled up all the sand we could scrape together with the shovel, till we had quite a pile of material that would tend to break a fall.[2] We arranged everything possible for a forced passage in the morning, and the animals found a few willows to browse and a few bunches of grass here and there, which gave them a little food, while the spring supplied them with enough water to keep them from suffering with thirst.

Early in the morning we took our soup hastily and, with ropes, lowered our luggage over the small precipice, then the children, and finally all the ropes were combined to make a single strong one about thirty feet long. They urged one of the oxen up to the edge of the falls, put the rope around his horns, and threw down the end to me, whom they had stationed below. I was told to pull hard when he started so that he might not light on his head and break his neck. We felt this was a desperate undertaking, and we fully expected to lose some of our animals, but our case was critical and we must take some chances. Bennett stood on one side of the ox, and Arcane on the other, while big Rogers was placed in the rear to give a regular Tennessee boost when the word was given. "Now for it," said Bennett, and as I braced out on the rope, those above gave a push and the ox came over, sprawling, but landed safely, cut only a little by some angular stones in the sandpile. "Good enough," said someone and I threw the rope back for another ox. "We'll get 'em all over safely," said Arcane, "if Lewis down there will keep them from getting their necks broken." Lewis pulled hard every time, and not a neck was broken. The sandpile was renewed every time and made as high and soft as possible, and very soon all our animals were below the falls. The little mule gave a jump when they pushed her and lighted squarely on her feet all right. With the exception of one or two slight cuts, which bled some, the oxen were all right and we began loading them at once.

Bennett and Arcane assisted their wives down along the little, narrow ledge which we used in getting up, keeping their faces toward the rocky wall, and feeling carefully for every footstep. Thus they worked along and landed safely by the time we had the animals ready for a march. We had passed without disaster the obstacle we most feared and started down the rough cañon, hope revived, and we felt we should get through. After winding around among the great boulders for a little while, we came to the two horses we had left behind, both dead and near together. We pointed to the carcasses, and told them those were the horses we brought for the women to ride, and that is the way they were cheated out of their passage. The bodies of the animals had not been touched by bird or beast. The cañon was too deep and dark for either wolves or buzzards to enter, and nothing alive had been seen by us in the shape of wild game of any sort. Firearms were useless here except for defense against Indians, and we expected no real trouble from them. From what we could see, it was my opinion that no general rain ever fell in that region. There was some evidence that water had at times flowed down them [the canyons] freely after cloudbursts or some sudden tempest, but the gravel was so little worn that it gave no evidence of much of a stream.

We hurried on as rapidly as possible so as to get into the Jayhawkers' beaten trail which would be a little easier to follow. When we reached the lowest part of the valley we had to turn south to get around a little slow-running stream of salt water that moved north and emptied into a salt lake. No source of the stream could be seen from this point, but when we reached a point where we could cross, we had a smooth, hard clay bed to march over.

PULLING THE OXEN DOWN THE PRECIPICE.

It seemed to have been, some day, a bed of mortar, but now [was] baked hard, and the hoofs of the oxen dented into it no more than half an inch. On our left hand was a perpendicular cliff, along which we traveled for quite a little way. The range of mountains now before us to cross was black, nothing but rocks, and extremely barren, having no water in it that we knew of, so when we reached the summit we camped[3] [and] tied all our animals to rocks, where they lay down and did not rise till morning. The women were so tired they were over two hours late, and we had the fire built, the soup cooked, and the beds made. As we did not stop at noon all were very hungry and ate with a relish. The poor animals had to go without either grass or water. When Old Crump and the party came in the men were carrying the babies and their wives were clinging to their arms, scarcely able to stand. When they reached the beds they fell at full length on them, saying their feet and limbs ached like a toothache. It seemed to be best for them to rest a little before eating. Mrs. Bennett said that the only consolation was that the road was getting shorter every day, but were it not for the children she would sooner die than follow the trail any farther. Their soup was carried to them in the bed, and they were covered up as they lay, and slept till morning. This day's walk was the hardest one yet, and probably the longest one of the whole journey, but there was no other place where we could find a place large enough to make a camp and free enough of rocks so that a bed could be made.

Rogers and I had the kettle boiling early and put in the last of the meat and nearly all that was left of the flour. At the next camp an ox must be killed. Just as it was fairly light I went about two hundred yards south where the dead body of Mr. Fish lay, just as he died more than a month before. The body had not been disturbed and looked quite natural. He was from Oscaloosa, Iowa.

The folks arose very reluctantly this morning and appeared with swollen eyes and uncombed hair, for there was no means of making a toilet without a drop of water except what we had used in getting breakfast. We set the soup kettle near the foot of the bed so the women could feed the children and themselves. Now as we loaded the oxen, it was agreed that Rogers and I should go ahead with all but Old Crump, and get in camp as soon as possible, and they were to follow on as best they could. There was a little water left in the canteens of Bennett and Arcane, to be given only to the children, who would cry when thirsty, the very thing to make them feel the worst.

We were to kill an ox when we reached camp, and as each of the men had an equal number on the start, each was to furnish one alternately and no disputing about whose were better or stronger, in any emergency.

Our road now led down the western slope of the mountain, and loose, hard, broken rocks were harder on the feet of our animals than coming up, and our own moccasins were wearing through. The cattle needed shoes as well as we. Anyone who has never tried it can[not] imagine how hard it is to walk with tender feet over broken rock. It was very slow getting along, at the best, and the oxen stumbled dreadfully in trying to protect their sore feet. At the foot of the mountain we had several miles of soft and sandy road. The sun shone very hot and, with no water, we suffered fearfully. A short way out in the sandy valley we passed again the grave of Mr. Isham, where he had been buried by his friends. He was from Rochester, New York. He was a cheerful, pleasant man, and during the forepart of the journey used his fiddle at the evening camps to increase the merriment of his jolly companions. In those days we got no rain, saw no living animals of any kind except those of our train, saw not a bird nor insect, saw nothing green except a very stunted sage and some dwarf bushes. We now know that the winter of 1849–50 was one of the wettest ever seen in California, but for some reason or other none of the wet clouds ever came to this portion of the state to deposit the most scattered drops of moisture.

Quite a long way from the expected camp, the oxen snuffed the moisture and began to hurry towards it with increased speed. A little while before it did not seem as if they had ambition enough left to make a quick move, but as we approached the water those which had no packs fairly trotted in their haste to get a drink. This stream was a very small one, seeping out from a great pile of rocks and maintaining itself till it reached the sands, where it disappeared completely. A few tufts of grass grew along the banks, otherwise everything surrounding was desolate in the extreme.

As soon as we could get the harness off the oxen, we went to look for our little buried sack of wheat which we were compelled to leave and hide on our way out. We had hidden it so completely that it took us quite a little while to strike its bed, but after scratching with our hands awhile, we hit the spot, and found it untouched. Although the sand in which it was buried seemed quite dry, the grain had absorbed so much moisture from it that the sack was nearly bursting. It was emptied on a blanket, and proved to be still sound and sweet.

Our first work now was to kill an ox and get some meat to cook for those who were coming later. We got the kettle boiling with some of the wheat in it, for the beans were all gone. We killed the ox, saving the blood to cook. Cutting the meat all off the bones, we had it drying over a fire as soon as possible, except what we needed for this meal and the next. Then we made a smooth place in the soft sand on which to spread the blankets, the first good place we had found to sleep since leaving Death Valley.

The next job was to make moccasins for ourselves and for the oxen, for it was plain they could not go on another day barefooted. We kept busy indeed, attending the fires under the meat and under the kettle, besides our shoemaking, and were getting along nicely about sundown, when Old Christian Crump appeared in sight, followed by the women and the rest of the party. The women were just as tired as ever and dropped down on the blankets the first thing. "How many such days as this can we endure?" they said. We had them count the days gone by, and look around to see the roughest part of the road was now behind them. They said that only five days had passed, and that two-thirds of the distance still remained untraveled, and they knew they could never endure even another five days' work like the last. We told them to be brave and be encouraged, for we had been over the road and knew what it was, and that we felt sure of being able to do it nicely. They were fed in bed as usual, and there they lay till morning. We men went to making moccasins from the green hide, and when we had cut out those for the men and women, the balance of the hide was used in preparing some also for the oxen, particularly the worst ones, for if I remember correctly there was not enough to go round.

The morning came, bright and pleasant, as all of them were, and just warm enough for comfort in that part of the day. The women were as usual, and their appearance would remind one quite strongly of half-drowned hens which had not been long out of trouble. Hair snarled, eyes red, noses swollen, and out of fix generally. They did not sleep well so much fatigued, for they said they lived over their hard days in dreams at night, and when they would close their eyes and try to go to sleep, the visions would seem to come to them half-waking and they could not rest.

There was now before us a particularly bad stretch of the country, as it would probably take us four or five days to get over it, and there was only one water hole in the entire distance. This one was quite salty, so much so that on our return trip the horses refused to drink it, and the little white one died next day. Only water for one day's camp could be carried with us, and that was for ourselves alone and not for the animals.

When the moccasins were finished in the morning we began to get our cattle together, when it was discovered that Old Brigham was gone, and the general belief was that the Indians had made a quiet raid on us and got away with the old fellow. We circled around till we found his track and then Arcane followed it while we made ready the others. Arcane came in with the stray namesake of the polygamous saint about this time, shouting, "I've got him! No Indians." The ox had got into the wash ravine below camp and passed out of sight behind, in a short time. He had been as easily tracked as if he walked in snow. There was larger sagebrush in the wash than elsewhere, and no doubt Brigham had thought this a good place to seek for some extra blades of grass.

Immediately south of this camp, now known as Providence Springs, is the salt lake to which Rogers and I went on the first trip and were so sadly disappointed in finding the water unfit to use.[4]

As soon as [we were] ready we started up the cañon, following the trail made by the Jayhawkers who had preceded us, and by night [we] had reached the summit but passed beyond, a short distance down the western slope, where we camped in a valley[5] that gave us good, large sagebrush for our fires and quite a range for the oxen without their getting out of sight. This being at quite a high elevation, we could see the foot, as well as the top, of the great snow mountain and had a general good view of the country.

This proved to be the easiest day's march we had experienced, and the women complained less than on any other night since our departure. Their path had been comparatively smooth, and with the new moccasins their feet had been well protected; they had come through pretty nicely. We told them they looked better, and if they would only keep up good courage they would succeed and come out all right to the land where there was plenty of bread and water and, when safely out, they might make good resolutions never to get in such a trap again. Mrs. Bennett said such a trip could never be done over again, and but for the fact that Rogers and I had been over the road and that she believed all we had said about it, she never would have had the courage to come thus far. Now, for the children's sake, she wished to live, and would put forth any effort to come through all right.

The next day we had a long cañon[6] to go down, and in it passed the dead body of the beautiful white mare Rogers had taken such a fancy to. The body had not decomposed, nor had it been disturbed by any bird or beast. Below this point the bed of the cañon was filled with great boulders, over which it was very difficult to get the oxen along. Some of them had lost their moccasins and had to suffer terribly over the rocks.

Camp was made at the saltwater hole, and our wheat and meat boiled in it did not soften and get tender as they did in freshwater.[7] There was plenty of salt grass above; but the oxen did not eat it any more than the horses did, and wandered around cropping a bite of the bitter brush once in a while, and looking very sorry. This was near the place where Rogers and I found the piece of ice which saved our lives. The women did not seriously complain when we reached this camp, but little Charlie Arcane broke out with a bad looking rash all over his body and, as he cried most of the time, it no doubt smarted and pained him like a mild burn. Neither his mother nor anyone else could do anything for him to give him any relief. We had no medicines and, if he or anyone should die, all we could do would be to roll the body in a blanket and cover it with a light covering of sand.

From this camp to the next water holes at the base of the great snow mountain, it was at least thirty miles, level as to surface, and with a light ascending grade. The Jayhawkers had made a well-marked trail, and it was quite good walking. The next camp[8] was a dry one, both for ourselves and the oxen, nothing but dry brush for them and a little dried meat for ourselves, but for all this the women did not complain so very much. They were getting used to the work and grew stronger with the exercise. They had followed Old Crump and the children every day with the canteens of water and a little dried meat to give them if they cried too much with hunger, and Arcane had led his ox day after day with a patience that was remarkable, and there was no bad temper shown by anyone. This was the way to do, for if there were any differences, there was no tribunal to settle them by.

In all this desert travel I did not hear any discontent and serious complaint, except in one case, and that was at the Jayhawkers' camp, where they burned their wagons at the end of the wagon road in Death Valley. Some could not say words bad enough to express their contempt and laid all the trouble of salt water to Lot's wife. Perhaps she was in a better position to stand the cursing than any of the party present.

The next day we reached the water holes[9] at the place where Rogers and I stole up to the campfire in the evening, supposing it to be Indians but finding there Captain Doty and his mess, a part of the Jayhawkers' band. By dipping carefully from these holes they filled again, and thus, although there was no flow from them, we gradually secured what water we needed for the camp, which was a small amount after so long a time without. There was some low brush here called greasewood, which grew about as high as currant bushes, and some distance up the mountain the oxen could find some scattered bunchgrass, which, on the whole, made this camp a pretty good one. The women, however, were pretty nearly exhausted, and little Charlie Arcane cried bitterly all day and almost all night. All began to talk more and feel more hopeful of getting through. The women began to say that every step brought them so much nearer to the house we had told them about on the other side, and often said the work was not so very hard after all. Really it was not so bad traveling as we had at first. We were now nine days from the wagons. "Are we halfway?" was the question they began to ask. We had to answer them that more than half the hard days were over, [even] if half the distance had not been traveled, and with the better walking and getting hardened to the work, they would get over the last half better than the first. One thing was a little hard. All of our beans and flour had been used up, and now the wheat was about gone also. We had cooked it, and it seemed best, trying to build up our strength where it was most needed for the greatest trials, and now we thought they would be able to get along on the meat. We had reached the base of the great snow mountain. It seems strange, with the mass of snow resting above, and which must be continually thawing more or less, [that] no ravines or large streams of water were produced, flowing down this side. It seemed dry all around its base, which is very singular, with the snow so near.

We had now our barren cañon to go down, and right here was the big trail coming down from the north, which we took and followed. We said all these good things about the road, and encouraged the people all we could to keep in good spirits and keep moving. We told them we thought we knew how to manage to get them safe over the road if they only fully endeavored to do it. We were all quite young, and not in the decline of life, as were most of them who had perished by the way. No reader can fully realize how much we had to say and do to keep up courage, and it is this, more than anything else that we did, which kept up the lagging energies and inspired the best exertion. I don't know but we painted some things a little brighter than they were and tried to hide some of the most disheartening points of the prospects ahead, for we found the mind had most to do with it after all. We have no doubt that if we had not done all we could to keep up good courage, the women would have pined away and died before reaching this far. Whenever we stopped talking encouragingly, they seemed to get melancholy and blue.

There was some pretty good management to be exercised still. The oxen were gradually growing weaker, and we had to kill the weakest one every time, for if the transportation of our food failed, we should yet be open to the danger of starvation. As it was, the meat on their frames was very scarce, and we had to use the greatest economy to make it last and waste nothing. We should now have to kill one of our oxen every few days, as our other means of subsistence had been so completely used up. The women contracted a strange dislike to this region and said they never wanted to see any part of it again.

As the sun showed its face over the great sea of mountains away to the east of Death Valley, and it seemed to rise very early for winter season, we packed up and started [south] on the big trail. Rogers and I took the oxen and mule and went on, leaving the others to accompany Old Crump and his little charges. Arcane had found it best to carry Charlie on his back, as it relieved the burning sensation caused by the eruption on his skin, which was aggravated by the close quarters of the pockets. This leaving the pockets unbalanced, Bennett had to carry his baby also. This made it harder for them, but everyone tried to be just as accommodating as they could and each one would put himself to trouble to accommodate or relieve others.

Rogers and I made camp when we reached the proper place, which was some distance from the mountain on a perfectly level plain where there was no water, no grass; nothing but sagebrush would grow on the dry and worthless soil. We let the oxen go and eat as much of this as they chose, which was very little and only enough to keep them from absolute starvation. The great trail had a branch near here that turned [west], and went up a ravine that would seem to reach the snow in a little while. This was believed to be impassable at this time of year. This route is known as Walker's Pass, leading over a comparatively low ridge, and coming out the south fork of the Kern River.

We made our camp here because it was as long a march as the women could make, and, for a dry one, was as good a location as we could find. The cool breeze came down from the snow to the north of us, not so very many miles away, and after a little it became uncomfortably cold. We gathered greasewood bushes and piled them up to make a windbreak for our heads. The oxen, even, would come and stand around the fire, seeming greatly to enjoy the warm smoke which came from burning the greasewood brush, which, by the way, burns about the best of any green wood. When we were ready to lie down, we tied the animals to bunches of brush, and they lay contentedly till morning.

To the [west] of us, a few miles away we could see some standing columns of rock,[10] much reminding one of the great stone chimney of the boiler house at Stanford Jr., University; not quite so trim and regular in exterior appearance, but something in that order. We reckon the only students in the vicinity would be lizards.

When the women arrived in camp they were very tired, but encouraged themselves that they were much nearer the promised land than they were in the morning. Mrs. Bennett said she was very careful never to take a step backward, and to make every forward one count as much as possible. "That's a good resolution, Sally," said Mr. Bennett. "Stick to it and we will come out by and by."

From near this camp we had a low range of mountains to cross, a sort of spur or offshoot of the great snow mountain that reaches out twenty miles or more to the southeast, and its extremity divides away into what seemed from our point of view a level plain. We had attained quite an elevation without realizing it, so gradual had been the ascent, and our course was now down a steep hillside and into a deep cañon.[11] In its very bottom we found a small stream of water only a few yards long, and then it sank into the sands. Not a spear of grass grew there, and if any had grown it had been eaten by the cattle which had gone before. This was the same place where Rogers and I had overtaken the advance portion of the Jayhawkers when we were on our outward trip in search of relief, and where some of the older men were so discouraged that they gave us their home addresses in Illinois so that we could notify their friends of their precarious situation, and if they were never otherwise heard from they [their friends] could be pretty sure they had perished from thirst and starvation when almost at their journeys' end.

The scenes of this camp on that occasion made so strong an impression on my memory that I can never forget it. There were poor dependent fellows without a morsel to eat except such bits of poor meat as they could beg from those who were fortunate enough to own oxen. Their tearful pleadings would soften a heart of stone. We shared with some of them even when we did not know the little store upon our backs would last us through. Our oxen here had water to drink, but nothing more. It might be a little more comfortable to drink and starve than both choke and starve, but there are no very pleasant prospects in either one.

Both ourselves and the oxen were getting barefoot and our feet very tender. The hill we had just come down was very rough and rocky and our progress very slow, every step made in a selected spot. We could not stop here to kill an ox and let the remainder of them starve, but must push on to where the living ones could get a little food. We fastened the oxen and the mule to keep them from wandering, and slept as best we could. The women and children looked worse than for some time, and could not help complaining. One of the women held up her foot and the sole was bare and blistered. She said they ached like a toothache. The women had left their combs in the wagons, and their hair was getting seriously tangled. Their dresses were getting worn off pretty nearly to their knees, and showed the contact with the ground that sometimes could not be avoided. They were in a sad condition so far as toilet and raiment were concerned. Life was in the balance, however, and instead of telling over sad things, we talked of the time when we would reach the little babbling brook where Rogers and I took such long draughts of clear, sweet water and the waiter at our dinner gave us the choice of crow, hawk, or quail, and where we took a little of all three.

In the morning we were off again down the cañon, limping some as we trod its coarse, gravelly bed with our tender feet and stiffened joints, but getting limbered up a little, after a bit, and enduring it pretty well. We set out to try to reach the bunch of willows out on the level plain, where the cattle could get some water and grass, but night overtook us at the mouth of the cañon, and we were forced to go into camp. This cañon is now called Red Cañon. This was on an elevated plain, with a lake nearby, but as we had been so often deceived by going to the lakes for water and finding them salty in every instance, or poison on account of strong alkali, we did not take the trouble to go and try this one.[12]

Near us was some coarse grass and wet ground where we found water enough for our moderate use, and the oxen, by perseverance, could get something to eat and drink. After supper we were out of meat and we would have to kill an ox to get some food for breakfast. In the night a storm came on, much to our surprise, for we had seen none since the night on the mountain east of Death Valley more than two months before. We tried to fix up a shelter to protect the children and ourselves, but were not very successful. We tried to use our guns for tent poles, but could not keep them in place. We laid down as close as pigs in cold weather, and covered up as best we could, but did not keep dry, and morning found us wet to the skin, cold and shivering. We gathered big sagebrush for a fire in the morning, and the tracks of our nearly bare feet could be plainly seen in the snow which lay like a blanket awhile over the ground, about two inches deep. Some lay in bed and we warmed blankets before the fire and put [the blankets] over them to keep them comfortable till the sun should rise and warm the air. We selected an ox and brought him up before the fire, where I shot him, and soon there was meat roasting over the fire and blood cooking in the camp kettle. We had nothing to season the blood pudding with but salt, and it was not very good, but answered to sustain life. We ate a hasty meal, then packed our animals and started for the willow patch about four miles away. The snow was about gone.

I stayed in camp to keep it till they could get through to the willows and [send] someone to come back with the mule to carry forward the portion of meat that could not be taken at first. We intended to dry it at the willows, and then we could carry it along as daily food over the wide plain we had yet to cross. Having carried the meat forward, we made a rack of willows and dried it over the fire, making up a lot of moccasins for the bare-footed ones while we waited. We were over most of the rocky road, [and] we calculated that our shoe making would last us through. This was a very pleasant camp. The tired ones were taking a rest. No one needed it more than our women and children, who were tired nearly out. They were in much better condition to endure their daily hardships than when they started out, and a little rest would make them feel quite fresh again. They understood that this was almost on the western edge of this desert country and this gave them good hope and courage.

This wonderful spot in the level plain, with a spring of pure water making an oasis of green willows and grass,[13] has been previously spoken of as "a spring of good water, and a little willow patch in a level desert away from any hill." In all our wanderings we had never seen the like before. No mountaineer would ever think of looking here for water, much less ever dream of finding a lone spring away out in the desert, several miles from the mountain's base. Where the range we just came through leaves the mother mountain stands a peak, seemingly alone, and built up of many colored rocks, in belts, and the whole looks as if tipped with steel.

Arcane's boy Charlie still suffered from his bogus measles or whatever else his disorder might be, and Bennett's little Martha grew more quiet and improved considerably in health, though still unable to walk, and still abdominally corpulent. The other two children, George and Melissa, seemed to bear up well and loved to get off and walk in places where the trail was smooth and level. Bennett, Arcane, and Old Crump usually traveled with the same party as the women, and as each of them had a small canteen to carry water, they could attend to the wants of the children and keep them from worrying and getting sick from fretfulness. They often carried the two younger ones on their backs to relieve and rest them from their cramped position on the ox.

Arcane used to say he expected the boys—meaning Rogers and I—would try to surprise the party by letting them get very near the house before they knew how near they were. "Be patient, Mr. Arcane," said we. "We can tell you just how many camps there must be before we reach it, and we won't fool you or surprise you in any way." "Well," said he, "I was almost in hopes you would, for I like to be disappointed in that way." "What do you think the folks will say when we tell them that our little mule packed most of the meat of an ox four miles from one camp to another?" "What will they say when we tell them that the oxen were so poor that there was no marrow in the great thigh bones?" Instead of marrow there was a thick, dark liquid, something like molasses in consistency, but streaked with different colors which made it look very unwholesome. Arcane said the whole story was so

152

incredible that he never should fight anyone, even if he should tell him he lied when he related the strange, sad truth. He said he had no doubt many a one would doubt their story, it was so much beyond what people had ever seen or heard of before, and they might be accused of very strong romancing in the matter.

They all felt more like talking; for we were thus far safe and sound, and though there was a desperate struggle of seventy-five miles or more from this place to the next water in the foothills. Possibly the snowstorms had left a little in some of the pools, but we made no calculations on any. The promised land we had so steadily been approaching, and now comparatively so near, gave us great hope, which was better than food and drink to give us strength.

There were surely two camps between this and the little pond John and I found among the cabbage trees, and not more than six by ten feet square. As we worked away at our footwear we talked more in an hour than we had in a whole day before. We were slowly leaving Death Valley behind us with its sad memories and sufferings. We were leaving behind the dead bodies of several who had traveled with us and been just as strong and hopeful as we. We had left behind us all our possessions in that terrible spot, and simply with our lives we hoped to escape, and trust to Providence and humanity on the other side. Arcane now admitted that they could not have got along half as well if we had not gone ahead and looked out the land. It was such a gain to know exactly where the next water hole was, so it could be steered for and struggled toward. He even went so far as to say they would have no chance alone and that, as he now saw the road, he was sure they would have all perished even before reaching as far as this. We had strong hopes of the morrow, when we would be all rested, all were shod, and would make every footstep count in our [southern] progress.

It seems quite a strange occurrence that the only two storms we had had since we turned westward on this route, November 4th,[14] were snowstorms, and that both had come while we were asleep, so that all our days were cloudless. Sometimes the sun was uncomfortably warm even in the heart of the winter. One would have naturally expected that the great rainfall all over the California coast in the winter of 1849–50, and the deep snows that came in the Sierra Nevada mountains the same winter, would have extended southerly the few hundred miles that separated the two places. Modern science has shown the tracks of the storms and partially explains the reasons for this dry and barren nature of this region. When rains do come they are so out of the regular order that they are called cloudbursts or waterspouts, and the washes in the cañons and their mouths show how great has been the volume of water that sometimes rushed down the slope. If clouds at a warm or moderate temperature float against these snow peaks, all the water they contain is suddenly precipitated. The country is an arid one and unless wealth should appear in the shape of mines, the country can never be inhabited. We considered ourselves very fortunate in finding the little pools and holes of water which kept us alive. It was not very good drinking water, but to us thirsty folks it was a blessing and we never passed it by on account of any little stagnant, bitter taste. Salt water we could not drink, of course, though we sometimes used it to cook with.

We were as well prepared next morning as possible for a move and the long walk before us, the last one between us and the fertile land. They all talked of how delighted they would be to see once more a running brook, green grass, and trees, and such signs of life as they had seen and been used to in the good land they had left behind. The women said they could endure the march of four or five days if when all over, they could sleep off the terrible fatigue and for once drink all the pure, sweet water they could desire. No more forced marches. No more gray road, stretching out its dusty miles as far as the eye could reach. The ladies thought the oxen would be as happy as themselves, and the little mule, the most patient one of the whole train, deserved a life of ease for her valuable services. This little, black, one-eyed lady wandered here and there at will, seeking for grass, but never going astray or getting far enough from the track to alarm us in the least. She seldom drank much water, was always ready, never got footsore, and seemed made expressly for such a life and for such a desert.

A good kettleful of soup for breakfast, dried meat fixed in packages, kegs and canteens filled with water, and we were ready for an advance.

There is one less ox to lead, and very little load for those we have, still the load is all such poor, weak fellows ought to bear. Old Crump was not thus favored by a gradually lightened load. He bore the same four children every day, faithfully, carefully, with never a stumble nor fall, as though fully aware of the precious nature of his burden.

In this new march John and I took the oxen and pushed on as usual, leaving the families to follow on, at a slower pace, the trail we made. The trail was slightly inclined. The bushes [are] stunted at the best, getting smaller as we proceed, and the horse bones, new and ancient, are now thickly scattered along the way. The soil is different from that we have had. We can see the trail, winding gently here and there, swept clean by the wind, and the surface is hard and good; but when the mule gets the least bit off of it she sinks six inches deep into the soft sand, and the labor of walking is immense. I stepped out to examine the peculiar soil, and found it finer than superfine flour. It was evident that a strong wind would lift it in vast clouds which might even darken the sky, but we were fortunate in this respect, for during all the time we were on this peculiar soil, there was no wind at all, and we escaped a sand-storm, a sort of storm as peculiar to this region as are blizzards to some of the states of the great West.

Our first night's camp[15] was out on the barren, waterless plain now known as the Mojave Desert. There were no shrubs large enough to make a fire of, and nothing to tie our cattle to, so we fastened all our animals together to keep them from scattering and getting lost. We ate a little dry meat and drank sparingly of the water, for our scanty stock was to last us another day, when we might reach prospective water holes. Starting early, John and I took all but Old Crump and the other travelers, and hurried on to try and find the water holes as early as possible. We, as well as the oxen, were very dry, for we left all the water we had with the party for the chil-dren, for they cannot endure the thirst as the older people can. We reached the camping place before night. Quite a time before we reached it, the cattle seemed to scent the water and quickened their pace, so we were confident it had not dried up. We got ahead of the oxen and kept there until we reached the little pond, and then guarded it to keep them from wading into it in their eagerness to reach some drink. They all satisfied their thirst, and then we removed the harness, built a fire of the dead cabbage trees which we found round about, laid down the beds and arranged them neatly, and had all nice-ly done before the rear guard came up, in charge of Captain Crump. The party was eager for water and all secured it. It was rainwater and no doubt did not quench thirst as readily as water from some living spring or brook. There was evidence that there had been a recent shower or snow to fill this depression up for our benefit. The Jayhawkers had passed not more than a half mile [west] of this spot, but no sign appeared that they had found it, and it was left to sustain the lives of the women and children.

It often occurs to me that many may read incredulously when I speak of our party eating the entire flesh of an ox in four or five days. To such I will say that one cannot form an idea how poor an ox will get when nearly starved so long. Months had passed since they had eaten a stomachful of good nutritious food. The animals walked slowly with heads down, nearly tripping themselves up with their long, swinging legs. The skin loosely covered the bones, but all the flesh and muscles had shrunk down to the smallest space. The meat was tough and stringy as basswood bark, and tasted strongly of bit-ter sagebrush the cattle had eaten at almost every camp. At a dry camp the oxen would lie down and grate their teeth, but they had no cud to chew. It looked almost merciless to shoot one down for food, but there was no alternative. We killed our poor brute servants to save ourselves. Our cattle found a few bunches out among the trees at this camp and looked some better in the morning. They had secured plenty of water and some grass.

Young Charlie Arcane seemed to grow worse rather than better. His whole body was red as fire, and he screamed with the pain and torment of the severe itching. Nothing could be done to relieve him, and if his strength lasted till we could get better air, water, and food he might recover, but his chances were very poor.

Not much rest at this camp, for in the morning we aimed to start early and reach the water in the foothills. We thought we could do it if we started early, walked rapidly, and took no resting spell at noon. Such a poor soil as this we were anxious to get away from, and walk once more on a soil that would grow something besides stunted sagebrush. From all appearances the Jayhawkers were here in about the same predicament Rogers and I were when we lost the trail. By their tracks we could see they had scattered wide and there was no road left for us to follow, and they had evidently tried to follow our former tracks. Having no trail to follow we passed on as best we could and came to a wide piece of land on which were growing a great many cabbage trees. The soil was of the finest dust with no grit in it, and not long before, a light shower had fallen, making it very soft and hard to get along in with the moccasins. The women had to stop to rest frequently, so our progress was very slow. Rogers and I had feet about as hard as those of the oxen, so we removed our moccasins and went barefoot, finding we could get along much easier in that way, but the others had such tender feet they could not endure the rough contact with the brush and mud. Only a few miles had been made before the women were so completely tired out that we had to stop and eat our little bit of dried meat and wait till morning. The little mule now carried all our stock of food, and the precious burden lightened every day. This delay was not expected, but we had to endure it and bear it patiently, for there was a limit to strength of the feeble ones of our party. We had therefore to make another barren camp. Relief seemed so near at hand we kept good courage and talked freely of the happy ending which would soon come. If we had any way to set a good table we would feast and be merry like the prodigal son, but at any rate we would be safe if we could reach the fertile shore.

When the sun went down we tied the mule and oxen to cabbage trees, and shortly after dusk lay down ourselves, for we had enjoyed a good fire made of the trunks of cabbage trees, the first really comfortable one in a long time. The air was cooler here, for we were on higher ground, and there was some snow on the range of mountains before us, which sent these cool breezes down to us, a change of climate quite pleasing.

For breakfast in the morning we had only dried meat roasted before the fire, without water, and when we started, each one put a piece in his or her pocket to chew on during the day as we walked along. As we went ahead the ground grew drier and the walking much improved. The morning over-head was perfectly lovely as away east, across the desert, the sun early showed his face to us. Not a cloud anywhere, not even over the tops of the high peaks where great white masses sometimes cluster but dissolve as soon as they float away, and there was not wind enough to be perceptible. We remarked the same lack of animal life which we had noticed on our first passage over this section, seeing not a rabbit, bird, or living thing we could use for food. Bennett had the same load in his gun he put there when we left the wagons, and all the powder I had burned was that used in killing the oxen we had slain whenever it became necessary to provide for our barren kitchen.

As we approached the low foothills the trail became better traveled and better to walk in, for the Jayhawkers who had scattered, everyone for himself apparently, in crossing the plain seemed here to have drawn together and their path was quite a beaten one. We saw from this that they followed the tracks made by Rogers and myself as we made our first trip westward in search of bread. Quite a little before the sun went out of sight in the west we reached our camping place in the lower hills at the [northern] slope of a range we must soon cross. Here was some standing water in several large holes,[16] that proved enough for our oxen, and they found some large sage-brush and small bushes round about, on which they browsed and among which they found a few bunches of grass. Lying about were some old skulls of cattle which had sometime been killed, or died. These were the first signs of the sort we had seen along this route. They might have been killed by Indians who doubtless used this trail.

The next day, in crossing the range before us, we reached the edge of the snow, which the sun had softened, and we dared not attempt to cross. Early in the morning, when it was frozen hard, the cattle could travel it very well. The snowbelt was five or six miles wide, and the snow two or three feet deep. This was a very good camping place except that we had to melt snow for all our water, but this being coarse and icy, it was not a great job, as we found enough dry juniper trees and twigs to make a very good fire. Here we also had to kill another ox. This one in its turn is Arcane's, and leaves him only two, and Bennett three, but we think that if we have no accident we shall get them along with us till we can get other food, as they have very light loads to pack. When the ox is killed and the meat prepared the mule has, for a time, a larger load than all the oxen have, but seems content and nips a bite of food whenever it can see a chance anywhere along the road, giving us no more trouble than a dog. And by the way, I think I have not mentioned our faithful camp dog, a worthy member of our party who stood watch always and gave us a sure alarm if anything unusual happened anywhere about. He was perhaps only one of a hundred that tried to cross the plains and had to be abandoned when they reached the upper Platte, where the alkali dust made their feet so sore they could not travel, and as they could not be hauled on wagons, they were left behind. But this dog Cuff did not propose to be left behind to starve, and crippled along after us, we doing all we could for him, and proved as tough as the best of us. Bennett and I had trained him as a hunting dog in the East, and he was very knowing and handy in every particular.

We were out of this camp at daylight. Very little rest for some of us, but we must make the best of the cool morning while the snow is hard, and so move on as soon as we can see the way. As it gets lighter and the sun comes up red and hot out of the desert, we have a grand view of the great spread of the country to [east] and of the great snow mountain to the [northwest] and [north], the peak[17] standing over the place where we left our wagons nineteen days before, on the edge of Death Valley. The glare of the sun on the snow makes us nearly blind, but we hurry on to try to cross it before it becomes so soft as to slump under our feet. It is two or three feet in the deepest places, and probably has been three times as deep when freshly fallen, but it is now solid and icy.

Our rawhide moccasins protected our feet from cold, and both we and the animals got along fairly well, the oxen breaking through occasionally as the snow softened up, but generally walking on the top as we did ourselves. The snowfield reached much farther down the [southern] slope than we had hoped, much farther than on the [northern] side. Before we got out of it, we saw the track of some animal which had crossed our route, but as it had been made some days before and now could be seen only as some holes in the surface, we could not determine what sort of an animal it was.

A mile or two down the hill we were at last out of the snow, and a little farther on we came to the little babbling brook Rogers and I had so long painted in the most refreshing colors to the tired women, with water, wood, and grass on every hand, the three greatest blessings of a camper's life. Here was where Rogers and I had cooked and eaten our meat of crow, quail, and hawk, pretty hard food, but then, the blessed water![18]

There it danced and jumped over the rocks singing the merriest song one ever heard, as it said, "Drink, drink ye thirsty ones your fill"—the happiest, sweetest music to the poor, starved, thirsty souls, wasted down almost to haggard skeletons. Oh! If some poet of wildest imagination could only place himself in the position of those poor, tired travelers to whom water in thick, muddy pools had been a blessing, who had eagerly drunk the fluid even when so salty and bitter as to be repulsive, and now to see the clear, pure liquid, distilled from the crystal snow, abundant, free, filled with life and health—and write it in words—the song of that joyous brook and set it to the music that it made as it echoed in gentle waves from the rocks and lofty walls, and with the gentle accompaniment of rustling trees—a soft, singing hush, telling of rest and peace and happiness.

New life seemed to come to the dear women. "Oh! What a beautiful stream!" say they, and they dip in a tin cup and drink, then watch in dreaming admiration the water as it goes hurrying down; then dip and drink again, and again watch the jolly, rollicking brook as if it were the most entertaining thing in the whole wide earth. "Why can't such a stream as that run out of the great snow mountain in the dry Death Valley" say they, "so we could get water on the way?"

The men have felt as glad as any of them, but have gathered wood and made a fire, and now a camp kettle of cut-up meat is boiling for our supper. It is not yet night, but we must camp in so beautiful a place as this, and though the food was poor, we were better off than we had been before.

Bennett proposed that I take the mule and go back to where we saw the track of the animal in the snow and follow it in hope that we might get some game, for we had an idea it might be an elk or bear or some large game, good to kill and give us better meat. So I saddled the mule and took the trail back till I came to the track, then followed it as best I could, for it was very dull and gave me no idea what it was. I traced [it] out of the snow and then in a blind way through bushes as high as the mule's back—chaparral we call it now—among which I made my way with difficulty. I could now see that the track was made by an ox or cow—perhaps an elk—I could not tell for sure, it was so faint. This chaparral covered a large piece of tableland, and I made my way through it, following the track for a mile or two, till I came to the top of a steep hill sloping down into a deep cañon and a creek, on the bank of which grew sycamore and alder trees, with large willows. I stopped here some minutes to see if I could see or hear the movement of anything. Across the creek I could see a small piece of perhaps half an acre of natural meadow, and in it some small bunches of sycamore trees. After a little I discovered some sort of a horned animal there, and I reckoned this was good enough game for me to try and capture, so [I] led the mule out to one side and down the hill near the creek, then tied her and crept along the bank, about four feet high, toward the little meadow. When about right, as I thought, I climbed up behind a bunch of sycamores, and when I slowly and cautiously raised up, I was within fifty yards of a cow or steer of some sort which I could dimly see. I put a ball square in its forehead and it fell without a struggle. I loaded again quick as possible, and there saw two other smaller cattle stepping very high as though terrified, but not aware of the nature or location of the danger. I gave a low whistle and one of them looked toward me long enough for me to put a ball in it. The third one was now behind a clump of sycamores, and I soon saw its face through a little opening not more than three inches wide. I made a shot, and wounded it, and then rushed up and gave it a fatal one.

I examined my game and found the first one was a poor old cow, but the others were yearlings, one of them very fat and nice, and I soon had the hindquarters skinned out, and all the fat I could find, which made a big load for the mule. It was now almost dark, and the next problem was to get back to camp again. The brushy hills would be terrible to cross with a load of meat, and by the way the ground lay I concluded our camp was on this same creek farther down.

The only way that seemed at all feasible was to follow the course of the stream if possible, rather than return [to] the course over which I had come. There were so many bushes and trees along the bank that I had to take to the bed and follow in the water, and as it was rocky and rough, and so dark I could not see well how to step, I stumbled into holes and pools up to my waist, wet as a rat. Coming to a small open place I decided I had better camp for the night and not attempt further progress in the darkness, and the decision was hastened by dark clouds, which began to gather, and a few sprinkles of rain began to come. There was a good patch of grass for the mule, but all was uncomfortable for me, with the prospect for a rainy night, but as wood was plenty I decided to make a fire and take the chances. I looked for matches and scratched one. No go—they were damp, and scratch as careful and quickly as I could, there was no answering spark or flame, and darkness reigned supreme. A camp without a fire in this wet place was not to be thought of, so I concluded I might as well be slowly working my way down along the stream, through thick brush and cold water, as to sit here in the cold and wait.

So the little mule and I started on, wading the creek in thick darkness, getting only the most dim reflected light from the sky through now and then an opening in the trees. I did not know then how easy it was for a grizzly to capture myself, the mule, and meat and have quite a variety for supper. But the grizzly stayed at home and we followed on through brambles and hard brush, through which it was almost impossible to force one's way. As it turned out, I was not in the track of the storm, and did not suffer much from it. Soon the cañon grew wider, and I could make out on the right hand a piece of tableland covered with brush that seemed easier to get through than the creek bed.

The hill up to the tableland was very steep, but not more than fifty yards high, and when the mule tried to get up she got along very well till near the top, when she slipped in the wet earth and never stopped till she reached the bottom and lay down. She was helped up to her feet again and we tried it in another place, I holding her from slipping when she stopped to rest, and at last we reached the top. The mule started on, seeming to follow a trail, but I could not see whether there was a trail or not, so thick was the darkness, but there was evidently something of the kind, for the brush was two or three feet high and very thick.

After proceeding some distance the mule stopped and did not seem to wish to go any farther. I was pretty sure there was something in front of her that blocked the way, and so worked my way through the brush and carefully past her. I could partly see and partly hear something just ahead, and in a moment found it was our good, faithful Cuff, and no frightful spook at all. The good fellow had discovered our approach and came out to meet us, and I am sure the mule was as glad as I was to see him. He crawled through the brush and smelled at the mule's load and then went forward in the trail, which we followed. It was a long time after midnight when we reached camp. There was a good fire burning, but all were asleep till I led the mule up to the fire and called out, "Wake up!" when they were, most of them, on their feet in a minute without stopping to dress, for all had slept a long time without taking off their clothes.

John took charge of the mule and unloaded it, telling me to get into his warm bed. I took off my wet clothes and told him to dry them, and then got between the dry, warm blankets in greatest comfort. Daylight came very quickly, it seemed to me, and before I finally rose, the sun had been up some hours before me. Before I fell asleep I could hear the women say, as they cut off the pieces of meat to roast, "See the fat! Only see how nice it is!" Quickly roasted on the coals they ate the delicate morsels with a relish and, most of all, praised the sweet fat. "We like to have it all fat," said they, showing how their system craved the nourishment the poor, starved beef could not give.

No one went to bed after I came, but all sat and roasted meat and ate till they were satisfied.

This sporting trip was quite different from deer hunting in Wisconsin, and nothing like looking for game in Death Valley, where nothing lived. It was the hardest night's work that ever came to me in many a day, and not the wild sport I generally looked for when on the chase. I felt pretty well when I got up, and a chunk of my last night's prize which had been roasted for me was eaten with a relish, for it was the best of meat and I, of course, had a first-class appetite. I had to tell them my last hunting story and was much praised as a lucky boy.

We would not be compelled to kill any more of our poor oxen in order to live. So far we had killed six of them, and there were five left. Our present situation was much appreciated, compared with that of a few days ago when we were crawling slowly over the desert, hungry, sore footed, and dry, when to lie [down] was far easier than to take steps forward. We felt like rejoicing at our deliverance and there was no mourning now for us. The surrounding hills and higher mountains seemed more beautiful to us. They were covered with green trees and brush, not a desert place in sight. The clear little singing brook ran merrily on its way, the happiest, brightest stream in all my memory. Wild birds came near us without fear, and seemed very friendly. All was calm, and the bright sunshine exactly warm enough so that no one could complain of heat or cold.

When ready to move it was announced that I had lost my saddle blanket in my adventure, so they substituted another one and I took the back track to the place where the mule slipped down the bank, and there I found it. I soon overtook them again just as they were going to camp on Mrs. Bennett's account, as she had been suddenly taken sick with severe pain and vomiting, something as Rogers and I had been after eating our first California cornmeal. The rich, fat meat was too strong for her weak stomach.

Arcane all along had an idea that Rogers and I meant to surprise them by leading them to believe the house we had visited was quite a distance off, and then to so manage it that it should appear upon their sight suddenly. We assured them it would take two or more camps before we could get there, and if Mrs. Bennett did not soon recover, even more than that. Our camp here was under a great live oak, the ground deeply covered with dry leaves, and nearby a beautiful meadow where our cattle and mule ate, drank, and rested, the oxen chewing their cud with such an air of comfort as had not come to them since leaving their far-off eastern pastures. They seemed as much pleased as anyone. They would lie down and rest and eat at the same time in perfectly enjoyable laziness.

Here we all rested and washed such clothes as we could do without long enough to dry, and washed our faces and hands over and over again to remove the dirt which had been burned and sweated in so completely as not to come off readily. We sat on the bank of the brook with our feet dangling in the water, a most refreshing bath, and they too began to look clean again. We often saw tracks of the grizzly bear about, but in our ignorance had no fear of them, for we did not know they were a dangerous animal. An owl came and hooted in the night, but that was the only challenge any wild beast or bird gave to our peaceful and restful camp. We were out of the dreadful sands and shadows of Death Valley, its exhausting phantoms, its salty columns, bitter lakes, and wild, dreary, sunken desolation. If the waves of the sea could flow in and cover its barren nakedness—as we now know they might if a few sandy barriers were swept away—it would be indeed a blessing, for in it there is naught of good, comfort, or satisfaction, but ever in the minds of those who braved its heat and sands, a thought of a horrid charnel house, a corner of the earth so dreary that it requires an exercise of strongest faith to believe that the great Creator ever smiled upon it as a portion of his work and pronounced it "very good." We had crossed the great North American continent from a land of plenty, over great, barren hills and plains to another mild and beautiful region, where, though still in winter months, we were basking in the warmth and luxuriance of early summer. We thought not of the gold we had come to win. We were dead almost, and now we lived. We were parched with thirst, and now the brightest of crystal streams invited us to stoop and drink. We were starved so that we had looked at each other with maniac thoughts, and now we placed in our mouth the very fat of the land. We had seen our cattle almost perishing, seen them grow gaunt and tottering, seen them slowly plod along with hanging heads, and only the supremacy of human will over animal instinct had kept them from lying down, never to rise again. Now they were in pastures of sweet grass, chewing the cud of content and satisfaction. Life which had been a burden grew sweet to us, and though it may be that our words of praise to Him, whose will was to deliver us out of the jaws of death, were not set nor formal, yet His all-seeing eye saw the truth in our hearts, and saw there the fullest expression of our gratitude and thankfulness. Who shall say the thanks that arose were less acceptable because not given on bended knees before gilded altars?

Though across the desert and evidently in the long-promised land, our troubles and trials were not through by any means, but evidently we were out of danger. Our lives seemed to be secure, and we were soon to meet with settlers who would no doubt extend to us the hand of human sympathy. Many long miles yet remained between us and the rivers in whose sands were hidden the tiny grains of gold we came to seek.

The rest in the lovely camp had answered to cause Mrs. Bennett to feel quite well again by the next morning, and we made ready to proceed. We had the trail of the Jayhawkers to follow, so the vines, brambles, and tangles which had perplexed Rogers and myself in our first passage were now somewhat broken down, and we could get along very well without further clearing of the road until the hills came down so close on both sides that there was no room except in the very bed of the stream. There was no other way, so we waded along after the oxen as best we could. Sometimes the women fell down, for a rawhide moccasin soaked soft in water was not a very comfortable or convenient shoe, however it might be adapted to hot, dry sands. The creek was shaded and the water quite cool. The trail, such as it was, crossed the creek often and generally was nothing else than the stream itself. The constant wading and wet, cold clothing caused the women to give out soon and we selected the first dry suitable place which offered food for the oxen as a place to camp.

Wood was plenty and dry, so a good fire was soon burning, and the poor women, wet to the waist and even higher, were standing before it, turning round and round to get warm and dry. Someone remarked that they resembled geese hanging before the fire to roast, as they slowly revolved, and it was all owing to their fatigue that the suggestor did not receive merited punishment then and there at their hands. As they got a little dry and comfortable they remarked that even an excess of water like this was better than the desert where there was none at all, and as to their looks, there were no society people about to point their fingers at them, and when they reached a settled country they hoped to have a chance to change their clothes, and get two dresses apiece, and that these would be long enough to hide their knees, which these poor tatters quite failed to do. One remarked that she was sure she had been down in the brook a dozen times and that she did not consider cold-water baths so frequently repeated were good for the health.

Young Charlie Arcane had been getting better for some days. No medicine had been given him, and it was no doubt the change of air and water that had begun to effect a cure. Arcane had a hard time of it to keep the brush from pulling George and Melissa off of Old Crump into the water. It was indeed one of the hardest days' work of the whole journey, but no one was low-spirited, and all felt very well. The camping place was in a deep cañon, surrounded by thick brush, so that no wind came in to chill us. Everybody was cook and nobody was boss. Not a cent of money among us, nor any chance to use any if we had possessed it. We had nice, sweet, fat meat, cooked rare or well done as each one preferred, and no complaints about the waiters. The conditions were so favorable, compared with the terrible Death Valley and its surroundings, that everyone remarked about it, and no one felt in the least like finding fault with the little inconveniences we were forced to put up with. It might cure an inveterate faultfinder to take a course of training in the desert.

The next day we did not wade half as much, and after a few hours of travel we suddenly emerged from the brush into a creek bottom which was much wider, with not a tree to obstruct our way. The soil was sandy and covered more or less with sagebrush, and the stream which had been strong and deep enough to make us very wet now sank entirely out of sight in the sandy bottom. The hills were thinly timbered on the left side but quite brushy on the right, and we could see the track of cattle in the sand. No signs of other animals, but some small birds came near, and meadowlarks whistled their tune, quite familiar to us but still sounding slightly different from the song of the same bird in the East. High in the air could be seen a large, sailing hawk or buzzard.

We stopped to rest at noon and noticed that the water ran a little in the creek bed; but by the time we were ready to start we found none with which to fill our canteens. No doubt this water was poured into the cañon somewhere near the place where we killed the three cattle, and we had got out of it before the flood came down. It was astonishing to see how the thirsty sand drank up the quite abundant flow.

The next day we came down to the point of hill that nearly crossed the valley, and we crossed the low ridge rather than make a longer trip to get around by way of the valley. As we reached the summit there appeared before us as beautiful a rural picture as one ever looked upon: a large, green meadow of a thousand acres, more or less, its southwest side bounded by low mountains, at the base of which oak trees were plenty, but no brush or undergrowth. It was like a grand old park, such as we read of in English tales. All over the meadow cattle of all sorts and sizes grazed, the "ringstraked and speckled" of old Jacob's breed being very prominent. Some lazily cropped the grass; some still more lazily reclined and chewed their cud, while frisky calves exercised their muscles in swift races and then secured their dinners from anxious mothers. We camped at once[19] and took the loads from all the animals that they might feed in comfort on the sweet grass that lay before them.

We tarried here perhaps two hours, till the cattle stopped eating, and amply enjoyed the scene. Never again would anyone of the party go back over that dreary desert, they said, and everyone wondered why all places could not be as green and beautiful as this one. I cannot half tell how we felt and acted, nor what we said in our delight over this picture of plenty. The strong contrasts created strong impressions, and the tongues so long silent in our dry and dreary trouble were loosened to say everything the heart inspired. Think as much as you can; you cannot think it all.

We felt much better after our rest, and the oxen seemed stronger and better able, as well as more willing, to carry their loads, so we soon prepared to move on down the valley, toward the house we had spoken of as the goal we were to reach. It was now the seventh day of March, 1850, and this date, as well as the fourth day of November, 1849, will always remain an important one in memory. On the last-named day we left the trail to take the unfortunate cutoff, and for four long months we had wandered and struggled in terrible hardship. Every point of that terrible journey is indelibly fixed upon my memory, and though seventy-three years of age on April 6, 1893, I can locate every camp, and if strong enough, could follow that weary trail from Death Valley to Los Angeles with unerring accuracy. The brushy cañon we have just described is now occupied by the Southern Pacific Railroad, and the steep and narrow ridge pierced by a tunnel through which the trains pass. The beautiful meadow we so much admired has now upon its border a railroad station, Newhall, and at the proper season some portion of it is covered with thousands of trays of golden apricots, grown in the luxuriant orchards just beyond the hills toward the coast, and here drying in the bright summer sun. The cattle in the parti-colored coats are gone, but one who knows the ground can see our picture.

Loaded up again we start down the beautiful grassy valley, the women each with a staff in hand, and everything is new and strange to us. Rogers and I know that we will soon meet people who are strangers to us, who speak a strange language of which we know nothing; and how we, without a dollar, are to proceed to get our food and things we need are questions we cannot answer nor devise any easy way to overcome. The mines are yet five hundred miles away, and we know not of any work for us to do nearer. Our lives have been given back to us, and now comes the problem of how to sustain them manfully and independently as soon as possible. If worse comes to worst we can walk to San Francisco, probably kill enough game on the way and possibly reach the gold mines at last, but the way is not clear. We must trust much to luck and fortune and the ever faithful Providence which rarely fails those who truly try to help themselves.

We began to think some very independent thoughts. We had a mule to carry our camp kettle and meat. Our cattle were now beginning to improve and would soon get fat; these could carry our blankets and odd loads, while Old Crump the Christian could still carry the children. Bennett and I knew how to hunt and had good rifles. So we could still proceed, and we determined that, come what may, *we will be victorious.*

These were some of the plans we talked over at our camps and resting places, and as we walked along. If we could get the two families fixed in some way so they could do without Rogers and I, we could strike for the mines quite rapidly and no doubt soon get ourselves on good footing. We were younger than the rest and could endure more hardship. We decided to remain together till we got to Los Angeles, and then see what is best.

We reached our camping place at the foot of the hill, about a hundred yards from the house we had so long striven to reach.[20] Here we unloaded in the shade of a large willow tree, and scarcely had we removed the harness from the oxen when the good lady of the house and her little child came down to see us. She stood for a moment and looked around her and at the two small children on the blankets, and we could hear her murmur *mucha pobre* (very poor). She could see our ragged clothes and dirty faces and everything told her of our extreme destitution. After seeing our oxen and mule, which were so poor, she said to herself *"flaco, flaco"* (so thin). She then turned to us, Rogers and I, whom she had seen before, and as her lively little youngster clung to her dress, as if in fear of such queer looking people as we were, she took an orange from her pocket and, pointing to the children of our party, wanted to know if we had given them the four oranges she sent to them by us. We made signs that we had done as she requested, when she smiled and said *"Buenos muchachos"* (good boys). In all this talk neither could say a word the other could understand, and the conversation was carried on by signs.

Arcane said to her, "Me Catholic," which she seemed partly to comprehend and seemed more friendly. About this time two men rode up and took a look at us. Arcane, who was a Mason, gave the Masonic sign, as he told me afterward, but neither of them recognized it. We used such words of Spanish as I had taken down in my pass book and committed to memory, and by motions in addition to these made them understand something of the state of affairs, and that Mr. French who had assisted us before had told us we could get some meat *(carne)* from them. These men were finely mounted, wore long leggins made of hide (dressed with the hair on, which reached to their hips), stiff hats with broad rims, and great spurs at their heels. Each had a coil of braided rawhide rope on the pommel of the saddle, and all these arrangements together made a very dashing outfit.

They seemed to understand what we had said to them, for they rode off with a rush and came back in a short time, leading a fine, fat, two-year-old heifer. When near our camp the rider who was behind threw his *riata* and caught both hind feet of the animal, when, by a sudden movement of the horses, the heifer was thrown. One of them dismounted, and at the command the horse backed up and kept the rope tight while the man went up to the prostrate beast and cut its throat. As soon as it had ceased struggling, they loosened their ropes and coiled them up. They came to us and pointed to the dead heifer in a way which said, "Help yourselves."

We were much gratified at the generosity of the people, and at once dressed the animal as it lay, cutting off some good fat pieces which we roasted over the fire and ate with a relish. It seemed as if meat never tasted so good as that did—sweet, fragrant, and juicy. If some French cook could only cook a steak that would smell and taste to his customers as that meal tasted to us, his art would be perfect. We separated a hindquarter and hung it from a tree, and when the lady came back we told her that the piece we had selected was enough for our present use, so she caused the remainder with the hide to be taken to the house. Toward night they drove up a lot of cows and calves and other cattle into their cattle yard, or corral, as it is called all over California, a stockade of strong oak posts set deep in the ground and close together, enclosing a space of about half an acre. The horsemen now rode in and began to catch the calves with their ropes. It seemed as if they were able to throw a rope over a calf's head or around either leg they desired, with better aim and at as great a distance as one could shoot a Colt's revolver, and we saw at once that a good rawhide rope, in the hands of an experienced man and well-trained horse, was a weapon in many respects superior to firearms of any kind. A man near the gate loosened the ropes and pushed the calves into a separate corral till they had as many as they desired.

Rogers watched the circus till it was over and then returned to camp, meeting on the way Bennett and Arcane, with their wives and children, carrying some blankets, for the good lady had invited them to come up to the house and sleep. They said we could go down and keep camp if old dog Cuff was willing, for they had left him guarding the property. He was pleased enough to have us come and keep him company, and we slept nicely, disturbed only a little by the barking of the house dogs and the hooting of an owl that came to visit our tree.

The people came back to camp in the morning and had their experience to relate. Their hosts first baked some kind of slapjacks and divided them among their guests; then gave them beans seasoned hot with pepper, also great pieces of squash cooked before the fire, which they said was delicious and sweet—more than good. Then came a dish of dried meat pounded fine, mixed with green peppers and well fried in beef tallow. This seemed to be the favorite dish of the proprietors, but was a little too hot for our people. They called it *chili con carne*—meat with pepper—and we soon found this to be one of the best dishes cooked by the Californians. The children were carefully waited on and given special attention by these good people, and it was nearly ten o'clock before the feast was over; then the household had evening worship by meeting in silence, except a few set words repeated by some in turn, the ceremony lasting half an hour or more. Then they came and wished them *buenas noches* in the most polite manner and left them to arrange their blankets on the floor and go to sleep.

The unaccustomed shelter of a roof and the restless worrying of the children, who required much attention—for the change of diet had about the same effect on them as on Rogers and myself when we first partook of the California food—gave them little sleep, but still they rested and were truly grateful for the most perfect hospitality of these kindhearted people.

In the morning the two horsemen and two Indians went to the corral, where the riders would catch a cow with their ropes and draw her head up to a post, binding it fast, while an Indian took a short piece of rope and closely tied the hind legs together above the gambrel joint, making the tail fast also. They had a large bucket and several gourds. The Indians then milked the cows they had made fast, getting from a pint to two quarts from each one, milking into a gourd and pouring into the bucket till they had all they desired. The calves were separated the night before so they could secure some milk. Cows were not trained to stand and be milked as they were at home. Setting down the bucket of milk before us, with some small gourds for dippers, we were invited to drink all we wished. This was a regular banquet to us, for our famished condition and good appetites made food taste wonderfully. When we made a sign of wishing to pay them for their great kindness they shook their heads and utterly refused. It was genuine sympathy and hospitality on their part, and none of us ever forgot it; the sight of a native Californian has always brought out thoughts of these good people, and respect and thankfulness to the race. This rancho at which we were so kindly entertained was called San Francisquito, or Little San Francisco Rancho.[21]

This morning Mr. Arcane, with our assistance, made an arrangement with these people to give them his two oxen; and they were to take him, and his wife and child, to the seashore to a place called San Pedro, from which place he hoped, in some way, to get passage to San Francisco in a sailing vessel. He had no money, and no property to sell, except perhaps his spyglass, worth about ten dollars. With this poor prospect before him he started for the sea. He bade Bennett's folks good-bye, then came to me and put a light gold ring on my finger, saying that it and his interest in the little mule were mine. Then he gave his silver watch to Rogers and said it was all he had to give him, but if he had a million dollars, he would divide [it], and still think it a small compensation for the faithful services we had rendered him. "I can never repay you," said he, "for I owe you a debt that is beyond compensation. You have saved our lives, and have done it when you knew you could get nothing for it. I hope we will meet again, and when we do you will be welcome. If you hear of me anywhere, come and see me, for I want to tell my friends who Manly and Rogers are, and how you helped us. Good-bye!" Tears in his eyes, voice full of emotion, and the firm clasp of his hand told how earnest he was, and that he felt more than he could speak.

He helped Mrs. Arcane on her horse, then gave Charlie to her, and amid waving hands and many *adios* from our newfound friends, with repeated "good-byes" from the old ones, they rode away. Mrs. Arcane could hardly speak when she bade us farewell, she was so much affected. They had about sixty miles to ride to reach the sea, and as she rode on a man's saddle, and was unused to riding, I knew she would be sadly wearied before she reached the coast.

Our little train now seemed much smaller. Three oxen and a mule were all our animals, and the adults must still walk, as they had done on our desert route. But we were comparatively happy, for we had plenty of good meat to eat, plenty of sweet water to drink, and our animals were contented and improving every day; grass and water seemed plenty everywhere. We put our luggage on the oxen and the mule, loaded the children on Old Crump as we had done before, and were ready to move again. Our good friends stood around and smiled good-naturedly at our queer arrangements, and we, not knowing how to say what our hearts would prompt us to, shook their hands and said good-bye in answer to their *"adios amigos"* as we moved away, waving hands to each other.

The man then detained me a little while to ask me more about the road we had come over, how far it was and how bad the Indians were, and other particulars. I told him by signs that we had been twenty-two days on the road, and that the *Indianos,* as they called them, had not troubled us, but that there was very little grass or water in all that land. He made a sort of map on the ground and made me understand he would like to go back and try to bring out the wagons we had left behind, and he wanted me to go back with him and help him. I explained to him, by the map he had made, and one which I made myself, that I considered it impossible to bring them over. He seemed much disappointed, and with a shrug of his shoulders said *"mucho malo"* (very bad) and seemed to abandon the idea of getting a Yankee wagon. They very much admired an American wagon, for their own vehicles were rude affairs, as I shall by and by describe. We bade each other many *adios,* and I went on my way, soon catching up with the little party. We had been informed that it was ten leagues, or thirty miles, to Los Angeles, whither we were now headed.

We had now been a whole year on the road between Wisconsin and California, much of the time with the ground for a bed, and though our meals had been sometimes scanty and long between, very few of us had missed one on account of sickness. Some, less strong than we, had lain down to perish and had been left behind, without coffin or grave; but we were here, and so far had found food to nourish us in some degree with prospects now of game in the future if nothing better offered. We still talked of going to the gold mines on foot, for with good food and rest our courage had returned, and we wanted to succeed.

Our camp this night was in a nice watering place, where dry oak wood was plenty and grass abundant. It was at the foot of the San Fernando Mountain, not rocky, as we had found our road some time before, but smooth and covered with grass. It was rather steep to climb, but an infant compared with the great mountains so rough and barren we had climbed on our way from Death Valley.[22] Our present condition and state of mind was an anomalous one. We were happy, encouraged, grateful, and quite contented in the plenty which surrounded us, and still there was a sort of puzzling uncertainty as to our future, the way to which seemed very obscure. In the past we had pushed on [with] our very best and a kind Providence had kept us. This we did now, but still revolved the best plans and the most fortunate possibilities in our minds. We talked of the time when we should be able to show hospitality to our friends and to strangers who might need our open hand, as we had needed the favors which strangers had shown us in the last few days.

We ate our supper of good meat with a dessert of good beans our kind friends had given us, and enjoyed it greatly. As we sat in silence a flock of the prettiest, most graceful birds came marching along, and halted as if to get a better view of our party. We admired them so much that we made not a move, but waited, and they fearlessly walked on again. We could see that there were two which were larger than the rest, and from twelve to twenty smaller ones. The little topknot on the head and their symmetrical forms made them specially attractive, and Mrs. Bennett and the children were much pleased. The beauty of the California quail is especially striking to one who sees them for the first time.

In the morning we began to climb the hill, getting along very well indeed, for our rawhide moccasins were now dry and hard, and fitted the foot perfectly. We did not try to make great speed, but kept steadily on, and as we were used to climbing, we reached the summit easily. From this elevation we could get a fine view of the big grassy plain that seemed to extend as far as the eye could reach and, not far from us, the buildings and gardens of the San Fernando Mission. If we could shut out the mountains, the landscape would remind us of a great western prairie. We never could get over comparing this country with the desolate Death Valley, for it seemed as if such strange and striking opposites could hardly exist.

We rested here a little while and then wound our way down the hill to the level land. A few miles brought us to the mission houses and the church of San Fernando. There was not much life about them; in fact, they seemed comparatively deserted, for we saw only one man and a few Indians. The man brought some oranges and gave the children one each. After a little rest we moved on over our road, which was now quite smooth and gently descending. Night overtook us in a place where there was no water, but we camped and suffered no inconvenience. A stream was passed next day, and a house nearby, unoccupied. The road now began to enter gently rolling hills covered with big grass and clover, which indicated rich soil, and we never got tired of talking about it.

At the top of these hills we had another beautiful view as far south and west as the eye could reach. Small objects, probably horses and cattle, were scattered about the plain, grazing in the midst of plenty. Our own animals were given frequent opportunities to eat, and again and again we rejoiced over the beauty. Of course it was not such a surprise and wonder as it was when such a view first burst upon our sight, but it pleased and delighted us ever. On the east was a snowcapped peak, and here we were in the midst of green fields of grass and wildflowers, in the softest climate of an early spring. These strong contrasts beat anything we had ever seen. Perhaps the contrast between the great snow mountain and the hot Death Valley was greater in point of temperature, but there the heat brought only barrenness, and of the two, the snow seemed the more cheerful. Here the vegetation of all sorts was in full balance with the balmy air, and in comparison, the snow seemed a strange neighbor. It was quite a contrast to our cold, windy March in Wisconsin, and we wondered if it is always summer here. We were satisfied that even if we could get no further, we could live in such a land as this. The broad prairie doubtless belonged to the United States, and we could have our share and own a little piece of it on very easy terms, and raise our own cattle and corn. If the people were all as kind as those we had met, we were sure at least of neighborly treatment. I have endeavored to write this just as it seemed to us then and not clothe the impressions with the cover of later experience. The impressions we then daily received and the sights we saw were stranger than the wildest fiction, and if it so strikes you, my friendly reader, do not wonder.

As we came over the hills we could see a village near the southern base and it seemed quite near us. It was a new and strange sight to us as we approached. The houses were only one story high and seemed built of mud of a gray color, the roofs flat, and the streets almost deserted. Occasionally a man could be seen, sometimes a dog, and now and then an Indian, sitting with his back to the house. The whole view indicated a thinly populated place, and the entire absence of wagons or animals was a rather strange circumstance to us. It occurred to us at first that if all the emigrants were gone, our reception might be a cool one in this city of mud. One thing was in its favor and that was its buildings were about fireproof, for they had earthen floors and flat roofs. We rested half an hour or so just outside, and then ventured down the hill into the street. We met an American almost the first man, and when we asked about a suitable camping place, he pointed out the way and we marched on. Our strange appearance attracted the attention of the children and they kept coming out of the houses to see the curious little train with Old Crump carrying the children and our poor selves following along, dirty and ragged. Mrs. Bennett's dress hardly reached below her knees, and although her skirts were fringed about the bottom, it was of a kind that had not been adopted as yet in general circle of either Spanish-American or good United States society. The shortness of the dress made the curious rawhide moccasins only the more prominent, and the whole makeup of the party was a curious sight.

We went down the hill a little farther to the lower bottom to camp, while the barefooted, bareheaded urchins followed after to get a further look at the strangers. Before we selected a suitable place, we saw two tents and some wagons which looked like those of overland travelers, and we went toward them. When within fifty yards, two men suddenly came to their feet and looked at our little party approaching as if in wonder, but at twenty steps they recognized Bennett and came rushing forward. "My God! It's Bennett," said they, and they clasped hands in silence while one greeted Mrs. Bennett warmly. The meeting was so unexpected they shed tears and quietly led the way back to camp. This was the camp of R. G. Moody and H. C. Skinner, with their families.[23] They had traveled together on the Platte and became well acquainted, the warmest of friends, and knowing that Bennett had taken the cutoff, they more than suspected he and his party had been lost, as no sight of them had come to their eyes. They had been waiting here six weeks in order to get some reliable news, and now Mr. Bennett answered for himself. Rogers and I, belonging to another party, were of course strangers.

Leaving them to compare notes, Rogers and I took charge of Old Crump, the oxen, and the mule, unpacked them, and arranged camp under a monstrous willow tree. Bennett and his wife were taken into Mr. Moody's tent, and an hour or so later when Mrs. Bennett appeared again, she had her face washed clean, her hair combed, and a new clean dress. It was the first time we had found soap, and the improvement in her looks and feelings was surprising. Bennett looked considerably cleaned up too, and appeared bright and fresh. The children had also been taken in hand and appeared in new clothes selected from the wardrobe of the other children, and the old dirty clothes were put in process of washing as soon as possible.

Supper came, and it was so inviting. There was real bread and it looked so nice, we smiled when it was offered to us. Mrs. Bennett broke pieces for the children and cautioned them not to eat too much. It did seem so good to be among friends we could talk with and be understood. After supper was over and the things cleared away we all sat down in a circle and Bennett told the story of where he had been these many days, on the cutoff that was to shorten the trail. Mr. Moody said he had about given the party up and intended to start up the coast tomorrow. The story was so long that they talked till they were sleepy and then began again after breakfast, keeping it up till they had a good outline of all our travels and tribulations. This Mr. R. G. Moody, his wife and daughter, Mrs. Quinby, and son, Charles, all lived in San Jose and are now dead. H. C. Skinner was a brother-in-law of Moody and also lived a long time in San Jose, but himself, son, and one daughter are now dead.

Rogers and I now took the packsaddle we had borrowed of Mr. French to use on our trip to Death Valley and return, and carried it to the saloon on the east side of the plaza, where we were to place it if we got back safely, and delivered it to the man in charge, with many thanks to Mr. French for his favors to us, and sent him word that we would always remember him and be ready to do him a similar or equal favor if ever we were able. We considered him a good, benevolent man, and such he [had] proved to be when he offered us fat oxen, good beans, and any other thing we needed. He told the people in the house who we were, which no doubt influenced them kindly in our favor when we arrived.

At the saloon there was a large room with tables in it and gambling going on actively. Money changed hands very rapidly, drinks at the bar were frequent, and the whole affair moved forward with the same regularity as any mercantile business. The door stood wide open and anyone could come and go at his pleasure. Quite a number of black-eyed, fair looking women circulated among the crowd, and this, to us, seemed quite out of place, for we had never seen women in saloons before. We watched the game awhile to see some losing and some gaining, the result being quite exciting; but as neither of us had any money, we could not have joined in the game had we been so disposed; so we looked on awhile and then took a seat on the ground outside of the house.

Here we talked over our chances of getting to the mines. All the clothes we had were on our backs and feet and those were the poorest of the poor. We had no money. I had the little black-eyed mule, and Rogers had the watch Arcane had given him. Mr. Moody had said it was five hundred miles to San Francisco, and a hundred and fifty miles farther to the mines, so that after the hard travel of a year we were still a long way off from the place we started for.

We could not see any way to make a living here. There was no land cultivated, not a fence, nothing to require labor of any kind. The valley was rich enough and produced great crops of grass, and the cattle and horses we had seen grazing seemed to be about all the use they put it to. It looked as if the people must live principally on meat. I thought if we could manage to get a little provision together, such as flour and beans, that I could pack these on the mule, and I was pretty sure I could find game that would be better meat than we had lived on during the last two months in the desert.

We looked around to see if we could find something to do to earn a little for a start, but were not successful. In our walk about this city of mud we saw many things that seemed strange to us. There were more women than men, and more children than grown-up people, while the dogs were plenty. At the edge of the town, near the river were some grapevines fenced in with living willows, interlaced in some places with dry vines. The Indians moved very moderately around and no doubt had plenty of beef to eat, with very few wants to provide for. We noticed some few people paying for small things at the stores with small money. The women all dressed much alike. The dress was of some cheap material, sandals on feet, and a kind of long shawl worn over the head and thrown over the shoulder. There seemed to be neither hoops nor corsets in their fashions. The men wore trousers of white cotton or linen, with a calico shirt, sandals, and a broad-rimmed snuff-colored hat. The Indians and their wives went bareheaded.

Near the end of the street we came to a boardinghouse and went in and sat down in the empty room. Soon a man came in, better dressed than ourselves, and much to our surprise it was one of the old Death Valley travelers, the Reverend J. W. Brier, whom I last saw in his lone camp in the desert, discoursing to his young sons on the benefits of an early education. I know the situation struck me very strangely, with death staring them in the face and he preaching!

We had a long talk about the hard journey we had each experienced. As his party had not waited, they had come through ahead of us. He said himself and Mr. Granger had started a boardinghouse when they arrived, and had been doing a good business. He said that as long as the emigrants continued to come he could get along very well. We asked him if there was any chance for us to work and get money to get some provisions to help us on the way to the mines. He said he could give work to one of us hauling water for the house with oxen and cart, and the one who could manage oxen was the man. I was an ox driver and so told him I would take his team and cart and set out with the work. He said he could pay fifty dollars a month, and I accepted the offer quickly, as I saw it was a good chance to build up my exhausted strength and flesh.

I turned the little mule out in the hill nearby and began my work. It was not hard, for the boarders were thinning out. The natives did not patronize this hotel very much, but grub disappeared pretty fast at my corner of the table, for my appetite began to be ravenous. There was not much variety to the food and very few luxuries or delicacies, which were hard to obtain on such a bare market, but all seemed satisfied with the food, and to me it tasted extra good.

Rogers went back to the old camp and helped them there, and I often went over after dark, when my work was done. Moody and Skinner had been active in trying to get Mr. Bennett ready to go up the coast with them. Bennett had sold his repeating rifle and with the proceeds and the help of his friends had got another ox, making two yoke for him. They fixed up a wagon for him, and yokes enough could be found where people had traded off their oxen for horses. Provisions enough had been gathered by Moody and Skinner for them all, and Rogers would go along with the party to help them with the teams.

I was left alone after they started, and it was my idea to quit when I had worked a month and, if my mule stayed with me, to start for the mines even if I went alone. The majority of the male inhabitants of this town had gone to the mines, and this accounted for the unusual proportion of women. We learned that they would return in November, and then the gambling houses would start up in full blast, for these native Californians seemed to have a great natural desire to indulge in games of chance, and while playing their favorite game of monte would lay down their last *real* (12½ cents) in the hope of winning the money in sight before them on the table.

As the boardinghouse business got dull I was taken over to a vineyard and set to work, in place of hauling water. The entire patch was as green as a meadow with weeds, and I was expected to clean them out. I inquired of Brier how he came to get hold of this nice property, and he said that during the war the soldiers had taken possession of this piece of ground, and had their camp here, so he considered it was government land, and therefore had squatted on it and was going to hold it and pay for it as regular government land, and that he already considered it his own, for said he, "I am an American, and this is a part of the public domain." "All right," said I, "I will kill weeds for you, if you wish, when I have time to spare and you don't want the oxen worked at any other work."

I could see every day that I was improving in health and weight and would soon become myself again, able to take the road to the mines. When about two weeks of my time had expired, two oldish men came to the house to stop for a few days and reported themselves as from Sacramento, buying up some horses for that market. Thus far they had purchased only six or eight, as they had found the price too high to buy and then drive so far to a market to sell again. They had about decided to go back with what they had and undertake some other kind of business. I thought this would be a pretty good chance for me to go, as I would have company, and so went to Brier and Granger and told them what I would like to do, and that with their permission I would quit and go on with them. They readily consented, for their money was coming in rather slow, and they paid me twenty-five dollars for half a month's work. This made me feel pretty rich and I thought this would give me food enough to reach the mines.

Having two or three days to get ready in, I began doing the best I could. I found an old saddletree[24] which had been thrown away, and managed to fix it up so I could use it. I also found an old gun some traveler had left, and with a little work I fitted the breech of that to my own gun, which was broken and had been roughly tied together with strips of rawhide. I now had a good, sound gun [even] if it was not very handsome. I bought a Spanish blanket, not so wide as ours, but coarse and strong, and having a hole in the center through which to put the head and wear it as a garment in case of storm, or at night. I went to a native store and bought a supply of *carne seca* (dried beef) and some crackers, put some salt in my pocket, and was now provisioned for another trip. I found my mule in the hills back of town, not far from where I left her, and the rest and good feed had made her look better and feel better, as well as myself.

The drovers had found two other men who wanted to go with them and help drive the horses for their board. I put my blanket on under the saddle, packed my little sack of meat and crackers on behind, and when I was in the saddle with my gun before me I considered I was pretty well fixed and able to make my way against almost anything. I said to myself that the only way now to keep me from getting to the gold mines was to kill me. I felt that there was not a mountain so high I could not climb, and no desert so wide and dry that I could not cross it. I had walked and starved and choked and lived through it, and now I felt so strong and brave I could do it again—any way to reach the gold mines and get some of the "dust."

I had not much idea how the gold from the mines looked. Everybody called it gold dust, and that conveyed an idea to me that it was fine as flour, but how to catch it I did not know. I knew other people found a way to get it, and I knew I could learn if anybody could. It was a great longing that came to me to see some of the yellow dust in its native state, before it had been through the mint.

At the last meal I took at the house, there were only a few at the table. Among them was a well-dressed Californian who evidently did not greatly fancy American cooking, but got along very well till Mrs. Brier brought around the dessert, a sort of duff. This the Californian tasted a few times and then laid down his spoon saying it was *no bueno,* and some other words I did not then understand, but afterward learned that they meant "too much grease." The fellow left the table not well pleased with what we generally consider the best end of a Yankee dinner, the last plate.

While here, I had slept in a small storeroom, where I made my pallet out of old rags and blankets. While I was looking round for material to make my bed I came across a bag partly full of sugar, brought from Chile. It was in very coarse crystals, some as large as corn. There were some other treasures and luxuries there that perhaps I was expected [to] guard. I, however, had a sweet tooth, and a handful or so of the sweet crystals found their way into my pocket.

I bade Mr. Brier and the rest good-bye and rode away to join my company.

CHAPTER XII

Dr. McMahon's Story

Leaving the little party whose wanderings we have followed so closely safely arrived in Los Angeles—their further history in California will be taken up later on—this narrative will go back to points when the original party was broken up and trace the little bands in their varied experiences. It will be remembered that the author and his friends, after a perilous voyage down Green River, halted at the camp of the Indian chief Walker, and there separated, the author and four companions striking for Salt Lake, while McMahon and Field remained behind, fully determined to go on down the river.

The story of these two men is told by McMahon in the following interesting letter.[1]

DEAR MANLY:

YOURS REQUESTING ME TO GIVE YOU A SYNOPSIS of the history of incidents, experience, and observations of our mutual friend, Richard Field, and myself, from the time you, John Rogers, Alfred Walton, and the Hazelrig brothers left us at the camp of the generous old Chief Walker on the west bank of the river near the mouth of the "great seven days cañon," is at hand.

You no doubt distinctly, and with pleasure, remember that unbroken friendship which existed among us up to the time of our separation and that we parted warm and tried friends.

Well, after you and your companions had left us, we set to work to prepare the canvas for the continuation of the voyage down the river. We drilled holes through the sides of the *Pilot*—you, I have no doubt, remember which that was, yours and mine, in which we took so many fearful risks, and *No. 2,* so that we might in case of necessity lash the two together. After a day or two Field lost courage and finally determined to go no farther down the river. Chief Walker, in the meantime, had repeated his friendly warnings appertaining to the great danger in going farther down the river. You will remember what he had told us about it before you left us.

You know that I was the biggest coward of the whole seven; but I assumed courage and told Field that I would go down the river alone; and, for a time, I thought I would do so; but after some reflection I concluded that, perhaps, discretion was the better part [of] valor, and reluctantly gave it up. We now decided to follow you, or to take some other unknown route and try to make our escape out of this most perilous condition.

We then set about, as you had done, to trade with Walker for a pony or two, and after much dickering Field succeeded in getting the afterwards famous, big, old, sore-backed mule. You may not remember him, but I do; and, notwithstanding his sore back, he made pretty good beef. I, with pins, needles, thread, a pocketknife, a handkerchief, etc., succeeded in getting a very nice, round, three-year-old, iron gray pony.

After making packsaddles, and getting almost ready to start, we were, through Walker's kindness and persuasiveness, overcome, and consented to go with him, feeling confident that we would not starve to death while with him. We did not now have Manly with his long experience, and his old, rusty, but always trusty, rifle as a sure defense against possible hunger and starvation.

The old chief, and, in fact, the whole tribe, seemed pleased when we consented to go with them. Preparations were now made, and all, except the horses and four head of cattle, was conveyed across the river in the two canoes which were lashed together, while the horses and cattle were forced to swim to the other side, where we camped for the night. Next morning the clever old chief had two good horses fitted up in good style for Field and I, which we rode all of the nine days that we remained with the band, while our own ran with the herd. Our baggage was carried on some of the chief's packhorses. We were, in fact, his honored guests, as will hereafter appear.

All were soon mounted and off to the buffalo fields, Walker having informed us that he intended going up into the buffalo country on the head-waters of Grand River, where he would remain until snow fell, when he would go to Salt Lake City or vicinity.

Leaving the river, we set out across a not entirely barren plain, for there was much sagebrush, and several varieties of cactus. Towards evening we came close up to the foot of a range of rugged, rocky mountains, where we found water and camped for the night. Field and I usually pitched our little muslin tent somewhere near our friends, where we could sleep without fear of man or beast, for I think someone of the reds was always on guard.

All went well for four or five days, when we all got entirely out of food except a few ounces of flour, which we had hidden away for a possible emergency. During the following two days and nights all were entirely without food except the two little children, whom you no doubt remember. We gave their mother a little flour now and then, which she mixed with a little milk which one of the cows afforded, for the little ones. These Indians did not seem to suffer for want of food; even when we were starving, they appeared happy and contented, and one young fellow would sing all day long while we were starving. During the second day of starvation and hard traveling over hot and barren deserts, the Indians killed a wildcat and two small rabbits. We got nothing. You will remember that all the arms of the seven men were lost in the river when the canoes were sunk, except your rifle and my double-barreled shotgun and revolver, so that Field and I had only the one gun, and neither of us knew anything about hunting. When we camped, one of the boys brought over to our tent a quarter of the cat, which was more than a fair share of the whole supply, as twenty-two of them had only the two little rabbits and three-quarters of the unfortunate cat. We boiled and boiled and boiled that cat's hind leg, but never got it done. We waited as long as we possibly could, gave up in despair and put a little flour into the broth to thicken it, and drank it. It was not good, but much better than the meat of the cat. That cat and the rabbits were all the twenty-four of us had to eat, after fasting two days, until late in the evening of the next day.

My people were religious, and when I was young the family was wont to observe fast days, but never did we have any such long fasts as these were. In the afternoon of the next day the old chief left the caravan and went on ahead of the train toward a chain of mountains, first giving some directions to the band, and taking one son with him. When we arrived in a small cañon in the edge of the mountains we found them with a fine mountain sheep, which they had killed and brought down to the dim, little-used trail where we camped; and after we had set up our little tent as usual, a short distance away from our friends, one of the young men brought to us about one-fourth of the sheep, while the twenty-two Indians had the rest.

You know that a good-sized mountain sheep would make a fair supper for twenty-four people, even though they had been starving three or four days; but this was a small one, and I think Field and I ate about half of the quarter. The twenty-two Indians soon devoured the three-fourths and all of the soft viscera, including the stomach and intestines, after which some of the boys came to our tent while we were stuffing what had been for several days our empty stomachs. We offered them part of our bounteous supply of mutton, having much more than we could eat; but no, they would not touch it until we were filled full, when they accepted what was left, and soon stowed it away. All were now pretty well filled up once more.

The next day was spent without food, traveling over rough mountains. Within a pass, late in the afternoon, we crossed the fresh trail of some other band of roving redskins, and Walker suspected who they were and went into camp early. The Indians had killed nothing that day, but I had killed a small rabbit which, unfortunately for it, came my way during the day. This we offered to the women for themselves and the little children; but they positively refused to accept it, insisting that they did not want it or need it, and that the small supply of milk from the cow was quite sufficient for the little ones, and the others spurned the offer to divide so little a thing, so we had it all to ourselves.

It appeared that these people were accustomed to go for long periods without food, and with little apparent inconvenience; but Field and I began to feel as I suppose Dr. Tanner felt after a few days' fasting, and began to wish that the old chief would get hungry and kill one of his large, fat steers, but he still held them in reserve.

Early the next morning, now nine days from the time we had left the river, the old chief took two of the young men and left camp, as we afterwards learned, to go in search of the Indians whose trail we had crossed the evening before. Sometime in the early part of the night, one of the young men returned and informed us that they had found the wandering tribe, and that we were to go back to their trail and follow it to their camp up in a southeast direction, Walker and one of the young men having remained with their newfound friends.

Field and I both felt greatly disappointed in not being able to proceed north; and in the meantime we had become very tired of the society of these people, notwithstanding the fact that they were exceedingly clever; but we were almost starved to death, and had about come to the conclusion that we would be obliged to make some change. We were still on the east side of, and considerable distance from, the river, and probably not more than one hundred or one hundred and twenty miles from the place where we parted from you.

The chief had sent particular instructions for us to go with the tribe; but, after canvassing the whole situation, we decided to part company with our good friends, proceed northward, and try to reach Fort Bridger[2] or some other settlement in the northwest, and so informed them, and requested the boys to bring in our mule and horse, which they did after failing to induce us to go with them.

Bright and early the next morning, they all, even the polygamous wives and little children, in apparent sorrow, bade us good-bye and were off, leaving us alone with our two poor, lonely, four-footed companions, who were very anxious to follow the band of horses. After the rather melancholy parting we arranged our packs, and about ten o'clock started out on what then seemed, and afterwards proved to be, a perilous voyage through deserts and over rough mountains. To avoid a high range of mountains, our course was for a time northeast, but after passing that range we bore to the northwest.

The days were quite warm, but the nights were cold. During the first day we killed and ate one small rabbit, and this, with a few seed buds gathered from wild rosebushes, constituted two days' rations. On the third we did not have even the rabbit or rose seed buds, but late in the afternoon we found some small red berries, similar in appearance to what I, in my childhood, knew and relished as Solomon's-seal berries. I being a natural coward, and fearing that they might poison me, did not eat any of them, but generously allowed my good friend to eat them all.

We had now been almost entirely without water for two days and nights. When night came on we picketed our animals in a grass plot and lay down near them to see that they did not get tangled in the ropes and hurt, or that some redskin, not having the fear of the Lord in his heart, did not come and take them away. About ten o'clock my companion began to complain of pain in his stomach and bowels, and was soon vomiting at a fearful rate, so violently, indeed, that I was apprehensive that he might die. If I had had an emetic I would have given it to him to have assisted nature in pumping those devilish little red berries out of him, for I felt quite sure that they were the cause of his illness. Perhaps it was fortunate that there was no medicine at hand, for if there had been I might have killed him with it.

He suffered most intensely, and soon became very thirsty, and there being no water within many miles of us, he appealed to me to bleed one of the animals and let him drink the blood; I refused; he insisted; I again refused; he commanded; I still refused. He swore, and called me almost everything except a good Christian; he even expressed the wish that I, his friend, might be sent to a certain place where the heat is most intense and the fire is never quenched.

At about eleven o'clock, when his pains were most severe, a dark cloud, the first we had seen for months, came over us, and a little rain began to fall. I at once opened our little camp kettle and turned the lid upside down, and into both kettle and lid there fell perhaps two or three teaspoonfuls of pure water, every drop of which I gave to the sufferer, whereupon he expressed thanks for another godsend, and at once apologized for bestowing unmerited abuse on me. He afterwards often asserted that he believed that the little rain cloud was sent by God for his special benefit, and that the water caught from that cloud was the sweetest and best that he had ever tasted. I did not doubt the latter half of the above statement, but I did have some doubt about the truth of the former half when I called to mind the scene which followed my refusal to bleed the horse. Whether the small quantity of water gave him much relief or not, I do not know, but I do know that he soon became better and slept some while I watched. He was quite feeble next morning when I put him on the old sore-backed mule, where he rode most of the time for the next four days, while the little horse carried our baggage and I led the way as usual, on foot.

For four days from the time Field ate the little red berries we did not have a drop of water except the two or three teaspoonfuls which the stingy cloud left to save the life of the "berry eater." We were still on the desert, or in the mountains east of the river, traveling hard during the day and burning up with fever in the night. There was plenty of drying grass in places, but our poor animals could not eat it any longer, for they, too, were burning up for want of water. Oh, how much I did wish that we had some camels from Arabia, which could have gone so much longer without water and traveled so much faster.

On the morning of the third day of starvation, we determined to change our course, and, if possible, reach the river once more, bearing to the left over a high, barren range of rocky mountains, and down into a plain of sand, sagebrush, and cactus. During the afternoon I shot a small rabbit, not much larger than a rat, which we carried until night, then broiled and tried to eat it, not because our appetites craved it, but hoping that it might strengthen and sustain us at least a little while longer. We were, however, so nearly burned up that there was not a sufficient flow of saliva to moisten the little bits of broiled meat in the mouth. Late that afternoon we fancied that our fast-failing brute companions scented water, or that they instinctively knew that it was not far away. They would raise their heads and extend their noses as if smelling, while their physical force and energy seemed renewed, and they certainly traveled faster.

That night we ate the little [rabbit], as before stated, more as a duty than as a pleasure. There was some green grass round about where we camped, or, more properly speaking, where we lay, for we did not erect our little tent, but the poor starving animals did not eat a bite of it, but stood over us as if in sympathy with us in our deplorable condition. We rose before the sun, being somewhat rested and refreshed, for the night had been cool, and took up our line of march: I, as usual, in the lead, then came the old mule guided by its precious owner, and lastly, the faithful little horse with the pack on his still quite round back; on over the still dry and barren plain we went, without a Moses, cloud, or pillar of fire to lead us.

About ten o'clock, through the hot glimmer of the down-pouring rays of the sun, we saw what appeared, and afterwards proved to be, a clump of cottonwood trees. Our hopes and courage were renewed, for we well knew the cottonwood usually grows near flowing water. There was no beaten pathway, no signs of animal life, no quails, no manna in that desert; but on we went, almost without a halt, and at one o'clock reached the cottonwood grove, immediately on the bank of the great river down which we had floated in our canoes more than a month before. On reaching the bank of the river we recognized objects which we had seen while on our way down.

We remembered that both men and horses might be water-foundered,[3] and that self-preservation is said to be the first law of nature; but it was difficult to prevent the famishing brutes from plunging into the river. We allowed them to take only a small quantity at first, and each of us took only a small cupful; then after a little time all took more, and the thirst was soon quenched. We were surprised to find how little water it took to satisfy the raging thirst of four days of continued fasting. The animals, after taking comparatively small quantities, seemed satisfied, and went off in search of grass.

We now had an abundance of water, but we well knew that water alone would not sustain life very long: therefore our next and most serious business was to determine how to prolong our lives. According to our map, our recollections of different objects, and present appearances, we were now a little above the mouth of the Uinta River, which comes in from the northwest, all of which proved true. Our little map pictured Fort Uinta[4] on the Uinta River about one hundred miles from where we were; but whether or not there were any human beings there, we did not know, and in order to determine, we must cross this great river and travel a hundred miles, and this seemed a perilous undertaking for us in our present starving condition; but after being refreshed by plenty of good water we determined to undertake it, hoping that good fortune might attend us.

After a little rest, the animals with grass, we packed up, and after Field had put on his once serviceable life preserver, he mounted the old mule behind the small pack and started to swim across the river. He took the lead in this instance for three reasons: first, we thought that the mule, being much older than the horse, had probably had more experience and therefore might be a much better swimmer; then Field had the advantage in having the life preserver; but the last and most potent reason was my fear of getting drowned. It was understood that I was to remain on shore and be ready to assist him if necessary, or until he had safely landed on the other side.

In he went, and the trusty old mule was swimming faithfully, and had reached the middle of the river, when Field, as he afterwards told me, to hurry the mule gave a gentle jerk on the bridle, when, to his utter astonishment, the mule made a complete somersault backwards, plunging Field, the pack, and himself entirely under the water, except his heels, which appeared above the water as his head went under. In a moment Field popped up and, after shaking his head as a swimmer will do after taking a plunge, cast about to take his bearings, or to determine just where he was, and began to paddle with his hands, much as he did when the canoes were upset on the river, or somewhat after the style of a swimming dog. On coming to the surface, the mule cast a glance at the still living, but unloaded, portion of his cargo, then made a beeline for the shore which he had so recently left. While Field continued to paddle and float down the river, I dismounted and followed along the bank, trying to encourage him to renewed efforts to float ashore. Finally he passed behind a clump of willows out of sight; but soon I heard him call for help and, on going a little farther down, found him stuck fast in the mud. I waded waist deep into that mud, and literally dragged him out, almost a mile below his starting point.

As we were struggling in this muddy swamp, Field said he wondered why some of this superfluous water was not distributed over those dry deserts from which we had so recently come. I told him, politely, that I thought that a man of his age, ability, opportunities, and nationality (you know he was quite proud of being an Englishman) ought to know why the moisture was not so distributed, and that I was too illiterate to enlighten him on that point, but that, when opportunity offered, he might consult someone who knew more of natural science than I did. I informed him that I had an idea that if any considerable portion of the water of that river had been distributed over that desert that we would not have had the experience of the last fifteen days, whereupon he very plainly intimated that I did not have much sense, or, in other words, he called me a d—d fool.

After reaching solid ground and resting for a little while, we returned to the place from which he had started out on his perilous voyage, and where I had hastily left my horse. We found the horse and mule quietly grazing with their packs on their backs. The faithful old mule had the appearance of having been wet, but was now almost dry, yet not so dry, internally, as he had been several days before.

What shall we do now? We are perhaps two hundred or more miles from any white settlement. We do not know that Fort Uinta is occupied. Shall we make another attempt to cross the river? I asked my brave friend if he was willing to again mount the mule and make another attempt, when he again exclaimed, "You must be a d—d fool!" I then, pretending to have a little courage, asked him if he would follow, provided I would lead, whereupon he declared most emphatically that under no conditions would he again attempt to swim across that river. I had not had his experience, but fear of being drowned was quite sufficient to prevent me from undertaking the perilous task, more especially after witnessing his failure.

Well, what next? We could not depend upon fishing and hunting, for we had no fishhooks, nor means of catching fish, and not more than a dozen loads of shot, and a little powder; so the matter of slaying one of our animal friends was now seriously debated, and, after thoroughly canvassing the whole situation, it was most reluctantly determined that, however hard, this must be done. No doubt our starving condition at that particular time had some weight in making this decision.

Then the question was, which of the animals shall be sacrificed? The mule was quite thin, and probably tough, while the little horse was young, and notwithstanding the many days it had, with all of us, starved and traveled without water, was still quite plump and round, and probably tender, or at the worst, not so tough as the poor old docile mule; so, at length we decided to kill the innocent little creature, jerk his flesh, pack it on the mule, and thereby try to save our own lives, for a time at least, and endeavor to reach some place of safety.

The matter of slaying the horse was determined by casting lots, neither being willing to perform that melancholy, but now absolutely necessary, act. It fell to my lot, and that was one of, if not the most, revolting act in my whole life's experience, for I had probably become as strongly attached to that little horse as man ever becomes attached to animal. I most reluctantly took the bridle in my left hand, my revolver in my right, stood directly in front of the poor, unsuspecting, innocent creature with the murderous pistol close to, and a little above, a line extending from eye to eye, and fired. When the smoke of the powder had cleared off a little, I saw at my feet the quivering, dying body. I staggered off a few steps and sat down, sick at heart.

Field walked several steps away, and turned his back upon the scene until after the fatal shot had been fired; then, after some little time, he entered upon his share of the enforced duty and, after having removed a portion of the skin, cut off some slices of flesh and brought them to a fire I had started.

We broiled and ate a little of it, not through desire or relish for it, but from a sense of duty, knowing that our lives depended upon it.

It is said that for many years Dr. Franklin refrained from eating flesh, having an idea that it was wrong to slay and eat the flesh of other creatures; but that he changed his mind, and his diet too, after having seen large fish devour small ones. I strongly suspect that if the doctor had been with us, or in a like condition, even before his conversion, he would more than likely have taken a little flesh, even though it had been a piece of his own favorite horse.

I said we only ate a little at first: I only ate a little for two reasons; first, I did not relish the food; second, I had heard of persons being killed by eating too much after fasting for a long time, and I had no desire to commit suicide just then. Field ate too much. Night came on, work was suspended, and we retired. The poor old lone and, no doubt, now lonely mule, having filled himself with grass, came up near the now terribly mutilated remains of his late companion, and looked on as Field continued his bloody work. Field, with an expression of sorrow, said, "If that mule could reason and look forward to the time when his body might be in a like condition as that of this horse, he would, no doubt, take to his heels, bid us a final farewell, and seek other society." But, fortunately for us, he did not know that he was to be held in reserve for our future security. He was securely tied up every night from that time until the day he was slain for our salvation.

Early in the night following that eventful day, my companion began to complain much as he had done on the night after he had eaten the little red berries; but there was no lack of water now, no need of a special rain cloud. I got up, heated water in our little camp kettle, applied hot cloths to his aching belly, and did everything else that either of us could think of for his relief. The pain was intense, and we feared that he would surely die, and earnestly prayed all the rest of the night that he might be relieved and get well. Towards morning most violent vomiting came on, which continued for thirty hours or more. He was not able to walk for three days, and during that time I nursed him, finished jerking the meat, and built a raft of some partly rotten logs which I found in the vicinity, on which we floated across the river on the fourth day after our arrival here. I also looked to the welfare of the mule, and prepared some bags in which to carry our jerk. Manly, I am sure that you know the meaning of the term "jerk" so that a definition of the word is not at all necessary.

The old logs of which the raft was made were remnants of log cabins, a number of which had been built and occupied more than half a century before, but by whom I do not know. Field remarked that the finding of these old rotting logs there was another godsend, as we then had neither ax, hammer, nor any tool of iron with which to cut down a tree. I bound these logs together with long strips cut from the hide of the dead horse. Paddles and poles were also provided. The mule was with difficulty driven across the river.

When the raft was landed on the west bank, the mule packed, and all about ready to start, I took the long strip of rawhide from the raft and tied one end of it around the mule's neck, mounting Field on the mule behind the large pack, which made the whole outfit look quite comical indeed. Before leaving the other side of the river I had discovered that the saddle girth was not very strong, so I cut a wide belt from the hide of the lately slaughtered horse and fitted it to the saddle as a girth, knowing that the pack, now containing all of our goods and a supply of more than a bushel of jerk, would be quite bulky, if not heavy, and more difficult to keep on the back of a mule than it is for the camel to maintain his hump on his back. This girth afterwards made us two or three pretty substantial meals, as did also the long strip of green, wet hide, one end of which I had tied round the mule's neck, allowing it to drag for a long distance through the hot, dry sand.

All being ready, I, as usual, took the lead, with my shotgun, which I always carried, but with which I seldom killed anything, on my shoulder. The old mule followed with his high, towering pack and Field almost hidden behind. It was noon, but we did not stop for dinner, but simply reached into one of the great bulging sacks, took out a piece of jerk, and ate it as we went marching on; no more trouble now about cooking. Late in the afternoon we reached Uinta River, and as my two-legged companion had grown very tired of the back of the four-legged one, we went into camp early. Our objective point was Fort Uinta, where we hoped to find military. We could not risk turning the mule loose at night, and the long strip of rawhide was designed and used to secure him, and yet to afford him liberty to graze while we slept. As you will see a little further on, both girth and lariat were used for a purpose not anticipated.

The second, third, fourth, and fifth days came and went, and we were trudging on, up the Uinta, through a mostly very barren country, with some little rich and fertile land. We saw signs of Indians often, but no Indians. There was much cottonwood, but little other timber. We saw some fish in the river which we coveted, but could not get. The main course of this river is from northwest to southeast. We traveled most of the way to the fort on Indian trails, some of which were much worn, but mostly at some much earlier period. Of course we had plenty of good water, and food, such as it was. Field did not walk two miles during those five days, but seemed to be fattening fast. I sometimes thought he might be just a little lazy, but I never told him so, for I realized that he had recently had a severe tussle with death.

Early in the morning of the sixth day we arrived at the abandoned old fort. There were only three log buildings, and they were in the shape of three sides of a hollow square, with portholes on the outer faces of the buildings, and doors entering each of them from the hollow square or court. Facing the vacant side of the court, the porthole from which I shot the wolf on the night after we had killed the mule would be on right-hand side. We were unable to determine whether this fort had been constructed and occupied by Americans or Mexicans, but from its apparent age, we were inclined to the opinion that it was Mexicans. It had not been occupied for, probably, three or four years. Some little farming had been done immediately around the fort. Surrounding the fort is a large body of fine, fertile land which I have no doubt has long since been occupied by Mormons or other enterprising people.

Having no means of subsistence here, we soon decided to push on towards Fort Bridger, and, after resting a few hours, set out following the larger fork of the river which comes almost directly from the north. We now believed that we were almost, if not exactly, due south of Fort Bridger. The river is small and very crooked; we crossed it many times within three days, and at the end of that time, found ourselves in the mouth of a rocky cañon, and after struggling for one whole day, we came to where the steep, high stone walls closed the little river in on both sides, rendering it impossible for us to proceed any farther.

We were now nearly out of food; the jerk was almost gone. A council was held, and it was decided that we should return to the fort and take chances of being rescued, or scalped by some roving band of reds, or starving to death. We at once set out on our return, full of disappointment and melancholy forebodings.

The next day found us without food: and now came into use the long, narrow strip of rawhide which first bound together the old, rotting logs of which the raft was made, then to secure the mule of nights. It was now almost as hard as bone, and nearly round, having been dragged through the hot sand while it was yet green and wet, closed up like a hollow tube with sand inside. Two or three yards of it at a time was cut into pieces about five inches long, the hair singed off, the sand scratched out, and these pieces were dropped into our camp kettle and cooked until the whole formed one mass of jelly or gluten which was, to us, quite palatable. When the lasso had all been thus prepared and eaten, the broad girth which had served so well in holding the packsaddle on the mule's back was cleaned, cooked, and eaten. These substitutes for jerk sustained us very well till we again arrived at the fort.

Another consultation was now held, and the question was—what shall we do now? We were again, apparently, at the starting point of another long, enforced fast. Our path seemed hedged in. The prospect was, indeed, very gloomy. Our only reasonable hope for even the temporary prolongation of our lives was centered in our ever faithful and always reliable old mule. We revolted at the idea of killing and eating him, but the last bit of the girth was gone. After canvassing the whole situation over and over, again and again, we finally, but most reluctantly, decided to kill the mule, and preserve all the soft parts, even the skin with all of its old scars, and then gather in whatever else we could find, and stay here until spring, or until good fortune might afford us some means [of] escape—till some Moses might come and lead us out of this wilderness, notwithstanding the fact that we had not borrowed any jewelry which we had failed to return.

There were signs of wolves in that vicinity, and it was decided that the mule be slain about ten paces distant and directly in front of one of the portholes of the fort with the idea that wolves might smell the blood and come there and subject themselves to being shot, and thereby afford us a chance to increase our stock of winter supplies in the form of wolf steak, or jerk. Accordingly the victim was led to the spot indicated, and there slain in the same manner, and with quite as much reluctance on the part of the slayer as on the occasion of the sacrifice of the little horse more than three weeks before. The body was skinned, cut up, and all taken within the building, nothing being left except the blood which had been spilled on the ground, and which was intended to attract wolves or, possibly, bears or other animals.

My now only living associate ridiculed the idea of killing wolves, and insisted that the flesh could not be eaten, stating the fact that even hogs would not eat the dead body of a dog, and insisted that a dog was only a tamed wolf. I reminded him of a cat which had been eaten. He finally agreed that, if I killed a wolf, he would get up and dress it, but said most emphatically that he would not sit up and watch for it; so he went to bed, that is, rolled himself up in a blanket on the ground in front of a good fire inside of the fort and went to sleep, while I sat with my rather untrustworthy double-barreled shotgun protruding through the porthole in full view of the spot before indicated. The night was clear, and the moon was shining in full splendor. It was probably eleven o'clock; Field had been snoring for a long time, when I heard something in the tall, dry grass, and soon a large, brownish gray wolf came into full view, with head up, apparently sniffing, or smelling, and cautiously approaching the fatal spot. When he reached it, and began to lick up the blood which was still on the surface of the ground, standing with his left side toward the fort, and in full view, I took deliberate aim, and fired, and he fell upon the ground without making any considerable noise.

The tired, sleeping man was aroused by the report of the gun, and rushed into the room where I was, in great excitement, thinking perhaps that some enemy had appeared and had just then commenced to bombard the fort; but when I explained to him that I had simply killed a wolf, he ran out towards it, and, arriving close to it, the wounded creature rose up on its hind feet and growled quite vigorously, which seemed to frighten Field as much as did the noise of the gun. He dashed back to the fort and, after having time to recover from his speechless condition, abused me most fearfully for having told him that I had killed a wolf. I then went out and put a load of shot into the wolf's head, and found that my first charge had passed through and broke both of its forelegs near the body. Field was so thoroughly frightened that I could not induce him to approach the dead animal for some time, and I do believe that that wolf haunted him as long as I knew him, for he seemed never to forget it.

After dressing it by the light of the moon, assisted by a torch, we retired. On viewing the plump body next morning Field exclaimed, "That's another godsend!" and notwithstanding his opinion that wolf could not be eaten, he found that wolf to be the best food we had eaten since we had assisted Walker and his tribe in eating the mountain sheep.

The French may eat their horses, but I do not want more horse flesh. The old mule made fair but quite coarse beef. While out on this little pleasure(?) excursion we ate horse, mule, wolf, wildcat, mountain sheep, rose seed buds, rawhide, a squirrel, fatty matter from the sockets of the mule's eyes and the marrow from his bones; but that ham of wildcat was certainly the most detestable thing that I ever undertook to eat. The marrow from the mule's bones was a real luxury.

We now had a pretty good stock of food, such as it was, but not enough to carry us through the winter on full rations; therefore we determined to try to add to it by hunting. One was to go out and hunt while the other would remain at home: we now had undisputed possession of the fort and it was our home. Field took the first day's outing while I occupied my time in drying and smoking meat. Late in the evening he returned, tired and worn out, having seen nothing worth shooting.

Next day came my turn to hunt. I took a lunch as he had done, consisting of jerked mule. I did not tell him so, but I had determined to make an excursion up the river to a point where we had seen some fresh trails and deer tracks some days before. When I was putting up my lunch my friend intimated that I was taking a very large amount for one lunch, but I told him that I might stay out late and that I did not intend to starve. I went, stayed all day, all night, and part of the next day, and returned as he had done, tired and discouraged, not having seen anything worth bringing in. In the evening of the first day out I found a trail which appeared to have been used daily by deer going to and from the river.

It occurred to me that they might go out early in the morning, so I secreted myself within gunshot of the trail behind an old, moss-covered log, where I slept comfortably; and when it was light enough in the morning to see a deer, I leveled my gun across the log in a position commanding the trail and waited and watched until nine o'clock, but nothing came upon that pathway that morning. After getting tired of watching and waiting I went down to the trail, where to my astonishment, I found the fresh tracks of a large bear, which must have passed by that way while I was sleeping. As a rule I do not like to be treated discourteously, but in this instance I felt glad that this stranger had passed me by.

On arriving at the fort late in the evening I found my friend in a terrible state of mental excitement. He said that he had not slept a minute during the whole of the night before. He had filled the door of his room with rails, and sharpened one end of a long stick which he intended to use, if necessary, as a weapon of defense. When I arrived he was again filling the door with rails. I had the gun, pistol, and big knife with me, so this was his only means of defense. He said he would not stay alone another night for all the gold in California.

I was much discouraged by our failures in hunting, and after a lengthy discussion we decided to make another attempt to cross the mountains and escape from what then seemed to us certain starvation. This was Thursday night and we set Monday as the time for starting. By Saturday night everything was in readiness for the start and Sunday we devoted to Bible reading, for we each still had a pocket Bible. As much of the flesh of the wolf and the lamented mule as we thought we could carry had been thoroughly jerked, and finding that we would not be overburdened by it, we economized by roasting and eating little scraps of flesh, the marrow from the bones, and even the head of the mule was roasted, the fragments of flesh scraped off and eaten, and Field found a rich, fatty substance in behind the eyes, which he ate.

We had a canteen in which our powder was carried, but the powder was nearly all gone, so we emptied it and used the canteen to carry water in.

Early Monday morning we loaded ourselves, mostly with jerked mule and wolf, leaving many useful things behind, bid adieu to Fort Uinta, and took up our line of march rather reluctantly.

My companion was not strong and we soon found it expedient for me to take on part of his burden. We rested often, and yet long before night he became so tired that we had to go into camp. Most of the day we had traveled on an old deserted trail. The nights being cold, we were under the necessity of keeping up a fire, as we had left our blankets at the fort. The next morning we made an early start and rested often. At about noon we found good shade and water, and the sun being quite hot, we stopped and rested in the shade for more than three hours, then trudged on till nearly night, when we found water and plenty of old, dry timber for fuel, and camped. Field expressed a wish that he had his old mule again, and I reminded him that he had a portion of it left in his knapsack, and that turnabout was fair play: as the mule had carried him for a long time when he was unable to walk, he should not object to carrying a portion of the mule now; whereupon he again plainly intimated that he thought I was a d—d fool. I kept up the fire and he slept until morning.

Another day was passed without any unusual occurrence; we traveled and ate at the same time as usual. Another day of pretty hard travel over sandy plains and rocky hills brought us to the foot of the mountain, where we had plenty of good water and an abundance of fuel. A little sprinkle of rain early in the evening was the first we had seen since the memorable night after Field had eaten the little red berries.

Early Saturday morning we filled our canteen with water and started up the mountain. I had been carrying most of the jerk, but the stock was running down quite rapidly. My companions' bag now being almost empty, and as he had little else to carry while I had the gun and some other things, including his heavy overcoat, I divided the jerk, putting about half of it into his sack. All day long we were climbing the mountain. Late in the afternoon I was several rods ahead of Field when he called to me to stop. I did so, and when he came up he appeared to be a little cross and insisted that we were not traveling in the direction formerly agreed upon. I requested him to let me see the little compass which he had in his pocket, and on examining it he found that he was mistaken; whereupon he muttered something which I thought was swear words, and then we went marching on. In a little while we were within the old snow limits, where we found large bodies of old, icy looking snow in places shaded by trees and rocks, and a little before dark went into camp. We gathered some old, dry timber and made a large fire, then some green fir limbs for a bed. When I began to prepare our bed on one side of the flaming logs, to my surprise Field began to prepare one on the other side of the fire. Neither had spoken since the occurrence of the little unpleasantness in the afternoon about the course of travel. Mutely each took his side of the fire.

We had always slept together except when he was sick and the night I had left him alone at the fort. Sometime in the night I became thirsty and got up and procured some snow, put it in our only tin cup and set it on some live coals to melt, and went to sleep. The snow melted, the water evaporated, the solder melted and left the tin. While I slept, my dumb friend woke up thirsty, took the tin cup, filled it with snow and put it on coals. The snow melted and the water ran out on the coals; his tongue let loose and he then denounced me as a knave, an ass, a fool, an unregenerate heathen, and what else I don't want to remember. I woke up alarmed and did not at first fully understand what had created the storm, but after having the bottomless cup dashed at my head, I realized the situation and began to try to apologize and explain the unavoidable and unfortunate circumstance; but no explanation would satisfy his now thoroughly "Johnny Bull" temper. After this little nocturnal disturbance had subsided, I, on my bed of fir branches with my feet towards the fire, soon fell into a sound sleep and knew nothing more of the world until the sun was shining. Whether or not my friend had cooled off I did not inquire; but I do know that there was an unusual coldness between us, for neither spoke to the other until about twelve o'clock and then, as will appear, our conversation was very short.

As we did not rise until late, no delay was made, but when each had his bag on his back and a nugget of jerk in his hand, we started up the side of the mountain as quiet as two deaf-mutes. There was no water to be had; our camp kettle had been left at the fort, and through my stupidity the cup had become useless, therefore we were obliged to eat the icy snow or endure the thirst. No new snow had yet fallen in this high altitude, although it was now nearing the end of October. These mountains were then heavily covered with pine and fir but the timber was not large. In some places where the snow had melted away, short green grass was found quite close to great banks of snow.

At about twelve o'clock we reached the summit of the great Uinta Range,[5] and I, being a little in advance of my still mute companion, halted to take a survey of the field before me. The top of the range here is bare of timber and there was no snow. When Field came up I broke the silence which had lasted since the little unpleasantness of the night before by suggesting that we attempt to cross the snow-covered range of mountains which now appeared north of us and probably fifty miles away, through what appeared to be a gap or low place in the great range of mountains. He replied, "You may go that way if you want to, but I am going this way," pointing in another direction, and quickly started off at an angle of about 45 degrees to the right, or directly northeast. I also started immediately, and when we were a few rods apart I said, "Good-bye; we may not meet again very soon." He replied "Good-bye," and within a few minutes we were out of sight and, in a very short time, beyond hailing distance.

This was the last I saw or heard of him until after each of us had undergone many more hardships, so I will now drop my friend but will hereafter devote a chapter to him, and give you an account of his experience as he afterwards gave it to me, detailing an account of many most interesting incidents. Fortunately we had divided the jerk, for nothing was said at this sudden and unexpected parting about anything which either had in his possession. I had an idea when I bade him good-bye that he would soon turn about and follow me.

After the unceremonious parting I immediately began to descend the north side of the mountain, which was very rough, rocky, and steep; but down, down, down I went into a deep, dark cañon, where I slept on the leaves under a fir tree, after having taken some landmarks. When it was light enough to see the objects I had noted to guide me, I set out and spent the day in crossing over hills and through deep cañons. In the evening I arrived at the foot of the range of mountains which I had seen from the point of our parting. The sun disappeared, dark clouds began to float over the mountains, and it was evident that a storm was approaching.

While it was yet light enough I took some landmarks or guiding points; and it was well I did so, for on the following morning when I woke I found it snowing quietly but heavily, and before it was light enough for me to see my guiding objects, there must have been six or more inches of new snow on the ground beyond my snug retreat under a sheltering pine. When it was light enough I rose from my comfortable bed, took my bearings as best I could without a compass, and started up the mountain through the rapidly accumulating bed of snow. The snow continued to fall nearly all day, and before night it was more than a foot deep.

All day long I struggled through a dense forest. Sometime in the forenoon I crossed the fresh trail of a large herd of elk, which forcibly reminded me that my sack was almost empty, and I vainly wished that one of these wild creatures might come my way, but I did not dare to follow the herd with the uncertainty of killing one, and the certainty of losing my way this dark, snowy day. In order to maintain my course during such dark days, I was under the necessity of looking ahead and observing trees or other objects in my line of travel.

That night I, as usual, slept under a pine tree where there was no snow. I saw no sign of fire in either of these ranges of mountains, nor did I see any signs of Indians on my trip over these two ranges. The next day as I approached the top of the mountain I found the timber much smaller, and mostly pine. There is much fertile land in some of the valleys between the two great ranges of mountains.

Early on the following morning I arrived at the bald, snow-covered summit. On my right and on my left were high, untimbered, snow-covered peaks. From this point I could overlook a vast territory extending over many hills, valleys, and smaller mountains where there was no snow; in fact, the snow only extended a few miles down the steep sides of the great range. As a rule there is more timber on the north than on the south side of mountains west of the Rockies; but it was the reverse here, for there was little timber on the north side of this range.

One more day's tramping brought me down into a large barren plain where I gathered some dry weeds for a bed and slept without food or water; the last bit of the mule or wolf, I know not which, I had eaten during the afternoon. I had had very little jerk for the last two or three days, and began to wish that I had another horse, mule, or even a wolf. For many days I had seen no living thing except when I looked into a small glass which I carried in my pocket, and then only saw a familiar shadow.

I spent another day without food, but had plenty of water; another night on a bed of green brush beside a good fire. The next day was bright and sunny, quite a contrast to the gloomy days I had spent in the mountains. For want of food I was becoming quite weak and was not able to travel as fast as usual. During the early part of the day I saw some tracks of an unshod horse, which renewed my courage and hope of redemption; and at about two o'clock in the afternoon I saw some dark spots on the plain a long distance away, but almost in the direction I was going. Hoping that these objects might be living creatures, I hurried on for a time, then sat down, and after having watched them for a time, I found that they changed positions, and that satisfied me to a moral certainty that they were living creatures, but what I could not tell. They might be horses, cattle, elk, deer, antelope, or buffalo; but no matter what, I must hurry on and try to reach them before night.

Late in the evening I determined that they were horses but could not yet tell whether they belonged to whites or Indians, or were wild. As I approached them they stopped grazing and started toward me, but soon disappeared in a deep gulch between us, which I had not noticed before. On arriving at the edge of the gulch or narrow valley I saw the horses in the vicinity of about fifteen or twenty wigwams which were all in a row on the bank of a little creek that ran through the gulch. Many Indians were sitting outside of their lodges, the weather being warm.

On first sight of the village, being not more than two hundred yards away, my heart fluttered just a little, not knowing whether the savages would scalp me or not; but, notwithstanding my natural cowardice, I at once determined to "beard the lion in his den," and walked as boldly as I could up to the lower end of the row of wigwams. Within a few feet of the nearest one, three young bucks met me and seemed to be anxious to know whence I came and whither I was going; whether right down from heaven, and if so what was my mission. They seemed as much surprised at my sudden appearance as I was on coming so suddenly upon them. My first and most important business was to determine whether they would give me something to eat, or eat me.

As the men, women, and children began to gather around me I heard someone halfway up the line of lodges call out, saying something which I did not understand, but on looking that way saw a man beckoning to me, as I thought, when the young men motioned for me to move on up the line. On arriving at the place indicated I found myself in the presence of one whom I then suspected, and afterwards found to be, the chief, who extended his royal right hand and greeted me in a most courteous and polite manner and then, with a graceful wave of his hand and a slight bow, indicated that I should precede him at the low open door into his royal palace, where he very politely introduced me to his wife, who proved to be a sensible, clever, courteous woman. She soon prepared something for me to eat, and after I had finished my supper, an Indian brought in two pistols and wanted me to take the cap tube from one and put it into the other, which I soon accomplished. He was much pleased, went out, and soon returned with ten or more pounds of elk meat which he tendered to me as compensation for my work, but the chief objected and insisted, as I understood him, that he had plenty and that I was his guest, but finally consented for me to accept part of the meat. I gave him to understand that I wanted to go to Fort Bridger.

A case of nice new blankets was opened, as it appeared to me, for my especial benefit. The chief, his lady, two sons almost grown, two or three wolfish looking dogs which forcibly reminded me of Field's terrible scare, and myself made up the number of lodgers in that mansion that night. Late that night some warriors who had been out on a campaign came home, and learning that there was a stranger within the gates, came to the king's palace to see him, and also to report that they had discovered some white barbarians in the vicinity who had dared to enter his domain without a special permit, and that they had sent a message to his highness informing him that they had a good assortment of blankets, cutlery, pins, needles, beads, etc., which his people might need or desire, and also a limited amount of "firewater," and that they would be pleased to receive his order for anything he might desire.

The fact of the presence of these palefaces in the vicinity was at once communicated to me, and early on the following morning I was informed that if it was my desire to cut short my stay at the palace, the king would take great pleasure in furnishing me means of conveyance, a proper escort, and a reliable guide who would safely conduct me to the camp of the accommodating merchants or Indian traders (but, in fact, Indian robbers.) Notwithstanding my reluctance in leaving the society of the noble ruler and his people, I most readily accepted his generous offer, and after breakfast, which consisted of elk meat and tobacco root in a combination stew which was very palatable, a fine steed with a good Mexican saddle and bridle was at the door. My escort, consisting of four mounted warriors, was ready, and after bidding my good friends farewell, I with some assistance mounted my charger and we were all off on a full run, up and down hill and across valley, at what seemed to me a fearful rate.

In less than two hours we entered the camp of the traders at full speed, dismounted, and found one man, a long Jake from Illinois, who could speak English. He had two wives (squaws), and several children which he claimed, but some of them were quite dark. His name was John Smith; not a very uncommon one. He was a very clever man, about thirty-five years old, was not a Mormon, but had taken the women in order to become popular with the Indians and to improve his opportunities for trade.

After getting something to eat, and learning something, through Smith, of my adventures, my escort made ready to return to their camp. Their trip, as Smith told me, was made solely for my accommodation and now I had nothing with which to compensate them; but as they were about to leave I took a large bandanna, the only one I had left, and tied it around the neck of the chief's son, he being one of the clever escorts. He at first refused to accept it, but when Smith told him that I desired him to take it as a token of regard, he accepted it with an expression of thanks, and after

I had bidden them all good-bye, they rode away as rapidly as we had come. I will always hold that chief and his people in kindly remembrance.

All of the other white men with Smith were French, and all had plenty of wives (squaws) and numerous slaves. The wives were not slaves, but they had slaves all around them. The whole tribe traveled about and lived much as other tribes did, only much better; for they lived by trading while the others lived by hunting and fishing. In this camp I ate bread for the first time in many weeks. At the end of three days after my arrival here, a caravan was ready to start for Fort Bridger for winter supplies for the traders. I was furnished with a good horse and saddle, and Smith, one of the Frenchmen, five slaves, twenty horses, and myself made up the caravan, and on the evening of the third day we reached the fort, where I was very kindly received.

Smith was a large man, had a good head, and some cultivation and apparent refinement, and treated his women and children well. He said he had been to his old home in Illinois since he had entered upon this kind of life, but was not contented there and soon returned to his Indian friends. He and those Frenchmen were as generous and hospitable as old Southern planters, and their kindness to me will not be forgotten while my memory lasts.

I was well treated at the fort, which is one hundred and sixteen miles from the point where the seven dug up the little flatboat from its sandy bed on the fifth day of August, just three months before, since which I had undergone many hardships, took many fearful risks, and traveled more than a thousand miles, far enough to have taken me from Green River to San Francisco.

On the morning of the seventh day of November I started with a government train for Salt Lake City, where I arrived on the fifteenth. I soon found a home with a prominent Mormon, a Scotchman named Archie Gardner, living in the fifth ward, on Mill Creek, one of the many small streams coming down from the mountains east of the city. Mr. Gardner was a clever gentleman about forty-five years old, had a sawmill up in the mountains, and was then building a flour mill only a few rods from his dwelling. I assisted him in completing the little flour mill and in attending it during the winter. Mr. Gardner had three wives, all living in one house, but occupying separate rooms at night. I usually attended the little mill until midnight, and Gardner made it part of my duty to go to his house and call him. He usually told me where I could find him, but not always, so at times I was under the necessity of rapping at more than one door before I found him.

He had the largest house in the ward, and the religious services were held there by Bishop Johnson, who also acted as justice of the peace in that ward. Gardner's family all ate at the same table over which the first wife presided. She was, indeed, mistress of the house, the other wives treating her with great respect, and all were, to all outward appearance, quite friendly. Gardner bestowed much attention on his first wife, though I always suspected that he was just a little more fond of the youngest one, and I did not blame him much, for she manifested strong affection for him even in the presence of the others, and yet there was no outward manifestation of jealousy.

The second, or the one I will call the second because she was in age between the others, and was the mother of the third, or youngest, a widowed mother and her daughter having been sealed to Gardner at the same time, the first wife having given her consent and standing with them at the triple matrimonial altar, and then and there joining in the sacred ceremony. As I was about to say, the second wife seemed to be pleased at the manifestation of affection for the common husband by the youngest wife, and No. 1 would in a good-humored way say, "My, Annie, don't be so demonstrative in the presence of other people," when the husband would laugh and go and kiss No. 1.

Gardner spent most of his leisure time, particularly during the day and evening, in his first wife's apartments with her and her children. He was a very religious man, and always had family prayers before retiring at night, and all persons about the house were expected to join, at least formally, in this service. The use of profane language was not allowed in or about the house.

Many of the higher church officers were entertained at Gardner's house and table, among whom were Brigham Young, George A. Smith, Heber C. Kimble, George Taylor, and Parley P. Pratt, with all of whom I formed some acquaintance. Brigham was a dignified, clever gentleman, not austere but kind and affable. Kimble was also a nice, genteel, genial, red-headed gentleman. Smith was a heavy man with a very large abdomen, dark hair, full beard, exceedingly jovial, and apparently always happy. Pratt was a small, rather slim, quick and athletic man, rather austere, refined, active and energetic. Taylor was a large man, highly intellectual, and rather unsociable. Kimble was my favorite notwithstanding the fact that he had fifteen wives, mostly young and handsome, all in one house, and my impression is that none of them had any children. I think it was conceded that his was the finest harem in Utah. He called me his young gentile, was very kind and affable, but he never invited me to inspect his harem.

About the first of December, 1849, Field arrived in Salt Lake City, and I will allude to a little matter in which he was concerned, after which I will give you a short account of his trip from the time we parted company until he arrived in Salt Lake, as he afterwards gave it to me. Soon after he arrived in the City of the Saints he heard of another who had recently arrived from the south and that he was located in the fifth ward on Mill Creek at the house of one Gardner, and at which house he soon arrived.

After staying with me for two or three days, he found employment in the family of the Apostle John Taylor. The family consisted of seven wives living in seven different houses. How many children there were I never knew, but there was one wife who did not have any. She was a fine specimen of English beauty. Taylor's women were nearly all English. It was the business of my friend to cut wood, and do chores generally for the Taylor family living in seven different places at the same time. Taylor was in Europe that winter looking after the interest of the Church, and possibly after a few more wives, and consequently could not, in person, attend to all of the necessities of the seven branches of his family. In his daily rounds looking after the seven woodpiles and other little matters appertaining to the comfort of the family in so many places, Field happened to come in contact with the English beauty, and the result was mutual love at first sight, notwithstanding the fact that this woman had passed and taken all of the solemn vows of the Lym house with the Apostle and his six other wives.

I do not think that my English friend had lost one iota of the fond recollection of his long-since dead English wife, the picture of whom he still carried near his heart; but, nevertheless, he and this seventh wife of the noted apostle fell heels over head in love. Field, as you know, was a well-developed, good-looking, intelligent man of forty. The woman was well developed, good-looking, and as smart as a steel-trap, and both being English, I was not at all surprised at their mutual admiration and infatuation, nor did I blame them much. I was entrusted with many closely sealed envelopes which I carried from one to the other. With my feeble assistance they tried to devise some method by which they might escape from the city before the apostle should return home; but the Danites were always on the alert, and they well knew that detection by the Danites of an attempt to get away together would lead to certain death to him and, if not to her, she would certainly have been returned to her polygamous state of bondage.[6] Spring came with little hope of escape, and they reluctantly parted with the mutual understanding that, if possible, she would make her escape and go to Sacramento, where he promised to keep his address. Ten months after the parting they had not met yet, and if they ever did it was after I had lost all further knowledge of him.

Mormon morals, exclusive of polygamy, are very good. I never saw a drunken man in Salt Lake City, and heard very little profane language there. The people were industrious and seemed happy. Their hospitality rivaled that of the old southern planters, and their charity was equal to that of other Christians.

I will now go back to the place where Field and I separated on the mountaintop and give you a short statement as he gave it to me, and while some things may border on the miraculous and seem somewhat incredible, I do not question the truth of his statements. When we parted so unexpectedly, he had about half of the jerked wolf and mule combined. I went north while he bore off in a northeasterly direction, and after traveling for three days came to the river at a point above where we lost our flatboat. He struggled on up the river without road or trail, and nothing to guide him except the little compass which he still carried in his pocket.

Two days more and his last bit of jerk was gone, starvation began to stare him in the face once more. He saw signs of Indians having crossed his pathless course, which gave him renewed courage. Soon after starting out next morning he was delighted to see a pony in the distance, grazing, and on coming up to it found one of its front legs broken. This, he said was another godsend. The poor pony seemed to fear him. It was probably an Indian pony, had its leg broken, and was left to die. He followed it for some time and finally got close to it and fired his revolver at its chest and wounded it, but it then left him with the blood flowing from its wound. After resting for a time he followed on and soon found it lying down, but not dead. He told me how innocent and helpless it appeared, and looked at him as if pleading with him not to inflict any more pain; but he felt that his life was in a balance with its, and after a little meditation he put the revolver to its forehead and ended its life and suffering. Then came the usual process of skinning, cutting up, and jerking, which took the balance of that day and part of the next.

Eight days more and he was again starving. On the ninth he arrived at the spot where we had dug up the little ferryboat which carried the seven adventurers far down the river more than three very long, dreary months before. Snow now covered the entire country, and all emigrants had long since gone by. His strength was failing fast but it would not do to linger there, so he arose and was about to start when he saw a poor old ox slowly coming towards him, and when it had come up near to him he discovered a wolf not far behind which seemed to be following the ox, but it soon turned and went away. Night was coming on and he was very hungry. Something must be done. The last cartridge had been exploded in killing the poor broken-legged Indian pony, and the revolver was no longer of use. The ox, though feeble, was probably yet stronger than the starving man.

Field feared that he was not able to catch the ox by the horns and hold it until he could cut its throat, so the next plan was to get hold of the animal's tail with one hand, and with the big knife in the other cut his hamstrings so as to disable him, and then cut his throat. The ox seemed fond of being rubbed and petted, so after a little time a firm hold on the tail was secured, and the big knife vigorously applied, but it was so very dull that he could not sever the tough old tendons. After sawing with the dull knife and being literally dragged for some distance, he became so much exhausted that he was obliged to relinquish his hold and see the excited old ox disappear.

In almost complete despair, Field spent the night beside a fire under one of those large cottonwoods, which I have no doubt you will remember even though it is now more than forty years since you saw them. He rose early next morning and started out on the well-beaten road towards the Golden West, but had only gone a few hundred yards when he was agreeably surprised to again behold the old ox approaching him, but so much exhausted that it could scarcely walk. The same, or some other, wolf was nearby, and had probably followed the poor old ox all night. When the ox came close to Field the wolf growled and again turned away as on the evening before. After the wolf had left, the ox seemed to be relieved.

It then occurred to the starving emigrant that he had a sharp razor in his kit with which he knew he could cut those tough tendons, provided he could get another hold on that tail. Field, as you probably remember, always kept his face cleanly shaved. Even while we were starving he would shave almost every day. The ox was tired and worn out and so was Field; but he got the razor ready and soon had hold of that tail again. Off went the ox, the keen razor was applied, soon the tendons parted, and down went the ox. But only half the victory was won, for the ox would raise up on his front feet and show fight; but after resting awhile the would-be victor rushed up, caught the poor beast by the horns, pushed him over on his side, held him down and cut his throat.

After a long, much needed rest, he cut out a piece of the poor beef, broiled and ate it, and then spent the remainder of the day in hunting out the small, lean muscles that still remained between the skin and bones of the poor old ox. The poor beef was jerked and put into the sack which on the following morning was thrown upon the back of its owner, and from which he fed for the next six days, at the end of which he arrived at Fort Bridger. From there he soon obtained a passage for Salt Lake City, arriving there on the second day of December, seventeen days after I had reached there, and finding me as before stated.

Sometime in the winter we formed an acquaintance of a gentleman named Jesse Morgan, a gentile, who had left Illinois in the spring of 1849 for California, but for some cause had been delayed and obliged to winter in the city of the Latter Day Saints. Morgan had a wife, a little child, a wagon, and two yoke of oxen, but no food nor money. Field and I arranged to furnish food for all for the trip from there to Sacramento, and assist in camp duties, drive the team, etc. We made the trip together and arrived in Sacramento in good condition on the fourth day of July, 1850, and pitched our tent under a large oak tree, where the state capitol now stands. I spent five months with a wholesale grocery and miners' supply firm, Elder and Smith, Fourth and J Streets, Sacramento, and three months in the mines as a drummer, or solicitor and collector, for the same firm. I returned to Sacramento and was almost ready to start home when the Scotts River excitement broke out.[7] I then went to the mines on Trinity River and associated myself in mining with Hiram Gould, a young Presbyterian clergyman who had laid aside the cloth for the time and engaged in mining. I remained in the mines until July 4th, 1851, exactly one year from the time I entered Sacramento, when I started home by way of Nicaragua. In due time, after an interesting trip, I arrived home and again entered upon the study of my chosen profession, graduated from an honorable college, and am now, as you know, practicing my profession on the seashore.[8]

M. S. McMahon

CHAPTER XIII

Story of the Jayhawkers

*In the foregoing chapters describing the trip across the deserts and moun-
tains, the author has had occasion many times to refer to the Jayhawkers.
Their history is in many respects no less remarkable and intensely interesting than that of his own party. The author has therefore collected many
notes and interviews with prominent members and presents herewith the
only written history of their travels.[1]*

THE LITTLE TRAIN AFTERWARD KNOWN BY THIS NAME was made up in the
state of Illinois in 1849, of industrious, enterprising young men who were
eager to see and explore the new country then promising gold to those who
sought [it]. The young men were from Knoxville, Galesburg, and other
towns.[2] Not all were influenced by the desire for gold. It was said that
California had a milder climate, and that pleasant homes could there be
made, and the long, cold winter avoided.

They placed some of the best men in position to manage for the
whole. The outfit was placed on a steamboat and transported to Kanesville,
on the Missouri River above Council Bluffs. Some of the company went
with the goods while others bought teams and wagons in western Missouri
and drove to the appointed place. Kanesville was a small Mormon camp,
while Council Bluffs was a trading post of a few log cabins on the riverbank,
inhabited mostly by Indians. There was no regular ferry at either place, and
our party secured a log raft which they used to get their wagons and provisions across, making the oxen swim. They asked all the questions they could
think of from everyone who pretended to know anything about the great
country to the west of them, for it seemed a great undertaking to set out into
the land they could see stretching out before them across the river. Other parties bound the same way also arrived and joined them. They chose a guide
who claimed to have been over the road before. When all were gathered

206

together the guide told them that they were about to enter an Indian country, and that the dusky residents did not always fancy the idea of strangers
richer than themselves passing through, and sometimes showed out some of
the bad traits the Indians had been said to possess. It would therefore be better to organize and travel systematically. He would divide the company into
divisions and have each division choose a captain, and the whole company
unite in adopting some rules and laws which they would all agree to observe.
This arrangement was satisfactorily accomplished, and they moved out in a
sort of military style. And then they launched out on the almost endless western prairie, said then to be a thousand miles wide, containing few trees, and
generally unknown.

These Illinois boys were young and full of mirth and fun which was
continually overflowing. They seemed to think they were to be on a sort of
everyday picnic and bound to make life as merry and happy as it could be.
One of the boys was Ed Doty, who was a sort of model traveler in this line.
A camp life suited him; he could drive an ox team, cook a meal of victuals,
turn a pan of flapjacks with a flop, and possessed many other frontier accom-
plishments. One day when Doty was engaged in the duty of cooking
flapjacks, another frolicsome fellow came up and took off the cook's hat and
commenced going through the motions of a barber giving his customer a
vigorous shampoo, saying, "I am going to make a Jayhawker out of you, old
boy." Now it happened at the election for captain in this division that Ed
Doty was chosen captain, and no sooner was the choice declared than the
boys took the newly elected captain on their shoulders and carried him
around the camp, introducing him as the Kingbird of the Jayhawkers. So
their division was afterwards known as the Jayhawkers, but whether the
word originated with them, and John Brown forgot to give them credit, or
whether it was some old frontier word, used in sport on the occasion, is
more than I will undertake to say; however, the boys felt proud of their title
and the organization has been kept up to this day by the survivors, as will
be related further on.

The first few days they got along finely and began to lose all feeling of
danger and to become rather careless in their guard duty. When the cattle had
eaten enough and lain down, the guards would sometimes come into camp
and go to sleep, always finding the stock all right in the morning and no
enemy or suspicious persons in sight. But one bright morning no cattle were
in sight, which was rather strange, as the country was all prairie. They went
out to look, making a big circuit, and found no traces till they came to the
river, where they found tracks upon the bank and saw some camps across the

river, a mile or so away. Doty had a small spyglass and, by rigging up a tripod of small sticks to hold it steady, they scanned the camps pretty closely and decided that there were too many oxen for the wagons in sight.

Some of the smartest of them stripped off their clothes and started to swim the stream, but landed on the same side they started from. Captain Doty studied the matter a little and then set out himself, being a good swimmer, and by a little shrewd management and swimming upstream when the current was strongest, soon got across to where he could touch bottom and shouted to the others to do the same. Soon all the swimmers were across.

They could now see that there were two trains on that side and that the farther one had already begun to move and was about a mile in advance of the nearest one. Doty said something must be done, and although they only were clothed in undershirts, they approached the nearest camp and were handed some overalls for temporary use. The men in this camp, on hearing about the missing oxen, said the fellows in the forward train went over and got them, for, they said, there were no wagons in sight and they must be strays. He said the forward train was from Tennessee, and that they had some occasion to doubt their honesty and had refused to travel with them any further. They said they were all old Missourians, and did not want other people's property, and if the boys found their cattle with the Tennesseeans, and wanted any help to get them back again, to call on them, and put in some good strong swear words for emphasis.

The boys, barefooted and with only overalls and shirts, started after the moving train, which they called to a halt when overtaken. The coarse grass was pretty hard to hurry through, clothed as they were. The train men were pretty gruff and wanted to know what was wanted. Captain Doty very emphatically told them he could see some of his oxen in their train, and others in the herd, and he proposed to have them all back again. The Jayhawker boys were unarmed but were in a fighting mood and determined to have the stock at all hazards, and if not peaceably, war might commence. The boys saw that the two trains were of about equal strength, and if worse came to worst they could go back and get their guns and men and come over in full force after their property, and they were assured the Missourians would help them, and a combination of forces would give them a majority and they could not be beaten by the Tennessee crowd. There was a good deal of talk, but finally when Doty demanded that their cattle be unyoked and the others separated from the herd, they yielded and gave them all their stock, some seventy head.

The Missourians had come up and heard the talk, and some of them went back and helped drive the cattle to the river, and deal out some double shotted thunder against the biggest scamps they had come across. It was quite a job to get the cattle across the river. They would go in a little way and then circle round and round like a circus, making no progress. They finally put a rope on one of them and a man led him as far as he could, which was more than halfway, and although they landed a good ways downstream, they got them all across safely, left their borrowed overalls in the hands of their friends, with a thousand thanks for valuable assistance, and plunged into the swift-running Platte, and swam back again to the northern side. They drove the straggling oxen back to camp with a sense of great satisfaction, and in turn received the praise of their friends, who said that Ed Doty was the best Jayhawker of the border.

This was the first unpleasantness and they were afterwards more cautious and stood guard all night, watching closely all the time, both night and day, for any signs of danger. Thus, in time, they reached Salt Lake, rather late in the season, but safe and sound, having escaped cholera or other disease, and in good spirits to surmount any further difficulties which might be met.

When the Jayhawkers reached Salt Lake it was found that it was not safe to try to go the regular northern route to California, as they were advised by those who seemed to know, as they might be snowed in on the Sierra Nevada mountains and perish.[3] The Mormons told them that the snow often fell there twenty feet deep, and some other stories likely to deter them from making the attempt. They also told them of a route farther south by which they could come into California at Los Angeles, or they could remain in Salt Lake until May, when it would be safe to try the mountain route again. After listening to the talk of the mountaineers who claimed to have been over the route and to know all about it, and camping some time to rest and learn all they could, they finally decided on taking the southern route. One Mormon told them of a place where they could make a cutoff and save five hundred miles, and if they would follow his instructions, they would find the route fully as good as the one usually traveled, which was not much better than a trail. The cutoff was so instilled into their minds that they had great confidence in the report and talked very favorably of taking it.

The man Williams made for them a map of the proposed route and explained it to them and others who had gathered at Salt Lake, and from the map they could see how much was to be gained in time and distance by taking that route.[4] A month or two of travel was indeed something to gain, and as the roads seemed similar in quality, the reasoning was very plausible. The map explained all the watering places and favorable things but said nothing about a desert, and as there was no one to tell them any unfavorable side to this plan, there were many who quite concluded to go this way, and among those who did so were the Jayhawkers, and the "Williams Short Route" was freely talked about as a settled thing by them.[5]

They now set about preparing to move. They sold, traded, and bought oxen till they had the best and fattest teams in Salt Lake Valley; selected good provisions, and plenty of them, so as to be safe in case of delay; and contended that nothing could stop them in a country where but little snow could be and water was as plentiful as shown on the map. They wanted to reach the gold mines and this was the shortest route and even if it was still considerably longer than the northern way, they said they would rather be moving along and thus gain time than to [remain] so long in camp with nothing to do by which they could earn a cent. There were here in Salt Lake ten times as many men as could find employment, and Brigham's saints would be pretty sure to get all of the odd jobs to the exclusion of the heretics.

To bring the matter to a determination, a paper was drawn up for those to sign who wanted to go the southern route and it was pretty generally signed. The Mormon elder, John Hunt, was consulted, and as he seemed to know the general southern route better than anyone else, he was prevailed upon to guide the train through on the Old Spanish Trail. This had never been used as a wagon road, but he thought it could be without much difficulty, and he said if they could secure him a fair-sized train he would go and conduct them through for ten dollars a wagon.[6] This proposition was accepted after some consideration, and all who wished to do so were given permission to join the train. In a few days there were one hundred and seven wagons enlisted for this route, including seven Mormons bound for San Bernardino.

Preparations for the trip now began in good earnest, and the Saints were liberally patronized in purchase of flour and meat, which were the principal things they had to sell. As their several wagons were loaded, they moved out in small lots to the south to keep in good fresh feed for their animals, and to move on slowly till all were ready, when they would join in one large body and proceed. The guide was in no special haste, as he said he wanted to wait a little later so the weather in the south would be cooler than they would be likely to find it if they pressed on at once. He said that in summer it was so hot that no white man could endure the heat. He said they could work slowly along the trail, and when the right time came he would move out himself, and that they might be assured that it would then be the coolest and best time in which to travel down there. So the company dallied along, and it was October before the whole train was made up at a point about a hundred miles south of Salt Lake.[7]

The complete organization was divided into seven divisions, each with its captain, and Division No. 1 was to lead the march the first day and then fall to the rear while No. 2 took the advance, and so continue till all had taken their turn. The leading party was to guard and care for the cattle and deliver them in the morning. The regulations were read aloud to the captains, and this rather large army of men, women, and children, with about five hundred head of stock, moved out very systematically. It would sometimes be fully ten o'clock before the rear division could make a start, and correspondingly late before they could get up with the main camp at night. They got along very well, but cleaned the country of grass for some distance each side of the trail as they swept along.

About the first of November Captain Smith overtook us with the pack train, and camped with us at night. He formed many acquaintances and told them he was going to take a shorter route and save five hundred miles, rather than take the long route by way of Los Angeles.[8] He had a map of his proposed route, and it was very much like the one we had. He also stated that it could probably be as easily traveled as the one by way of Los Angeles, and as a consequence of his talk, cutoff fever began to rage in camp again. Some got very enthusiastic in the matter and spoke publicly in favor of following Captain Smith when he should come to the place when his short route turned away from the other trail. His plan grew so much in favor that when the place was reached, a hundred wagons turned out into the Smith trail, leaving Captain Hunt only the seven Mormon wagons bound for San Bernardino. Hunt stood at the forks of the road as the wagons went by and said to them, "Good-bye, friends. I cannot, according to my agreement, go with you, for I was hired for this road, and no other was mentioned. I am in duty bound to go even if only one wagon decides to go." When the last wagon had passed him he still stood talking with several who had chosen the new way and told them they were taking a big risk, for they did not know very much about the route, and he had been thinking that they might find it pretty rough and hard to get over the first time. He said that if all decided to go that way he would go and help them, even if they went to h—ll, but as it was, he could not. He wished them luck and the two trains parted company.

At the end of three days of travel on the Smith trail they came to the top of a long, steep hill. The trail went down and down, and they saw no way of crossing the terribly deep cañon that was before them. So they went into camp and sent explorers out to investigate and find a crossing if possible.[9]

On the second day the explorers began to return with very unfavorable reports, and many who found their progress thus blocked turned about and started to follow Hunt. Most of the wagons which remained had each one or more of their men out exploring and could not turn back until their return. Several of the Jayhawkers, having once started on this route, were very anxious to get through on it if a way could be found for them to do it, and therefore searched farther and with greater determination than the others. When they returned they reported they had found a way around the head of the cañon and they believed it to be the right way. The map Williams had given them did not show this cañon and they believed it to be correct, and that the real road led around at the place which they had found, and no further trouble would be met.

Acting on this report about twenty wagons, including the Jayhawkers, concluded to go ahead. "We can beat the other fellows a month," said they, and so they hitched up and pulled out in a northerly direction, feeling in good spirits and hopeful of success.

They named this place Mt. Misery.[10] While camped here, a lone and seemingly friendless man died and was buried. None seem now to remember his name, but think he was from Kentucky. He was low with consumption and not strong enough to endure the hardships of the journey.[11]

About the third night, the Jayhawkers were overtaken by seven more wagons owned by A. Bennett and friends, J. B. Arcane and family, two men named Earhart and a son of one of them, and one or two other wagons.

The Jayhawkers' train was made up of men from many states, but seemed well united and was as complete as when they first started. The author was with the party that came up in the rear, which had started later but traveled faster on account of having a road broken for them. He visited the leaders in camp when they were discussing the necessity of forming a new traveling compact to help and protect each other on the road. Those who had no families were objecting to being bound to those who had women and children with them. They argued that the road would be hard and difficult and those wagons with women and children would require more assistance than they would be able to render in return. They said they [the wagons with women and children] could go back and follow Hunt, who was on a better road, and they could proceed with more safety.

Among those with this train was Reverend J. W. Brier, his wife, and three children. He objected to being turned back and said he did not want to be assisted, but would go with them and do his part and take care of himself. The author listened to the various speeches without speaking and became satisfied that it would end in everyone looking out for himself in case of hard times. He went over to their camp again the next night and wished to ask them why they were steering so nearly due north. He said to them that they were going toward Salt Lake rather than California, and that the Bennett party did not feel inclined to follow them any farther in that direction. They replied that their map told them to go north a day or more and then they would find the route as represented. They would then turn west and reach Owen's Lake and from there, there would be no more trouble. The Jayhawker crowd seemed to think they could go anywhere and no difficulty could happen which they couldn't overcome. Bennett's little train turned west from this point and the Jayhawkers went on north, but before night they changed their minds and came following on after Bennett, whom they over-took and passed, again taking the lead.

Thus far the country had been well watered and furnished plenty of grass, and most of them talked and believed that this kind of rolling country would last all the way through. The men at leisure scattered around over the hills on each side of the route taken by the train, and in advance of it, hunt-ing camping places and making a regular picnic of it. There were no hard-ships, and one man had a fiddle which he tuned up evenings and gave plenty of fine music. Joy and happiness seemed the rule, and all of the train were cer-tainly having a good time of it.

But gradually there came a change as the wagon wheels rolled west-ward. The valleys seemed to have no streams in them, and the mountain ranges grew more and more broken, and in the lower ground a dry lake could be found, and water and grass grew scarce—so much so that both men and oxen suffered. These dry lake beds deceived them many times. They seemed as if containing plenty of water, and off the men would go to explore. They usually found the distance to them about three times as far as they at first sup-posed, and when at last they reached them they found no water, but a dry, shining bed, smooth as glass, but just clay, hard as a rock. Most of these dry lakes showed no outlet, nor any inlet for that matter, though at some period in the past they must have been full of water. Nothing grew in the shape of vegetables or plants except a small, stunted, bitter brush.

Away to the west and north there was much broken country, the mountain ranges higher and rougher and more barren, and from almost every sightly elevation there appeared one or more of these dry lake beds.[12] One night, after about three days of travel, the whole of the train of twenty-seven wagons was camped along the bank of one of these lakes, this one with a very little water in it, not more than one-fourth or one-half an inch in depth and yet spread out to the width of a mile or more.[13] It was truly providential, for by digging holes along the border, the water would run into them and prove abundant for all, both oxen and men. If it had proved dry, as so many before had proved, or if we had been a few days earlier or later, we might not have found a drop. This proved to be the last time the whole twenty-seven wagons were gathered in one camp together.

The author came into camp about nine o'clock in the evening after climbing many peaks and taking a survey of the surrounding country with a fieldglass. Men from nearly every mess came to him to inquire what he had seen. They asked all sorts of questions and wanted an opinion as to the advisability of trailing across the prairie directly west, which then seemed easy. They were told that from what could be seen from the summit of buttes both north and south of the camp, ranging a hundred or so miles in almost every direction, it was believed no water could be found between the present camp and a range of mountains which could be seen crossing the route far to the west.[14] "Well," said Captain Doty of the Jayhawkers, "I don't like to hear such discouraging talk from Manly, but I think we will have to steer straight ahead. The prospect for water seems to be about the same, west or south, and I cannot see that we would better ourselves by going north." When morning came Captain Doty and his party yoked up and set out straight across the desert, leaving seven wagons of the Bennett party still in camp.

For some time all of us had seen in the range ahead an appearance of a pass, or lower place in the mountain, and we had got to calling it Martin's Pass, naming it after Jim Martin.[15] There was a snowcapped peak just to the south of it, and the pass, now apparently exactly west of the lake camp, seemed to the Jayhawkers easy to reach. Their wills were strong enough and they were running over with determination and energy enough to carry them over any plain, no matter how dry or barren, or over any mountain, no matter how rugged and steep.

Five days they traveled, without finding water, and [the] small supply they took along had been consumed. For lack of water they could not eat or sleep. The oxen gathered round the little fire and seemed to beg for water; they had no cud to chew unless it was the cud of disappointment. The range of mountains they had been aiming for still seemed far away, and the possible show for reaching it seemed very poor indeed, and the prospect of any water hole between them and the mountains poorer yet. Hope was pretty near gone. Martin's mess unyoked their oxen from the wagons, put some small packs on their own backs, and loaded some upon the backs of the oxen, and turned south toward the nearest snowy mountain they could see,[16] the same one towards which the Bennett party steered from the lake camp.

The Doty party kept their courage longer and kept on straight ahead for another day, and then camped, almost without hope. No rest came to them, nor sleep. Towards morning, as they stood around the fire, a stray cloud appeared and hid the stars and, shortly after, began to unload a cargo of snow it carried. They spread out every blanket and brushed up every bit they could from the smooth places, kindled a little fire of brush under the camp kettles, and melted all the snow all of them could gather, besides filling their mouths as fast as ever they could, hoping that it would fall in sufficient quantities to satisfy themselves and the oxen, and quench their dreadful thirst. Slowly the cloud moved, scattering the snowflakes till they felt relieved. The last time the author conversed with a member of this party was in 1892, and it was conceded that this storm saved the lives of both man and beast in that little band of Jayhawkers. It was like manna falling from heaven, and as surely saved their lives as did the manna of the Bible save the lives of the tribes of Israel. They had no reason to expect a storm of rain or snow, but [it] came to them just as they were perishing. A little farther on they came to a small stream of water and, as the bed showed only a recent flow, it must also have come from the little local storm further up the mountain. They used this water freely, even though it was not very good, and it acted on them very much like a solution of Glauber's salts.[17]

They decided at first that they had better follow the stream southward, but after a little time, feeling the sickness caused by the water, they saw it was no advantage and turned west again, bearing to the north toward a sort of pass they could now see in the mountains in that direction. This stream is now known as the Amargosa, or bitter river.[18]

The new direction in which they marched gave them an uphill route for thirty or forty miles, rough and barren, with no water or grass. There was no road or trail to follow, the oxen were as weak as their owners from drinking the bitter water, and the road needed some clearing and breaking in places before the wagons could pass. They moved quite slowly and reached the summit on the second night with the loss of a single ox. The author would say here that this was the last ox which was allowed to die without using the flesh for food, and it was from this same one he cut a steak to eat on Christmas eve, 1849.

From the summit they took a way down a dark, deep cañon having a steep slope and very rocky and bad, but down which the oxen drew their loads much easier than when they came up, reaching water on the third day, where there were many springs and a sort of coarse grass for the oxen. The place is now known as Furnace Creek. The Jayhawkers passed on, and here at these very springs was where the author overtook the Reverend J. W. Brier delivering a lecture to his children on the benefits of an early education, as referred to in his narrative.

As the Jayhawkers drove out of this Furnace Creek Cañon, the valley into which they came was very narrow, the high, snowcapped mountain before them seemed steeper and rougher than ever, so steep in fact that it could not be ascended by a man on foot. A short distance below could be seen a lake containing water,[19] and the pass toward which they had been directing their course seemed to the north of them. They therefore turned their course in that direction. The road was sandy, and the brush that grew on it was only a few inches high. On their way they came to an abandoned Indian camp occupied by one poor old blind red man. He would hold his mouth open like a young bird begging for something to eat. One man dropped kernels of parched corn into his mouth, but instead of eating them, he quickly spit them out; it seemed that he had been left to die and could not or would not. His hair was white as snow. His skin looked about the color of a smoked ham, and so crippled was he that he crawled about like a beast,[20] on all fours. It was barely possible that he had been left to watch, and that his great infirmities were only pretended, but they seemed genuine enough, and were doubtless true. They left him in peaceable possession of the spot and traveled on.

They approached the base of the mountain in front of what they had all along supposed to be a pass, and found, as they had lately begun to suspect, that there was no pass that their wagons could be taken through, and they must be abandoned. The camp was poor. What little water there was had a salty taste, and they could only find here and there a bunch of the poorest grass. The oxen stood around as if utterly dispirited, and would sometimes make a faint effort to pick up and eat some of the dry brush that grew around the desolate camp. This camp is now known to be in the northern part of Death Valley, but then they knew no names for anything, but if dreariness and absence of life and threatened danger all around were any indication, they might well have named it Death Valley, as was afterwards done by the party with whom the author traveled.[21]

The party had been brave till now, but when they realized that they must make pack animals of themselves and trudge on, they knew not where, perhaps to only a lingering death, the keen edge of disappointment cut close, and they realized how desolate they were. They felt much inclined to attribute all their troubles to the advice of the Mormon. Some said that the plan was thus to wipe so many more hated gentiles out of the way, and wishes were deep and loud that the Mormons might all be buried out of sight in the Great Salt Lake. They thought Lot's wife must have been turned to salt in the neighborhood, everything was so impregnated with saline substances, and the same result might come to them.[22] But the inherent manhood of the little band came to their relief and they determined not to die without a struggle for escape and life.

They killed some of their oxen, and took the wood of their wagons and kindled fires to dry and smoke the flesh so it would be light and easy to carry with them.[23] They scattered all surplus baggage around the ground, carefully storing and saving the bit of bread that yet remained and dividing it equally among the party. They also divided the tea, coffee, rice, and some such things, and each one agreed that he could not ask aught of his neighbor more. Knapsacks were improvised from parts of the wagon canvas, and long strips of canvas were made into a sort of pack harness for the oxen. It was a sad sight to see the strong and vigorous young men of a few days ago reduced to such straits; almost skeletons now, with no hope of nourishment to invigorate them.[24] They made canteens by sewing a couple of small powder cans in cloth, with a band to go over the shoulders.

The Jayhawkers were still making their preparations when the Martin party and Reverend J. W. Brier and family came up to their camp, having taken a circuit around farther to the south. The Martin party was already in marching order and this camp was so poor that they did not wait, but gave all their oxen they had left to Mr. Brier and said they could get on faster without them. They took a straight course over the hills and up the mountain, saying they believed they had provisions enough upon their backs to last them through, and that nothing should check their progress till they reached the other side, where, they said, were fertile valleys and plenty of chance to live.[25]

The Doty party, or Jayhawkers, when they were ready, started first a northerly course to find a more favorable place to cross the range and drove their oxen with them, each with a small pack. They soon came to some good water, and after refreshing themselves turned westward to cross the great mountain before them.[26] Both men and oxen were shod with moccasins made of rawhide to protect the feet against sharp rocks. They could see no trail but merely picked out the best way to go.[27] While climbing the steep mountainside they came across a dead ox left by some party that had gone before them. They cut out the tongue and some of the best meat and ate it to eke out their own small stock, and carried some pieces with them, but soon threw it all away but enough for a roast for supper.

When it was getting dark they were almost at the summit, but there was no good camping place, and they saw a small firelight at a little distance and went to it, finding a poor lone camper taking care of himself.[28] They camped here also. It seemed as if there were many men from the various parties scattered all around the country, each one seeking out the path which seemed to suit best his tender feet or present fancy, steering west as well as mountains and cañons would permit, some farther north, some farther south, and generally demoralized, each thinking that as a last resort he would be able to save his own life. It seemed to be a question of will and endurance, strong hearts, and keeping the body in motion. The weak and faint must fail, and the strong said to the weak, "Stand up; be a man; don't fall down," and so the strong spurred on the weak and kept them up as best they could.

Down the mountain they went, on the west side, and instead of Los Angeles, which some of them expected to see, they saw only a salt lake in the midst of a barren desert valley and their route lay directly across it.[29] They traveled in several directions as they went across. One went across the valley on a strip of dried mud between two small lakes. Others followed down along the east side of the lake near the foot of the mountain, where they found some good water and an old Indian camp.[30] They found some mesquite beans, which they did not know were of much use, but really, if they had known how to fix them up a little, they would have been good food.

Captain Doty's mess crossed between the lakes on the strip of dry mud while others went on where it was still soft and left marks of their footsteps. Both parties turned up a small cañon on the west side and began the ascent of a black and barren range, containing no water, but in the bed of the ravine near the summit they found some damp sand and tried to dig with their hands to find some of the precious fluid.[31] But no water came, and in the morning, one of their number, Mr. Fish, died and was left unburied on the barren rocks. No doubt his bones could be found there today.

Turning west again, they had a downgrade over a most barren and rocky road for many miles. The prospect from this point was anything but cheering. To the left a large lake could be seen, and from their previous experience they concluded it to be salt,[32] and the valley they were coming to was very sandy, and the hardest sort of footing for men and animals as weak as those of the party were. It must be crossed before there was any possibility of water and, when across, it was quite uncertain whether they could obtain any. One of their number had already died of thirst and fatigue and all were suffering terribly.

The valley seemed about eight miles across and before they were halfway over, Mr. Ischam (one of their party) sat down, perfectly exhausted, and said he could not take another step. No one was able to assist him or give him a drink of water, and they could not tarry to see if rest would refresh him. They could only look sadly at him and pass on in silence, for he seemed fast wasting away.[33] The thought came to everyone that perhaps it would be his turn next to sit down and see the others pass on. In fact the probability of any more of them living another day was very poor, for they all grew weaker and weaker with every hour, and no one knew how many hours must pass before they could hope for water. There was not moisture enough in their poor bodies to make tears, and no one dare open his mouth, lest all the moisture suddenly evaporate and respiration cease.

Those who had no cattle took different courses to reach the hills and mountains on the west side of this valley, hoping there to find water and signal to the others if they were successful. All except the two men managed to get across, and finding no water, the packs were taken from the oxen and they were driven to the lake which appeared on the left.[34] Reaching the lake they found the water red in color and so strong of alkali that no man or beast could take a single swallow. They drove the cattle back again with sad hearts and almost despondent, for in the rough, dry rocks of the mountains there seemed no signs of water. But they were saved again. Those who bore farthest to the right in their course to the mountains, steering toward a pile of tremendous rocks, found a little stream of good water, which flowed only a short distance and then sank into the sand.[35] This good news spread rapidly, and all soon gathered at the little streamlet. It was slow work getting water for them all, but by being patient they were all filled up. Some took two canteens of water and hurried back to Mr. Ischam, whom they found still alive, but his mouth and throat so dry and parched and his strength so small that he was unable to swallow a single drop, and while they waited he breathed his last. With their hands and feet they dug away the sand for a shallow grave, placed the body in it, covered it with his blankets, and then scraped the sand back over again to make a little mound over their dead comrade. Perhaps if he could have walked a mile farther he might have lived, and but for the little trickling stream of water from the rocks they might all be dead, so slight were the circumstances that turned the scale to balance toward life or death.

There was so little feed for oxen that they could gain no strength, but were much refreshed by the water and could still travel. One was killed here, and the meat, poor as it was, gave the men new strength. They all guessed it to be at least fifty miles to the base of the great snow mountain before them,

and what there was between no one could tell, for there were hills and valleys between.[36] Leaving the little spring, their course led first up a small
cañon, and when they reached the summit of the ridge a small valley covered with sagebrush was before them, the most fertile spot they had seen for
a long time.[37] The descent to this valley was through another cañon, which
was filled with large boulders for much of the way, and over these it seemed
almost impossible to get the cattle.[38] They had seen no water since leaving
the little stream, and the plain they were now approaching seemed thirty
miles wide, with no signs of streams or springs. However, just at the foot of
the cañon, they found a small water hole, but the water was so salty that even
the oxen refused to drink it.[39]

They decided to make a push across the plain and endeavor to reach
the other side in two days, and they knew there could be no water on its
even expanse.[40] The plain seemed quite an upgrade from where they were to
the base of the mountain.

On the second day they all reached the point they were aiming for
except Reverend J. W. Brier and family, and they came in one day behind.
Everyone looked out for himself and had no time nor strength to spare to
help others. Here on a small bench overlooking the country to the south and
east but still a long distance from the snow, they found some holes of water,[41]
and some bunchgrass a little farther up the hill. Here was a large trail[42] coming from the north and leading from this point [southward]. There were no
signs of recent use, but there were many indications that it was quite ancient
and had been considerably traveled in time past. This was quite encouraging
to many of them and they declared they would follow this trail which would
surely lead to someplace well known, in a better country. They cared not
whether it led to California, Mexico, or Texas, only that they might get out
of this country which seemed accursed. Anyplace where they could get
something to eat and drink would be better than this.

Mr. and Mrs. Brier had some pretty hard struggles to get along, and
everyone of this party has ever been loud in praise of the energy and determination of the brave little woman of the Brier mess. All agreed that she was
by far the best man of the party. She was the one who put the packs on the
oxen in the morning. She it was who took them off at night, built the fires,
cooked the food, helped the children, and did all sorts of work when the
father of the family was too tired, which was almost all of the time. They all
said that he, like other ministers, had fallen out with any work but that of the
tongue, and seemed perfectly willing for someone else to do the work. Mrs.
Brier had the sympathy of everyone, and many would have helped her if they

could. She waited on her big husband with untiring zeal, and still had time to care for the children with all of a mother's love. It seemed almost impossible that one little woman could do so much. It was entirely to her untiring devotion that her husband and children lived. Mr. Brier had but little sympathy or help from anyone but her. Some were quite sarcastic in their remarks about the invalid preacher who never earned his bread by the sweat of his brow, and by their actions showed that they did not care very much whether he ever got through or not. They thought he ought to have asserted his manliness and taken the burden on himself, and not lean upon his delicate and trusting wife as he seemed to do. All are sure that it is to his faithful wife the Reverend J. W. Brier owed his succor from the sands of that desert.[43]

Looking back on the scenes of that day, the way the selfish dispositions of people were made manifest is almost incredible. Everyone seemed to think only of saving his own life, and every spark of human sympathy and kindness seemed extinguished. A man would drink the last cup of water even if his neighbor choked.[44]

This camp was the same one which the author mentions in his narrative, to which Rogers and himself crept so silently and carefully at night to ascertain whether the occupants were friends or foes. They were much pleased to find it was Captain Doty of the Jayhawkers and his mess, who had remained behind to dry the flesh of an ox they had killed when it could travel no longer. The others had gone on ahead,[45] following the trail, leaving these to follow. They stayed here two days, and it was while waiting here that the Reverend J. W. Brier came up, as before related, and they all went on together when they moved.

Nearly every man had carried a gun in the early days of the expedition, hoping to kill game and to be well armed in case of attack by Indians or enemies, but they began to find that they were useless encumbrances, and first one and then another would throw away his firearms as a burden too great for a weary man to bear. There was no game, and the poor weak men hardly deemed their own lives worth defending against an enemy when a day or two of lack of water would end the matter, of life at any rate.

As they slept they dreamed the most tantalizing dreams of clear, rippling brooks of water; of wading knee deep in the most beautiful of ponds; of hoisting the old moss-covered bucket from some deep, old well; of breaking and eating great white loaves of bread; of surrounding the home table with its load of steaming beans and bacon, fragrant coffee, and delicious fried cakes. With such dreams of comfort, they awoke to realize more fully the terrors of their dry and swollen throats, the discomfort of empty stomachs.

Water and food were the great riches of life to them then. Had piles of twenty-dollar pieces been on the one hand and a bucket of cold water on the other there is no doubt of the choice that would have been made.

Seven or eight miles from this place were two branches to the trail. One led into the mountains toward the snow, and the other still bore southerly.[46] They could see that some other party who had no oxen to drive had taken the more [westerly] route, which seemed to lead more directly in the direction of the mines of California. Those who came later with animals thought it would be folly to try to cross the deep snow they could see on the mountains before them and concluded that it would be safer to the south of the snow line, braving the danger of scarcity of water, rather than to perish in the snow. Captain Doty was willing to attempt the [western] branch of the trail if the others so decided, but the general feeling was in favor of the more plain and open trail which led away from the snows. It is known that this [western] branch led over what is known as Walker's Pass, coming out at the Kern River.

Taking then the southern branch, the party passed through a range of low mountains, and then the country before them seemed quite level for a hundred miles.[47]

They expected they would find much difficulty on account of water, as their experience had taught them that it was very scarce in such locations, but this trail, when they came to follow it, led them for eight or ten miles over a level piece of high land that looked as if it might have slid down from the high mountain at some day long past, and this easily traveled road brought them at last to the top of a steep hill, down which they went and found, near the bottom, a small, weak stream of water, but no grass, and but little fuel of any kind. (This was the same camp at which Rogers and the author overtook the advance party.) Here they killed an ox, which made a good meal for all, and not much remained over, for many had no oxen and were getting out of all sorts of provisions. They depended much on the generosity of their fellow travelers. Many of them stood back, and waited till those who owned the food were satisfied, and were very grateful when they were invited to take even the poorest morsels.

They could count the oxen and make a pretty close guess of how many days they could live in this way, even with the best probable fortune favoring them, and to the best of them there was but little hope, and to those who were dependent it seemed as if the fate of Fish and Ischam might be theirs almost any day. When the author conversed with them at this camp he found them the first really heartbroken men he had ever seen. Some were men of middle age who had left good farms that gave them every need, and these they had left to seek a yellow phantom, and now there were yellow phantoms of a different sort rearing their dreadful forms all about them. They called themselves foolish gold hunters to forsake a land of plenty for a chance to leave their bones in a hot desert. More eyes than one filled with tears, and hopes in more than one breast vanished to almost nothing. More than one would gladly have placed himself back where he could have been assured of the poorest fare he ever saw upon his farm, for bread and water would have been an assurance of life, of which there seemed to be really but little expectation here.

When they left this camp in the cañon, the trail was between two high rocks, rising like walls on each side. In one place they were so near together that an ox could hardly squeeze through. In a very short time they came to a bunch of willows growing out in the open ground. The little bunch or grove was forty or fifty feet in diameter, and in the center was a spring of water. The center of the clump had been cleared out, making a sort of corral of bushes, enclosing the spring.[48] On the outside there was quite a little growth of grass, which was a fortunate thing for their poor beasts.

Away in the distance, rising up a little against the [southern] sky, they could see mountains with snow on them, and it seemed as if it were a journey of five or six days to reach them,[49] but the good water and the grass bolstered up their spirits wonderfully, for there was present relief and rather better prospects ahead. They were pretty sure that the wide plain held no water. Everything that would hold the precious drink was filled, and the best preparations made for what they believed was to be the final struggle for life. They rested one day and prepared for the very worst that might [be] before them. Early in the morning, when they could see plainest, they looked across the expanse before them and really it did not seem quite so barren, hot, and desolate as the region they had passed, and they talked and hoped that this would be the last desert they must cross and that Los Angeles lay just beyond the sunny ridge they could dimly see ahead. There were some fears that more than one would not live to answer roll call on the other side, but it was the last hope, and worth an earnest, active trial.

Early in the morning, much refreshed, they started on again with rather sober faces. That night one man insisted on sleeping with his clothes and boots all on—for, he said, if he died, he wanted to die in full dress. Another day and some thought they could see trees on the mountains ahead of them, and this renewed their courage greatly. In the middle of the day they suffered greatly with the heat, and the dry air seemed to drink up every bit of moisture from everybody.[50] When they killed an ox, they saved the blood and ate it. The intestines, cleaned with the fingers, made food when roasted on the fire, and pieces of hide, singed and roasted, helped to sustain life. The water was nearly all gone. Only [those with] power of will and strength of body had kept any. Captain Asa Haines sat down one day and said he could go no farther, but his comrade, L. D. Stephens, who had kept a little rice, a little tea, and a dry crust of bread for time of need, took a little water in a cup and made some soup, which he forced his friend to eat, and soon he revived and was able to move on again. That was true friendship.

The next night Stephens himself awoke and seemed perishing with thirst. He crawled over to Doty's bed and begged for just one sip of water. Doty, in the goodness of his heart, took his canteen from under his head [and] divided the last few drops with him, and the death which threatened him was held off. Captain Doty found it necessary to talk very seriously to those who mourned and talked of failing. He never gave up in the least. He encouraged all to make every step they could and know no such word as fail. When they said that death would be easier than life, he told them [that was] so, but that life was possible if they only willed it, and a better life than had been theirs. And so he kept them encouraged and kept them putting one foot before the other, pointing out the ever lessening distance to the mountain before them. He appealed to their manhood. "Be men," said he, "be brave and courageous, and you have more strength than you believe." Thus by example and words he proved to be a true captain to his little band.

Their water was all gone, every drop, and still the foothills seemed far away. The supply of meat ran out. Tom Shannon killed an ox, and when those who had cattle had taken some, the others who had none were told to divide the rest. There was no water to dress or cook it, but it helped to sustain life. Entrails, bones, sinews, bits of hide and everything was used. One man was seen with an ox horn, burning the end in the fire and gnawing away at the softened portion. It was something terrible to see human beings eating what the dogs would cast aside. One man saw some moist looking earth on the shady side of a bunch of brush and he dug down and got a handful of it, from which he tried to suck the moisture. He failed, and the bad taste of the earth made him suffer more than before. Many bones of horses and cattle now appeared along the trail. They seemed to have been there a long time, and some were partly decayed. On this waterless stretch one of their number, a Frenchman, wandered off, searching for water in little hollows or puddles, and never came back to camp. He was supposed to be dead, but ten years afterward some surveyors found him in a Digger Indian camp.

An idea how selfish men will get under such circumstances may be gained by relating that on one occasion when an ox was killed, the liver was carried to the brave little Mrs. Brier for herself and children, and she laid it aside for a few moments till she could attend to some other duties before cooking it. Darkness coming on meanwhile, some unprincipled, ungallant thief stole it, and only bits of offal and almost uneatable pieces were left to sustain their lives. That anyone could steal the last morsel from a woman and her children surpasses belief, but yet it was plain that there was at least one man in the party who could do it.[51] No one can fully understand or describe such scenes as this unless he has looked into just such hungry looking, haggard eyes and faces, a mixture of determination and despair, the human expression almost vanishing, and the face of a starving wolf or jackal taking its place. There are no words to paint such a state of things to him who has never seen and known [them].

But there were true men, true, charitable hearts in that little band. Though death stared them in the face, they never forgot their fellow men. As they slowly crawled along, many would wander here and there beside the trail and fall behind, especially the weaker ones, and many were the predictions that such and such a one would never come up again, or reach the camp. Then it was that these noble souls, tired almost beyond recovery themselves, would take water and go back to seek the wandering ones and give them drink and help them on. More than one would thus have perished in the sands but for the little canteen of water carried back by some friend. Only a swallow or two would often revive their failing strength and courage, and with slow step they would move on again. How much good a crust of bread would have done such a poor creature. Bread there was none—nothing but the flesh of their poor oxen, wasted and consumed by days of travel and lack of food till it had no goodness in it. Even the poor oxen, every night seemed to be the end of their walking; every morning it was feared that that would be the last time they would be able to rise upon their feet.

Already five or six days had passed since they left the camp at the willows where they had their last supply of water, and still they were on the desert. The journey was longer than they had expected, partly owing to the slow progress they had made, for there were frequent stops to rest or they could not move at all. The mountains seemed nearer every day, and the trees were outlined more plainly each morning as they started out. Captain Doty used every circumstance to encourage them. He would remark upon the favorable signs of water in the hills before them, and the hope that there might be some game to provide better meat than that of starving oxen. Thus he renewed their hope and kept alive their courage. He must have had a great deal of fortitude to hide his own sad feelings, for they must as surely have come to him as to anyone, and to keep up always an air of hope, courage, and determination to succeed. If he had been a man of less spirit and good judgment it is very probable that many more would have been left by the wayside to die.

About this point, the trail, which had been growing fainter and fainter, seemed to vanish entirely. One could move in almost any direction, to right or left as he chose, and because of this, previous travelers had doubtless scattered and thus left no trail. It was thought best that this company should spread out and approach the mountains in as broad a front as possible so as to multiply the chances of finding water, and so they started out in pairs, some to the right and some to the left, each selecting the point where water seemed most probable.

Tom Shannon and a companion were one of these pairs. Tom was one of the few who still stuck to his gun, for he felt that it might save his life sometime. He and his companion separated about a mile, each looking at all points that showed the least sign of water. Suddenly a jackrabbit started from a bush, the first game Shannon had seen for more than a month. He pulled the rifle on him as he was making some big bound and had the good luck to nearly split his head open. Rushing up to his game he put his mouth to the wound and sucked the warm blood as it flowed, for it was the first liquid he had seen; but instead of allaying his fearful thirst it seemed to make it worse and he seemed delirious. A little way up the gulch he saw a rock and a green bush and steered for it, but found no water. He sat down with his back to the rock, his rifle leaning up nearby, pulled his old worn hat over his eyes, and suffered an agony of sickness. He realized that life was leaving his body, and there he sat with no power to move and no desire to make an effort. It seemed as if he could see plain before him all the trail from where he sat, back over all the deserts, mountains, and rivers to the old place in Illinois. He entirely forgot the present, and seemed unconscious of everything but the pictures of the past. The mind seemed growing freer from its attachment to the body and at liberty to take in his whole past life, and bright scenes that had gone before. How long he sat thus he knows not. His companion was fortunate in finding water, and when he had refreshed himself he set out to find poor Tom, of whom he could see nothing. Going toward where he heard the shot, he followed on till he saw him at the rock, almost doubled up, with his face concealed by his hat. "Oh! Tom!" said he, but there came no answering motion, and going nearer he called again and still no answer and no sign. Poor Tom had surely passed on to the better land, thought he, and salvation was so near. He approached and lifted the hat rim. There was a movement of the eyes, a quivering of the muscles of the face, and a sort of semiunconscious stare such as precedes approaching dissolution.

Quickly holding back his head he poured water between his lips from his canteen and it was swallowed. Then a little more, and then some more, and life seemed coming back again into a troublesome world, bringing pain with it, and the consciousness of a suffering body. After a time he felt better and was helped to his feet, and together they went to the water hole, where they made a fire and cooked the rabbit, which was the first savory meat they had tasted for a long time. Tom felt better and told his companion how he felt after tasting the warm rabbit's blood, and how he had nearly gone off into the sleep of death.

"If you had been a little longer finding me," said Tom, "I should soon have been out of this sad world." They fired a signal gun, looked down at the bones of the rabbit, drank more water, and gradually felt new life coming to them. The mountains seemed more fertile, and there was brush and grass nearby, timber farther up, and still higher a cap of snow extending far along the range, both [west] and [east]. Towards night on this eventful day the scattered travelers began to come slowly into camp, attracted by the guns and the smoke of the fire made by those who first found the water. Some were nearly as far gone as Tom Shannon was, and great caution had to [be] used in giving them water on their empty stomachs. One man named Robinson became so weak before he got near camp that his companions placed him on the back of one of the animals and a man walked on either side to catch him if he fell off. When they got within a mile of the water he insisted that he was strong enough to take care of himself and not be watched every minute, and they relaxed their vigilance. He soon fell off, and when they went to him he refused to be put back on the animal again or to walk any farther. "Just spread my blankets down," said he, "and I will lie down and rest a little and after a while I will come along into camp." So they left him and pushed on to water, and when they were a little refreshed, went back to him with water, and to help him to come in, but when they came to him they found him dead.[52] He did not seem to have moved after he had lain down. He did not seem so bad off as Shannon was when he lay down, and probably a few swallows of water at that time would have saved his life. It seemed sad indeed, after so much suffering and striving to get along, that he should die within a mile of water that would have saved his life. If he had possessed a little more strength so that the spark of life could have remained a little longer, the cooling moisture from the canteen would have revived it, and a little rest would have placed him on his feet again. They had no tools to dig a grave, not even a knife, for they had left every weight in camp, so they covered him closely in his blankets and sadly returned to their friends. They had all along hoped that the Frenchman who had wandered away would come in, but he never came. There were several water holes scattered around at this point, which seemed to be a sort of sunken place in the hills, and quite large brush could be obtained for fire and grass for the oxen. Those who had been good hunters and had thrown away their rifles as useless burdens now began to look at hills before them and think that game might be found in them, as well as water. There were only one or two guns in the whole party.[53] They thought that this must surely be the edge of the great desert they had crossed, and only the snowy range before them could be the obstacle that separated them from Los Angeles.

One day from here would bring them to the edge of the snow, and they debated as to the best course to pursue. Some of them were fearful they could not cross the snow with the oxen, for it seemed to be quite deep. The best place to cross seemed directly [southwest] of them.[54] South was a higher peak, and to the north it was surely impassable. There seemed to be a faint sign of a trail from this point towards the lowest point in the snow mountains. There were some bones of cattle around the springs, which they thought was an indication that in years gone by there had been some traveling on this trail. There surely would be water in the snow which could be got by melting it, and on the whole it seemed best to make the attempt to cross at the lowest place. There were no signs of travel, except the trail which had not been used in years, nor signs of civilization except the bones.

Starting from the water holes, which showed no signs of having been used for several years, their next camp was, as they had calculated, on the edge of the snow, where they found plenty of dry juniper trees for fire and, of course, plenty of water. Here they killed an ox and fed the hungry so that they were pretty well refreshed. This was an elevated place and they could look back over the trail across the desert for what seemed to them a hundred miles, and the great dangers of their journey were discussed. Said one of them to Tom Shannon, "Tom, you killed the first game we have come across in two months. Even the buzzards and coyotes knew better than to go out into the country where the cursed Mormon saint sent us numbskulls." Another said that while they had been seeking a heaven on earth, they had passed through purgatory or perhaps a worse place still, nearer the one from which sulphurous fumes arise, and now they hoped that there might be a somewhat more heavenly place beyond the snow. One who had been silent seemed awakened by inspiration and spoke in impromptu lines somewhat as follows, as he pointed out to the dim distance:

> "Yonder in mountains' gray beauty,
>   Wealth and fame decay.
> Yonder, the sands of the desert,
> Yonder, the salt of the sea,
> Yonder, a fiery furnace,
> Yonder, the bones of our friends,
> Yonder the old and the young
>   Lie scattered along the way."

Some even confessed the desperate thoughts that had come to their minds when they were choking and starving. We have mentioned four of the train who had perished beside the trail and it will be remembered that one party of eleven started out on foot before the wagons were abandoned by the rest of the party. Nothing was heard of these for seven years, but long afterward nine skeletons were found at the remains of a camp, and the other two were afterward seen in the goldfields. When spoken to about this party, they burst into tears and could not talk of it. So it is known that at least thirteen men perished in the country which has well been named Death Valley.[55]

People who have always been well fed, and have never suffered from thirst till every drop of moisture seemed gone from the body so they dare not open their mouth lest they dry up and cease to breathe, can never understand, nor is there language to convey the horrors of such a situation. The story of these parties may seem like fairy fables, but to those who experienced it all, the strongest statements come far short of the reality. No one could believe how some men, when they are starving, take on the wild aspect of savage beasts and that one could never feel safe in their presence. Some proved true and kind and charitable, even with death staring them in the face, and never forgot their fellow men. Some that seemed weakest proved strongest in the final struggle for existence.

Early next morning, before the sun rose, they started to cross the snow, leaving their comrade Robinson behind, rolled up in his blankets, taking his everlasting sleep so far as the troubles of this world are concerned. What the day would bring forth very few could have any idea. Go on they must, and this direction seemed most promising. If the snow should prove hard enough to hold up the oxen, they could probably cross before night, but if compelled to camp in the snow it was a doubtful case for them.

The snow held them as they advanced on it, but grew a little softer as the sun got higher. The tracks of both men and animals were stained with blood from their worn-out feet. When they turned the summit they found more timber, and the ravine they followed was so shaded that the force of the sun was broken, and they really did not suffer very much from slumping through the snow, and so got safely over. Not far below the snow they found a running brook of clear, sweet water, with willows along the banks and trees on the hill, the first really good water for a month or two. This is the same camp where Rogers and his companion ate their meal of quail, hawk, and crow a few days before, and these travelers knew by the remains of the little campfire that they were following on the trail of the two men who had gone before.

This place was so great an improvement on the camps of the past that all hands began to talk and act more rational as hope dawned more brightly on them. Those who had guns branched off to search for game, but found they were too weak for that kind of work, and had to sit down very often to rest. When they tried to run, they stumbled down and made very poor progress.

Captain Doty, Tom Shannon, and Bill Rude sat down to rest on a bold point above the creek. While there, three wild horses came along within easy range, and thinking they would form better meat than the oxen, each man picked his animal and all fired simultaneously, bringing them all to the ground. This seemed a piece of glorious luck, and all rushed in like wolves after a wounded animal. It was not very long before each had a chunk of meat in his hand, and many a one did not stop from eating because it was not cooked. Some declared they never ate anything so delicious in all their lives before, and wondered why horses were not used as food instead of hogs and cattle. As they satisfied their ravenous appetites they ate more like beasts than like men, so nearly were they starved, and so nearly had their starving condition made them fall from their lofty estate.

As they passed on down this cañon they found it very brushy, and on the dry leaves under the wide-spreading trees they saw signs of bear and perhaps other animals. There were some swampy places where it was grassy, and into these the cattle rushed with great eagerness for the food they had so long suffered for. Some of Mr. Brier's cattle went in, and in tramping around for food sank deep into the mud and could not be coaxed out again. Mrs. Brier threw clubs at them, but they did not seem inclined to pay much attention to her attacks, so she was forced to go in after them herself, and in so doing also sank into the mud and could not get out without assistance. All this time her reverend husband sat outside on the hard ground at a safe distance, but did not offer any help. Probably if an extended and learned lecture on the effects of gravitation would have done any good, he would have been ready with prompt and extended service to one whom he had promised to love and cherish.

About this time L. D. Stephens came along and, seeing the condition of the unfortunate woman, at once went to her assistance and helped her to dry land. Brier himself never made a move nor said a word. Stephens looked terribly cross at him and remarked to his companions that if the preacher himself had been the one stuck in the mud, he would have been quite inclined to leave him there for all of helping him.

The cañon grew narrow as they descended, and the brush thicker, so that to follow the bed of the stream was the only way to get along. The cattle seemed to scent a bear and stampeded in terror through the brush in various directions, all except one which was being led by a rope. They tried to follow the animals in a desperate effort to recover them and a few blankets they had upon their backs, but could only make slow progress. Tom Shannon and two others found a fresh bear track and determined to follow it awhile in the hope of having revenge on the cause of their mishap with the oxen. They took their blankets and kept the trail till night, when they camped, but were at so great an elevation that a snowstorm came with six inches of snow, so they could no longer follow the track.

They were very hungry and on the way back came across some wild cherries, which had dried perfectly dry as they hung on the bushes. These they picked and ate, cracking the seeds with their teeth, and declaring them to be the best of fruit. Good appetites made almost anything taste good then. They got back to the creek next day pretty nearly starved and with neither a bear nor runaway oxen to reward them for their two days' hard work.

Wood and water were plenty, but grass was scarce and their oxen had to live on brush and leaves, but this was infinitely better than the stunted and bitter shrubs of the desert. They came out of the brush at last into the open bottomland where the brook sank out of sight in the sand, and sagebrush appeared all about. From this [place] on, over the elevated point which projected out nearly across the valley, their experience and emotions in coming in sight of vast herds of cattle feeding on rolling grassy hills, or reclining under great oak trees scattered over the more level lands, were much the same as came to the author and his party when the same scene was suddenly opened to them. Signs of civilization and of plenty so suddenly appearing after so many weeks of suffering and desolation were almost enough to turn their heads, and more than one of the stouthearted pioneers shed tears of joy.

Only a few days before, they could scarcely have believed it possible to find a spot so lovely.

But to hungry, more than half-starved men, points of artistic beauty and sober reflections over the terrors of the past found little place, and their first thought was to satisfy the cravings of hunger, which were assuredly none the less when they beheld the numerous fat cattle all around them. There was no one to ask or to buy from, and to kill and eat without permission might be wrong and might get them into difficulty, but one might as well ask a starving wolf to get permission to slay and eat when a fat lamb came across his path as to expect these men to take very much time to hunt up owners. When life or death are the questions that present themselves, men are not so apt to discuss the right or wrong of any matter.

Tom Shannon and a couple of others did not wait long at any rate, but crawled down the creek bed till they were opposite a few fine animals and then crept up the bank very near to them. Two or three shots rang out and as many fine cattle were brought down. The live cattle ran away and the hungry men soon had the field to themselves. Much quicker than can be told, the men had fat pieces of meat in their hands, which they devoured without cooking. The men acted like crazy creatures at a barbecue—each one cut for himself with very little respect for anyone. The boldest got in first and the more retiring came in later, but all had enough and gradually resumed more human actions and appearance.

They had hardly finished their bloody feast when they saw a small squad of men on horseback advancing toward them, and as they came near it was quite plain that they were all armed in some way. All had lassoes at their saddles, some had old-fashioned blunderbusses, and nearly everyone had a machete, or long bladed Spanish knife. As the horsemen drew near they formed into something like military order and advanced slowly and carefully. It was pretty evident they thought they were about to encounter a band of thieving Indians, but as they came closer they recognized the strangers as Americans and passed the compliments with them in a rather friendly manner.

Some of the Jayhawkers had been in the Mexican War and understood a few words of Spanish, and by a liberal use of signs were able to communicate with the armed party and tell them who they were, where they were going, and the unfortunate condition in which they found themselves. The men did not seem angry at losing so few of their cattle, and doubtless considered themselves fortunate in not suffering to the extent of some hundreds as they did sometimes by Indian raids, and invited the whole party down to the ranch house of the San Francisquito Rancho, of which this was a part.[56]

Arrived at the house, the ranchmen brought in a good, fat steer, which they killed, and told the poor Americans to help themselves and be welcome. This was on the fourth day of February, 1850.

The whole party remained here to rest themselves and their oxen for several days, and were royally entertained by the people at the ranch. They talked over the plans for the future, and considered the best course to pursue. They thought it would be wise to keep their oxen, for these would now improve in flesh, and as they had no money with which to buy food, they might still rely on them in further travels. The best oxen had survived, for the failing ones were selected to be killed when they were forced to have food. The weaker of their comrades had perished in the desert, and the remainder of the train consisted of the strongest men and the strongest oxen, and there seemed to be no question but that they could all live in this country where grass and water were both abundant, and [there was] every sign of more or less wild game.

Those of the company who had no cattle made their way directly to Los Angeles, and from thence to the coast, from which most of them reached San Francisco by sailing vessel. Those who had no money were given a passage on credit, and it is believed that all such debts were afterwards honestly paid.

Captain Doty made a proposition to buy out the oxen of some who had only one or two, giving his note for them payable in San Francisco or anywhere up north they might chance to meet, and many of them accepted and went to the coast. In this way Doty secured oxen enough to supply one for each of those who decided to go with him. They decided to use them for pack animals to carry their blankets, and to proceed slowly toward the mines, killing game, if possible, and permitting their animals to graze and improve in condition as they moved.

There must have been from twenty-five to forty people gathered at the ranch. Among them was the Reverend J. W. Brier, who seemed to want to impress it on the new California friends that he was the man of all others to be honored. The ranchman was a good Catholic, and Brier tried to make him understand that he, also, was very devout. He said, and repeated to him very often, "Me preacher," but he did not succeed very well in impressing the good Californian with the dignity of his profession, for he could talk no Spanish and was not highly gifted in sign language.

When they went away they had no way to reward their good friends, who had been friends indeed to them. They could only look their thanks and express themselves in a very few words of Spanish. *"Adios Amigos,"* said they to the scantily clothed travelers as they set out on their way to the mines.

They followed down the course of the river that flowed through the valley, the Santa Clara River, and knew that it would take them to the sea at last. Before they reached the mission of San Buena Ventura,[57] near the sea, they ran out of meat again, for they had failed to find game as they had expected, and Captain Asa Haines took the chance of killing a Spanish cow that looked nice and fat. They camped around the carcass and ate, and smoked the meat that was left. While [they were] thus engaged, two horsemen approached and, after taking a good look at the proceedings, galloped off again. When the party arrived at the mission they were arrested and taken before the *alcalde* to give an account of their misdeeds. They realized that they were now in a bad fix, and either horn of the dilemma was bad enough. They could not talk Spanish; they had no money; they had killed somebody's cow; they were very hungry; they might be willing to pay but had no way of doing it; they did not want to languish in jail, and how to get out of it they could not understand. Luck came to them, however, in the shape of a man who could speak both English and Spanish, to whom they told their story and who repeated it to the *alcalde,* telling him of their misfortunes and unfortunate condition, and when that officer found out all the circumstances he promptly released them, as he did not consider them as criminals. The cow was probably worth no more than ten dollars.

At Santa Barbara they found a chance to trade off some of their oxen for mares, which were not considered worth much,[58] and managed the barter so well that they came out with a horse apiece and a few dollars besides, with which to buy grub along the road. They depended mostly on their guns for supplying them with food. They supposed they were about three hundred miles from San Francisco,[59] and expected to meet with but few people except at the missions, of which they had learned there were a few along the road. At these there was not much to be had except dried beef. However, they managed to use the guns with fair success, and at last arrived safely at Stockton, where they sold some of their horses for more than double what they cost, and with a small number of horses they packed on to the gold mines.

Those of the party who went to Los Angeles managed in one way or another to get through on schooners, and many of them, after a year or two of hard work, made some money and returned to their homes in Illinois. It is hardly necessary to add that they did not return via Death Valley.

Some years afterward the members of this party who had returned to their eastern homes formed themselves into an organization which they called the Jayhawkers' Union, appointed a chairman and secretary, and each year everyone whose name and residence could be obtained was notified to be present at some designated place on the fourth day of February, which was the date on which they considered they passed from impending death into a richly promising life. They always had as good a dinner as Illinois could produce, cooked by the wives and daughters of the pioneers, and the old tales were told over again.

One part of the program was the calling of the roll and such reports and letters as had come to hand. The following is a list of the members of the party so far as can be ascertained, as gathered from recollections and from the reports of the meetings of the reunions.

LIST OF JAYHAWKERS

The following named were living, so far as known, in 1893: John B. Colton and Alonzo C. Clay, of Galesburg, Ill.; Deacon Luther A. Richards, of Woodhull, Ill.; Chas. B. Mecum, of Ripley, Iowa; John W. Plummer, of Tulon, Ill.; Edward Bartholomew, Urban P. Davidson, John Grosscup, and L. Dow Stephens, of San Jose, Calif.; Harrison Frans and Thomas Shannon, of Los Gatos, Calif.; J. W. Brier and wife, Lodi, Calif.; three children of Mr. Brier.

The following are supposed to be dead: Asa Haines, Knoxville, Ill.; Sidney P. Edgerton, formerly of Blair, Nebr.; Thomas McGrew, John Cole, Wm. B. Rude, Wm. Robinson, and Alex. Palmer, of Knoxville, Ill.; Marshall B. Edgerton, late of Galesburg, Ill.; Wm. Ischam, of Rochester, N.Y.; Mr. —— Fish, of Oskaloosa, Iowa; John L. West, Aaron Larkin, Capt. Edwin Doty, and Bruin Byram, of Knoxville, Ill.; Mr. ——Carter, of Wis.; Geo. Allen, Leander Woolsey, and Chas. Clark, of Henderson, Ill.; Mr. [Frederick] Gretzinger, of Oskaloosa, Iowa; and a Frenchman whose name is unknown.

There were some others connected more or less with the party at some part of the trip, but not coming in with the Jayhawker organization. So far as learned, their names are as follows: John Goller, Jim Woods, and Jim Martin of Miss.; Ed Croker of N.Y.; David Funk, Mr. Town, Henry Wade, wife and three children,[60] Nat Ward, John D. Martin, of Tex.; Old Francis, a Frenchman, Fred Carr, and Negro "Joe," from Miss.

There were a great many reports about finding rich mines about this time, and these stories have been magnified and told in all sorts of ways since then, and parties have returned to try to find the great riches.

Among the Jayhawkers were two Germans who could speak but little English and probably for this reason kept apart from the remainder of the party.

One day, after the wagons were abandoned, these German fellows were marching along alone with their packs on their backs in the warm sun, suffering very much for want of water and food, when one of them sat down on a hillside in pretty nearly absolute despair, while the other man went down into a ravine hoping to find a puddle of water in the rocky bottom somewhere, though it was almost a forlorn hope. All at once he called out to his partner on the hill, "John, come down here and get some of this gold. There is a lot of it." To this poor John Goller only replied, "No, I won't come. I don't want any gold, but I would like very much to have some water and some bread." And so they left the valuable find and slowly walked on, pulling through at last with the rest of them, and reaching Los Angeles.

The man who found the gold went to the Mission of San Luis Rey[61] and started a small clothing store, and sometime afterward was killed. John Goller settled in Los Angeles and established a wagon shop in which he did a successful business. He was an honest, industrious man and the people had great confidence in him. He often told them about what his partner had said about finding the gold in the desert, and the people gave him an outfit on two or three occasions to go back and relocate the find, but he did not seem to have much idea of location, and when he got back into the desert again, things looked so different to him that he was not able to identify the place, or to be really certain they were on the same trail where his companion found the gold.

The author saw him in 1860 and heard what he had to say about it, and is convinced that it was not gold at all which they saw. I told him that I more than suspected that what he saw was mica instead of gold and that both he and his partner had been deceived, for more than one man not used to gold had been deceived before now. "No sir!" said he, "I saw lots of gold in Germany, and when I saw that, I knew what it was." The author went back over that trail in 1860 and sought out the German on purpose to get information about the gold. He could not give the name of a single man who was in the party at that time, but insisted that it was gold he saw and that he knew the trail.[62]

The author was able to identify with reasonable certainty the trails followed by the different parties, but found no signs of gold formation except some barren quartz, and this after an experience of several years in both placer and quartz mines. So honest John Goller's famous placer mine still remains in the great list of lost mines, like the Gunsight Lead and other noted mines for which men have since prospected in vain.

CHAPTER XIV

Alexander Erkson's Statement and the Experience of Edward Coker

Alexander Combs Erkson was one of the pioneers of 1849, having left the state of Iowa in the month of May, when he assisted in organizing a company known as the Badger Company at Kanesville, the object being mutual assistance and protection. This company joined the Bennett party, mentioned so prominently in this history, at the Missouri and traveled with them or near them to the rendezvous near Salt Lake, where the new company was organized for the southern trip taken by the Death Valley party—the Jayhawkers and others. As the experience of Mr. Erkson was in some respects different from that of the parties mentioned, he having taken a different route for a part of the way, it was thought best to embody it in this history. The following was dictated to the editor of this book, and as Mr. Erkson died before the written account could be revised by him, it is the best that can possibly be obtained.[1]

MR. ERKSON'S STATEMENT

WE ARRIVED AT THE MORMON CAMP near Salt Lake, Salt Lake City, in the month of August. Several of us went to work getting out lumber for Brigham Young while we were waiting and resting. The Mormons all advised us not to undertake to go on by the northern route, and as the travelers gathered at this point, they canvassed the situation. We used our teams when we were at work for Brigham and assisted in building a dam across a cañon where he intended to build a woolen mill. I earned about a hundred dollars by my work, which was paid to me in ten-dollar pieces of a gold coin made by the Mormons. They were not like the U.S. coins. I remember one side had an eye and the words "Holiness to the Lord."[2]

We entered into an agreement with Captain Hunt, a Mormon, to pilot us through, and turned all our gold into that company, thus bringing none of the Mormon gold with us. We went on with the company as has been related in the foregoing pages, till we arrived at Mt. Misery, so named by us, when we took the back track, while Mr. Manly and the others went on as they have related. We had meetings by the light of a green-wood fire, and the matter was talked up in little knots of people, and then someone would get up and speak. One J. W. Brier, a preacher, was the principal blower. "You are going wrong!" said he. "We should go west, and in six weeks we will be loaded with gold!"

Hunt got a little confused at a place called Beaver Meadows, or Mountain Meadows, and thought perhaps he could find a new road. Several men were sent out to look, and some of us in camp played ball for amusement while we were waiting. Hunt's men came back and said there were no prospects of a new road, and he said he knew the southern route and believed it would be safe to go that way.[3]

He told us that we must decide the next day. When we came to the road where we were to separate, he filed off on his road, and the others filed off on their road, and then came back with their whips in their hands. I had filed in after Hunt, and they tried to convince me that I was very wrong. A Mr. Norton of Adrian, Michigan, promised Mrs. Erkson a horse to ride if she would go, and so I left Hunt and turned in on the other road, the hindmost wagon. (This is going back a little with the history and bringing it up to Mt. Misery.) On my way back from Mt. Misery I climbed up on a big rock and inscribed the date—Nov. 10, 1849.[4]

In our journey we came to what is called "The Rim of the Basin," and traveled along on that a distance till we came to the Santa Clara River and saw where the Indians had raised corn and melons. We followed on down that stream and found our teams gradually failing. Noting this we decided to overhaul our loads and reject a lot of things not strictly necessary to preserve life. I know I threw out a good many valuable and pretty things by the roadside. I remember six volumes of Rollin's *Ancient History,* nicely bound, with my name on the back, that were piled up and left.[5] We followed along near the Santa Clara River till it emptied into the Virgin River.[6] It was somewhere along here that we first saw some yucca trees. The boys often set fire to them to see them burn.

The Virgin River was a small stream running on about the course we wanted to travel, and we followed this course for thirty or forty miles. We found plenty of wood and water and mesquite. After a while the river turned off to the left, while we wanted to keep to the right, so we parted company there. We heard of a river beyond, which they called the Big Muddy, and we went up a little arroyo, then over a divide to some tableland that led us down to the Big Muddy.[7] We made our wagons as light as possible, taking off all the boards and stakes we could possibly get along without. William Philipps and others were placed on short allowance.[8] They had an idea that I had more provisions in my wagon than I ought to have, but I told them that it was clothing that we used to sleep on. I divided among them once or twice. When we reached the Muddy we stopped two or three days, for there was plenty of feed. It was a narrow stream that seemed as if it must come from springs. It was narrow between banks, but ran pretty deep, and a streak of fog marked its course in the morning. We understood it was not very far from where we left the Virgin River to the Colorado, some said not more than fourteen miles, and that the Colorado turned sharply to the south at that point. Mr. Rhynierson and wife had a child born to them on the Virgin River, and it was named Virginia.

It was a gloomy trip the whole time on the Muddy. I lost three or four head of cattle, all within a day and a night. Mrs. Erkson walked to lighten the load and would pick all the bunches of grass she saw and put them on the wagon to feed the oxen when we stopped. I let them pass me, and stopped and fed the cattle, and slept ourselves. It was said that we ran great risks from Indians, but we did not see any. I had at this time only two yoke of oxen left.

We overtook the party next morning at nine o'clock, having met some of them who were coming back after us. All were rejoiced that we had come on safely. Here I met Elisha Bennett and told him my story. He said he could sell me a yoke of oxen. He had a yoke in J. A. Philipps' team and was going to take them out. He said nothing in particular as to price. I said that I wanted to see Mr. Philipps and talk with him about the matter, for he had said Bennett should not have the cattle. I went over to see him and spoke to him about Bennett's cattle and he told me they had quarreled and I could have them, and so we made a bargain. I gave twenty dollars for the cattle, the last money I had, and as much provisions as he could carry on his back. They were making up a party to reach the settlements at the Williams ranch, and I made arrangements for them to send back provisions for us. About thirty started that way—young men, and men with no families with them.

I got along very well with my new team after that. It was about forty miles from water to water, and I think we camped three times. At one place we found that provisions had been left, with a notice that the material was for us, but the redskins got the provisions. We struck a spring called——,[9] a small spring of water, and a child of some of the party died there and was buried.

We then went more nearly south to find the Mojave River, for we hoped to find water there. It was very scarce with us then. We had one pretty cold day, but generally fine weather, and to get along we traveled at night, and a party struck the Mojave. Here there was some grass, and the mustard was beginning to start up and some elder bushes to put forth leaves. I picked some of the mustard and chewed it to try to get back my natural taste. Here the party divided, a part going to the left to San Bernardino and the remainder to the right to Cucamonga. I was with the latter party and we got there before night.

Rhynierson said to one of the party, "Charlie, you had better hurry on ahead and try to get some meat before the crowd comes up." Charlie went on ahead and we drove along at the regular gait, which was not very fast about these times. We saw nothing of Charlie and so I went to the house to look for him and found him dead drunk on wine. He [Rhynierson] had not said a word to them about provisions. That wine wrecked us all. All had a little touch of scurvy, and it seemed to be just what we craved. I bought a big tumbler of it for two bits and carried it to my wife. She tasted it at first rather gingerly, then took a little larger sip of it, and then put it to her lips and never stopped drinking till the last drop was gone. I looked a little bit surprised and she looked at me and innocently asked, "Why! Haven't you had any?" I was afraid she would be the next one to be dead drunk, but it never affected her in that way at all. We bought a cow here to kill, and used the meat either fresh or dried, and then went on to the Williams, or Chino, ranch. Colonel Williams was glad to see us, and said we could have everything we wanted. We wanted to get wheat, for we had lived so long on meat that we craved such food. He told us about the journey before us and where we would find places to camp. Here we found one of the Gruwells.[10] We camped here a week, meeting many emigrants who came by way of Santa Fe.

We went on from here to San Gabriel, where we stayed six weeks to rest and recuperate the cattle. In the good grass we found here they all became about as fat as ever in a little while. Here the party all broke up and no sort of an organization was kept up beyond here. Some went to Los Angeles, some went on north, trading off their cattle for horses, and some went directly to the coast. We went to the Mission of San Fernando, where we got some oranges, which were very good for us. There is a long, tedious hill there to get over. We made up ten wagons. By the time we reached the San Francisquito Ranch,[11] I had lost my cattle. I went down to this ranch and there met Mr. and Mrs. Arcane getting ready to go to San Pedro. We came north by way of Tejon Pass and the Kern River, not far from quite a large lake, and reached the mines at last. I remember we killed a very fat bear and tried out the grease, and with this grease and some flour and dried apples Mrs. Erkson made some pretty good pies, which the miners were glad to get at a dollar and even two dollars apiece.

> *Mr. Erkson followed mining for about a year and then went into other business, until he came to Santa Clara Valley and began farming near Alviso. He has been a highly respected citizen and progressive man. He died in San Jose in the spring of 1893.*
>
> *Edward Coker was one of a party of twenty-one men who left their wagons, being impatient of the slow progress made by the ox train, and organized a pack train in which they were themselves the burden carriers. They discarded everything not absolutely necessary to sustain life, packed all their provisions into knapsacks, bravely shouldered them, and started off on foot from the desert to reach California by the shortest way.*
>
> *Among those whom Mr. Coker can recollect are Captain Nat. Ward, Jim Woods, Jim Martin of Missouri, John D. Martin of Texas, "Old Francis," a French Canadian, Fred Carr, Negro "Joe" and some others from Coffeeville, Mississippi, with others from other states.*
>
> *Mr. Coker related his experience to the author somewhat as follows.*[12]

THE EXPERIENCE OF EDWARD COKER

ONE OTHER OF THE PARTY WAS A COLORED MAN who joined us at the camp when we left the families, he being the only remaining member of a small party who had followed our wagon tracks after we had tried to proceed south. This party was made up of a Mr. Culverwell, who had formerly been a writer in a government office at Washington, D.C., a man named Fish claiming to be a relative of Hamilton Fish of New York, and another man whose name I never knew.[13] He, poor fellow, arrived at our camp in a starving condition and died before our departure. The other two unfortunate ones died on the desert, and the colored man reported that he simply covered their remains with their blankets.[14]

I well remember that last night in camp before we started with our knapsacks and left the families,[15] for it was plain the women and children must go very slow, and we felt we could go over rougher and shorter roads on foot and get through sooner by going straight across the Sierra Nevada mountains. Our condition was certainly appalling. We were without water, all on the verge of starvation, and the three poor cattle which yet remained alive were objects of pity. It seemed almost a crime to kill the poor beasts, so little real food was there left on their skeleton frames. They had been so faithful and had plodded along when there seemed no hope for them. They might still serve to keep the party from starvation.

It was at this camp that Mr. Ischam died. The night before our departure he came wandering into camp and presented such an awful appearance, simply a living skeleton of a once grand and powerful man. He must have suffered untold agony as he struggled on to overtake the party, starving and alone, with the knowledge that two of his companions had perished miserably of starvation in that unknown wilderness of rocks and alkali.[16]

Our journey on foot through the mountains was full of adventure and suffering. On our arrival at the shores of Owen's Lake, not a man of the party had a mouthful of food left in his pack, and to add to our difficulties we had several encounters with the hostile Indians. There was a fearful snowstorm falling at Owen's Lake[17] on the evening that we arrived there, and we could make no fire. The Indians gathered around us and we did not know exactly what to make of them, nor could we determine whether their intentions were good or bad. We examined the lake and determined to try to ford it,[18] and thus set out by the light of the moon that occasionally peeped out from behind the clouds, while the red devils stood howling on the shore.

The following morning we found what was then known as the Fremont Trail, and by the advice of some friendly Indians who came into our camp, we kept [on] the "big trail" for three days and came to Walker's Pass.[19] While on this trail we were followed at night by a number of wild Indians, but we prudently avoided any collisions with them and kept moving on. Going on through the pass we followed the right-hand branch of the trail, the left-hand branch leading more to the south and across a wide plain. We soon came to a fair-sized stream, now known to be the south fork of the Kern River, which we followed until we came to its junction with a larger river, the two making the Kern River.[20] Here we were taken across by some friendly Indians who left the missions farther west during the Mexican War and took to their own village, located at the foot of the Sierra Nevada mountains. At this village we were on exhibition for several hours with an audience of five hundred people, or more, of the red men, and on the following morning we commenced the ascent of the mountains again, the Indians furnishing us with a guide in the person of an old Piute. He brought us over the range, through the snow, and over the bleak ridges, in the month of December, 1849,[21] and we made our first camp at an Indian village in Tulare Valley, a few miles south of where Porterville now stands.[22]

From this Indian village we walked on until we arrived at the present site of Millerton[23] on the south bank of the San Joaquin River. Our sufferings were terrible from hunger, cold, and wet, for the rains were almost continual at this elevation, and we had been forced several times to swim. The sudden change from the dried-up desert to a rainy region was pretty severe on us. On our arrival at the San Joaquin River we found a camp of wealthy Mexicans, who gave us a small amount of food and seemed to want us to pass on that they might be rid of us. I can well believe that a company of twenty-one starving men was the cause of some disquietude to them. They gave us some hides taken from some of the cattle they had recently slain, and from these we constructed a boat and ferry rope, in which we crossed the river, and then continued our journey to the mining camp on Aqua Frio, in Mariposa County.[24]

It is very strange to think that since that time I have never met a single man of that party of twenty-one. I had kept quite full notes of the whole trip from the state of New York to the mines and included my early mining experience up to the year 1851. Unfortunately this manuscript was burned at the Russ House fire in Fresno, where I also lost many personal effects.

In the year 1892 Mr. Coker was living in Fresno, or near that city, in fairly comfortable health, and it is to be hoped that the evening of his days, to which all the old pioneers are rapidly approaching, may be to him all that his brightest hopes pictured.

CHAPTER XV

The Author Again Takes up the History

Having followed the various little parties into which the great train had resolved itself when it began to feel the pressure of suffering and trouble which came with contact with the desert, followed them in their various ways till they came through to the Pacific slope, the travels and experiences of the author are again resumed.

It will be remembered that he had rested at Los Angeles, working for Mr. Brier, who had temporarily turned boardinghouse keeper, and finally made arrangements with some drovers to assist in taking a small stock of horses north to the mines. His story is thus continued:

WE FOLLOWED THE WAGON ROAD WHICH THE COMPANIES that had gone on before had made, and got along very well. At night I acted independently—staked out my mule and ate my meal of dried meat and crackers—then joined the others around a large fire, and all seemed to enjoy the company. After a few days the two men who owned the horses proposed to me to let my mule carry the provisions, and they wanted me to ride one of their horses that was not carrying a pack, as they said it would keep it more gentle to ride it.

To please the old gentleman from Sacramento, I agreed to the proposition, for I thought perhaps by being accommodating I could get along more pleasantly.

Thus we traveled on, over rolling hills covered with grass and wildflowers, and I was much pleased with all that I could see. For the first two days we did not pass a house, which shows how thinly settled the country was. Cattle were often seen, and sometimes horses, but people were very scarce. In time we went down a long, steep hill, then across a wide valley that supported a rank growth of vegetation, and came to a mission called San Buena Ventura (good luck.)[1] Here the men seemed scarce but Indians and

244

dogs plenty. The houses were of the same sort as at Los Angeles, except the church, all made of dried mud, and never more than one story high.

As we journeyed along we came to the seashore, the grandest sight in the world to me, for I had never before seen the ocean. What a wide piece of water it was! Far out I could see small waves coming toward the shore, and the nearer they came the faster they seemed to rush and at last turned into great rollers and breakers, which dashed upon the rocks or washed far up the sandy shore with a force that made the ground tremble. There was no wind and I could not see what it could be that so strangely agitated the water. Here the waves kept coming, one after another, with as much regularity as the slow strokes of a clock. This was the first puzzle the great sea propounded to me, and there under the clear, blue sky and soft air I studied over the ceaseless, restless motion and the great power that was always beating on the shore. I tasted the water and found it exceedingly salty, and I did not see how anything could live in it and not become in the condition of pickled pork or fish. Where was the salt to make this mighty brine pond, and why did it keep so when the great rivers kept pouring in their torrents of fresh waters? I did not understand, and these are some of the thoughts that came to the boy who had been raised upon the prairie, and to whom the great ocean was indeed an unknown sea.

We followed along the road and in time came to another village and mission called Santa Barbara.[2] The village was near the shore, and the church farther back upon an elevated piece of ground near the foot of the mountain, overlooking the town and sea and much of the country to the south, west, and east. The mountain was high and rough, and a point ran out into the sea, making a sort of harbor. This town was built much as the others had been, except perhaps the mission, which seemed better. The roofs were as flat as the floors and were covered with a sort of tar which made them waterproof. The material of the houses was sun-dried bricks, two feet long by one foot wide and four to six inches thick. There was no lime in the mortar of this mason work, and the openings in the walls had iron bars across them instead of sash and glass. Dried hides were spread upon the floors, and there was a large earthen jar for water, but not a table, bedstead or chair could be seen in the rooms we saw. A man came along, rode right in at the door, turned around and rode out again. The floor was so hard that the horse's feet made no impression on it. Very few men, quite a number of Indians, more women, and a still larger quantity of dogs made up the inhabitants.

Leaving here, the road led back from the seashore and over quite a level tableland covered with a big growth of grass and some timber, and then down to the sandy shore again, where the mountain comes so close that we were crowded down to the very water's edge. Here the never-tiring waves were still following each other to the shore and dashing themselves to pieces with such a noise that I felt awed to silence. What a strange difference in two parts of the earth so little distance from each other! Here was a waste of waters, there was a waste of sands that may sometime have been the bottom of just such a dashing, rolling sea as this. And here, between the two, was a fertile region covered with trees, grass, and flowers, and watered with brooks of fresh, sweet water. Paradise and Desolation! They surely were not far apart. Here I saw some of the queer things that wash on shore, for we camped close to the beach.

It was a circumstance of great interest to me to see the sun slowly go down into the great ocean. Slowly and steadily it went, getting redder and redder as it went down, then it just touched the distant water, and the waves dashed over more and more of its face till all was covered. Were it not for the strong, bright rays that still shot up across the sky, one might think it was drowned forever, but in the morning it came up over the mountaintop, having apparently made half the circuit of the globe.

Soon after this the road left the shore and turned into the mountains. Another mission was on this road, Santa Ynez, situated in a beautiful place but apparently in decay, for the men had gone to the mines, leaving the Indians, women, and dogs, as in other places. San Luis Obispo was another mission similarly inhabited, but the surroundings did not seem so pleasant as those we had seen before, although it bore signs that considerable [work] had been done. From here our road bore still more north, and we had a long mountain to work over, very rocky, and in some places barren.[3]

San Miguel[4] was a mission situated on the bank of a dry stream that evidently had seen plenty of water earlier in the season. The surrounding country was covered with scattered timber. Soledad was another place where there were some improvements; [it was] located on a small river, but nearly deserted like the other places. Prospects at the gold mines were so favorable that every man felt an irresistible desire to enrich himself, and so they left their families at the missions and in the towns, and rushed off to the mines. Nearly all of them expected to return by winter. I think I must stop right here and tell about the California carriages, of which I had seen several at Los Angeles and at the missions along our road. The first time I saw one it was a great curiosity, I assure you. The wheels were cut off the end of a sycamore log, a little over two feet in diameter and each section about a foot long. The axle was a piece of wood eight inches square with a tongue fastened to it, long enough to be used with a yoke of oxen, and the ends of the axle were roughly rounded, leaving something of a shoulder. The wheels were retained in place by a big linchpin. On the axle and tongue was a strong frame of square-hewed timbers answering for bed pieces, and the bottom was of rawhide tightly stretched, which covered the whole frame. Tall stakes at each corner of the frame held up an awning in hot weather. The yoke was fastened to the horns of the oxen by strong, narrow strips of rawhide, and the tongue was fastened to the yoke in the same way. The driver was generally an Indian, armed with a small pole six or eight feet long, who marched on before, the oxen following after. I saw many a wagon like this, the platform well filled up with women and children, and a pack of dogs following along behind, slowly rolling over the country, and this is the way they traveled when they went visiting friends who lived a few miles in the country. Sometimes the wheels gave perfectly agonizing shrieks as they revolved, and when they made so much noise that their strong Spanish nerves could stand it no longer, if there was any green grass to be found, the drivers would crowd in a quantity around the axle, and there was generally room for a good lot of it, to answer for a lubricator.

We passed on from Soledad and shortly rose into the tableland we had seen for some time before us. From here we could look north for a long way with no hill or mountain in sight; but our road led along on the east side of this treeless plain, so thickly covered with grass that we recalled some of the old tales of the grassy plains. We passed a landholder's house on the road, then crossed a range of low mountains and came to the mission of San Juan (St. John), situated near the foothills, overlooking a level, rich-appearing extent of valley land with a big vegetable growth all over it; in some places wild mustard stood thickly and was from four to ten feet high. I thought what a splendid place it would be for the Yankees who are fond of greens.[5]

This was the first place since we left Los Angeles where we could buy any kind of breadstuff, and we were here enabled to get a change of diet, including greens. This seemed to be one end or side of another valley, and as we went along it seemed to widen away to the east; but our course was to the north, and we followed the road. The architecture of all the buildings except the churches was all the same, being built of the sun-dried adobes, or bricks, made by mixing up a clay mud with tough grass and letting it get dry and hard. We saw the same kind of roof material as before, a sort of mineral tar which I supposed they must find somewhere about.

I could imagine why the houses were built in this way, for when the Jesuit missionaries first came in, they found the country occupied by Indians who used their arrows to good effect, as they were jealous of all outside occupation. The early settlers evidently made the walls of their dwellings thick and strong enough to resist all kinds of weapons used by Indians. They could not set fire to them for they were fireproof and arrow-proof, and the hostile Indian could dance on the roof without being able to get in or do any injury. Thus the poor Indian was fairly beat and eventually became a better Indian.

The Indians of what is now Nevada and Arizona used to come over into these rich valleys and clandestinely capture a band of a hundred or more head of cattle or horses and make their escape. They were often followed by the herders, but if they did not overtake the thieves before they got into the deep cañons of the mountains, they would usually turn back and let them go rather than be led into ambush in some strange, narrow place where escape would be impossible and they might be filled with arrows. No doubt the trail we had followed across the plains, where there were so many horses' bones, was one of these trails, along which the thieving Indians took their booty, which died upon the trip.

Our road from here was near the foothills on the west side of a level, grassy, thinly timbered valley, and as we advanced we noticed that the timber grew more plentiful and the trees larger, without much underbrush. We also noticed that the vegetation was ranker and no doubt the soil was very rich. We then came to a point where the mountain reaches out almost across the valley to meet the mountain on the east side. Here we found a gravelly creek with but little water, but as soon as we passed this point we saw the valley suddenly widening out, and beautiful groves of live oak trees scattered all around. The vegetation here was very rank, the mustard ten feet high in places, making it difficult to see out of the road. This was perhaps the strongest contrast to the arid desert that we had seen.

As we went on down the valley, the hills seemed to stand farther and farther back, as if to make more room for those who would soon settle in this fertile place, and we soon came in sight of the village or pueblo of San Jose (St. Joseph),[6] where we camped. Here we learned that the two owners of the horses intended to go to San Francisco instead of Sacramento, and as we considered the former place a very poor one for a penniless person to go, we concluded to break up the company camp and each do the best he could for himself, for our objective point was the gold mines, and the sooner we reached them the better.

The drovers who had been anxious to have us go with them and help them now began to talk about a settlement with us, as if they had done us great favors, and called on the other fellows to help pay for their board upon the way. When they came to me they said my share would be an ounce. This struck me hard, but they said I had ridden their horse all the way and the charge was very low. I told them I had furnished the most of the provisions I had eaten, and my mule had packed a good load all the way, which I considered worth as much as the use of the horse. But they refused to allow me anything for the use of the mule and became very urgent in their demand for money.

These men were evidently of the tribe of Skinflint, who had no souls, or they would not have attempted to rob an almost penniless emigrant in this way of the last few dollars he had and all the hope he had of reaching the mines. I did not desire to give up to such narrow principles as this and hesitated, but they were bound to have the money or make a quarrel, and talked pretty loud of the way they collected debts in Sacramento, so that to avoid trouble and get out of the clutches of such mean scoundrels as these, I counted out sixteen dollars, almost every cent I had, and reluctantly gave them to my enemy. I immediately mounted my mule and, without stopping to say good-bye, rode off. I may have quoted a part of the speech Captain Hunt made when the party wanted to leave the trail and take the cutoff, especially that part where he alluded to their going to h—l. I very much fear the little piety my mother taught me was badly strained on that occasion, and I thought of a good many swear words, if I did not say them, which I suppose is about as bad. I could see how cunningly they had managed to get me to ride their horse that it might serve as the foundation for a claim on me for about all the money I had in the world.

I hitched my mule in the edge of the town and went in to look at the place. The houses were situated very much as in other places we had come through—scattered around over much ground and built low, but had a different style of roof, a peaked or sloping one, and covered with half-round tile two feet or more long and an inch thick. One course of these would be laid with the hollow side up, and then a course with the hollow side down, covering the joints of the lower course. This allowed the air to circulate freely and was proof against rain. I saw no flat roofs such as I had seen down along the coast. I saw one gambling house and about all the men in town were gathered there, and some women, too. This was the busiest place in town and situated near the plaza. This was the largest town I had yet been in. There seemed to be plenty of women and lots of dogs, but the men were as scarce as they had been in any of the towns—gone to the gold mines to make a stake. I took in the sights pretty well, and there were a great many new things for me to see and, when pretty well satisfied, concluded I would go back to my mule and camp in someplace just out of town for the night.

Before I reached my animal, whom should I meet but my old travel-ing companion John Rogers, whom I thought to be a hundred miles away by this time. We shook hands heartily and he told me that Bennett, Moody, and Skinner were camped not far off, and he was still with them. He wore a pair of blue overalls, a blue woolen shirt, and the same little narrow-rimmed hat he had worn so long. I observed, too, that he was barefoot, and told him I had a dollar or two which he could take and get some shoes. He said it was no use, for there was not a pair of shoes in the town to buy, and he had not found any material of which he could make himself a pair of moccasins. I told him how I had been swindled coming up, and he was about as angry as I had been. I think if I had known that my friend John Rogers had been so near I should have bidden the rascals an unceremonious good-bye and we would have been able to hold our own on a claim for the services of myself and mule.

We went up to the place where our people were camped, perhaps a mile above town on the bank of a river, nearly dry, but where plenty of wood, water, and grass were at hand; such a place as we had looked for in vain for many a weary day upon the desert. This was as far above Death Valley as a king above a pauper, and we hoped never to see such a country again.

In camp we talked about moving on to the mines. Rogers said he was going to start next day, and in answer to exclamations of surprise that he should start off alone, he said that some fellows camped a little way down the river were going to start and he had made arrangements to go with them, as the Bennett party would not go yet for a week. In the morning he shook hands and bade us good-bye and good luck, and started off down the river bank, lost to us, as it proved, for many years.

The next day, as we were all sitting on the ground, I felt a sort of mov-ing of the earth under me and heard a rumbling sound that seemed very queer. It seemed there was a motion also to the trees around us. We all started and looked a little frightened, and Skinner said he believed it was an earth-quake, for he said he could see the motion in a sort of wave. It was gone in half a minute. Moody said, "How do you like California now?" I said I thought this part of it was a pretty good place, for there was plenty of wood, water, and grass, and that was better than we had seen in some places.

He then went on to say that he had heard Mr. Bennett's story of their sufferings and narrow escape from death, and it was the most wonderful story he had ever heard. He said the idea of Mrs. Bennett walking over such a country for twenty-two days was almost beyond belief, for he would not have thought her able to walk one-third the distance. He never knew before how much women could do when they were called to do it, and they proved in emergencies to be as tough as anybody. He said if he ever got back home he should move to give them all the rights and privileges of men for sure.[7]

One day I mounted my mule for a ride to the eastern foothills, and sat down on a little incline and overlooked the valley, a beautiful landscape, while my mule cropped the rich grasses in a circle described by the rope which confined him. I was always a great admirer of nature, and as I sat there alone I could see miles on miles of mammoth mustard waving in the strong breeze which came down over the San Francisco Bay just visible to the northward, and on the mountain summits to the west, [I] could see tall timber reaching up into the deep blue of the sky. It was a real contented comfort to be thus in the midst of luxuriance and beauty, and I enjoyed it, coming as it did at the end of the long and dreary road I had been traveling for the past twelve months. Up the Platte; across the Rockies; down the Green River cañons in my canoe; across the mountains to Salt Lake; out over the "Rim of the Basin," and across the desert, guided only by the fact that we knew the Pacific Ocean was to the west of us, and choosing our road as best we could in view of the lofty, snow-clad, impassible mountains; seeing thirteen of our comrades lie down never to rise again and, when hope and strength were almost gone, to suddenly come out into a fertile region on the seventh of March, 1850.[8] How I wished the fellows who slept in Death Valley could have seen this view. The change from all that barrenness and desolation to this beautiful, fertile country, covered with wildflowers and luxuriant live oaks, was as strong a contrast as one could imagine, a sudden coming from purgatory to paradise in the space of a single hour.

I woke up from my dreamy thoughts, mounted my mule, and rode to camp. As I rode along, the nimble ground squirrel, with his keen black eye, would climb to the top of the high mustard stalks to get a better view and, suspicious of an enemy within his almost undisputed territory, disappear in a wink to his safe underground fortress. Fat cattle and horses would appear before me a moment and then, with a wild look and high heads, dash through the tall mustard out of sight.

Next day my trip was toward the western hills, and before I came to them, [I] was confronted with an extensive stretch of chaparral brush, absolutely impenetrable, which I must go around or stop my progress in this direction. These thickets were a regular paradise for grizzly bears, for within the protection of this matted and thorny growth, he is as safe as is the soldier in the rocky fort of Gibraltar. I soon found a way around the brush and rose high enough so that a backward look over the valley was charming, quite as much so as the eastern side. I wandered over the grassy hills covered with great scattering oaks, and came to a grove of mammoth trees, six feet or more in diameter, with tops reaching two hundred or three hundred feet toward the blue sky. They seemed to me to be a kind of cedar, and were far larger and taller than any trees I had ever seen in the forests of Vermont, Michigan, or Wisconsin, and in my long journey from the East the route had been principally through a country devoid of good timber. [To] a stranger in a strange land, everything was new and wonderful. After satisfying my inquiring mind I returned to camp again, and soon learned that my newly discovered trees were the famous redwoods,[9] so greatly prized for their valuable qualities.

Taking the most direct course to camp I came, when within two or three miles of San Jose, to a large extent of willows so thick, and so thickly woven together with wild blackberry vines, wild roses, and other thorny plants, that it appeared at first as if I never could get through. But I found a winding trail made by the cattle through the bushes and mustard, and this I followed, being nearly scared occasionally by some wild steers as they rushed off through the thickets. I got through safely, though it would have been difficult to escape a wild, enraged steer or a grizzly, had I met him face to face even with a rifle in hand. I could see nowhere but by looking straight up, for the willows were in places fifty feet high and a foot in diameter. The willows where I came from were mere bushes, and these astonished me. This bit of brush is still locally known as The Willows, but the trees are all gone and the ground thickly covered with orchards and fine residences, the land selling at from one thousand to two thousand dollars per acre.

The sun rose without a cloud, and a little later the sea breeze from the bay blew gently over the valley, making the climate perfectly delightful in its temperate coolness, a true paradise on earth, it seemed to me, if I was able to judge or set a value upon so beautiful a spot; and surely I had seen all sorts, good and poor, desert and valley, mountain and plain.

But I was poor in purse, and resolved I would seek first the gold mines and secure gold enough to buy a piece of this valley afterward.

When I had seen what was to be seen about San Jose, I had a talk with my friends and found that Mr. Bennett favored going on to the mines at once and that Moody and Skinner thought they would remain a little while at least.

I went along in company with Bennett, and when we got a little way from San Jose, on the road to the mission, the road seemed walled in on both sides with growing mustard ten or twelve feet high and all in blossom. How so much mustard could grow, and grow so large, I could not understand. I had seen a few plants in the gardens or fields which people used for greens, and here seemed to be enough to feed the nation, if they liked mustard greens.

The second day out we passed the big church at Mission San Jose[10] and soon left the valley and turned into the mountains and, when partway over, we came to a stream which we followed up and came out into Livermore Valley, where we found a road to follow. Houses were scarce, and we camped a mile or so before we got to the Livermore ranch buildings. There was very little sign of life about the place, and we soon went out of the valley and into the mountains again.

The first sign of settlement we saw when partway through the mountains was a stone corral, but no house or other improvements. The next place was a small house made of willow poles set in the ground and plastered over with mud. This rejoiced in the name of "Mountain House." This wayside inn looked like a horse thief's glory; only one or two men, a quarter of an elk hanging on a pole, and no accommodations for man or beast. There was very little water, nothing to sell as well as nothing wanted. On the summits of the mountains as we passed through we saw, standing like guards, many large buck elks.

It was now fifteen miles to the San Joaquin River, and a level plain lay before us. When our road turned into the river bottom, we found the water too deep to get through safely, so we concluded to go on and try to find some place where we could cross. On our way droves of antelopes could be seen frolicking over the broad plains, while in the distance were herds of elk winding their way from the mountains towards the river for water. When far away, their horns were the first things visible, and they much resembled the dry tops of dead pine trees, but a nearer view showed them to us as the proud monarchs of the plain.

When we came up opposite the mouth of the Merced River we concluded to try again to cross. The river here, as below, was out of its banks, and the overflowed part was quite wide, which we had to pass through before we could reach the river proper.

I waded in ahead of the team and sounded the depth of the river so as not to get in too deep water, and avoid, if possible, such accidents as might otherwise occur. Sometimes the water was up to the wagon bed and it looked a little doubtful of our getting through in safety, but we made it at last.

We found a narrow strip of dry land along the riverbank. A town was on the east side of the San Joaquin River, just below where the Merced River came in. I think this place was called Merced City.[11] This so-called city contained but one residence, a tent occupied by the ferryman. We crossed the sluggish stream and for the privilege paid the ferryman ten dollars for toll. The road was not much used and the ferry business seemed lonesome.

Here we camped for the night. The mosquitoes soon found us, and they were all very hungry and had good teeth. They annoyed me so that I moved my lodgings to the ferryboat, but here they quickly found me and troubled me all night. These insects were the first I had seen since I left the lower Platte River, and I thought them as bad as on the Mississippi.

From here the road led up the Merced River near the bottom, and as we came near groves of willows, big, stately elk would start out and trot off proudly into the open plains to avoid danger. These proud, big-horned monarchs of the plains could be seen in bunches scattered over the broad meadows, as well as an equal amount of antelope. They all seemed to fear us, which was wise on their part, and kept out of rifle shot. As [we] were not starving as we were once, I did not follow them out on the open plain, for I thought I could get meat when we were more in need.

We followed up the river bottom and saw not a single house until we reached the road leading from Stockton to the Mariposa mines, where we found a ferry and a small store. Here we learned that some men were mining a few miles up the river, so we drove on until we found a little work being done in a dry gulch near the riverbank. We made our camp at this spot and had plenty of wood, water, and grass. We found there was something to be learned in the art of gold mining. We had no tools nor money, and had never seen a speck of native gold and did not know how to separate it from the dirt nor where to search for it. We were poor, ignorant emigrants. There were two or three men camped here. One of them was more social than the rest and we soon got acquainted. His name was Williams, from Missouri. He came down to the river with a pan of dirt, and seeing me in my ignorance trying to wash some as well, he took the pan from me and very kindly showed me how to work so as to let the dirt go and save the gold. When he had the pan finished, a few small, bright scales remained. These to me were curious little fellows and I examined them closely and concluded there was a vast difference between gold and lead mining. Williams became more friendly and we told him something about our journey across the plains, and he seemed to think that we deserved a good claim. He went to a dry gulch where a Spaniard was working and told him that all of California, now that the war was over, belonged to Americans and he must leave. Williams had his gun in his hand and war might follow, so Mr. Spaniard left and his claim was presented to Bennett and myself.

Williams had been twice to Santa Fe from Missouri and had learned the Spanish language and could swear at them by rote if necessary. We now began work almost without tools, but our ground we had to work was quite shallow and Williams helped us out by loaning us some of his tools at times. We soon succeeded in scratching together some of the yellow stuff and I went down to the store and bought a pan for five dollars, a shovel for ten dollars, and a poor pick cost me ten dollars more. This took about two ounces of my money.

We now worked harder than ever for about three weeks, but we could not save much and pay such high prices as were charged. Our gulch claim was soon worked out, and as the river had fallen some, we tried the bar, but we could only make four or five dollars a day, and the gold was very fine and hard to save. We bought a hindquarter of an elk and hung it up in a tree and it kept fresh till all of it was eaten.

Some others came and took up claims on the bar, and as the prospects were not as good as was wished, three of us concluded to go and try to find a better place. The next day was Sunday and all lay in bed late. Before I rose I felt something crawling on my breast, and when I looked I found it to be an insect, slow in motion, resembling a louse, but larger. He was a new emigrant to me and I wondered what he was. I now took off my pants and found many of his kind in the seams. I murdered all I could find, and when I got up I told Williams what I had found. He said they hurt nobody and were called *piojos,* more commonly known as body lice.[12]

We started on our prospecting tour and went northeast to a place now called Big Oak Flat.[13] This was at the head of a small stream and there were several small gulches that emptied into it that paid well. This flat was all taken up and a ditch was cut through to drain it. A shipload of gold was expected to be found when it was worked. A small town of tents had been pitched on both sides of the flat. One side was occupied by gamblers, and many games were constantly carried on and were well patronized. On the opposite side of the flat were many small tents, and around on the hillside some mules and jacks were feeding.[14] One of the little long-eared donkeys came down among the tents and went in one and commenced eating flour from the sack. The owner of the flour ran to the tent, took his shotgun and fired a load of buckshot into the donkey's hams. The animal reeled and seemed shot fatally. I now looked for a battle to commence, but the parties were more reasonable. The price of the animal was fully paid, and no bloodshed as I expected there surely would be.

We now prospected further east, but nothing good enough was found. The place we looked over was where the town of Garota now stands.[15] We concluded to go back, have a council, and go somewhere else. On our way back we stopped to get dinner. While I was around the fire, barefoot, I felt something crawl up my instep, and it proved to be another of those *piojos* of Williams'. I now thought these torments must be all over this country.

Gold dust was used to transact all business; all the coin was in the hands of the gentlemen gamblers. Most miners found it necessary to have a small pair of scales in the breast pocket to weigh the dust so as not to have to trust someone who carried lead weights and often got more than his just dues. Gold dust was valued at sixteen dollars an ounce.[16]

We now thought it would be best for two of us to take our mules and go down in the small hills and try to get some elk meat to take with us, as our route would be mostly through the unsettled part of the country, and no provisions could likely be procured, so Mr. Bradford of New Orleans and myself took our mules and went down where the hills were low and the game plenty. We camped in a low ravine, staked out our mules, and stayed all night without a fire, believing that when we woke in the early morning some of the many herd of elk then in sight would be near us at daylight, and we could easily kill all we wanted without leaving camp, but we were disappointed. Hundreds of the big horned fellows were in sight, but none in rifle shot, and there was no chance for us to get any nearer to them. We got near a couple of antelope and Mr. Bradford, who was a brag shot and had the best gun, proposed to kill them as we stood. The larger of the two was on his side and much nearer than the smaller one, but we fired together just as we stood. Bradford's antelope ran off unhurt: mine fell dead in its tracks. Bradford bragged no more about his fine gun and superior marksmanship.

We went back to camp with the little we had killed and soon got ready to start north. Bennett was to go with his team to Sacramento and wait there until he heard from us.

Four of us, mounted on mules, now started on our journey along the foothills without a road. We struck the Tuolumne River at a ferry. The stream was high and rapid and could not be forded, so we had to patronize the ferryman, and give him half an ounce apiece. We thought such charges on poor and almost penniless emigrants were unjust.

The point we were seeking to reach was a new discovery called Gold Lake on Feather River, where many rich gulches that emptied into it had been worked, and the lake was believed to have at least a shipload of gold in it. It was located high in the mountains and could be easily drained and a fortune soon obtained if we got there in time and said nothing to anyone we might meet on the road. We might succeed in getting a claim before they were all taken up. We followed along the foothills without a road, and when we came to the Stanislaus River we had to patronize a ferry and pay half an ounce each again. We thought their scale weights were rather heavy and their ferrymen well paid.

We continued along the foothills without any trail until we struck the road from Sacramento to Hangtown. This sounded like a bad name for a good village, but we found it was fittingly named after some ugly devils who were hanged there.[17] The first house that we came to on this road was the Mormon Tavern. Here were some men playing cards for money, and two boys, twelve or fourteen years old, playing poker for the same and trying in every way to ape the older gamblers and bet their money as freely and swear as loud as the old sports. All I saw was new and strange to me and became indelibly fixed on my mind. I had never before seen such wicked boys, and the men paid no attention to these fast American boys. I began to wonder if all the people in California were like these, bad and wicked.

Here we learned that Gold Lake was not as rich as reported,[18] so we concluded to take the road and go to Coloma, the place where gold was first found on the American River.[19]

We camped at Coloma all night. Mr. Bradford got his mule shod and paid sixteen dollars, or in the mining phrase, an ounce of gold dust. I visited the small town and found that the only lively business place in it was a large gambling house, and I saw money (gold dust) liberally used—sometimes hundreds of dollars bet on a single card. When a few hundred or thousand were lost, more would be brought on. The purse would be set in the center of the table and the owners would take perhaps twenty silver dollars or checks, and when they were lost, the deposited purse would be handed to the barkeeper, the amount weighed out, and the purse returned. When the purse was empty, a friend of the bettor would bring another, and so the game went on almost in silence. The game called monte seemed to be the favorite. How long these sacks of gold lasted or who eventually got the whole I never knew. This was a new country with new people, and many seemed to be engaged in a business that was new, strange, and hazardous. The final result of all this was what puzzled me.

We now followed the road up the mountain to Georgetown.[20] Here was a small village on the summit of the ridge and it seemed to be in a prosperous mining section. After some inquiry about a good place to work we concluded to go down a couple of miles northeast of town on Cañon Creek and go to work if vacant ground could be found. There was a piece of creek bottom here that had not been much worked. Georgia Flat above had been worked and paid well, and the Illinois and Oregon cañons that emptied into the bottom here were rich, so we concluded to locate in the bottom. Claims here in the flat were only fifteen feet square. I located one and my notice told others that I would go to work on it as soon my partner came from Sacramento. I sent my partner, Mr. Bennett, a note telling him to come up.

While waiting for Mr. Bennett I took my pan and butcher knife and went into a dry gulch out of sight of the other campers and began work. As the ground was mostly bare bedrock, by scratching around I succeeded in getting three or four pans of dirt a day. The few days I had to wait for Bennett I made eight dollars a day until my claim was worked out.

I then went to Georgetown to meet Bennett and family, and soon after my arrival they came well and safe. All of them, even to the faithful camp dog, Cuff, were glad to see me. Old Cuff followed me all around town, but when we got ready to start for camp the dog was gone and could not be found. Someone had hidden him away, knowing he could not be gotten any other way, for six ounces would not have bought him. We had raised him in Wisconsin, made him a good deer dog, and with us he had crossed the dry and sandy deserts. He had been a great protection to Bennett's children on the plains, and company for us all.

We now located claims on the creek bottom. The channel of the creek was claimed by Holman of Alabama and the Helms brothers of Missouri. They had turned the stream into a ditch in order to work the bed of the stream, believing that their claims had all the gold in them. Our claims joined theirs.

Mr. W. M. Stockton, who left his family in Los Angeles, came with Mr. Bennett and went to work with us. As everything here was very high, we concluded to let Mr. Stockton take the team and go to Sacramento for provisions for our own use. Flour and meat were each fifty cents a pound; potatoes, twenty-five cents a pound; and onions, one dollar and twenty-five cents each. Onions and potatoes eaten raw were considered very necessary to prevent and cure scurvy, which was quite a common complaint. Whiskey, if not watered, cost one dollar a drink.

Our claims were about ten feet deep. The bottom was wet and a pump needed, so we went to a whip sawmill and got four narrow strips one by three and one by five and twelve feet long, paying for them by weight, the price being twelve cents a pound. Out of these strips we made a good pump by fixing a valve at the end and nailing a piece of green rawhide on a pole, which answered for a plunger, and with the pump set at 45 degrees it worked easily and well. One man could easily keep the water out and we made fair wages.

In the creek bottom Mr. Bush of Missouri had a saloon. The building was made mainly of brush, with a split piece for a counter, and another one for a shelf for his whiskey keg, a box of cigars, a few decks of cards, and half a dozen glasses, which made up the entire stock of trade for the shop. In front was a table made of two puncheons with a blanket thrown over all, and a few rough seats around. There was no roof except the brush, and through the dry season none was needed except for shade.

There were also at this place five brothers by the name of Helms, also from Missouri. Their names were Jim, Davenport, Wade, Chet, and Daunt. These men, with Mr. Holman, owned the bed of the stream, and their ground proved to be quite wet and disagreeable to work. Mr. Holman could not well stand to work in the cold water, so he asked the privilege of putting in a hired man in his place, which was agreed to. He then took up a claim for himself outside of the other claims, and this proved to be on higher bedrock and dry, and paid even better than the low claims where the Helms brothers were at work. This was not what the Helms boys considered exactly fair, as Holman seemed to be getting rich the fastest and, as there was no law to govern them, they held a free-country court of their own, and decided the case to suit themselves. So they ordered Holman to come back and do his own work. No fault was found with the hired man but what he did his work well enough, but they were jealous and would not be bound by their agreement.

But this decision did not satisfy all parties, and it was agreed to submit the case to three men, and I was chosen one of them. We held court on the ground and heard both sides of the story, after which we retired to the shade of a bunch of willows to hold council over the matter, with the result that we soon came to a decision in favor of Mr. Holman. About this time one of the Helms boys began to quarrel with Holman and grew terribly mad, swearing all kinds of vengeance, and making the cañon ring with the loudest kind of Missouri oaths. Finally he picked up a rock to kill Holman, but the latter was quick with his pistol, a single-shot dueling piece, and as they were not more than ten feet apart, Helms would have had a hole in him large enough for daylight to shine through if the pistol had not misfired. We stopped the quarrel and made known our decision, whereupon Helms went off muttering vengeance.

We now went back to our work again at our claims, mine being between Helms's cabin and the saloon. Holman stopped to talk a little while on my claim while I was down below at work, and soon Helms came back again in a terrible rage, stopping on the opposite side of the hole from Holman, swearing long and loud, and flourishing a big pistol, with which he threatened to blow Holman into purgatory. He was so much enraged that he fairly frothed at the mouth like a rabid dog. The men were about twenty feet apart, and I at the bottom of the hole ten feet below, but exactly between them. It seemed to me that I was in some little danger, for Helms had his big pistol at full cock and, as it pointed at me quite as often as it did at anybody, I expect I dodged around a little to keep out of range. Helms was terribly nervous, and trembled as he cursed, but Holman was cool and drew his weapon deliberately, daring Helms to raise his hand or he would kill him on the instant. Helms now began to back off, but carefully kept his eye on Holman and continued his abuse as he went on to the saloon to get something to replenish his courage. Holman, during the whole affair, talked very calmly and put considerable emphasis into his words when he dared Helms to make a hostile motion. He was a true Alabamian and could be neither scared nor driven. He soon sold out, however, and went to a more congenial camp, for he said these people were cowardly enough to waylay and kill him unawares.

Soon after this unpleasantness, a man and wife who lived in Georgetown came into notice, and while the man made some money mining, his wife did a good stroke of business washing for the boys, who paid her a dollar a shirt as laundry fees. As she began to make considerable money, the bigger—if not better—half of this couple began to feel quite rich and went off on a drunk, and when his own money was spent he went to his wife for more, but she refused him, and he, in his drunken rage, picked up a gun nearby and shot her dead.

All of a sudden the Helms boys and others gathered at the saloon, took drinks all around, and did a good deal of swearing, which was the biggest portion of the proceedings of the meeting; and then they all started off toward town, swearing and yelling as they struggled up the steep mountainside—a pack of reckless, backwoods Missourians who seemed to smell something bloody.

It was near night when they all came back and gathered around the saloon again. They were all in unusual good humor as they related the adventures of the afternoon, and bragged of their bravery and skill in performing the little job they had just completed, which consisted in taking the murderer out to the first convenient oak tree and, with the assistance of some sailors in handling the ropes, hoisting the fellow from the ground with a noose around his neck and, to the "heave, yo heave" of the sailor boys, pulling the rope that had been passed over an elevated limb. They watched the suspended body till the last spark of life went out, and then went back to town leaving the corpse hanging for somebody else to cut down and bury. They whooped and yelled at the top of their voices as they came down along the mountain trail, and at the saloon they related to the crowd that had gathered there how they had helped to hang the —— who had killed his wife. They said justice must be done if there was no law, and that no man could kill a woman and live in California. They imagined they were very important individuals, and veritable lords of creation.

These miners, many of them, were inveterate gamblers and played every night till near daylight, with no roof over them, and their only clothes a woolen shirt and overalls, which must have been a little scanty in the cool nights which settled down over the mountain camp; but they bore it all in their great desire for card playing.

Nearby there were three men who worked and slept together, every night dividing the dust, which each put into a purse at the head of his bed. One day the news came to the saloon that one of the purses had been stolen. The Helms boys talked it over and concluded that as one of the men had gone to town, he might know something about the lost dust; so they went to town and there, after a little search, found their man in a gambling house. After a little while they invited him to return to camp with them, and all started together down the mountain; but when about halfway down, they halted suddenly under an oak tree and accused their man of knowing where his partner's money was. This he strongly denied, and was very positive in his denial till he felt the surprise of a rope around his neck, with the end over a limb and beginning to haul pretty taut in a direction that would soon elevate his body from the ground, when he weakened at their earnestness and asked them to hold on a minute. As the rope slackened he owned up he had the dust and would give it up if they would not send the news to his folks in Missouri. This was agreed to and the thief was advised to leave at once for some distant camp, or they might yet expose him. He was not seen afterward.

The boys bragged a good deal of their detective ability after this, and said that a little hanging would make a —— thief tell the truth even if it did not make an honest man of him, and that a thief would be lucky if he got through with them and saved his life. Their law was "Hanging for Stealing."

The Helms brothers were said to be from western Missouri, and in early days were somewhat of the border-ruffian order and, of course, preferred to live on the frontier rather than in any well-regulated society. As the country became settled and improved around them, they moved on. A schoolhouse was an indication that the country was getting too far advanced for them.

They crossed the plains in 1849 and began mining operations near Georgetown in Placer County.[21] It was well known that they were foremost in all gambling, and in taking a hand in any excitement that came up, and as a better class of miners came in, they moved on, keeping ahead with the prospectors, and just out of reach of law and order. If anyone else committed a crime they were always quite eager to be on the vigilance committee, and were remarkably happy when punishing a wrongdoer. When any of their number was suspected, it was generally the case that they moved quickly on and so escaped. It was reported, however, that one of their number was in the hands of the vigilance committee, and hanged, in Montana.

After a time, it is said, they went down to southern California and settled on the border of the Colorado desert, about seventy-five miles east of San Diego, in a mountainous and desert region. Here they found a small tribe of Indians and, by each marrying a squaw, they secured rights equal to any of them in the occupation of the land. This was considered pretty sharp practice, but it suited them and they became big chiefs and medicine men, and numerous dusky descendants grew up around them.

It is said that their property consists of extensive pasturelands on which they raise cattle, and that they always go well armed with pistol, rifle, and riata. It is said that some of the Indians undertook to claim that the Helms brothers were intruders, but that in some mysterious way accidents happened to most of them [these Indians] and they [the brothers] were left without any serious opposition.

They are very hospitable and entertaining to people who visit them, provided they do not know too much about the men or their former deeds or history. In this case ignorance is bliss and it is folly, if not dangerous, to be too wise. They have made no improvements, but live in about the same style as the Indians and about on a level with them morally and intellectually.

There may be those who know them well, but the writer only knows them by hearsay and introduces them as a certain type of character found in the early days.

As I was now about barefoot, I went to town to look for boots or shoes. There were no shoes, and a pair of the cheapest boots I found hanging at the door were priced to me at two ounces. This seemed a wonderful sum for a pair of coarse cowhide boots that would sell in the States for two dollars and fifty cents, but I had to buy them at the price or go barefoot.

While rambling around town I went into a round tent used as a gambling saloon. The occupants were mostly men, and one or two nice-appearing ladies, but perhaps of doubtful reputation. The men were of all classes—

lawyers, doctors, preachers and such others as wanted to make money without work. The miners, especially sailors, were eager to try to beat the games. While I was here, the table was only occupied by a sailor lying upon it and covered with a green blanket. All at once the fellow noticed a large *piojo* walking slowly across the table and, drawing his sheath knife, made a desperate stab at him, saying, "You kind of a deckhand can't play at this game."

Our claims, by this time, were nearly worked out, and I thought that I had upward of two thousand dollars in gold, and the pile looked pretty big to me. It seemed to me that these mines were very shallow and would soon be worked out, at least in a year or two. I could not see that the land would be good for much for farming when no irrigation could be easily got, and the Spanish people seemed to own all the best land as well as the water, so that a poor fellow like myself would never get rich at farming here.

Seeing the matter in this light, I thought it would be best to take my money and go back to Wisconsin, where government land was good and plenty, and with even my little pile I could soon be master of a good farm in a healthy country, and I would there be rich enough. Thus reasoning, I decided to return to Wisconsin, for I could not see how a man could ever be a successful farmer in a country where there were only two seasons, one wet and the other long and dry.

I went out and hunted up my mule, which I had turned out to pasture for herself, and found her entirely alone. After a little coaxing I caught her and brought her with me to camp, where I offered her for sale. She was sleek and fat and looked so well that Helms said that if I could beat him shooting, he would buy both mule and gun; so three or four of us tried our skill. My opponents boasted a good deal of their superior marksmanship, but on the trial, which began at short range, I beat them all pretty badly. Helms was as good as his word and offered me twelve ounces for my gun and mule, which I took. I thought a great deal of my fat little one-eyed mule, and I thought then, as I think now, how well she did her part on the fearful road to and from Death Valley.

Helms was now going to the valley to have a winter's hunt, for here the snow would fall four feet deep and no mining work could be done till spring, when he would return and work his claim again.

I now had all in my pocket, and when I got ready to go, Mrs. Bennett was much affected at knowing that I would now leave them, perhaps never to return to them again. She clasped me in her arms, embraced me as she would her own son, and said, "Good luck to you—God bless you, for I know that you saved all our lives. I don't suppose you will ever come back, but we may come back to Wisconsin sometime and we will try to find a better road than the one we came over. Give my best regards to all who inquire after us." She shook my hand again and again with earnest pressure, and cried and sobbed bitterly. As I climbed the mountain she stood and watched me so long as I was in sight, and with her handkerchief waved a final adieu. I was myself much affected at this parting, for with Mr. and Mrs. Bennett [it] had been really a home to me; she had been to me as a mother, and it was like leaving a home fireside to go away from them. I was now starting out among strangers, and those I should meet might be the same good friends as those whom I had left behind. Mr. Bennett and I had for many years been hunting companions; I had lived at his house in the East, and we never disagreed but had always been good friends. I had now a traveling companion whose home was in Iowa County, Wisconsin, where I had lived for several years, and we went along together by way of Greenwood,[22] where there was a small mining town built of tents, many of which were used as gambling places. These places were occupied by gentlemen, some of whom wore white shirts to distinguish them, I presume, from the common herd of miners from whom they won their dust.

We crossed the American River at Salmon Falls,[23] and walked thence on to Sacramento City, which was the largest town we had seen on the coast. The houses were all small wooden ones, but business seemed to be brisk, and whiskey shops and gambling houses plenty. One game played with three cards, called three card monte, was played openly on the streets, with goods boxes for tables. Everyone who came along was urged to bet by the dealer, who would lay out his cards face up so all could see them, then turn them over and shuffle them and say, "I'll bet six ounces that no one can put his finger on the queen." I watched this awhile and saw that the dealer won much oftener than he lost, and it seemed to be a simple and easy way to make a living when money was plenty.

We strolled around town looking at the sights and the different business places, the most lively of which had plenty of music inside, lots of tables with plenty of money on them, and many questionable lady occupants. These business places were liberally patronized and every department flourishing, especially the bar. Oaths and vulgar language were the favorite style of speech, and very many of the people had all the whiskey down them that they could conveniently carry.

We got through the town safely and at the river we found a steamboat bound for San Francisco, and the fare was two ounces. The runners were calling loudly for passengers, and we were told we could never make the trip any cheaper, for they had received a telegram from below saying that no boat would come up again for two days. I said to him, "I can't see your telegram. Where is it?" At this he turned and left us. He had thought, no doubt, that miners were green enough to believe anything. In the course of an hour the smoke of a steamer was seen down the river, and this beat out the runners, who now offered passage for half an ounce.

At this time there was no telegraph and the delay was a lucky one for us. We took passage and went to San Francisco that night, where we put up at a cheap tavern near where the Custom House now stands.

Here we learned that we would have to wait two days before a ship would sail for Panama, and during this time we surveyed the town from the hilltops and walked all over the principal streets. It was really a small, poorly built, dirty looking place, with few wharves, poor cheap hotels, and very rough inhabitants. There were lots of gambling houses full of tables holding money, and the rooms filled with pretty rough-looking people, except the card dealers, most of whom wore white shirts and a few sported plug hats. There was also a "right smart sprinkling" of ladies present who were well dressed and adorned with rich jewelry, and their position seemed to be that of paying teller at the gambling tables.

The buildings seemed to be rather cheap, although material was very expensive, as well as labor, mechanics of all sorts getting as much as ten or twelve dollars per day for work. Coin seemed to be scarce, and a great deal of the money needed on the gambling tables was represented by iron washers, each of which represented an ounce of gold.

I noticed some places in the streets where it was muddy, and a narrow walk had been made out of boxes of tobacco, and sometimes even bacon was used for the same purpose. Transportation from the city to the mines was very slow and made by schooner. Shiploads of merchandise had arrived and been unloaded, and the sailors having run away to the mines, everything except whiskey and cards was neglected. Whiskey sold at this place for fifty cents a drink.

A man at the tavern where we stopped tried hard to sell me a fifty-vara lot there in the edge of the mud (near where the Custom House now stands) for six hundred dollars.[24] I thought this a pretty high price and besides, such a lot was no use to me, for I had never lived in town and could not so easily see the uses to which such property could be put. It seemed very doubtful to me that this place would ever be much larger or amount to much, for it evidently depended on the mines for a support, and these were so shallow that it looked as if they would be worked out in a short time and the country and town both be deserted. And I was not alone in thinking that the country would soon be deserted, for accustomed as we all had been to a showery summer, these dry seasons would seem entirely to prevent extensive farming. Some cursed the country and said they were on their way to "good old Missouri, God's own country." Hearing so much, I concluded it would be wise not to invest, but to get me back to Wisconsin again.

The steamer we took passage in was the *Northerner,* advertised to sail on the twenty-ninth day of November, 1850. The cabin room was all engaged, and they charged us nine ounces for steerage passage; but I did not care as much about their good rooms and clean sheets as I would have done at one time, for I had been a long time without either and did not care to pay the difference. When we were at the ship's office we had to take our turns to get tickets. One man weighed out the dust, and another filled out certificates.

When the callers began to get a little scarce, I looked under the counter, where I saw a whole panful of dust, to which they added mine to make the pile a little higher. They gave out no berths with these tickets, but such little things as that did not trouble us in the least. It was far better fare than we used to have in and about Death Valley, and we thought we could live through anything that promised better than the desert.

The passenger list footed up four hundred and forty, and when all got on board, at about ten o'clock in the morning, there was hardly room for all to stand up comfortably. It seemed to me to be a very much overcrowded boat in which to put to sea, but we floated out into the current with all the faces toward the shore, and hats and handkerchiefs waving good-bye to those who had come down to see the home goers safely off.

As we passed out through the wonderful Golden Gate and the outgoing current met the solid sea, each seemed wrestling for the mastery, and the waves beat and dashed themselves into foam all around us, while the spray came over the bows quite lively, frightening some who did not expect such treatment. When we had passed this scene of watery commotion and got out into the deeper water, the sea smoothed down a great deal; but seasickness began to claim its victims, at first a few, then more and more, till the greater part were quite badly affected. I had a touch of it myself, but managed to keep my feet by bracing out pretty wide, and hugging everything I could get hold of that seemed to offer a steady support, and I did not lie down until after I had thrown my breakfast overboard.

By the time dark came, nearly everyone was on his back, mostly on deck, and no one asleep. All were retching and moaning bitterly. Some, who had a few hours before cursed California, now cursed the sea, and declared that if they could induce the captain to turn about and put them back on shore again, they would rather creep on their hands and knees clear back to old Missouri over rocks and sand than to ride any farther on such a miserable old boat as this one was.

Next morning the decks looked pretty filthy, and about all the food the passengers had eaten was now spread about the decks in a half-digested condition. Most of the passengers were very sick. With the early daylight the sailors coupled the hose to the big steam pump, and began the work of washing and scrubbing off the decks, and though many begged hard to be left alone as they were, with all the filth, a good flood of salt water was the only answer they received to their pleading, and they were compelled to move, for the sailors said they could not change their orders without the captain, and he would not be out of bed till ten o'clock or later. So the cursing and swearing went for naught, and the decks were clean again. There were no deaths to report, but there were very few to do duty at the tables in eating the food prepared for them. After a few days the tables filled up again, and now it took them so long to eat that there had to be an order for only two meals a day or there would not have been a chance for all to get something. They were terribly hungry now, and everyone seemed to try his best to take in provisions enough to last him for at least twelve hours.

As the fellows began to get their sea legs on, they began to talk as if they were still in California, and could easily manage any little boat like this, and could run things as they did when they crossed the plains, where no sheriff, court, or judge had anything to say about matters, and all law was left behind. They began to act as if they were lords over all they could see, and as many of them were from the southern states, they seemed to take an especial pride in boasting of how they did as they pleased, about like the Helms brothers. They talked as if they could run the world—or the universe even—themselves, without assistance.

One morning at breakfast, when the table was full and the waiters scarce, some of these fellows swore and talked pretty rough, and as a waiter was passing, a blue blood from New Orleans rose in his seat and called for sugar, holding the empty bowl in his hand, but the waiter passed on and paid no attention, and when a mulatto waiter came along behind him, the angry man damned him the worst he could, ordering him to bring a bowl of sugar, quick. This waiter did not stop and the Louisiana man threw the bowl at the waiter's head, but missed it, and the bowl went crashing against the side of the ship. I expected surely the captain and his men would come and put the unruly fellow in irons, and there might be a fight or a riot, so I cut my meal short and went on deck about as soon as I could do so, thinking that would be a safer place. But the captain seemed to know about how to manage such fellows, and never left his stateroom, which I think was a wise move. The darky did not make his appearance at table afterwards, and the man who threw the bowl said that colored folks had to mind a gentleman when he spoke to them, or fare worse.

The captain now got out his passenger list, and we all had to pass through a narrow space near the wheelhouse and everyone answer to his name and show his ticket. This made work for about one day. Some stowaways were found and put down into the hole to heave coal. One day the captain and mate were out taking an observation on the sun when a young Missourian stepped up to see what was being done, and said to the captain, "Captain, don't you think I could learn how to do that kind of business?" The captain took the young man's hand and looked at his nails, which were very rough and dirty, and said, "No, my lad; boys with such fingernails can't learn navigation." This made a big laugh at the brave lubber's expense.

Many of the seasick ones did not get up so soon, and some died of that, or something else, and their bodies were sewed up in blankets, with a bushel of coal at their feet to sink them, and thrown overboard. The bodies were laid out on a plank at the ship's side, the captain would read a very brief service, and the sailors would, at the appropriate time, raise the end of the plank so that the body slid off and went down out of sight in a moment.

In due time we went into the harbor of Acapulco for water and coal. Here nearly everyone went on shore, and as there was no wharf for the vessel to lie to, the native canoes had many passengers at a dollar apiece for passage money. Out back of town there was a small stream of clear water which was warm and nice to bathe in, and some places three or four feet deep, so that a great many stripped off for a good wash, which was said to be very healthful in this climate. Many native women were on hand with soap and towels, ready to give anyone a good scrubbing for *dos reales,* (twenty-five cents) and those who employed them said they did a good, satisfactory job.

As I returned to town the streets seemed to be deserted, and I saw one man come out on an adjoining street and, after running a few steps, fall down on his face. Hearing the report of a gun at the same time, I hurried on to get out of danger, but I afterward learned that the man was a traveling gambler who had come across the country from Mexico, and that he was killed as he fell. No one seemed to care for him.

Near the beach were some large trees, and under them, dancing was going on to the music of the guitar. There were plenty of pretty Spanish girls for partners, and these and our boys made up an interesting party. The girls did not seem at all bashful or afraid of the boys, and though they could not talk together very much they got along with the sign language; ladies seemed very fond of the *Americanos.*

There was a fort here, a regular moss-backed old concern, and the soldiers were barefooted and did not need much clothing.

The cattle that were taken on board here were made to swim out to the ship, and then, with a rope around their horns, hoisted on deck, a distance of perhaps forty feet above the water. The maddened brutes were put into a secure stall ready for the ship's butcher. The small boys came around the ship in canoes, and begged the passengers to throw them out a dime, and when the coin struck the water they would dive for it, never losing a single one. One man dropped a bright bullet and the boy who dove for it was so enraged that he called him a d—d gringo (Englishman). None of these boys wore any clothes.

This town, like all Spanish towns, was composed of one-story houses, with dry-mud, fireproof walls. The country around looked very mountainous and barren, and comfortably warm.

After two days we were called on board, and soon set sail for sea again; and now, as we approached the equator, it became uncomfortably warm and an awning was put over the upper deck. All heavy clothing was laid aside, and anyone who had any amount of money on his person was unable to conceal it; but no one seemed to have any fear of theft, for a thief could not conceal anything he should steal, and no one reported anything lost. There was occasionally a dead body to be consigned to a watery grave.

A few days out from here and we were again mustered as before to show our tickets, which were carefully examined.

It seemed strange to me that the water was the poorest fare we had. It was sickish-tasting stuff, and so warm it would do very well for dishwater.

There were many interesting things to see. Sometimes it would be spouting whales; sometimes great, black masses, rolling on the water, looking like a ship bottom-upward, which some said were blackfish. Some fish seemed to be at play, and would jump ten feet or more out of the water. The flying fish would skim over the waves as the ship's wheels seemed to frighten them; and we went through a hundred acres of porpoises, all going the same way. The ship plowed right through them, but none seemed to get hurt by the wheels. Perhaps they were emigrants like ourselves in search of a better place.

It now became terribly hot, and the sun was nearly overhead at noon. Sometimes a shark could be seen alongside, and though he seemed to make no effort, easily kept up with the moving ship. Occasionally we saw a sea snake navigating the ocean all by himself. I did not understand how these fellows went to sea and lived so far from land. The flying fish seemed to be more plentiful as we went along, and would leave the water and scud along before us.

We had evening concerts on the forecastle, managed by the sailors. Their songs were not sacred songs, by any means, and many of them hardly fit to be heard by delicate ears. We again had to run the gauntlet of the narrow passage and have our tickets looked over, and this time a new stowaway was found, and he straightway made application for a job. "Go below, sir" was all the captain said. Several died and had their sea burial, and some who had been so sick all the way as not to get out of bed proved tough enough to stand the climate pretty well.

As we were nearing Panama, the doctor posted a notice to the mast cautioning us against eating much fruit while on shore, as it was very dangerous when eaten to excess. We anchored some little distance from the shore and had to land in small boats managed by the natives. I went in one and, when the boat grounded at the beach, the boatman took me on his back and set me on shore, demanding two dollars for the job, which I paid, and he served the whole crowd in the same way. The water here was blood warm, and they told me the tide ran very high.

This was a strange old town to me, walled in on all sides, a small plaza in the center, with a Catholic church on one side, and the other houses were mostly two story. On the side next to the beach was a high, thick wall which contained cells that were used for a jail, and on top were some dismounted cannon, long and old-fashioned.

The soldiers were poor lazy fellows, barefoot, and had very poor looking guns. Going out and in, all had to pass through a large gateway, but they asked no questions. The streets were very narrow and dirty and the sleeping rooms in the second story of the houses seemed to be inhabited by cats. For bedclothes was needed only a single sheet. On the roofs all around sat turkey buzzards, and anything that fell in the streets that was possible for them to eat was gobbled up very quickly. They were as tame as chickens, and walked around as fearless and lordly as tame turkeys. In consideration of their cleaning up the streets without pay, they were protected by law. One of the passengers could not resist the temptation to shoot one, and a small squad of soldiers was soon after him, and came into a room where there were fifty of us, but could not find their man. He would have been sent to jail if he had been caught. We had to pay one dollar a night for beds in these rooms, and they counted money at the rate of eight dimes to the dollar.

The old town of Panama lies a little south at the edge of the sea, and was destroyed by an earthquake long ago, I was told. To me, raised in the North, everything was very new and strange in way of living, style of building, and kind of produce. There were donkeys, parrots, and all kinds of monkeys in plenty. Most of the women were of very dark complexion, and not dressed very stylishly, while the younger population did not have even a fig leaf, or anything to take its place. The adults dressed very economically, for the days are summer days all the year round, and the clothing is scanty and cheap for either sex.

The cattle were small, pale red creatures, and not inclined to be very fat, and the birds mostly of the parrot kind. The market plaza is outside the walls, and a small stream runs through it, with the banks pretty thickly occupied by washerwomen. All the washing was done without the aid of a fire.

On the plaza there were plenty of donkeys loaded with truck of all sorts, from wood, green grass, coconuts, and sugar-cane to parrots, monkeys, and all kinds of tropical fruits. Outside the walls the houses were made of stakes interwoven with palm leaves, and everything was green as well as the grass and trees. Very little of the ground seemed to be cultivated, and the people were lazy and idle, for they could live so easily on the wild products of the country. A white man here would soon sweat out all his ambition and enterprise, and would be almost certain to catch the Panama yellow fever.[25] The common class of the people here, I should say, were Spanish and negro mixed, and they seem to get along pretty well; but the country is not suitable for white people. It seems to have been made on purpose for donkeys, parrots, and long-heeled negroes.

The cabin passengers engaged all the horses and mules the country afforded on which to ride across [to] the Chagres River, so it fell to the lot of myself and [my] companion to transfer ourselves on foot, which was pretty hard work in the hot and sultry weather. My gold dust began to grow pretty heavy as I went along, and though I had only about two thousand dollars, weighing about ten pounds, it seemed to me that it weighed fifty pounds by the way that it bore down upon my shoulders and wore sore places on them. It really was burdensome. I had worn it on my person night and day ever since leaving the mines, and I had some little fear of being robbed when off the ship.

Our road had been some day paved with cobblestones.[26] At the outskirts of the town we met a native coming in with a big, green lizard, about two feet long, which he was hauling and driving along with a string around its neck. I wondered if this was not a Panama butcher bringing in a fresh supply of meat.

271

When we reached the hills on our way from Panama, the paved road ended and we had only a mule trail to follow. The whole country was so densely timbered that no man could go very far without a cleared road. In some places we passed over hills of solid rock, but it was of a soft nature, so that the trail was worn down very deep, and we had to take the same regular steps that the mules did, for their tracks were worn down a foot or more. On the road we would occasionally meet a native with a heavy pack on his back, a long staff in each hand, and a solid, half-length sword by his side. He, like the burro, grunted every step he took. They seemed to carry unreasonably heavy loads on their backs, such as boxes and trunks, but there was no other way of getting either freight or baggage across the isthmus at that time.

It looked to me as if this trail might be just such a one as one would expect robbers to frequent, for it would, of course, be expected that Californians would carry considerable money with them, and we might reasonably look out for this sort of gentry at any turn of the trail. We were generally without weapons, and we should have to deliver on demand, and if anyone was killed, the body could easily be concealed in the thick brush on either side of the trail, and no special search for anyone missing would occur.

About noon one day we came to a native hut, and saw growing on a tree nearby something that looked like oranges, and we made very straight tracks with the idea of picking some and having a feast, but some of the people in the shanty called out to us and made motions for us not to pick them for they were no good; so we missed our treat of oranges and contented ourselves with a big drink of water and walked on.

After a little more travel we came to another shanty made of poles and palm leaves, occupied by an American. He was a tall, rawboned, cadaverous looking, wayside renegade who looked as if the blood had all been pumped out of his veins, and he claimed to be sick. He said he was one of the Texas royal sons. We applied for some dinner and he lazily told us there were flour, tea, and bacon and that we could help ourselves. I wet up some flour and baked some cakes, made some poor tea, and fried some bacon. We all got a sort of dinner out of his pantry stuff, and left him a dollar apiece for the accommodation. As we walked on my companion gave out and could carry his bundle no longer, so I took it, along with my own, and we got on as fast as we could, but darkness came on us before we reached the Chagres River and we had to stay all night at a native hut. We had some supper consisting of some very poor coffee, crackers, and a couple of eggs apiece, and had to sleep out under a tree where we knew we might find lizards, snakes, and other poisonous reptiles, and perhaps a thieving monkey might pick our pockets while we slept.

Before it was entirely dark many who rode horses came along, many of them ladies, and following the custom of the country, they all rode astride. Among this crowd was one middle-aged and somewhat corpulent old fellow, by profession a sea captain, who put on many airs. The old fellow put on his cool white coat—in fact, a white suit throughout—and in this tropical climate he looked very comfortable, indeed, thus attired. He filled his breast pocket with fine cigars, and put in the other pocket a flask with some medicine in it which was good for snakebites and also tending to produce courage in case the man, not used to horseback riding, should find his natural spirits failing. The rest of his luggage was placed on pack animals and, in fact, the only way luggage was carried in those days was either on the backs of donkeys or men.

All was ready for a start, and the captain in his snow-white suit was mounted on a mule so small that his feet nearly touched the ground. The little animal had a mind of his own, and at first did not seem inclined to start out readily, but after a bit concluded to follow his fellow animals, and all went well.

The rider was much amused at what he saw—sometimes a very lively monkey, sometimes a flock of parakeets or a high-colored lizard—and so he rode along with a very happy air, holding his head up, and smoking a fragrant Havana with much grace. The road was rough and rocky, with a mud hole, now and then, of rather uncertain depth. At every one of these mud holes the captain's mule would stop, put down his head, blow his nose, and look wise, and then carefully sound the miniature sea with his forefeet, being altogether too cautious to suit his rider, who had never been accustomed to a craft that was afraid of water.

At one of these performances, the mule evidently concluded the sea before him was not safe, for when the captain tried to persuade him to cross, his persuasions had no effect. Then he coaxed him with voice gentle, soft, and low, with the result that the little animal took a few very short steps and then came to anchor again. Then the captain began to get slightly roiled in temper, and the voice was not so gentle, sweet, and low, but it had no greater effect upon his craft. He began to get anxious, for the others had gone on, and he thought perhaps he might be left.

Now, this seafaring man had armed his heels with the large Spanish spurs so common in the country, and bringing them in contact with the force due to considerable impatience, Mr. Mule was quite suddenly and painfully aware of the result. This was harsher treatment than he could peaceably submit to and, at the second application of the spurs, a pair of small hoofs were very high in the air and the captain very low on his back in the mud and water, having been blown from the hurricane deck of his craft in a very sudden and lively style. The philosophical mule stood very still and looked on while the white coat and pantaloons were changing to a dirty brown, and watched the captain as he waded out, to the accompaniment of some very vigorous swear words.

Both the man and beast looked very doubtful of each other's future actions, but the man shook the water off and bestowed some lively kicks on his muleship, which made him bounce into and through the mud hole, and the captain, still holding the bridle, followed after. Once across the pool the captain set his marine eye on the only craft that had been too much for his navigation and said, "Vengeance should be mine," and in this doubtful state of mind he cautiously mounted his beast again and fully resolved to stick to the deck hereafter, at all hazards. He hurried on and soon overtook the train again, looking quite like a half-drowned rooster. The others laughed at him and told him they could find better water a little way ahead, at the river, and they would see him safely in. The captain was over his pet, and made as much fun as any of them, declaring that he could not navigate such a bloody craft as that in such limited sea room, for it was dangerous even when there was no gale to speak of.

The ladies did not blush at the new and convenient costumes which they saw in this country, and laughed a good deal over the way of traveling they had to adopt. Any who were sick were carried in a kind of chair strapped to the back of a native. Passengers were strung along the road for miles, going and coming. We would occasionally sit down awhile and let the sweat run off while a party of them passed us. Some were mounted on horses, some on mules, and some on donkeys, and they had to pay twelve dollars for the use of an animal for the trip.

Our night at this [last] wayside deadfall was not much better than some of the nights about Death Valley, but as I was used to low fare, I did not complain as some did. This seemed a wonderful country to a northern-raised boy. The trail was lined on both sides with all kinds of palms and various other kinds of trees and shrubs, and they were woven together in a compact mass with trailing and running vines. The trees were not tall, and the bark was as smooth as a young hickory. The roots would start out of the tree three feet above the ground and stand out at an angle, and looked like big planks placed edgewise.

It seemed as if there were too many plants for the ground to support, and so they grew on the big limbs of the trees all around, the same as the mistletoe on the oak, only there were ever so many different kinds.

The weather was very clear, and the sun so hot that many of the travelers began to wilt and sit down by the roadside to rest. Many walked along very slowly and wore long faces. The road from Panama to Crucez, on the Chagres River, was eighteen miles long, and all were glad when they were on the last end of it. The climate here seems to take all the starch and energy out of a man's body, and in this condition he must be very cautious or some disease will overtake him and he will be left to die without burial for his body if he has no personal friends with him.

We started on the next morning, and on our way stepped over a large ship anchor that lay across the trail. I suppose the natives had undertaken to pack it across the isthmus and found it too heavy for them. Perhaps it was for Captain Kidd, the great pirate, for it is said that he often visited Panama in the course of his cruising about in search of treasures.

Passing along a sandy place in the trail, a snake crossed and left his track, big as a stovepipe it seemed to be, and after this we kept a sharp watch for big snakes that might be in waiting to waylay us for game.

There were plenty of monkeys and parrots climbing and chattering around in the trees. The forest is here so dense that the wind never blows, and consequently it never gets cool. The sun, ever since we got down near the equator, was nearly overhead, and the moon seemed to be even north of us.

When we reached the Chagres River we hired a boat of an Irishman for the trip down. I wondered if there was a place on earth so desolate that the "Paddy" would not find it. The boat for the journey cost two hundred dollars, and would hold passengers enough so that it would cost us ten dollars each, at any rate, and perhaps a little more. Two natives had charge of the boat and did the navigating. There were two ladies among the passengers, and when the two natives, who I suppose were the captain and mate of the craft, came on board, clad very coolly in Panama hats, the ladies looked at them a little out of the corners of their eyes and made the best of it. Our two navigators took the oars and pulled slowly down the stream.

Nothing but water and evergreen trees could we see, for the shore on either hand was completely hidden by the dense growth that hung over and touched the water. On a mud bar that we passed a huge alligator lay, taking a sunbath, and though many shots were fired at him, he moved away very leisurely. No one could get on shore without first clearing a road through the thick brushes and vines along the bank. On the way one of our boatmen lost his hat, his only garment, into the river, and overboard he went, like a dog, and soon had it and climbed on board again. I wondered why some of the big alligators did not make a snap at him.

The water in the run looked very roily and dirty, and no doubt had fever in it. The only animals we saw were monkeys and alligators, and there were parrots in the trees. The farther we went down the stream the wider it became, and the current slacker, so that we moved more slowly with the same amount of rowing. At a place called Dos Hermanos (two brothers) we could see a little cleared spot near the bank, which seemed to be three or four feet above the water. There were no mountains nor hills in sight, and the whole country seemed to be an extensive swamp. It was near night that we came to a small native village of palm huts, and here our boatmen landed and hid themselves, and not being able to find them, we were compelled to stay all night, for we dared not go on alone. The place looked like a regular robbers' roost, and being forced to sleep outside the huts, we considered it safest to sleep with one eye open. We would have gone on with the boat, only that we were afraid the river might have more than one outlet, and if we should take the wrong one we might be too late for the steamer, which even now we were afraid would not wait for us, and getting left would be a very serious matter in this country.

We had very little to eat, and all we could buy was sugar cane, bananas, monkeys, and parrots. We kept a sharp eye out for robbers, keeping together as much as we could, for we knew that all returning Californians would be suspected of having money. Most all of them were ready for war except myself, who had no weapon of any kind. All of these people had a bad name, and every one of them carried a long-bladed knife called a machete, with which they could kill a man at a single blow. But with all our fears we got through the night safely, and in the morning found our boatmen, who had hidden away. We waited not for breakfast, but sailed away as soon as we could, and reached Chagres, near the mouth of the river, before night.[27]

The riverbanks here are not more than three feet high, and farther back the land fell off again into a wet swamp of timber and dense vegetable growth. The town was small and poorly built, on the immediate bank, and the houses were little brush-and-palm affairs, except the boardinghouse, which was T-shaped, the front two stories high, with a long dining room running back, having holes for windows, but no glass in them.

Before the bell rang for meals, a long string of hungry men would form in line, and at the first tap would make a rush for the table, like a flock of sheep. After all were seated, a waiter came around and collected a dollar from each one, and we thought this paid pretty well for the very poor grub they served afterwards.

No ship had as yet been in sight to take us away from this lowest, dirtiest, most unhealthful place on earth, and the prospect of remaining here had nothing very charming about it. The river was full of alligators, so the bathing was dangerous, and the whole country was about fit for its inhabitants, which were snakes, alligators, monkeys, parrots, and lazy negroes. It could not have been more filthy if the dregs of the whole earth had been dumped here, and cholera and yellow fever were easy for a decent man to catch.

My companion and I went out on the beach a mile or two to get the saltwater breeze, and leave the stinking malaria for those who chose to stay in the hot, suffocating village, and here we would stay until nearly night. [28] Across a small neck of water was what was called a fort. It could hardly be seen, it was so covered with moss and vines, but near the top could be seen something that looked like old walls. There was no sign of life about it, and I should judge it was built at some very early day. Surely there was nothing here to protect, for the whole country did not seem able to support even a few barefooted soldiers. Some men who wandered along up the riverbank, following a path, said they had seen some dead human bodies thrown into the swamp and left, probably because it was easier than putting them underground.

For a bedroom I hired a little platform which a storekeeper had placed before his store, where I slept, and paid a dollar for the privilege. Someone walked around near me all night, and I dared not close more than one eye at a time for fear of losing a little bag of gold dust. This little bag of gold was getting to be a great burden to me in this sickly climate, and the vigilant guard I had to keep over so small a treasure was very tiresome.

The second night no steamer came, but on the third morning the steamer was riding at anchor three or four miles out, and soon after a ship came in from the Atlantic end of the Nicaragua route with one thousand passengers, there being no steamer there for them to take a passage home on, and so they had to come here for a start. This filled the little town to overflowing, but as the ship that had arrived was the *Georgia,* one of the largest afloat, all could go if they only could endure the fare.

We now had to go in small boats from the shore to the ship, and the trip cost two dollars and a half. I waited till I had seen some of the boats make a trip or two and then, choosing one that had a sober skipper, I made the venture. It was said that one drunken boatman allowed his boat to drift into some breakers and all were lost.

I tell you I was overanxious to get out of this country, for I well knew that if I stayed very long I should stay forever, for one like myself, raised in a healthful climate, could not remain long without taking some of the fatal diseases the country was full of.

We made the trip to the vessel safely, and as our boat lay under the ship's quarter—the men holding the ropes—I looked up, and when I saw the swinging rope ladder on which I was expected to climb up to the ship's deck, it seemed a pretty dangerous job; but I mustered up courage and made the attempt. The sea was pretty rough out here for the small boats, and the ship rolled some, so that when persons tried to get hold of the ladder they were thrown down and sometimes hurt a little. A man held on to the lower end of the ladder so that the one who was climbing might not get banged against the side of the ship and have his breath knocked out of him. I mounted the ladder safely and climbed away like a monkey, reaching the deck all right. Ladies and weak people were hauled up in a sort of chair with a block and rope.

It took the most of two days to get the people on board, and when they were counted up there were one thousand four hundred and forty, all told. This steamer had a very long upper deck and a comparatively short keel, and rolled very badly; and as for me, I had swallowed so much of the deadly malaria of the isthmus that I soon got very seasick, and the first day or two were very unpleasant. I went to the bar and paid two bits for a glass of wine to help my appetite, but it stayed with me no longer than time enough to reach the ship's side. When night came the decks were covered with sleepy men, and if the weather had been rough and all sick, as was the case when we left San Francisco, we should have had more filthy decks than we had even on that occasion.

Approaching the harbor at Havana, Cuba, we seemed to be going head foremost against a wall of solid rock, but when within speaking distance, an officer came in sight on the fort right before us and shouted through his speaking trumpet, saying, "Why don't you salute us?" Our officer said, "You know us well enough without." Our ship had a small cannon on the forecastle but did not choose to use it, and I suppose the Cuban officer felt slighted. We now turned short to the right and entered the beautiful harbor, which is perfectly landlocked and as still as a pond. The city is all on the right side of the bay and our coal yard was on the left, at a short wharf at which we landed.

A lot of armed soldiers were placed a short distance back on the high ground and no one was allowed to go beyond them. We now had a port officer on board who had entire charge of the ship, and if anyone wanted to go to the city, across the bay two or three miles, he had to pay a dollar for a pass. This pass business made the blue bloods terribly angry, and they swore long and loud, and the longer they talked the madder they got, and more bitter in their feelings, so that they were ready to fight (not with sugar bowls this time).

The weather here was very warm and the heat powerful, and as these fellows saw there was only one course to be pursued if they wanted to get on shore, they slowly took passes good for all day and paid their dollar for them, and also another dollar each to the canoemen to take them to the city. Myself and companion also took passes and went over.

Arriving at the city we walked a short distance and came to the plaza, which is not a very large one. Here was a single grave nicely fenced in, and across the plaza were some large, two-story houses, in front of which was stationed a squad of cavalry, standing as motionless as if every man of them was a marble statue. We kept on the opposite side of the street, and chancing to meet a man whom we rightly supposed to be an Englishman, we inquired about the grave on the plaza and were informed that it was that of Christopher Columbus, the discoverer of America.

Just then we noticed the cavalry moving up the street at a slow gallop, and so formed that a close carriage was in the center of the squad. As they rushed by and we gazed at them with purely American curiosity, our new English friend raised our hats for us and held them till the cavalcade had passed, merely remarking that the governor general was within the carriage. We spoke perhaps a bit unpleasantly when we asked him why he was so ungentlemanly in his treatment of us as to remove our hats, but he said, "My friends, if I had not taken off your hats for you as a friend, some of those other fellows would have knocked them off, so I did for you an act of greatest kindness, for everyone removes his hat when the governor general passes." He also informed us that the special occasion for this rather pompous parade was the execution of some criminals at a park or prison not far away, and that this was done by beheading them.

Our friend proposed that we also walk out in that direction, and we went with him to the edge of the city, but when he turned into a bypath that did not seem much frequented, we declined to follow farther, and turned back along the open road. The path looked to us a sort of robber's route, and not exactly safe for unarmed men like us in a strange country.

The man followed us back and took us into a large, airy saloon, in the center of which a big fountain was playing, and the great basin in which the water fell was filled with beautiful fish. Our friend called for an iced drink for each of us, and as we sat at the table we tasted it and found it rather intoxicating. For this they charged us one dollar each, but we noticed that our friend paid nothing, and we set him down as a sort of capper [shill], after the style we had seen at the gold mines. We sat a few minutes and then so coolly bade our friend good-bye that he had not the face to follow us further, and continued our walk about the streets, which seemed to us very narrow, and the houses generally two stories high.

A chaise passed us, containing two young ladies with complexions white and fair, and eyes and hair black, in striking contrast. The carriage was drawn by two horses tandem, the horse in the shafts being mounted by a big negro of very dignified appearance, dressed in livery and having top boots that came to his knees. This was the only vehicle of the kind we saw on the streets.

We did not dare to go very far alone, for with our ignorance of the Spanish language we might go astray and not get back to the ship within the lifetime of our passes, and not knowing how much trouble that might cause us, we were naturally a little timid; so we took a boat back to the ship, and when on board again we felt safe. We had only about four dollars cash left.

A big gang of darkies were coaling the ship. Each one carried a large tub full of coal upon his head and poured it down into the ship's hold. All the clothes these fellows wore was a strip of cloth about their middle. When they were let off for dinner they skimmed off all they could get from the ship's slop barrel, which stood on the wharf alongside, to help out their very scanty food. The overseer stood by them all the time with a big whip and made them hurry up as fast as possible, talking Spanish pretty vigorously, and though we could not understand, we made up our minds that a good part of it was swearing.

The next morning the steamship *Prometheus* came in and tied up near us, and soon word was brought that she would take the New Orleans passengers onboard and sail immediately for that port. It now occurred to me that I could get nearer home by going up the Mississippi River than by way of New York, so I went on board the *Prometheus,* and we soon sailed out of the harbor, passing under the gate of the fortress called, I think, San Juan de Ulloa.[29]

Nothing special occurred during our passage till we were near the mouth of the Mississippi River, when, in the absence of a pilot boat or tug, our captain thought he would try to get in alone, and as a consequence we were soon fast in the mud. The captain now made all the passengers go aft, and worked the engine hard but could not move her at all. The tide was now low, and there was a prospect that we should have to wait [a] full six hours to get away. We worked on, however, and after a few hours a tug came to our assistance and pulled us out of the mud and towed us into the right channel, up which we steamed on our way to New Orleans, one hundred twenty miles away.

The country on both sides of us was an immense marsh—no hills in sight, no timber, nothing but the same level marsh or prairie. When we were nearer the *Crescent City,* some houses came in sight; then we passed General Jackson's battlefield, and in due time reached the city.

On board this ship I became acquainted with Dick Evans, who lived in the same county that I used to in Wisconsin, near Mineral Point, so the three of us now concluded to travel together.

New Orleans seemed to be a very large city. Near the levee a large government building was in course of construction for a customhouse. It was all of stone, and the walls were up about two stories. We put up at a private boardinghouse, and the first business was to try and sell our gold dust. So we went to the mint[30] and were told we would have to wait ten days to run it through the mill, and we did not like to wait so long. We were shown all through the mint and saw all the wonders of coin making. Everything seemed perfect here. Beautiful machinery was in operation, making all sizes of gold coins, from a twenty-dollar piece down. Strips of gold bands about six feet long and of the proper thickness for twenty-dollar pieces are run through a machine which cuts out the pieces, and when these are cut they can stamp out the pieces as fast as one can count.

This was the most ingenious work I ever saw, and very wonderful and astonishing to a backwoodsman like myself, for I supposed that money was run in molds like bullets.

As we could not wait, we went to a bank and sold our dust, getting only sixteen dollars per ounce, the same price they paid in California.[31] We now took the cars and rode out to Lake Pontchartrain[32]—most of the way over a trestlework. We found a wharf and warehouse at the lake, and a steamer lay there all ready to go across to the other side. The country all about looked low, with no hills in sight.

When we returned to the city we looked all about, and in the course of our travels came to a slave market. Here there were all sorts of black folks for sale; big and little, old and young, and all sorts. They all seemed good-natured, and were clean, and seemed to think they were worth a good deal of money. Looking at them a few minutes sent my mind back to St. Joseph, Missouri, where I saw a black sold at auction. From my standpoint of education, I did not approve of this way of trading in colored people.

We continued our stroll about the city, coming to a cemetery, where I looked into a newly dug grave to find it half full of water. On one side were many brick vaults above ground. The ground here is very low and wet, and seemed to be all swamp. The drainage was in surface gutters, and in them the water stood nearly still. It seemed to me such water must have yellow fever in it.

For a long way along the levee the steamboats lay thick and close together, unloading cotton, hemp, sugar, hoop poles, bacon, and other products, mostly the product of negro labor.

Here our friend Evans was taken sick, and as he got no better after a day or two, we called a doctor to examine him. He pronounced it a mild case of yellow fever. His skin was yellow in places, and he looked very bad. The doctor advised us to go on up the river, saying it was very dangerous staying here with him. Evans gave me most of his money and all of his gold specimens to take to his wife, and [said] when he got well he would follow us. We bade him good-bye, and with many wishes for his speedy recovery we took passage on a steamer for St. Louis. This steamer, the *Atlantic,* proved to be a real floating palace in all respects. The table was supplied with everything the country afforded, and polite and well-dressed darkies were numerous as table waiters. This was the most pleasant trip I had ever taken, and I could not help comparing the luxuriance of my coming home to the hardships of the outward journey across the plains and our starvation fare.

Our boat was rather large for the stage of water this time of year, and we proceeded rather slowly, but I cared little for speed, as bed and board were extra good, and a first-cabin passage in the company of friends, many of whom were going to the same part of Wisconsin as myself, was not a tedious affair by any means.

At night gambling was carried on very extensively, and money changed hands freely as the result of sundry games of poker, which was the popular game.

We reached St. Louis in time, and here was the end of our boat's run. The river had some ice floating on its surface, and this plainly told us that we were likely to meet more ice and colder weather as we went north. We concluded to take the Illinois River boat from here to Peoria, and paid our passage and stepped on board. We were no more than halfway through this trip when the ice began to form on the surface of the water, and soon became so thick and strong that the boat finally came to a perfect standstill, frozen in solid.

We now engaged a farm wagon to take us to Peoria, from which place we took regular stages for Galena.[33] Our driver was inclined to be very merciful to his horses, so we were two days in reaching that town, but perhaps it was best, for the roads were icy and slippery, and the weather of the real winter sort. From here we hired a team to take four of us to Plattville, and then an eighteen-mile walk brought me to Mineral Point, the place from which I started with my Winnebago pony in 1849. I had now finished my circle and brought both ends of the long belt together.

I now went to a drug store and weighed Mr. Evans's specimens, wrapping each in a separate piece of paper, with the value marked on each, and took them to his wife, to whom I told the news about her husband. In two weeks' time he came home sound and well.

I was quite disappointed in regard to the looks and business appearance of the country. It looked thinly settled, people scarce, and business dull. I could not get a day's work to do, and I could not go much farther on foot, for the snow was eight or ten inches deep, and I was still several hundred miles from my parents in Michigan. So my journey farther east was delayed until spring. The hunting season was over, and when I came into Mineral Point without a gun and wore good clothes, making a better appearance than I used to, they seemed to think I must be rich and showed me marked attention, and made many inquiries about their neighbors who started for California about the same time I did. The young ladies smiled pleasantly when near me, and put on their best white aprons, looking very tidy and bright, far superior to any of the ladies I had seen in my crooked route from San Francisco through Acapulco, Panama, the West Indies, and along the Mississippi.

After a few days in town I went out into the neighborhood where I used to live and stopped with Mr. E. A. Hall, who used to be a neighbor of Mr. Bennett, as he had invited me to stay with himself and wife, who were the only occupants of a good house, and all was pleasant. But notwithstanding all the comfort in which I was placed, I grew lonesome, for the enforced idleness on account of the stormy weather was a new feature in my life and grew terribly monotonous.

After some delay I concluded to write to my parents in Michigan and give them a long letter with something of a history of my travels, and to refresh my memory I got out my memorandum I had kept through all my journey.

As my letter was liable to be quite lengthy I bought a quantity of foolscap paper and began.[34] I took my diary as my guide, and filled out the ideas suggested in it so they would understand them. I soon ran through with my paper and bought more, and kept on writing. The weather was cold and stormy, and I found it the best occupation I could have to prevent my being lonesome; so I worked away, day after day, for about a month, and I was really quite tired of this sort of work before I had all the facts recorded which I found noted down in my diary. My notes began in March, 1849, in Wisconsin, and ended in February, 1852, on my return to Mineral Point. I found, as the result of my elaboration, over three hundred pages of closely written foolscap paper, and I felt very much relieved when it was done. By the aid of my notes I could very easily remember everything that had taken place during my absence, and it was recorded in regular form, with day and date, not an incident of any importance left out, and every word as true as gospel. I had neither exaggerated nor detracted from any event so far as I could recollect.

I now loaned Mr. Hall, with whom I lived, six hundred dollars to enable him to cross the plains to California and try to make his fortune. To secure this I took a mortgage on his eighty-acre farm, and he set out to make the journey. I had another eighty acres of land near here which I bought at government price before going to California, but I could not now sell it for what it cost me. When I went away I had left my chest and contents with my friend Samuel Zollinger, and he had kept it safely, so I now made him my lawful agent. I placed my narrative and some other papers in the chest and gave the key into his charge, while I went north, across the Wisconsin River, to visit my old hunting and trapping friend, Robert McCloud. Here I made a very pleasant visit of perhaps a week, and the common prospects of the country were freely talked over. It seemed to us as if the good times were still far off; every day was like Sunday so far as anything going on: no money in circulation, many places abandoned, and, like myself, many had gone to California to seek gold instead of lead. (The mines at Mineral Point are mostly of lead, with some copper.)

Looking at matters in this light, it did not need a great deal of McCloud's persuasion to induce me to go back with him to California, all the more so as my little pile seemed to look smaller every day, while three or four years ago it would have seemed quite large. Deciding to go, I wrote to Mr. Zollinger to send the account I had written to my parents in Michigan, reading it first himself, and admonishing him not to lend it. I also wrote to my parents telling them what they might look for in the mails, and cautioning them never to have it printed, for the writing was so ungrammatical and the spelling so incorrect that it would be no credit to me.

I afterward learned that, in time, they received the bundle of paper and read it through and through, and circulated it around the neighborhood till it was badly worn, and laid it away for future perusal when their minds should incline that way. But the farmhouse soon after took fire and burned, my labor going up in smoke.

When the news of this reached me, I resolved to try to forget all the trials, troubles, and hardships I had gone through, and which I had almost lived over again as I wrote them down, and I said to myself that I would not talk about them more than I could help, the sooner to have them vanish, and never write them down again, but a few years ago an accident befell me so that I could not work, and I backslid from my determination when I was persuaded so earnestly by many friends to write the account, which appeared a few years ago in *The Santa Clara Valley,* now *The Pacific Tree and Vine,* edited by H. A. Brainard, at San Jose, California.[35] The diary was lost, and from memory alone the facts have been rehearsed [related], and it is but fair to tell the reader that the hardest and worst of it has never been told nor will it ever be.

CHAPTER XVI

Off to the Mines Again

MCCLOUD AND I NOW TOOK HIS SKIFF, and for two days floated down the Wisconsin River till we reached the Mississippi, boarded the first steamboat we could hail, and let our own little craft adrift. In due time we reached St. Louis and boarded another steamer for New Orleans.

At a wood yard about dark, a lot of negroes, little and big, came on board to sell brooms. The boat's clerk seemed to know negro character pretty well, so he got out his violin and played for them. For a while the young colored gentry listened in silence, but pretty soon he struck a tune that suited them, and they began to dance in their own wild style.

In seven days from St. Louis we landed in New Orleans, and found the government steamer, *Falcon,* advertised to sail in two days. We went together to one of the slave warehouses. Outside and in, all was neat and clean, and any day you could see men, women, and children standing under the shed as a sign of what they had within, and the painted signs "For Sale" displayed conspicuously. We were very civilly treated, and invited to examine the goods offered for sale. There were those of all ages and all colors, for some were nearly white and some intensely black, with all the shades between. All were to be sold separately, or in families, or in groups, as buyers might desire. All were made to keep themselves clean and neatly dressed, and to behave well, with a smile to all the visitors whether they felt like smiling or not. Some seemed really anxious to get a good master, and when a kind, pleasant looking man came along they would do their utmost to be agreeable to him and inquire if he did not want to buy them. We talked it over some between ourselves, and when we thought of the market and the human chattels for sale there, McCloud spoke up and said, "I am almost persuaded to be an abolitionist."

I now went on board the steamer *Falcon,* in command of a government officer, to try to learn something about the family of Captain Culverwell who perished alone in Death Valley. He told me he had once belonged to the Navy and had his life insured and, as I was an important witness for his family, I wanted to learn where they lived. The captain looked over a list of officers, but Culverwell's name was not there. I then wrote a letter to Washington stating the facts of his death, and my own address in Sacramento, California. I also stated that I would assist the widow if I could, but I never received an answer.

We soon started down the river, having on board about one hundred passengers, men going to work on the Panama Railroad.[1] At Chagres we found a small, stern-wheeled river steamer and took passage on it for Gorgona, as far as the steamer could well go up the river.[2] While going up, we met a similar boat coming down and, being near a short bend, they crashed together, breaking down our guards severely, but fortunately with no damage to our wheel. A few miles above this a dark, passing cloud gave us rain in streams, and we had to drift in near shore to wait for the storm to pass. I never before saw water fall so fast, and yet in half an hour the sun was out and burning hot.

Before we reached Gorgona we got acquainted with a man named John Briggs from Wisconsin, and Lyman Ross from Rhode Island, and concluded to travel in company. Our fare thus far was ten dollars, and two horses to Panama, for which we paid twelve dollars each. We now rode and walked turnabout, and when we inquired about the road, we were told that being once in it we could not possibly get out except at the other end, and would need no guide, and at the end of a very disagreeable day's work, we reached the big gate at Panama and entered the ancient city.[3]

We waited but little here before taking the steamer *Southerner*, bound for San Francisco. Three days after we sailed away, one of our passengers went overboard, a corpse, and three or four more died and were buried alongside before we reached Acapulco.

Here we took on water and coal and were soon at sea again. McCloud soon had to take his place in the sick ward, and I attended him most of the time, but was not allowed to give him anything without a permit from the doctor, and the long delays between the administrations of medicine made the sickness hard to endure. The sick could see the dead sewed up in blankets with a bucket of coal for a weight; then resting on a plank, with sailors on each side, the mate would read the brief services appropriate to a burial at sea, the plank was tilted, and the lifeless body slid down into the depths. Such scenes were no benefit to the suffering, for each might think his turn was next, when a bright hope and prospect would be better for his recovery.

One forenoon the fire gong rang out sharply, and all was in confusion, supposing the ship to be on fire, but nothing could be seen but a dense fog except as a gentle wind lifted it a little, and there, dead ahead, was a rocky island against which it seemed we must dash to destruction, for there was no beach and very little chance for anyone to be saved. Ten minutes more in this direction and we were lost, but the officers quickly changed the course, and we passed the pile of rocks, scarcely a rifle-shot away. Whose fault it was, this danger so miraculously avoided, we did not know—the captain's or the imperfect chart—and opinions were freely given both ways.

About those days the air felt cooler, the fog less dense, and the foggy rainbows we had seen so much when the sun tried to shine were scarce, while a more northern wind created a coolness that made sick folks feel refreshed and hopeful. It gave me a chance to cheer up my sick friend, who was still in bed, and tell him it would continue to be cooler as we went.

On the Fourth of July the officers produced the ship's full supply of flags, and the sailors climbed high and low, fastening them to every rope, till we had a very gay Independence Day appearance. In this gay dress we steamed into San Diego harbor to leave the mail for a few soldiers stationed there, and get their letters in return.

I could see no town in San Diego, but a beautiful harbor, and some poor-looking mustard wigwams some way off seemed to contain the good people of that place.

A boat with a small crew pulled out and came alongside to get the mail and deliver theirs, and then we turned to sea again. The country all around this beautiful little harbor looked mountainous and extremely barren, and no one wanted to go on shore.

About dark we had made sufficient offing and turned northward, plowing through large fields of kelp.[4] The next morning the forward watch announced land ahead, which could dimly be seen as the fog rose. The officers rushed on deck and could see not far ahead a sandy beach, and a moment more showed that we were headed directly for it, and that it was not more than a quarter of a mile away. Quickly the helmsman was given orders to steer almost west instead of the north course he had been following. He was asked why he kept on his north course when he saw danger ahead and answered, "It is my business to steer according to orders, even if the ship goes ashore, and I cannot change course unless ordered to." The captain now examined his chart and decided he was in San Pedro harbor, off Los Angeles.

The sun came out bright and clear a little later, and I got McCloud out of his bed and gave him a seat at the ship's side, where he could see the green, grassy hills near the beach and larger hills and mountains farther back. We could see cattle feeding in the nearest pastures, and the whole scene was a pleasant one; and as we sat on the eastern side of the ship and snuffed the cool breeze which came from the north, we thought we were comparatively happy people, and hoped that, if no accident befell, we would soon be at the end of our voyage.

On the seventh day of July, 1851, we entered the Golden Gate, this being my second arrival in California. On our trip from Panama seven or more had died and been buried at sea, but the remainder of us were quite safe and sound. We found the heart of the city still smoking, for a fire had broken out on July fourth and burned extensively, and these broad, blackened ruins were the result. Some said the work had been done by the Sidney "ducks" and their numerous helpers, who were really the rulers of the city. The place now looked much worse than it did when I left in November before. These Sidney "ducks" were English convicts from Australia, and other thieves and robbers joined them as agreeable companions, making a large class that seemed to glory in destruction and a chance for booty.[5]

I walked around over the hills, where I could see the burned district and the destruction of so much valuable property, and when I thought the civil law was not strong enough to govern, it seemed to me it would be a good place for such men as the Helms brothers of Georgetown to come down and do a little hanging business, for they could here find plenty to do, and they could carry out their plan of letting no guilty man escape.

About four o'clock one afternoon, we went aboard the Sacramento steamer, *Antelope,* paying our passage with half an ounce apiece, and were soon on our way past the islands and up the bay. When we were beyond Benicia, where the riverbanks were close, McCloud sat watching the shore and remarked that the boat ran like a greyhound and, it seemed to him, beat the old ocean steamer pretty bad.

He seemed to be nearly well again, and complimented me as the best doctor he ever saw. Since he had been sick I had paid him all the attention I could, and he gave me all the praise I deserved, now that he was getting to feel himself again.

At Sacramento we changed to another boat bound for Marysville,[6] which place we reached without special incident. Here we invested in a four-ounce donkey, that is, we paid four ounces of gold for him, just an ounce apiece for four of us—W. L. Manly, Robert McCloud, Lyman Ross, and John Briggs. We piled our blankets in a pack upon the gentle four-ounce donkey, and added a little tea and coffee, dried beef, and bread, then started for the

Yuba River, ourselves on foot. We crossed the river at Park's Bar, then went up the ridge by way of Nigger Tent, came down to the river again at Goodyear Bar, then up the stream to Downieville. This town was named after John Downie, a worthless drunkard. I remember that he once reformed, but again backslid, and died a drunkard's death.[7]

We found this a lively mining town about sixty miles above Marysville, on the North Fork of the Yuba River, and only reached by a pack trail, but everything was flush here, even four aces. The location was a veritable Hole-in-the-Ground, for the mountains around were very high, and some of them wore their caps of snow all summer, particularly those on the east. The gold dust we found here was coarser than it was where I worked before, down south on the Merced River. Before I came to California I always supposed that gold dust was really dust, and about as fine as flour.

We went up the North Fork about a mile or two above town and camped on Wisconsin Flat to begin our mining operations.[8] Our luck was poor at first, and all except myself were out of money and more or less in debt to me. We made expenses, however, and a little more, and as soon as Mr. Ross got his small debt paid, he said he was discouraged [with] mining and, with blankets on his shoulders, started up the trail towards Galloway's Ranch, on the summit south of town. Mr. Ross said the work was too hard for him, for he was not strong enough to handle pick and shovel, and he believed he could go down to Sacramento and make more by his wits than he could here. I went with him to town, and saw him start off with a fair load on his back, and watched him as he toiled up the steep mountain trail for about two miles, when he went out of sight.

The rest of us kept on mining. Our luck was not very good, but we persevered, for there was nothing to be gained by fainting by the way. I went into an old abandoned shaft about ten feet deep and found the bottom filled with a big quartz boulder and, as I had been a lead miner in Wisconsin, I began drifting, and soon found bedrock, when I picked up a piece of pure gold that weighed four ounces.[9] This was what I called a pretty big find, and not exactly what I called gold dust. It was quite a surprise to me, for the gravel on the bedrock was only about three or four inches thick.

We kept on drifting for some time, sometimes making good wages, and on the whole so satisfactory that we concluded to stay. We now located some claims back in the flat where the ground would be thirty feet deep and would have to be drifted. These we managed to hold until winter, and in the meantime we worked along the river and could make something all the time.

We put in a flume between two falls on the Middle Fork, but made only wages, and I got my arm nearly broken, and had to work with one hand for nearly a month.

One afternoon I went crevicing up the river, and found a crevice at the water's edge about half an inch wide, and the next day we worked it out, getting forty ounces, and many of the pieces were about an inch long and as large around as a pipe stem.

Winter was now nearby, and we set to work to build a cabin and lay in a stock of grub, which cost quite a good deal, for the self-raising flour which we bought was worth twenty cents a pound, and all kinds of hog meat fifty cents, with other supplies in proportion. Our new claims now paid very well. Snow came down to the depth of about four feet around our cabin, but as our work was underground, we had a comfortable place all winter.

In the spring McCloud and I went to Sacramento and sold our chunks of gold (it was all very coarse) to Page, Bacon & Co., who were themselves surprised at the coarseness of the whole lot. When our savings were weighed up, we found we had made half an ounce a day, clear of all expenses, for the entire year. We now took a little run down to San Francisco, also to Santa Clara, where we stayed a night or two with Mr. McCloud's friend, Mr. Otterson, and then went back to our claims again. In taking care of our money we had to be our own bankers, and the usual way was to put the slugs we received for pay into a gallon pickle jar, and bury this in some place known only to our particular selves, and these vaults we considered perfectly safe. The slugs were fifty-dollar pieces, coined for convenience, and were eight-sided, heavy pieces. In the western counties the people called them "adobies," but among the miners they were universally known as "slugs."[10]

The winter proved a little lonesome; the miners mostly stayed at home and worked. During the year we had been here, I had not seen a respectable woman in this mining country. There were few females here, and they were said to be of very doubtful character. As a general thing people were very patient with their wickedness, but not always.

Twice only in the history of California were women made the victims of mob violence, once at Los Angeles and once at Downieville. The affair at the last-named place occurred in 1851, and the victim was a pretty little Spanish woman named Juanita. She and her husband, like many another couple at that time, kept a monte game for the delectation of the miners who had more money than sense, but beyond this fact absolutely nothing was said against her character.

There was an English miner named Cannon living in town, who was very popular among a large number of gamblers and others. He got drunk one night and about midnight went to the house occupied by the Spanish woman and her husband and kicked the door down. Early the following morning he told his comrades that he was going to apologize to the woman for what he had done. He went alone to the house, and, while [he was] talking with the husband and wife, the woman suddenly drew a knife and stabbed Cannon to the heart. What had been said that provoked the deed was never known, further than that Juanita claimed she had been grossly insulted.

She was given a mock trial, but the facts of the case were not brought out, as the men who were with Cannon were too drunk to remember what had happened the previous night. It was a foregone conclusion that the poor woman was to be hanged, and the leaders of the mob would brook no interference. A physician examined Juanita and announced to the mob that she was in a condition that demanded the highest sympathy of every man, but he was forced to flee from town to save his life.[11] A prominent citizen made an appeal for mercy, but he was driven down the main street and across the river by a mob with drawn revolvers and with threats of instant death. The well-known John B. Weller[12] was in town at the time, and was asked to reason with the mob, but refused to do so.

The execution was promptly carried out. A plank was put across the supports of the bridge over the Yuba, and a rope fastened to a beam overhead. Juanita went calmly to her death. She wore a Panama hat and, after mounting the platform, she removed it [and] tossed it to a friend in the crowd, whose nickname was Oregon, with the remark, "*Adios amigo.*" Then she adjusted the noose to her own neck, raising her long, loose tresses carefully in order to fix the rope firmly in its place, and then, with a smile and wave of her hand to the bloodthirsty crowd present, she stepped calmly from the plank into eternity. Singular enough, her body rests side by side, in the cemetery on the hill, with that of the man whose life she had taken.

On Sundays Downieville was full of men, none very old and none very young, but almost everyone of middle age. Nearly every man was coarsely dressed, with beard unshaved, and many with long hair, but on any occasion of excitement it was not at all strange to see the coarsest, roughest looking one of all the party mount a stump and deliver as eloquent an address as one could wish to hear. On Sunday it was not at all unusual for some preacher to address the moving crowd, while a few feet behind him would be a saloon in full blast, and drinking, gambling, swearing, and vulgar language could be plainly seen and heard at the same time, and this class of people seemed to respect the Sunday preacher very little. The big saloon was owned by John Craycroft, formerly a mate on a Mississippi River steamboat, who gained most of his money by marrying a Spanish woman and making her a silent partner.

One enterprising man who was anxious to make money easily took a notion to try his luck in trade, so, as rats and mice were troublesome in shops and stores, he went down to the valley and brought up a cargo of cats, which he disposed of at prices varying from fifty to one hundred dollars each, according to the buyer's fancy.

During the summer Kelley the fiddler came up in the mines to make a raise, and Craycroft made him a pulpit about ten feet above the floor in his saloon, having him to play nights and Sundays at twenty dollars per day. He was a big, uneducated Irishman who could neither read nor write, but he played and sang and talked the rich Irish brogue, all of which brought many customers to the bar. In the saloon could be seen all sorts of people dealing different games, and some were said to be preachers. Kelley stayed here as long as he could live on his salary, and left town much in debt, for whiskey and cards got all his money.

One of the grocers kept out a sign, "CHEAP JOHN, THE PACKER," and kept a mule to deliver goods, which no other merchant did, and in this way gained many friends, and many now may praise the enterprise of Cheap John, the Packer. Prices were pretty high in those days. Sharpening picks cost fifty cents; a drink of whiskey one dollar; and all kinds of pork, fifty cents per pound. You could get meals at the McNutty house for one dollar. The faro and monte banks absorbed so much of the small change that on one occasion I had to pay five dollars for a two-dollar pair of pants in order to get a fifty-dollar slug changed.

No white shirts were worn by honest men, and if any man appeared in such a garment, he was at once set down as a gambler, and with very little chance of a mistake. One Langdon had the only express office, and brought letters and packages from Sacramento. I paid one dollar simply to get my name on his letter list, and when a letter came I had to pay one dollar for bringing it up, as there was no post office at Downieville.

Newspapers were eagerly sought for, such was the hunger for reading. The western folks bought the St. Louis papers, while eastern people found the *New York Tribune* a favorite. One dollar each for such papers was the regular price. It may seem strange, but aside from the news we got from an occasional newspaper, I did not hear a word from the East during the two years I remained on Yuba River.

Our evenings were spent in playing cards for amusement, for no reading could be got. The snow between Marysville and Downieville was deep and impassable in winter, but we could work our drifting claims very comfortably, having laid in a stock of provisions early in the season, before snowfall. The nights seemed tediously long and lonesome, for when the snow was deep no one came to visit us, and we could go nowhere, being completely hemmed in. All the miners who did not have claims they could work underground went down below the winter snow line to find work, and when the snow went off, came back again and took possession of the old claims they had left.

After the snow went off, three German sailors came up and took a river claim a short distance above us on a north fork of the north fork of the stream, where one side of the cañon was perpendicular and the other sloped back only slightly. Here they put logs across the river, laid stringers on these, and covered the bottom with fir boughs. Then they put stakes at the sides and rigged a canvas flume over their bridge through which they turned the whole current of the river, leaving a nearly dry bed beneath. This we called pretty good engineering and management on the part of the sailor boys, for no lumber was to be had, and they had made themselves masters of the situation with the material on hand.

They went to work under their log aqueduct, and found the claim very rich in coarse gold. They went to town every Saturday night with good, big bags of dust, and as they were openhearted fellows, believing that a sailor always has the best of luck, they played cards freely, always betting on the Jack and Queen, and spent their money more easily than they earned it. They were quite partial to the ladies and, patronizing the bar and card tables as liberally as they did, usually returned to camp on Monday or Tuesday with a mule-load of grub and whiskey as all the visible proceeds of a week's successful mining; but when Saturday night came around again, we were pretty sure to see the jolly sailors going past with heavy bags of gold. They left one nearly pure piece of gold at Langdon's Express office that weighed five pounds, and another as large as a man's hand, of the shape of a prickly-pear leaf.

They worked their claim with good success until the snow water came down and forced them out. I went one day to see them, and they took a pan of dirt from behind a big rock and washed it out, getting as much as two teacupfuls of nuggets, worth perhaps a thousand dollars. When they went away, they said they would go to Germany to see their poor relatives and friends, and one of them really went home, but the other two had spent all their money before they were ready to leave San Francisco. These men were, without doubt, the inventors of the canvas flume, which was afterward used so successfully in various places.

While I was still here, the now famous Downieville Butte quartz mine was discovered, but there was no way then of working quartz successfully, and just at that time very little was done with it, but afterward, when it was learned how to work it and the proper machinery introduced, it yielded large sums of bullion.

The miners had a queer way of calling every man by some nickname or other instead of his true name, and no one seemed offended at it, but answered to his new name as readily as to any.

It was nearly fall when we found we had worked our claims out, and there were no new ones we could locate here, so we concluded to go prospecting for a new locality. I bought a donkey in town of a Mr. Hawley, a merchant, for which I paid sixty dollars, and gave the little fellow his old master's name. We now had two animals, and we packed on them our worldly goods and started south up the mountain trail by way of the "city of six," where some half-dozen men had claims, but the ground was dry and deep, so we went on.

We still went south, down toward the middle Yuba River and, when about halfway down the mountainside, came to a sort of level bench, where some miners were at work but hardly any water could be had. They called this Minnesota.[13] We stayed here a day or two, but as there seemed to be no possible further development of water, concluded to go on further. Across the river we could see a little flat, very similar to the one we were on, and a little prospecting seemed to have been done on the side of the mountain. We had a terribly steep cañon to cross, and a river also, with no trail to follow, but our donkeys were as good climbers as any of us, so we started down the mountain in the morning and arrived at the river about noon. Here we rested an hour or two and then began climbing the brushy mountainside. The hill was very steep, and the sun beat down on us with all his heat, so that, with our hard labor and the absence of any wind, we found it a pretty hot place.

It was pretty risky traveling in some places, and we had to help the donkeys to keep them from rolling down the hill, pack and all. It took us four hours to make a mile and a half or two miles in that dense brush, and we were nearly choked when we reached the little flat. Here we found some water, but no one lived here. From here we could see a large flat across a deep cañon to the west, and made up our minds to try to go to it. We went around the head of the cañon and worked through the brush and fallen timber, reaching our objective point just as night was coming on. This flat, like the one we had left, was quite level and contained, perhaps nearly one hundred acres. Here we found two men at work with a Long Tom—Mr. Fernay and Mr. Bloat.[14] They had brought the water of a small spring to their claim and were making five or six dollars per day. We now prospected around the edge of this flat and, getting pretty fair prospects, concluded we would locate here if we could get water.

We then began our search for water and found a spring about three-quarters of a mile away, to which we laid claim and, with a triangle level, began to survey out a route for our ditch. The survey was satisfactory, and we found we could bring the water out high on the flat, so we set to work digging at it, and turned the water in. The ground was so very dry that all the water soaked up within two hundred yards of the spring.

By this time we were out of grub, and someone must go for a new supply, and as we knew the trail to Downieville was terribly rough, I was chosen as the one to try to find Nevada City, which we thought would be nearer and more easily reached.[15] So I started south with the donkeys, up the mountain toward the ridge which lies between the middle and south Yuba Rivers, and when I got well on the ridge I found a trail used some by wagons, which I followed till I came to a place where the ridge was only wide enough for a wagon and, at the west end, a faint trail turned off south into the rolling hills. I thought this went about the course I wanted to go, so I followed it, and after two or three miles came to the south Yuba River. This seemed to be an Indian trail, no other signs on it. I climbed the mountain here, and when I reached the top I found a large tent made of blue drilling, and here I found I was four or five miles from Nevada City with a good trail to follow. The rolling hills I then passed through are now called North Bloomfield and at one time were known as Humbug.[16]

I started along the trail and soon reached the city, where I drove my donkeys up to a store, which had out the sign "Davis & Co." I entered and, inquiring the prices of various sorts of provisions such as flour, bacon, beans, butter, etc., soon had selected enough for two donkey-loads. They assisted me in putting them in packs, and when it was ready I asked the amount of my bill, which was one hundred and fifty dollars. This I paid at once, and they gave me some crackers and dried beef for lunch on the way. Davis said, "That is the quickest sale I ever made, and here the man is ready to go. I defy anyone to beat it." Before sundown I was two or three miles on my way back, when I found some grass and camped for the night, picketed the animals, ate some of Mr. Davis' grub for supper, and arranged a bed of saddle blankets. I arrived at camp the next day about sundown.

Next day I went on up the divide and found a house on the trail leading farther east, where two men lived, but they seemed to be doing nothing.

There were no mines and miners near there, and there seemed to be very little travel on the trail. The fellows looked rough, and I suspected they might
be bad characters. The stream they lived near was afterward called Bloody
Run, and there were stories current that blood had been shed there.[17]

Here was a section of comparatively level land for the mountain divide,
and a fine spring of good, cold water, all surrounded by several hundred acres
of the most magnificent sugar pines California ever raised, very large, straight
as a candle, and one hundred feet or more to the lowest limbs.[18] This place
was afterward called Snow Tent,[19] and S. W. Churchill built a sawmill at the
spring and had all this fine timber at the mercy of his ax and saw, without
anyone to dispute his right. He furnished lumber to the miners at fifty dollars or more per thousand feet.

Bloody Run no doubt well deserves its name, for there was much talk
of killing done there. I, however, went up and talked to the men and told
them I wished to hire a crosscut saw for a few days to get out stuff for a cabin,
and agreed to pay two dollars a day for the use of it till it came back.

We cut down a large sugar pine, cut off four six-foot cuts, one twelve-
foot cut, and one sixteen-foot cut, and from these we split out a lot of boards
which we used to make a V-shaped flume,[20] which we placed in our ditch,
and thus got the water through. We split the longer cuts into two-inch planks
for sluice boxes, and made a small reservoir, so that we succeeded in working
the ground. We paid wages to the two men who worked, and two other men
who were with us went and built a cabin.

I now went and got another load of provisions and, as the snow could
be seen on the high mountains to the east, I thought the deer must be
crowded down to our country, so I went out hunting and killed a big, fat
buck, and the next day three more, so fresh meat was plenty.

About this time a man came down the mountain with his oxen and
wagon, wife, and three or four children, the eldest a young lady of fifteen
years. The man's name was H. M. Moore. We had posted notices, according
to custom, to make mining laws, and had quite a discussion about a name for
the place. Some of the fellows wanted to name it after the young lady,
"Minda's Flat," but we finally chose "Moore's Flat" instead, which I believe is
the name it still goes by.[21] Our laws were soon completed, and a recorder chosen to record claims. We gave Mr. Moore the honor of having a prospecting
town named after him because he was the first man to be on hand with a wife.

I became satisfied, after a little, that this place would be a very snowy place,
and that from all appearances it would fall from two to four feet deep, and not
a very pleasant place to winter in. An honest acquaintance of mine came along,

Samuel Tyler, and to him I let my claim to work on shares and made McCloud my agent, verbally, while I took my blankets and started for the valley.

The first town I passed through was a newly discovered mining town called French Corral.[22] Here I found an old Wisconsin friend, William Sublet, the foster father of the accomplished wife of Mayor S. W. Boring of San Jose. From here I went to Marysville. The storm had been raging high in the mountains for some days, and the Yuba River rising fast, overflowing its banks as I walked into town, and the next day the merchants were very busy piling their goods above high-water mark. I went to a hotel and called for a bed. "Yes," says the landlord. "Is your name John or Peter?" I told him William, which he set down in his book, and we went upstairs to the best room, which was fitted up with berths three tiers high on each side and only one or two empty ones. He looked around for covers, but none could be found unoccupied, but one fellow was sound asleep and snoring awfully, so he took the blanket off from him, saying, "He won't know a thing about it till morning, be jabers, so don't say a word."

Next morning the river was booming, its surface covered with all sorts of mining outfit such as flume timber, rockers, various qualities of lumber, pieces of trees as well as whole ones, waterwheels, and other traps. The river between Downieville and here must have been swept clean of all material that would float, including Long Toms. The water continued to rise till it covered the plaza, and in two days a steamer came up and sailed across the public square. This looked like a wet season to me, and when the boat was ready to go down the river I went on board, bound for Sacramento. Here it was also getting terribly wet and muddy, and the rain kept pouring down. In the morning I worked my way up J Street and saw a six-mule team wading up the streets, the driver on foot, tramping through the sloppy mud, occasionally stepping in a hole and falling his whole length in the mud. On the street where so much trouble was met by the teamsters, a lot of idlers stood on the sidewalk, and when a driver would fall and go nearly out of sight, they would, like a set of loafers, laugh at him and blackguard him with much noise, and as they were numerous, they feared nothing.

Suddenly a miner who had lately arrived from the mountains raised his room window in the second story of a house, put out one leg and then his body as far as he could and, having nothing on but his nightclothes, shouted to the noisy crowd below, "Say, can't you d—d farmers plow now?" At this he dodged back quickly into his window, as if he expected something might be thrown at him. The rain continued, and the water rose gradually till it began to run slowly through the streets, and all the business stopped except gambling and drinking whisky, which were freely carried on in the saloons day and night.

While here in Sacramento I was sufficiently prompted by curiosity to go around to the place on J Street where the legislature was in session. I stood some time outside the enclosure listening to the members, who were in earnest debate over a question concerning the size of mining claims. They wanted them uniform in size all over the state, but there was some opposition, and the debate on this occasion was between the members from the mining counties on one side and the "cow" counties on the other. The miners took the ground that the claims were of different richness in the different mining localities, and that the miners themselves were the best judges of the proper size of claims, and were abundantly able to make their own laws, as they had done under the present mining customs, and their laws had always been respected, making any further legislative action unnecessary.

While this wrangle was going on, Captain Hunt, of San Bernardino (our guide from Salt Lake in 1849), came along and stopped where I stood, shaking me heartily by the hand, inquiring where I was from, and when I told him I was from the mines, he said he thought the cow county fellows were trying to make the miners some trouble. I told him the present mining regulations suited us very well and, after he had talked with me a little, he went inside and whispered to some of the silent members that the miners wanted no change, for he had just consulted a miner to that effect. When occasion offered he called for a vote, which resulted in the defeat of the cow counties and a postponement of the measure indefinitely.[23]

My next move was to try to find a dryer place, so I took a boat for Benicia, then for Stockton, where I found a sea of mud, so that a man needed stilts or a boat to cross the street.

Here in a livery stable I found my old Platte River boss, Charles Dallas, for whom I drove in 1849, but he did not seem to know me and took no notice of me, but talked "horse" and horse-racing to the bystanders very loudly. I suppose that Dallas had made money and did not care for a poor ox driver, and on my part I did not care very much for his friendship, so I walked away and left him without a word.

Every way I looked was a sea of black, sticky mud; dogs mired in the streets and died, and teams and animals had forsaken the usual route of travel. The gambling houses and saloons were crowded, gum boots in demand, and the only way to get out of town was by water. I took this way out, and on the same boat by which I came, going to San Francisco. This was high and dry enough to be above the highest floods of Yuba, Sacramento, or San

Joaquin, but all business except the saloons was dull. Fronting on Portsmouth Square was the Hall of Corruption. Inside was a magnificently furnished bar, more than one keeper, and various gambling tables, most of them with soiled doves in attendance.[24] The room was thronged with players and spectators, and coin and dust were plenty. The dealers drew off their cards carefully, and seemed to have the largest pile of coin on their side.

I climbed Russian Hill to take a look over the city. It seemed poorly built, but the portion that had been burned in July 1852 had been built up again. The business part was near the beach and north of Market Street.

I had never lived in a town and did not know its ways, so I strolled around alone, for without acquaintances I did not know where to go nor what to look for. I therefore thought I would see some other part of the country. I found that a schooner was about to sail for San Pedro, near Los Angeles. I took hold of a rope to help myself on board, when it gave way and I found myself floundering in the water. They helped me out and the captain gave me a dry suit to put on. I was profoundly grateful for the favor, and found him a generous man.

We sailed away and stopped at Monterey for twenty-four hours, which gave me a good chance for a good look at the capital's houses, which were of adobe, and to find that this city was also liberally supplied with gambling, card and billiard tables. The majority of the people were Spanish and fond of gaming, and the general appearance of the place was old and without good improvements, though there were more two-story houses than in most places in California.

Some houses were of stone, but more of adobe, and there seemed to be no fertile country round, and the hills about had small pines[25] on them.

Some of the sailors went out and gathered a large bag of mussels and clams, from which they made a liberal allowance of chowder for the table. After seven or eight days we arrived in San Pedro and found the town to consist of one long adobe house. The beach was low and sandy, and we were wet somewhat in wading through a light surf to get on shore. We had on board a Mr. Baylis, who we afterward learned came down with Captain Lackey on a big speculation, which was to capture all the wild goats they could on Catalina Island and take them to San Francisco for slaughtering.

The goats were easily captured and taken on board the schooner, and thence to shore, but many were drowned in the transit, and when driven to San Francisco, the dead were scattered all along the route. Although wild they seemed to lack the vitality that tame goats possess. The speculation proved a disappointment to the projectors.[26]

At the adobe house, kept by a Spaniard, we had breakfast, then shouldered our packs for the march of ten leagues[27] to Los Angeles, for there was no chance to ride. It was night before we reached the City of Angels, and here I stayed a day to take a look at the first city I saw in California in March 1850.

I inquired for my mining companion, W. M. Stockton, who worked with Bennett and myself near Georgetown in 1850, and found he lived near the old mission of San Gabriel, nine miles away, whither I walked and found him and family well and glad to see me. He had jumped an old pear orchard which was not claimed by the mission fathers, although it was only three-fourths of a mile away. The trees were all seedlings and very large, probably fifty or more years old. Some of the mission buildings were falling down since they had been abandoned, and the Americans would go to these houses and remove the tile flooring from the porches and from the pillars that supported them. These tiles were of hard, burned clay, in pieces about a foot square, and were very convenient to make fireplaces and pavements before the doors of their new houses. Outside the enclosed orange and fig orchard at this place were some large olive and fig trees, apparently as old as the mission, being a foot or more in diameter and about fifty feet high. I had never seen olives, and when I saw these trees covered with plenty of fruit about the size of damson plums, I took the liberty of tasting it, and found it very disagreeable, and wondered of what use such fruit could be.

Mr. Stockton fenced his orchard by setting posts and tying sycamore poles to them to keep the stock away, built an adobe house on the claim, and called the property his. I went to work for him at once, pruning the trees, which improved their appearance, and then turned on a little stream of water which ran through the place and on down to the mission. With this treatment the trees did well without cultivation.

I bought one-half the stock, consisting of some Spanish cows, one yoke of oxen, and some horses, worked enough to pay my board, watched the stock, and still had plenty of time to ride around over the adjoining country.

When the pears were ripe, the Spanish men, women, and children eagerly bought them at twenty-five cents per dozen, and some Sundays the receipts for fruit sold would be as high as a hundred dollars. That, taken to town, would bring from five to eight dollars per box, the boxes being a little larger than those in present use. An Indian woman, widow of a Mr. Reed, claimed a vineyard near the orchard, and laid claim to the whole property, so Stockton gave her one thousand dollars for a quit-claim deed.

Nearby was a small artificial lake made by a dam of cobblestones, laid in cement across a ravine, which was built perhaps fifty years before, and yet the tracks of a child who had walked across before the cement was dry were plainly seen.

Stockton and I visited Mr. Roland, an old settler who lived south of San Gabriel River, and stayed all night with him, finding him very sociable and hospitable. All his work was done by Indians who lived nearby and had been there as long as he. He had a small vineyard and raised corn, squashes, melons, and all that is necessary for his table, having also a small mill nearby for grinding corn and wheat without bolting. The Indians made his wine by tramping the grapes with their feet in a rawhide vat hung between four poles set in the ground. The workmen were paid off every Saturday night, and during Sunday he would generally sell them wine enough to get about all the money back again. This had been his practice for many years, and no doubt suited Mr. Roland as well as the redmen.

Roland was an old Rocky Mountain trapper who came to California long before gold was discovered, and during the evening the talk naturally ran to the subject of early days.

Mr. Roland related that while his party were in camp in the upper Colorado, they were visited by a small band of Indians who professed friendship and seated themselves around the fire. Suddenly they made an attack and each trapper had an Indian to contend with, except Mr. Roland, who was left to be dispatched afterwards. But as he ran, a squaw among them followed him, and after a while overtook him and showed friendship. He had neither gun or knife and so concluded to put faith in the woman, who safely guided him in a long tramp across the desert, where they both came near starving but finally reached Los Angeles Valley, when the brave squaw mingled with her own people and he lost sight of her forever.

No white man could alone have traversed that desert waste and found food enough to last him half the journey.

He gradually learned to speak Spanish and was granted the piece of land he applied for and where he then lived; married a Spanish girl, with whom he had a happy home and raised a large family and grew rich, for they were both industrious and economical. The first wife died, and he was persuaded to marry a Texas widow, and now had to buy the first carriage he ever owned, and furnish a fine turnout and driver for the lady, who wore much jewelry and fine clothes, and spent money freely. Roland was not a society man, his thoughts and habits were different from his wife's, and he stayed at home, better contented there.

There were many other pioneers in the neighborhood: Dan Sexton, Colonel Williams of Chino Ranch, Workman, B. D. Wilson, Abel Stearns,

Temple, Wolfskill, and many others; Scott and Granger were lawyers. Granger was the same man who read the preamble and resolutions that were to govern our big train as we were about to start from Utah Lake.

Scott was quite a noted member of the bar, and when General Winfield Scott ran for president, some wideawake politicians caused the uneducated Spaniards to vote for their favorite lawyer instead of the redoubtable general, and they did this with a good will, for they thought the famous *abogado* was the best man, and thus the manipulators lost many votes for the real candidate.[28] Scott was afterward retained by many of the Spaniards to present their claims for their land to the U.S. government and was considered a very able man.

Mr. Stockton related that when he left his family here to go to the mines, he rented one-half a house of Michael Blanco, who had a Spanish wife and children, and these and his own were of course constant playmates. When he returned in the fall he found his children had learned to speak Spanish and nearly forgotten English, so that he had to coax them a great deal to get them to talk to him at all, and he could not understand a word they said.

I now tried to learn the language myself. I had money to loan, and the borrowers were Spanish who gave good security and paid from 5 to 25 percent interest per month, on short time. Mrs. Stockton assisted me very much as an interpreter.

I bought young steers for eight dollars each and gradually added to my herd. I got along well until next spring, when the beef-eating population began to steal my fat cattle, and seemed determined I should get no richer. The country was overstocked with desperate and lawless renegades in Los Angeles, and from one to four dead men was about the number picked up in the streets each morning. They were of low class, and there was no investigation, simply a burial at public expense.

The permanent Spanish population seemed honest and benevolent, but there were many bad ones from Chile, Sonora, Mexico, Texas, Utah, and Europe, who seemed always on an errand of mischief, a murder, thieving, or robbery.

Three or four suspicious looking men came on horseback and made their camp near the mission under an oak tree, where they stayed some time. They always left someone in camp while the others went away every day on their horses, and acted so strangely that the report soon became current that they were stealing horses and running them off to some safe place in the mountains till a quantity could be accumulated to take to the mines to sell. On this information the Vigilance Committee arrested the man in camp and brought him to a private room, where he was tried by twelve men, who found him guilty of horse stealing and sentenced [him] to be hung at once, for horse stealing was a capital offense in those days.

To carry out the sentence they procured a cart, put a box on it for a seat, and with a rope around his neck and seated on the box, the condemned man was dragged off by hand to an oak tree not far away, whither he was followed by all the men, women, and children of the place, who where nearly all natives. While preparations were being made under the tree, someone called out that men were riding rapidly from the direction of Los Angeles and, from the dust they raised, seemed to be more than usually in haste. So it was proposed to wait till they came up. It was soon known that an Indian had been sent to Los Angeles to give news to the man's friends there, and they had come with all the speed of their horses to try to save his life. They talked and inquired around a little and then proposed the question whether to hang him or to turn him over to the lawful authorities for regular trial. This was put to a vote and it was decided to spare him now. So the rope was taken off his neck, and he was turned over to Mr. Mallard, the mission justice of the peace, much to the relief of the fellow who saw death staring him in the face.

The Santa Anita Ranch, now owned by E. J. Baldwin, was owned by Henry Dalton, an Englishman, who came with a stock of goods worth $75,000 years before, but now had only the ranch left. The Azuza, a short distance south, was occupied by his brother.[29]

I became well acquainted with many of these old California natives, and found them honest in their dealings, good to the needy, and in all my travels I never found more willing hands to bestow upon relatives, friends, or strangers ready relief than I saw among these simple natives. Their kindness to our party, when we came starving from the desert in 1850, can never be praised enough, and as long as I shall live, my best wishes shall go with them.

I was one day riding with Vincent Duarte down toward Anaheim, when he suddenly dismounted to kill a large tarantula by pelting him with stones. It was the first one I had seen and seemed an overgrown spider. I asked him if the thing was harmful, and he replied with considerable warmth, *"Mucho malo por Cristianos,"* and I wondered if the insect knew saints from sinners.

This spring we concluded to go to the Mormon settlement at San Bernardino and secure some American bulls to improve our stock, and starting late one day, I rode as far as the Azuza Rancho, where I stayed all night with Mr. Dalton, reaching the holy city, a branch of Brigham Young's harem, next day. Here I found a town of log houses in a circle, enclosing a plaza. There was a passage between the houses. I stopped at the principal hotel, kept by a vigorous and enthusiastic Mormon woman, who delighted to preach the doctrine.

Walking around on the outside of the fortifications I came across Captain Hunt, the man who was hired in the fall of 1849 to bring the big train from Salt Lake to San Bernardino. I told him who I was, and what I wanted, and he seemed to know me, inviting me in the most friendly and social manner to take supper with him, which I did. He sat at the head of the table and introduced me to his three wives. The furnishing of the house was cheap and common, but the table was fairly provided for. He said he would help me to find the animals I wanted, and in the morning showed me two which he had that were young and suitable, and a larger one which he said I could have if I could drive him.

I soon found out that I had better move or sell my cattle, for with all the watching I could do, they gradually disappeared, and hungry thieves who could live on beef alone visited my little band of cattle too often and took what they wanted, and I could not detect them. I soon sold to four buyers from the north, L. D. Stephens, David Grant, Sam Craig, and Mr. Wilson, and hired out with my two horses to help them drive the band north, at a salary of a hundred dollars per month.

Disposing most of my money with Palmer, Cook & Co., I went to see my mine at Moore's Flat. There were two boats leaving at about the same time, one for Stockton and one for Sacramento, the latter of which I took, and Rogers the other. Both landed at Benicia, and when we swung away from that wharf, Rogers and I saluted each other with raised and swinging hats, shouted a good-bye, and I have never seen him since.

At Moore's Flat I found my mine well and profitably worked by Mr. Tyler and, as his lease was not out, I returned to San Jose, as I had learned from Rogers that Mr. A. Bennett was at Watsonville and Mr. Arcane at Santa Cruz, and I desired to visit them. I rode back across the country and found Mr. Bennett and family at the point where the Salinas River enters Monterey Bay. They were all well and were glad to see me, for they did not know I was in California. Mrs. Bennett was greatly affected at our meeting and shed tears of joy as she shook hands.

Bennett had a nice Whitehall boat and we had a genuine happy time hunting, fishing, and gathering clams, and also in social visits among the neighbors and old acquaintants, among them one Jacob Rhodehouse of Wisconsin.

While here I rode my horse around to Monterey and to Carmel Mission, where I stayed two or three days with Mr. Gourley, a brother of Mrs.

William M. Stockton, who was here engaged in raising potatoes. I walked along the beach near some rocky islands near the shore, and on these rocks were more sea lions and seals than I supposed the whole ocean contained—the most wonderful show of sea life on the California coast. Returning, I stayed all night at the crossing of the Salinas with a colored family who gave me good accommodations for self and horse. I heard afterward that this family was attacked by robbers and all but one murdered.

Mrs. Bennett's father, D. J. Dilley, lived near here also, and I had not seen him since the time in Wisconsin when he hauled my canoe over to the river, in 1849. One day while fishing on the beach we found the body of a man, which we carried above the tide and buried in the sand.

I gave one of my horses to George Bennett, and went over to Santa Cruz, where I found Mr. and Mrs. J. B. Arcane and son Charles in a comfortable home, well situated, and overjoyed to see me.

He [Mr. Arcane] knew everyone in town, and as we went about he never failed to introduce me to everyone we met as the man who helped himself and family out of Death Valley and saved their lives. Arcane was a very polite Frenchman and knew how to manage such things very gracefully, but with all his grace and heartiness, it made me feel quite a little embarrassed to be made so much of publicly and among strangers. He took me in his buggy, and we drove along the beach, and to the limekiln of Cowel & Jordan, also to the courthouse when court was in session.

Upon the hill I met Judge Watson, the father of Watsonville, and a Mr. Graham, an old settler and landowner, and on this occasion he pulled a sheet of ancient, smoky-looking paper from beneath his arm, pointed to a dozen or so of written lines in Spanish and then, with a flourish of the precious document in Watson's face, dared him to beat that, or get off his land. I must say that never in my life was I better entertained than here.

From Santa Cruz I crossed the mountain on a lonely and romantic trail to San Jose again, finding very few houses on the road. Here I went to work for R. G. Moody, building a gristmill on the banks of the Coyote Creek, to be run by water from artesian wells. When the mill was done I went for my horse, and on my return I ran very unexpectedly upon Davenport Helms, to whom I had sold my little black mule in 1850. Our talk was short, but he told me he had killed a man in Georgetown and the sheriff was looking for him. He was now venturing to town for tobacco and would hurry back to the hills again, where he was herding cattle.

He said he kept them off at one time by getting in a piece of chaparral and presenting his gun to them when they came near; they dared not advance on him. Then he laughed and said, "And all the time my gun was empty, for I did not have a d—d thing to put into it. I tell you, they don't catch old Davenport. Now don't you tell on me. Good-bye." I saw him no more after that. The town of San Jose was now more of a town than it was a few years before. The "forty thieves" and others commenced building a city hall of brick on the top of old adobe walls, and this was the principal improvement, except the Moody mill near the Sutter house, one street north of Julian.

After finishing work on the mill, I drew my money from the bank in San Francisco and started for the mines on horseback. Near French Camp,[30] on the east side of the San Joaquin Valley, many cattle were feeding on the plains, and among them, much to my surprise, I found Old Crump, the ox that brought Bennett's and Arcane's children safe through from Death Valley in February 1850. He was now fat and sleek and as kind and gentle as when so poor upon the terrible journey. I got off my horse, and went up to him, and patted my old friend. I was glad to find him so contented and happy, and I doubt not that he too was glad. I met a man nearby and asked him about the ox, and he said that the owner would not sell him nor allow him to be worked, for he knew of the faithful part he performed in the world and respected him for it.

At Sacramento I deposited my money with Page, Bacon & Co., a branch of the St. Louis firm of the same name, considered the safest bank in the United States. Their bills were taken in payment of government land. Some rascals had some counterfeit bills on their bank and traded them off for gold with the Missourians who were going home, and the poor fellows found themselves poor on arrival.

Going to my mine, where I left only a cabin or two, I found quite a village with two hotels and a post office.

News soon came that the banks had closed their door, and Page and Bacon also, so I concluded that I was broke.[31] The "Pikers" said Page and Bacon could not, nor would not fail, but news was against them. The boys now tried to persuade me to go to Sacramento and try to get my money and, if I succeeded, to bring up a good stock of goods, and they would buy of me in preference to anyone else. On this showing I went down, and finding my old friend Lyman Ross (well known in San Jose), who was keeping a fruit store, I told him my business and he took me to L. A. Booth, Carrol & Co., and I stated to him the facts about my money in the bank and the doors closed. I told him if he would assist me, I would buy two thousand dollars' worth of his goods, and send them to Moore's Flat. I endorsed the certificate over to him, and in half an hour he came back with the coin. How he got it I never knew, but he did me a great favor, and we have been good friends ever since. I was no merchant, nor had I any mercantile education, so I took lessons from Mr. Booth and allowed him to make out for me a bill of goods such as he well knew I needed. With these we loaded up two six-mule teams, and started for the mountains.

I had about seven hundred dollars left besides paying for the goods, but I felt a very little troubled as to my prospect for success, for it was a new business to me. Mr. Booth, in a business way, was a true father to me, and the much needed points in trade which he gave me were stored away for the use I knew I would make of them. Of all those whom I bear in grateful remembrance, none stand higher than this worthy man.

I went first direct to Nevada City to take out a license that I might best protect myself against oppositions, and from there I had a walk of eighteen miles over a rough mountain trail to my selected place of business. Climbing the great hill of the South Fork Yuba River, I often tired and sat down to rest, and I used this time to study my bill of goods and add the freight and profit to the cost, so as to be well posted and able to answer all questions readily when I unloaded the stock. The new trade seemed quite a task to learn, but I felt that I was compelled to succeed, and I worked manfully at it.

When I reached Moore's Flat I found that the boys had rented a store for me, and their welcome was very hearty when they found how lucky I had been in securing my money and starting out as their "grub supplier."

Four of us now located some mining claims, and began a tunnel both to drain the ground and to work through the bedrock. This we named the Paradise, and we expected that three or four months would elapse before we made it pay, but there was in truth two years of solid rock work before we got under the ground, but it paid well in the end.

The largest nugget of gold ever found before this time was a quartz boulder from the Buckeye sluice, about eight by ten inches in size and, when cleaned up at the San Francisco mint, the value was about ten thousand dollars.

Two of my partners in the work, L. J. Hanchett and James Clark, ran out of funds at the end of the first year, and I took as much of the expense as I could upon my own shoulders.

About this time, learning by a letter from her father that Mrs. Bennett was lying at the point of death at Mr. L. C. Bostic's in San Jose, I left Hanchett in charge of my business, and in four days I stood beside the bedside of my friend, endeared through the trials when death by thirst, starvation, and the desert sands stared us in the face with all its ghastliness.

She reached out her arms and drew me down to her, and embraced me and said in a faint whisper, "God bless you—you saved us all till now, and I hope you will always be happy and live long." She would have said more, but her voice was so weak she could not be heard. She was very low with consumption, and easily exhausted. I sat with her much of the time at her request and though, for her sake, I would have kept back the tears, I could not always do it. Two doctors came, one of them Dr. Spencer, and as I sat with my face partly turned away, I overheard Dr. Spencer say to his assistant, "He is a manly man."

This presence and the circumstances brought back the trying Death Valley struggles, when this woman and her companions and the poor children, so nearly starved they could not stand alone, were only prevented from sitting down to die in sheer despair by the encouraging words of Rogers and myself, who had passed over the road, and used every way to sustain their courage.

She died the following day; with Mr. Bennett, I followed her remains to Oak Hill Cemetery, where she was buried near the foot of the hill, and a board marked in large letters, "S. B." (Sarah Bennett), placed to mark the mound. The grave cannot now be found, and no records being then kept, it is probably lost.

I went home with Mr. Bennett to his home near Watsonville, and spent several days meeting several of our old Death Valley party and Mr. D. J. Dilley, Mrs. Bennett's father. Mrs. Bennett left surviving her a young babe.

I returned to Moore's Flat and soon sold out my store,[32] taking up the business of purchasing gold dust direct from the miners, which I followed for about two years, and in the fall of 1859 sold out the business to Marks & Powers. I looked about through Napa and Sonoma Counties and finally came to San Jose, where I purchased the farm I now own, near Hillsdale, from Bodley & McCabe, for which I paid $4,000.

In the fall of the same year my old friend W. M. Stockton of Los Angeles County persuaded me to come down and pay him a visit. His wife had died and he felt very lonely. I had been there but a few days when my old friend A. Bennett and his children also came to Stockton's. The children had grown so much I hardly knew them, but I was glad indeed to meet them.

I found Mr. Bennett to be a poor man. He had been persuaded to go to Utah, being told that a fortune awaited his coming there, or could be accumulated in a short time. He gave away the little babe left by his wife to Mrs. Scott, of Scott's Valley, in Santa Cruz County, and sold his farm near the mouth of the Salinas River. With what money he had accumulated, he loaded two four-mule teams with dry goods, put his four children into his wagon, and went to Cedar City, Utah.

He gave a thrilling account of passing through Mountain Meadows, where he saw, here and there, little groups of skeletons of the unhappy victims of the great massacre at that place of men, women, and children by J. D. Lee and his Mormon followers, and told me the terrible story, which I here omit.

Smarting under the terrible taxation of one-tenth of everything, Bennett grew poorer and poorer and at last resolved that he must go away, but his wife could not leave her own people,[33] and so he set off with his children, somewhat afraid he might be shot down, but he reached Los Angeles County in safety. One daughter married a lawyer in San Bernardino and died a few years afterwards. The other married a Captain Johnson of Wilmington, and Bennett and two sons went to Idaho.

A few years ago, in passing from San Jose to the coast, my wife[34] and I spent Sunday at Scott's Valley. Mrs. Scott invited us to visit them in the evening at the house, when all would be at home. Mrs. Scott was the lady to whom Bennett gave his girl baby when he started away for Utah, and I felt very anxious to see her now she was grown up. Mrs. Scott introduced us, and I sat and looked at the little woman quite a long time, but could not see that she resembled either father or mother. My mind ran back over the terrible road we came, and I pictured to myself the woman as she then appeared.

I studied over our early trials, crossing the plains, over the deserts, and our trying scenes out of Death Valley, and turned all over in my mind for some time, and finally all came to me like a flash and I could clearly see that the little lady was a true picture of her mother. I now began to ask questions about her folks. She said her father lived near Belmont, Nevada, and her grandfather died at Monte, Los Angeles County, California. Our visit now became very interesting and we kept a late hour.

CHAPTER XVII

The Pioneers,
Their Character and Influence

SINCE WRITING THE CONNECTED STORY WHICH has thus far appeared, I turn back to give some incidents of life in the mines and some description of those pioneer gold days.

I have spoken of Moore's Flat, Orleans Flat, and Woolsey's Flat, all similarly situated on different points of the mountain, on the north side of the ridge between the South and Middle Yuba River, and all at about the same altitude.[1] A very deep cañon lies between each of them, but a good mountain road was built around the head of each cañon, connecting the towns. When the snow got to be three or four feet deep, the roads must be broken out and communication opened, and the boys used to turn out en masse and each one would take his turn in leading the army of road breakers. When the leader got tired out, someone would take his place, for it was terrible hard work to wade through snow up to one's hips, and the progress [was] very slow. But the boys went at it as if they were going to a picnic, and a sort of picnic it was when they reached the next town, for whisky was free and grub plenty to such a party, and jollity and fun the uppermost thoughts. On one such occasion, when the crowd came through Orleans Flat to Moore's Flat, Sid Hunt, the butcher, was in the lead as they came in sight of the latter place, and both he and his followers talked pretty loud and rough to the Moore's Flat fellows, calling them "lazy pups" for not getting their road clear. Hunt's helper was a big, stout, loud-talking young man named Williams, and he shouted to the leader, "Sid Hunt, toot your horn if you don't sell a clam." This seemed to put both sides in good humor, and the Orleans fellows joined in [and had] plenty to eat and drink, [then] rested and went home. Next day, both camps joined forces and broke the road over to Woolsey's Flat, and the third day, crowded on toward Nevada City, and when out and across Bloody Run—a stream called thus because some dead men had been found at the head of the stream by the early settlers and it was suspected the guilty murderers lived not far off—they turned down into Humbug, a town now called Bloomfield, and as they went down, the snow was not so deep. They soon met Sam Henry, the express man, working through with letters and papers, and all turned home again.

A young doctor came to Moore's Flat and soon became quite popular and, after a little while, purchased a small drugstore at Orleans Flat. In this town there lived a man and his family and, among them, a little curly-headed girl, perhaps one or two years old. She was sick and died and was buried while the ground was covered thick with snow. A little time after, it was discovered that the grave had been disturbed, and on examination no body was found in the grave.

Then it was [that] a searching party was organized and threats of vengeance made against the grave robber if he should be caught. No tracks were found leading out of town, so they began to look about inside, and there began to be some talk about this Dr. Kittridge as the culprit. He was the very man, and he went to his drugstore and told his clerk to get a saddle horse, and take the dead child's body in a sack to his cabin at Moore's Flat, and conceal it in a back room. The clerk obeyed and, with the little corpse before him on the horse, started from the back door, and rode furiously to Moore's Flat, and concealed the body as he had been directed.

Some noticed that he had ridden unusually fast and, having a suspicion that all was not right, told their belief to the Orleans Flat people, who visited the doctor at his store and accused him of the crime, and talked about hanging him on the spot without a trial. At this the doctor began to be greatly frightened and begged piteously for them to spare his life, confessing to the deed, but pleading in extenuation that it was for the purpose of confirming a question in his profession, and wholly in the interest of science that he did it, and really to spare the feelings of the parents that he did it secretly. He argued that no real harm had been done, and some of his friends sided with him in this view. But the controversy grew warmer, and the house filled up with people. Some were bloodthirsty and needed no urging to proceed to buy a rope and use it. Others argued, and finally the doctor said that the body had not been dissected, and if they would allow him and appoint a committee to go with him, he would produce the body, and they could decently bury it again, and there it might remain forever. This he promised to do, and all agreed to it, and he kept his word, thus ending the matter satisfactorily, and the doctor was released. But the feeling never died out. The doctor's friends deserted him, and no one seemed to like to converse with him. At the saloon he would sit like a perfect stranger, no one noticing him, and he soon left for new fields.

The first tunnel run at Moore's Flat was called the Paradise, and had to be started low on the side of the mountain in order to drain the ground, and had to be blasted through the bedrock for about two hundred feet.

Four of us secured ground enough by purchase so we could afford to undertake this expensive job, and we worked on it day and night. Jerry Clark and Len Redfield worked the day shifts and Sam King and William Quirk the night shifts. When the tunnel was completed about a hundred feet, the night shift had driven forward the top of the tunnel as a heading, leaving the bottom, which was about a foot thick or more, to be taken out by the day shift. They drilled a hole about two feet horizontally to blast out this bench. King would sit and hold the drill between his feet, while Quirk would strike with a heavy sledge. When the hole was loaded, they tamped down the charge very hard so as to be sure it would not blow out but lift the whole bench. One day when they were loading a hole, King told Quirk to come down pretty heavy on the tamping, so as to make all sure, and after a few blows given as directed, there was an explosion and Quirk was forced some distance out of the tunnel, his eyes nearly put out with dirt blown into them, and his face and body cut with flying pieces of rock. He was at first completely stunned, but after a while recovered so as to crawl out, and was slowly making his way up the hill on hands and knees when he was discovered and helped to his cabin, where his wounds were washed and dressed.

Then a party with lighted candles entered the tunnel to learn the fate of King, and they found him lying on the mass of rock the blast had lifted, dead. On a piece of board they bore the body to his cabin. There was hardly a whole bone remaining. A cut diagonally across his face, made by a sharp stone, had nearly cut his head in two. He had been thrown so violently against the roof of the tunnel, about six feet high, that he was completely mashed.

He had a wife in Massachusetts, and as I had often heard him talk of her, and of sending her money, I bought a one-hundred-dollar check and sent it in the same letter which bore the melancholy news. King had a claim at Chip's Flat[2] which he believed would be very rich in time, so I kept his interest up in it till it amounted to five hundred dollars and then abandoned the claim and pocketed the loss. We made a pine box, and putting his body in it, laid it away with respect. I had often heard him say that if he suffered an accident, he wished to be killed outright and not be left a cripple, and his wish came true.

After this accident the blacksmith, working for the Paradise Company, was making some repairs about the surface of the air shaft, and among his tools was a bar of steel an inch square and eight or ten feet long, which was thrown across the shaft, and while working at the whim wheel, he slipped and struck this bar, which fell to the bottom of the shaft, a hundred feet deep, and the blacksmith followed. When the other workmen went down to his assistance, they found that the bar of steel had stuck upright in the bottom of the shaft and, when the man came down, it pierced his body from hip to neck, killing him instantly. He was a young man, and I have forgotten his name.

Those who came to California these later years will not many of them see the old apparatus and appliances which were used in saving the gold in those primitive days. Among them was the old rocker. This had a bottom about five feet long and sixteen inches wide, with the sides about eight inches high for half the length, and then sloped off to two inches at the end. There was a bar about an inch high across the end to serve as a riffle, and on the higher end of this box was a stationary box fourteen inches square, with sides four inches high and having a sheet iron bottom perforated with half-inch holes. On the bottom of the box were fastened two rockers like those on the baby cradle, and the whole had a piece of board or other solid foundation to stand on, the whole being set at an angle to allow the gravel to work off at the lower end with the water. A cleat was fastened across the bottom to catch the gold, and this was frequently examined to see how the work was paying, and taking out such coarse pieces as could be readily seen. To work the rocker, a pan of dirt would be placed in the square screen box, and then with one hand the miner would rock the cradle while he poured water with the other from a dipper to wash the earth. After he had poured on enough water and shaken the box sufficiently to pass all the small stuff through, he would stir over what remained in the screen box, examining carefully for a nugget too large to pass through the half-inch holes. If the miner found that the dirt did not pay, he took his rocker on his back and went on in search of a better claim.

Another way to work the dirt was to get a small head of water running in a ditch, and then run the water and gravel through a series of boxes a foot square and twelve feet long, using from one to ten boxes as circumstances seemed to indicate. At the lower end of these boxes was placed the Long Tom, which was about two feet wide at the lower end, and having sides six inches high at the same point. The side pieces extend out about three feet longer than the wooden bottom, and are turned up to a point, some like a sled runner, and this turned-up part has a bottom of sheet iron punched full of holes, the size of the sheet iron being about three feet by sixteen inches.

The miners shovel dirt into the upper end of the boxes slowly, and regulate the water so that it dissolves the lumps and chunks very thoroughly before it reaches the Long Tom, where a man stands and stirs the gravel over and, if nothing yellow is seen, throws the washed gravel away, and lets the rest go through the screen. Immediately below this screen was placed what was called a riffle box, two by four feet in size with bars four inches high across the bottom and sides, and this box is set at the proper angle. Now, when the water comes through the screen, it falls perpendicularly in this box with force enough to keep the contents continually in motion and, as the gold is much heavier than any other mineral likely to be found in the dirt, it settles to the bottom, and all the lighter stuff is carried away by the water. The gold would be found behind the bars in the riffle box.

These methods of working were very crude, and we gradually became aware that the finest dust was not saved, and many improvements were brought into use. In my own mine the tailings that we let go down the mountainside would lodge in large piles in different places, and after lying a year, more gold could be washed out of it than was first obtained, and some of it coarser, so that it was plainly seen that a better way of working would be more profitable. There was plenty of ground called poor ground that had much gold in it but could not be profitably worked with the rocker and Long Tom. The bedrock was nearly level, and as the land had a gradual rise, the banks kept getting higher and higher as they dug farther in. Now, it was really good ground only down close to the bedrock, but all the dirt had some gold in it, and if a way could be invented to work it fast enough, such ground would pay. So the plan of hydraulic mining was experimented upon.

The water was brought in a ditch or flume to the top of a high bank, and then terminated in a tight box. To this box was attached a large hose made by hand out of canvas, and a pipe and nozzle attached to the lower end of the hose. Now, as the bank was often a hundred feet or more high, the water at this head, when directed through the nozzle against the bank, fairly melted it away into liquid mud. Imagine us located a mile above the river on the side of a mountain. We dug, at first, sluices in the rock to carry off the mud and water and, after it had flowed in these a little way, a sluice box was put in to pass it through. These were made on a slope of one in twelve, and the bottom paved with blocks three inches thick, so laid as to make a cavity or pocket at the corner of the blocks. After passing the first sluice box, the water and gravel would be run in a bedrock sluice again, and then into another sluice box and so on for a mile, passing through several sluice boxes on the way. Quicksilver³ was placed in the upper sluice boxes, and when the particles of gold were polished up by tumbling about in the gravel, they combined with the quicksilver, making an amalgam.

The most gold would be left in the first sluice boxes but some would go on down to the very last, where the water and dirt was run off into the river. They cleaned up the first sluices every week, a little farther down every month, while the lower ones would only be cleaned up at the end of the season.

In cleaning up, the blocks would be taken out of the boxes, and every little crevice or pocket in the whole length of the sluice cleaned out, from the bottom to the top, using little hooks and iron spoons made for the purpose.

The amalgam⁴ thus collected was heated in a retort which expelled the quicksilver in vapor, which was condensed and used again.

When they first tried hydraulic work, a tinsmith made a nozzle out of sheet iron, but when put in practice, instead of throwing a solid stream, it scattered like a shotgun, and up at Moore's Flat they called the claims where they used it the shotgun claims.

From that time great improvements were made in hydraulic apparatus until the work done by them was really wonderful.

In 1850 there lived at Orleans Flat and Moore's Flat, in Nevada County, a few young, energetic, and very stirring pioneers in the persons of lads from ten to fifteen years of age, always on the search for a few dimes to spend, or add to an already hoarded store, and the mountain air, with the wild surroundings, seemed to inspire them always with lively vigor, and especially when there was a prospect of a two-bit piece not far ahead.

In winter, when the deep snow cut off all communication with the valley, our busy tinner ran short of solder, and seeing a limited supply in the tin cans that lay thick about, he engaged the boys to gather in a supply and showed them how they could be melted down to secure the solder with which they had been fastened, and thus provide for his immediate wants. So the boys ransacked every spot where they had been thrown, under the saloon and houses, and in old dump holes everywhere, till they had gathered a pretty large pile, which they fired as he had told them, and then panned out the ashes to secure the drops of metal, which had melted down and cooled in small drops and bits below. This was remelted and cast into a mold, made in a pine block, and the solder made into regular form. About one-third was made up thus in good and honest shape.

But the boys soon developed a shrewdness that if more fully expanded might make them millionaires, but in the present small way they hoped to put to account in getting a few extra dimes. They put a big chunk of iron in the mold and poured in the melted solder, which enclosed it completely, so that when they presented the bright silvery bar to the old tinker, he paid the price agreed upon, and they divided the money between them and then, in a secure place, they laughed till their sides ached at the good joke on the tinman.

In due time the man found the iron core in his bar of solder, and thought the joke such a good one that he told of it in the saloon, and had to spend at least five dollars in drinks to ease off the laugh they had on him as the victim of the young California pioneers. And these young fellows—some have paddled their own canoes successfully into quiet waters and are now in the fullness of life, happy in their possessions, while some have been swamped on the great rushing stream of business, and dwell in memory on the happy times gone by.

The older pioneers in these mining towns were, in many respects, a peculiar class of men. Most of them were sober and industrious, fearless and venturesome, jolly and happy when good luck came to them, and in misfortune stood up with brave, strong, manly hearts, without a tear or murmur. They let the world roll merrily by, were ever ready with joke, mirth, and fun to make their surroundings cheerful.

Fortunes came and went; they made money easily, and spent it just as freely, and in their generosity and kindly charity the old expression "He has a heart like an ox" fitted well the character of most of them.

When luck turned against them they worked the harder, for the next turn might fill their big pockets with a fortune, and then the dream of capturing a wife and building up a home could be realized, and they would move out into the world on a wave of happiness and plenty. This kind of talk was freely carried on around the campfire in the long evenings, and who knows how many of these royal good fellows realized those bright hopes and glorious anticipations? Who knows?

The names come back in memory of some of them, and others have been forgotten. I recall Washington Work, H. J. Kingman, A. J. Henderson, L. J. Hanchett, Jack Hays, Seth Bishop, Burr Blakeslee, [and] Jim Tyler, who was the loudest laugher in the town, and as he lived at the Clifton House, he was called "The Clifton House Calf." These and many others might be mentioned as typical good fellows of the mining days. The biggest kind of practical joke would be settled amicably at the saloon after the usual style.

One day Jack Hays bought a pair of new boots, set them down in the store, and went to turn off the miners' supply of water. When he returned he found his boots well filled with refuse, crackers, and water. This he discovered when he took them up to go to dinner, and as he poured out the contents at the door, a half-dozen boys across the street raised a big laugh at him and hooted at his discomfiture. Jack scowled an awful scowl, and if he called them "pukes" with a few swear words added, it was a mild way of pouring out his anger. But after dinner the boys surrounded him and fairly laughed him into a good humor, so that he set up drinks for the crowd.

Footraces were a great Sunday sport, and dog fights were not uncommon. One dog in our camp was champion of the ridge, and though other camps brought in their pet canines to eat him up, he was always the top dog at the end of the scrimmage, and he had a winning grip on the forefoot of his antagonist.

A big "husky" who answered to the name of Cherokee Bob came our way and stopped awhile. He announced himself a footracer, and a contest was soon arranged with Soda Bill of Nevada City, and each went into a course of training at his own camp. Bob found some way to get the best time that Bill could make, and comparing it with his own, said he could beat that [time] in [a] race. So when it came off, our boys gathered up their money, and loaded down the stage, inside and out, departing with swinging hats and flying colors, and screaming in wild delight at the sure prospect of doubling their dust. In a few days they all came back after the style of half-drowned roosters.

Bob had thrown the race and skipped with his money before they could catch him. Had he been found, he would have been urgently hoisted to the first projecting limb, but he was never seen again. The boys were sad and silent for a day or two, but a look of cheerful resignation soon came upon their faces as they handled pick and shovel, and the world rolled on as before.

One fall we had a county election, and among the candidates for office was our townsman, H. M. Moore, from whom Moore's flat secured its name. He was the Democratic nominee for county judge, and on the other side was David Belden, he whom Santa Clara County felt proud to honor as its superior judge, and when death claimed him, never was man more sincerely mourned by every citizen.

The votes were counted, and Belden was one ahead. Moore claimed another count, and this time a mistake was discovered in the former count, but unfortunately it gave Belden a larger majority than before, and his adversary was forced to abandon the political fight.

In the [eighteen]-fifties I traveled from the North Yuba River to San Bernardino on different roads and made many acquaintances and friends. I can truly say that I found many of these early comers the most noble men and women of the earth. They were brave, else they never would have taken the journey through unknown deserts and through lands where wild Indians had their homes. They were just and true to friends, and to real enemies, terribly bitter and uncompromising. Money was borrowed and loaned without a note or written obligation, and there was no mention made of statute laws as a rule of action. When a real murderer or horse thief was caught, no lawyers were needed nor employed, but if the community was satisfied as to the guilt and identity of the prisoner, the punishment was speedily meted out, and the nearest tree was soon ornamented (?) with his swinging carcass.

Many of these worthy men broke the trail on the rough way that led to the Pacific coast, drove away all dangers, and made it safer for those who dared not at first risk life and fortune in the journey, but, encouraged by the success of the earliest pioneers, ventured later on the eventful trip to the new goldfields. I cannot praise these noble men too much; they deserve all I can say, and much more too, and if a word I can say shall teach our new citizens to regard with reverent respect the early pioneers who laid the foundations of the glory, prosperity, and beauty of the California of today, I shall have done all I hope to, and the historian of another half-century may do them justice, and give to them their full meed of praise.

As long as I have lived in California I have never carried a weapon of defense and never could see much danger. I tried to follow the right trail so as to shun bad men and never found much difficulty in doing so. We hear much of the Vigilance Committee of early days. It was an actual necessity of former times. The goldfields not only attracted the good and brave, but also the worst and most lawless desperadoes of the world at large. England's banished convicts came here from the penal colonies of Australia and Van Diemen's Land.[5] They had wonderful ideas of freedom. In their own land the stern laws and numerous constabularies had not been able to keep them from crime. A colony of criminals did not improve in moral tone, and when the most reckless and daring of all these were turned loose in a country like California, where the machinery of laws and officers to execute them was not yet in order, these lawless Sidney ducks, as they were called, felt free to rob and murder, and human life or blood was not allowed to stand between them and their desires.[6] Others of the same general stripe came from Mexico and Chile, and Texas and Western Missouri furnished another class almost as bad.

The Vigilance Committee of San Francisco was composed of the best men in the world. They endured all that was heaped upon them by these lawless men, and the law of self-protection forced them to organize for the swift apprehension and punishment of crime, and the preservation of their property and lives. No one was punished unjustly, but there was no delay, and

319

the evildoer met his fate swiftly and surely. Justice was strict, and the circumstances were generally unfavorable to thoughts of mercy. I was in San Francisco the day after Casey and Cory[7] were hung by the Vigilance Committee. Things looked quite military. Fort Gunny-bags[8] seemed well protected and no innocent man in any danger. I was then a customer of G. W. Badger & Lindenberger, clothiers, and was present one day in their store when some of the clerks came in from general duty, and their comrades shouldered the same guns and took their places on guard. The Committee was so truly vigilant that these firebugs, robbers, and cutthroats had to hide for safety.

Those who came early to this coast were mostly brave, venturesome, enduring fellows, who felt they could outlive any hardship and overcome all difficulties; they were of no ordinary type of character or habits. They thought they saw success before them and were determined to win it at almost any cost. They had pictured in their minds the size of the pile that would satisfy them, and brought their buckskin bags with them, in various sizes, to hold the snug sums they hoped to win in the wonderful goldfields of the then unknown California.

These California pioneers were restless fellows, but those who came by the overland trail were not without education and refinement; they were indeed, many of them, the very cream of Americans. The new scenes and associations, the escape from the influence of home and friends, of wife and children, led some off the dim track, and their restlessness could not well be put down. Reasonable men could not expect all persons under these circumstances to be models of virtue. Then, the Missouri River seemed to be the western boundary of all civilization, and as these gold hunters launched out on the almost trackless prairies that lay westward of that mighty stream, many considered themselves as entering a country of peculiar freedom, and it was often said that "law and morality never crossed the Missouri River." Passing this great stream was like the crossing of the Rubicon in earlier history, a step that could not be retraced, a launching to victory or death. Under this state of feeling many showed the cloven foot and tried to make trouble, but in any emergency good and honest men seemed always in the majority, and those who had thoughts or desires of evil were compelled to submit to honorable and just conclusions.

There were some strange developments of character among these travelers. Some who had, in long attendance at school and church, listened all their lives to teachings of morality and justice, and at home seemed to be fairly wedded to ideas of even rights between man and man, seemed to experience a change of character as they neared the Pacific coast. Amiable dispositions became soured, moral ideas sadly blunted, and their whole make-up seemed changed, while others who at home seemed to be of rougher mold developed principles of justice and humanity, affection almost unbounded, and were true men in every trial and in all places. A majority of all were thus fair-minded and true.

Men from every state from New Hampshire to Texas gathered on the banks of the Missouri to set out together across the plains. These men, reared in different climates, amid different ways and customs, taught by different teachers in schools of religion and politics, made up a strange mass when thus thrown together; but the good and true came to the surface, and the turbulent and bad were always in a hopeless minority. Laws seemed to grow out of the very circumstances and, though not in print, flagrant violations would be surely punished.

Some left civilization with all the luxuries money could buy—fine, well-equipped trains of their own, and riding a fat and prancing steed which they guided with gloved hands—and seemed to think that water and grass and pleasant camping places would always be found wherever they wished to stop for rest, and that the great El Dorado would be a grand pleasure excursion, ending in a pile of gold large enough to fill their big leather purses. But the sleek, fat horse grew poor; the gloves with embroidered gauntlet wrists were cast aside; the trains grew small; and the luxuries vanished; and perhaps the plucky owner made the last few hundred miles on foot, with blistered soles and scanty pack, almost alone. Many of these gay trains never reached California, and many a pioneer who started with high hopes died upon the way, some rudely buried, some left where they fell upon the sands or rocks.

Those who got through found a splendid climate and promising prospects before them of filling empty stomachs and empty pockets, and were soon searching eagerly for yellow treasure. When fortunate, they recovered rapidly their exhausted bodies to health and strength, and gained new energy as they saw prosperity.

Prospectors wandered through the mountains in search of new and suitable gold diggings, and when they came to a miner's cabin, the door was always open, and whether the owner was present or absent they could go in, and if hungry, help themselves to anything they found in shape of food, and go away again without fear of offense, for under such circumstances the unwritten law said that grub was free.

By the same unwritten law, stealing and robbery, as well as murder, were capital offenses, and lawless characters were put down. Favors were freely granted, and written obligations were never asked or given, and business was governed by the rules of strictest honor. The great majority of these pioneers were the bone and sinew of the nation, and possessed a fair share of the brains. In a personal experience with them, extending from early days to the present time, I have found them always just and honorable, and I regret that it is not within my ability to give the praise they deserve. When a stranger and hungry, I was never turned away without food, and my entertainment was free and given without thought of compensation or reward.

In the chambers of my mind are stored up the most pleasant recollections of these noble men whose good deeds in days gone by have earned for them the right to a crown of glory of greatest splendor.

These noble souls who came here forty years ago[9] are fast passing away across the Mystic River, and those who trod on foot the hot and dusty trail are giving way to those who come in swiftly rolling palace cars, and who hardly seem to give a thought to the difference between then and now.[10] Those who came early cleared the way and started the great stream of gold that has made America one of the richest nations of the world.

I have a suggestion to make to the descendants of these noble pioneers: that to perpetuate the memory of their fathers, and do reverence to their good and noble deeds in the early history of this grand state, there should be erected upon the highest mountaintop a memorial building, wherein may be inscribed the names and histories of the brave pioneers, so they may never be blotted out.

THE JAYHAWKERS[11]

THE MOST PERFECT ORGANIZATION OF THE PIONEERS who participated, more or less, in the scenes depicted in this volume is that of the Jayhawkers, and, strange to say, this organization is in the East and has its annual meetings there, although the living members are about equally divided between the East and the Pacific Coast. As related elsewhere, February 4th is the day of the annual meeting, for on that day they reached the Santa Clara Valley.

It is greatly regretted that a more direct and complete account of the Death Valley experience of the Jayhawkers could not have been obtained for this work. To be sure, it was from the lips of living witnesses told in many conversations, but no doubt many striking incidents were left out. It is, however, a settled thing that these and other individuals with whom he [the author] was immediately connected were more intimately connected with the horrors of the sunken valley, which was given its name by them, than were any other persons who ever crossed that desert region.

It will be considered that this was the most favorable time of year possible, and that during the spring or summer not one would have lived to tell the tale.

The author, to his best, has done his duty to all, and concludes with the hope that this mite[12] may authenticate one of the saddest chapters in the history of the Golden State.

CONCLUSION

THIS STORY IS NOT MEANT TO BE SENSATIONAL, but a plain, unvarnished tale of truth—some parts hard and very sad. It is a narrative of my personal experience and, being in no sense a literary man or making any pretense as a writer, I hope the errors may be overlooked, for it has been to me a difficult story to tell, arousing as it did sad recollections of the past. I have told it in the plainest, briefest way, with nothing exaggerated or overdone. Those who traveled over the same or similar routes are capable of passing a just opinion of the story.

Looking back over more than forty years, I was then a great lover of liberty, as well as health and happiness, and I possessed a great desire to see a new country never yet trod by civilized man, so that I easily caught the gold fever of 1849, and naught but a trip to that land of fabled wealth could cure me.

Geography has wonderfully changed since then. Where Omaha now stands there was not a house in 1849. Six hundred miles of treeless prairie without a house brought us to the adobe dwellings at Fort Laramie, and four hundred, more or less, were the long miles to Mormondom, still more than seven hundred miles from the Pacific coast. Passing over this wilderness was like going to sea without a compass.

Hence it will be seen that when we crossed a stream that was said to flow to the Pacific Ocean, myself and comrades were ready to adopt floating down its current as an easier road than the heated trail, and for three weeks, over rocks and rapids, we floated and tumbled down the deep cañon of Green River till we emerged into an open plain and were compelled to come on shore by the Indians there encamped. We had believed the Indians to be a warlike and cruel people, but when we made them understand where we wanted to go, they warned us of the great impassable Colorado cañon, only two days ahead of us, and pointed out the road to "Mormonee" with their advice to take it. This was Chief Walker, a good, well-meaning redman, and to him we owed our lives.

Out of this trouble we were once again on the safe road from Salt Lake to Los Angeles, and again made [an] error in taking a cutoff route, and striking across a trackless country because it seemed to promise a shorter distance, and where thirteen of our party lie unburied on the sands of the terribly dry valley. Those who lived were saved by the little puddles of rainwater that had fallen from the small rain clouds that had been forced over the great Sierra Nevada mountains in one of the wettest winters ever known. In an ordinary year we should have all died of thirst, so that we were lucky in our misfortune.

When we came out to the fertile coast near Los Angeles, we found good friends in the native Californians who, like good Samaritans, gave us food and took us in, poor, nearly starved creatures that we were, without money or property from which they could expect to be rewarded. Their deeds stand out whiter in our memories than all the rest, notwithstanding their skins were dark. It seems to me such people do not live in this age of the world which we are pleased to call advanced. I was much with these old Californians, and found them honest and truthful, willing to divide the last bit of food with a needy stranger or a friend. Their good deeds have never been praised enough, and I feel it in my heart to do them ample justice while I live. The work that was laid out for me to do, to tell when and where I went, is done. Perhaps in days to come it may be of even more interest than now, and I shall be glad I have turned over the scenes in my memory and recorded them, and on some rolling stone you may inscribe the name of WILLIAM LEWIS MANLY, born near St. Albans, Vermont, April 6, 1820,[13] who went to Michigan while yet it was a territory, as an early pioneer; then onward to Wisconsin before it became a state, and for twelve long, weary months traveled across the wild, western prairies, the lofty mountains, and [the] sunken deserts of Death Valley, to this land which is now so pleasant and so fair, wherein, after over forty years of earnest toil, I rest in the midst of family and friends, and can truly say I am content.

THE END

William Lewis Manly

ALTHOUGH MANLY SPENT MUCH OF THE REMAINDER of his life farming in the Santa Clara Valley, his adventures did not end with the mining experiences detailed in *Death Valley in '49*. In November 1860, Manly, Asabel Bennett, and Caesar Twitchell retraced the forty-niner route to the Panamint Mountains, west of Death Valley. They were searching for Charles Alvord, who had been abandoned in that area by his comrades (including Bennett) when he could not locate the fabulously rich lode he had found on a previous prospecting expedition. The rescue party camped at Redlands Spring, just above Ox-Jump Fall. Bennett and Alvord had built a ramp to take their pack animals over the dry fall, which enabled the rescuers to climb the fall—the same one that the Bennett and Arcane party had pushed their oxen over in February 1850.

Miraculously, Alvord wandered into his rescuers' camp. Finding him well, the four continued to prospect in the Panamints but could not find the lode they were seeking. Bennett and Twitchell took the mules back to civilization to replenish their supplies, but their return was barred by a heavy snowfall that closed the mountain passes. Manly and Alvord finally headed out of the desert on foot and survived only by Manly's hunting ability—their only food was jackrabbits. Alvord developed a boil on his knee and could hardly walk. While Manly and Alvord were recuperating at Indian Wells Spring (at the base of the Sierra Nevada), Dr. S. G. George and his prospecting party arrived. They loaned Alvord one of their mounts and all went together to the San Joaquin Valley.

In March 1861, Manly, Alvord, and a mining friend left Visalia and took their supplies in a wagon over the Greenhorn Mountains, across Walker Pass, north to Owens Little Lake, and thence east with pack animals to the Coso Mining District, where they prospected the Coso Range until early July. While there, they received news that the nation was at war with itself—the

War of the Rebellion, which we now call the Civil War. Manly then spent the rest of July hunting deer and grizzly bear in the southern Sierra Nevada.

The following year, on July 10, 1862, Manly (age 42, though the marriage license gives Manly's age as 40) married Mary Jane Woods (age 36) of Lodi, California. History is mute on how Manly and Mary met. They settled on Manly's 250-acre farm at Hillsdale, south of San Jose on the Monterey road, not far from where Manly had helped Mr. Moody set up his gristmill in 1850. He had paid about sixteen dollars per acre for the farm in 1859.

From 1875 to 1889 Manly is listed in the San Jose city directories as a farmer. About 1886, he had an accident that prevented him from working his farm and, while convalescing, wrote "From Vermont to California," which was published in monthly installments in *The Santa Clara Valley* over the next three years. *Death Valley in '49,* the compiled, enlarged, and edited version of these installments, was published in 1894, selling for two dollars a copy (today, a single copy in pristine condition sells for seven hundred dollars).

By 1898 Manly was quite ill and could no longer feed himself. Three years later he fell and broke his hip, which confined him to a wheelchair for the rest of his life. He died on February 15, 1903, after a heart attack and was buried in Woodbridge Cemetery, just north of Lodi, next to his wife, who had died the year before.

Manly left a considerable estate—$41,667 (about $800,000 now, adjusted for inflation). In the estate were a gold watch and chain Manly had given his wife, today in the possession of a descendant of Mary's family. Among other belongings, Manly's executors liquidated three wagons ($55), four horses ($76), a sulky plow ($10), and one wheelchair ($14). His estate included stock in the Farmers Union and the Garden City Bank, and he held notes for loans to several friends.

JOHN HANEY ROGERS

Between 1854, when Manly and Rogers saw each other at Benicia, and January 1895, they were out of touch. We know very little about Rogers' life after the Death Valley ordeal. We do know that he recorded the sale of eighty acres southwest of Merced for the sum of one hundred and fifty dollars in 1860, and that on April 26, 1894, his account of the trip through Death Valley was printed in the *Merced Star.*

In *Death Valley '49ers,* Frank Latta quotes John Flanagan (eighty-four years old in 1941), who knew Rogers after 1880. Flanagan said Rogers was a bachelor as long as he knew him, and he had high praise for the old pioneer.

Yes, I knew Big John Rogers for many years. He was as fine an old pioneer as ever lived. He was a lonely old fellow, an old bachelor....Rogers had been salivated in the mines by breathing mercury fumes while retorting amalgam. Both of his feet were cut off at the instep. But that did not keep him from making a living. He was an excellent separator man. He tended separator on stationary threshing machines all over this country until they were replaced by combines....Between harvest seasons he worked at carpentering or at any kind of mechanical work. He was a good mechanic. He always earned his way. He never sponged off anyone and he never accepted charity. He was a good butcher and used to slaughter for the Ellis family....I never knew of him to drink at all. He was a kind, generous old fellow and a square shooter if there ever was one.

On January 14, 1895, Rogers sent a man to Manly's home to let Manly know his Death Valley compadre was still alive, inviting Manly to visit him. In June of that year Manly took the train to Merced for a reunion, where he found that Rogers "like myself was an old man with a hairy face and walked with a cane." Manly further related that:

John looked me over and after a short pause said, "Lewis, is this really you?" And I replied, "Yes, if you are John."...His eyes ran over as he grasped my hand, the big tears rolling down his cheeks, for the lost was found....

Manly commented in 1900 that Rogers "writes me he thinks he is better-looking than the picture [he sent, and]...he is called, where he lives, Big John Rogers." It appears Rogers still had a sense of humor.

About 1905, when Rogers was eighty-four years old, he was admitted to the county hospital. By this time he had lost the sight of one eye and the other was seriously deteriorating. A sad story appeared in the December 29, 1906, issue of the *Merced Evening Sun*:

JOHN ROGERS TIRES OF LIFE
Attempted Suicide Friday as a Result of Physical Infirmities

Overburdened with an abundance of physical ailments, John Rogers, pioneer resident of this locality, slashed himself into ribbons with a razor at the county hospital yesterday in an attempt to end his troubles. He was found a few minutes afterward rapidly bleeding to death. His neck was gashed in six different places, though the blade had failed to touch a vital part. The desperate man had also inflicted three wounds upon each of his arms at the elbow joints. County physician Castle was promptly summoned and after stanching the flow of blood stitched the wounds. Rogers is not expected to live, though today he seems to be gaining strength.

The unfortunate man is eighty-four years of age and was one of the first inhabitants of this locality. About a year ago he was admitted to the county hospital and many times since then he has threatened to take his life....Little attention was paid him, the statement being accredited to his wandering mind. David Matthews, the steward, however, was informed of the threat and only yesterday searched the old man and his quarters for weapons. Only an old knife was found, which Rogers used to cut tobacco, and which was so dull that it would be almost impossible to cut any tougher substance with it. He was allowed to retain that. But Rogers had cunningly concealed a razor in some mysterious place and it was that instrument which he used with such terrible effect a short time afterward. The weapon was his own property and he had never intimated that he possessed it during all the time he had been in the hospital.

An addendum to this article said that Rogers had died about one o'clock that afternoon. In a letter to Manly, he had provided his own epitaph: "[he] will not need any pocket in his shroud, as he will take nothing with him."

Bennett Family

At the time of the 1850 California census, the Bennett family was living in Illinois Canyon, near Georgetown in El Dorado County. After leaving the mines, the Bennetts settled at Moss Landing, north of Monterey, where two more children were born: John Rogers in 1853 and Barbara Ellen (Ella) in 1854. When Ella was about three years old, Sarah Ann Bennett became ill and was taken to San Jose. Manly, having heard from her father that she was dying, rushed from Moore's Flat and arrived in time for a final farewell.

In late summer of the same year, Bennett sold his property, loaded two wagons with calico and other goods to trade with the Mormons, left Ella with Anna (Mrs. George Edwin) Scott of Scotts Valley, and drove with his four older children to Utah. They traversed the Salt Lake–Los Angeles Trail north from Los Angeles—the same trail that Captain Hunt had successfully led seven wagons over in 1849 after one hundred wagons, including the Bennetts, ceded from his train to take the disastrous shortcut to Walker Pass. Bennett and his children now passed through Mountain Meadows, where, three weeks before, Mormons and local Indians had murdered and mutilated one hundred and twenty members of the Fancher wagon train. Wolves and coyotes had scavenged the corpses and strewn them about the meadow.

After arriving in Utah and finding it difficult to be a gentile entrepreneur there, Bennett joined the Church of Jesus Christ of Latter-day Saints, married a Mormon woman, and settled in Cedar City. In April 1858, he guided the Mormons' White Mountain Expedition over part of the forty-niner trail that he had helped pioneer through southwestern Utah Territory. One of the springs Bennett led them to, west of today's Panaca, Nevada, was given his name. Around the campfires Bennett entertained his companions with tales of his 1849 travails.

Many members of the expedition had been involved in the Mountain Meadows massacre, and from them Bennett learned the story behind the rotting corpses he and his children had seen. By the end of summer 1858, Bennett was reunited with his family. Soon after, having experienced the heavy tithing required by the Church, having learned the truth about the massacre of the Fancher train, and not wanting his daughters to enter polygamous marriages, Bennett left his wife and the Church and returned to Los Angeles with his children.

From Los Angeles Bennett led prospectors into the Death Valley area, probably in the spring of 1860. It was on this trip that Charles Alvord found a promising vein of ore but failed to share this discovery with his partners. Upon returning to Los Angeles, he sent the ore sample to San Francisco, and it assayed extremely high in gold. When Alvord's partners discovered he had held out on them, they forced him to return to the desert to reveal his discovery. When he could not find it, they angrily abandoned him in the Panamint Mountains. When Manly learned of Alvord's plight, he initiated the successful expedition to rescue him.

After moving from place to place for many years, Bennett settled in Idaho Falls, Idaho, where he died at about eighty-four years of age. His oldest daughter, Melissa J. Bennett, married Judge Horace Cowan Rolfe in Los

Angeles about 1862. Martha Ann Bennett, who had celebrated her second birthday in Death Valley, married Johan F. C. Johansen (changed to John F. C. Johnson) in 1868, a few months after the death of her sister Melissa. Martha died February 27, 1910, in Wilmington, California. George Bennett was listed in the census for Belmont, in Nye County, Nevada, in 1875 and 1880. He is reported to have died March 10, 1884. John Rogers Bennett died February 25, 1904. Barbara Ellen (Ella) Bennett married George E. Gushee in 1874 and died January 20, 1923, in Oakland.

ARCANE (ARCAN) FAMILY

The Arcans (Manly consistently spelled the name Arcane, but Arcan is the spelling on the family tombstones) settled in Santa Cruz, California, where Abigail Arcan gave birth to Julia, named in honor of Juliet Brier, on July 1, 1850; Abigail had been five months pregnant when she started the arduous trek out of Death Valley. Julia lived just nineteen days and was the first person to be buried in the new Evergreen Cemetery. Her gravestone is still at the family plot. Ten years later, Abigail gave birth to Julia Madaline, and a year after that, Abigail (Abby) Carolyn was born.

John constructed a building at today's Soquel and Pacific Avenues, then called the Arcan block, and opened a gunsmith shop. He died in 1869, about twenty years after the family struggled out of Death Valley.

Charlie Arcan married at age nineteen and fathered five children. After his first wife died, he married Etta Berry Emery. He was employed as a machinist and later owned a bar in Santa Cruz. He died in 1907 at the age of fifty-nine.

A rare treasure that Abigail carried out of Death Valley was a linen tablecloth that she had woven. She probably covered the family with it during the snowstorm near the El Paso Mountains and may have wrapped Charlie in it when he suffered from his burning rash. Abigail used the cloth for special occasions, and it was bleached white with many washings. It is now in the possession of a distant relative.

WADE FAMILY

The Wade family was the only group of argonauts that succeeded in getting a wagon (possibly two) out of Death Valley. Harry Wade, a professional coachman, probably knew more than most of the emigrants about the care of dray animals and equipage; his riding horse and the family milk cow also apparently survived as far as Death Valley. Harry, Mary, and their four children exited Death Valley through the southern end, camped at the Mojave River, and crossed Cajon Pass to Los Angeles, arriving in February 1850. Manly knew the Wades had made it out of Death Valley with at least one wagon, yet he never mentions it in any of his reminiscences. After using the wagon to earn some money carrying freight from Los Angeles to San Pedro, the family headed for the mines.

Harry George Wade, who was fifteen years old in Death Valley, later built a deep-water wharf on San Francisco Bay, where goods could be loaded into wagons directly from ships. Charles Elliot Wade, eleven years old in Death Valley, went into farming after marrying Stefana Alviso in 1863. Almira Wade, age nine in Death Valley, married Jacob Ortley and had eleven children. Richard Angus Wade ran a stagecoach and livery business and was hired as a driver when James Lick built his mountain observatory. He married Marie Berryessa. In 1883 Harry Wade (Senior) died from a self-inflicted gunshot wound, according to a letter from Jayhawker Lorenzo Dow Stephens to John Colton in 1884. Mary Wade died six years later.

BRIER FAMILY

James Welsh Brier, a Methodist minister from Indiana, married Juliet Wells in 1839. Grace Leadingham described James Brier, in the *Pacific Historian,* as "tactless, idealistic, somewhat impractical, honest, courageous, venturesome, more than a little egotistical, tender in his own way." Reverend Brier was remembered proudly by his second son, who also became a minister: "My father had always been active, enterprising, and irrepressible. He…had never known what it meant to be discouraged." Juliet (Julia) Brier was an extraordinary person. She was small—115 pounds—and was greatly admired by the young Jayhawkers. She was said to be "a deeply religious person" who "had a keen mind and memory and could quote scripture by chapters."

While struggling along the fabled shortcut, Reverend Brier became noticeably ill in the Searles Valley area, and by the time the argonauts were out of the desert he had lost seventy-five pounds and needed two canes to support himself. Apparently he suffered from diabetes and was lucky to survive his desert ordeal.

When the Briers reached Los Angeles, they sold some of their cattle and purchased a half-interest in a boardinghouse, but by 1852 they were in Marysville. In addition to their three sons, Christopher Columbus, John Wells, and Kirke White, who were born before the family left for California, three daughters were born to the Briers.

Reverend Brier returned to Death Valley in 1873 as a guide for some miners, and letters that he later wrote for the Jayhawker reunions are invaluable firsthand resources, now housed in the Jayhawker Collection in the Huntington Library. The same cannot be said for John Brier's reminiscences or those of Juliet Brier. John said of his mother, "those events are...mingled and confused in her memory," and although he, a six-year-old when in the desert, did his best, the results muddy the research waters.

Reverend Brier died in Lodi in 1898, but Juliet lived to host the Jayhawker reunion in 1902. She died in 1913, just four months before her one-hundredth birthday.

Information on other members of the Death Valley forty-niner party can be found in proceedings of the Death Valley Conferences on History and Prehistory, in the Jayhawker Collection at the Huntington Library, and in books listed in the bibliography on page 367.

LeRoy and Jean Johnson

Chapter I

1. In the early 1600s, the Crown of England granted Plymouth Company the right to settle American soil between the 38th and 45th degrees north latitude; thus, Vermont's northern boundary became "five-and-forty north degrees." Vermont, the fourteenth state, was admitted to the Union on February 18, 1791.

2. William Lewis Manly's birth date is given incorrectly as April 20th on the last page of the original edition of this book. The last page also spells his last name "Manley," which is how the name appears in the original's text and copyright page. However, it is "Manly" on the original's cover, title page, and autographed photo, and "Manly" in all forty hand-written and signed letters in the Jayhawker Collection (at the Huntington Library in San Mateo, California). William Lewis Manly was called Lewis by his family.

   Doris Holloway Sleath, a descendant of Manly's youngest brother, Allen Clark, traced the family's roots back to 1066, when a Jon De Mandelie accompanied William the Conqueror in his conquest of England. Over time, the family name changed from Mandelie to Manley and finally, in some branches of the family, to Manly. One sibling's tombstone, in the Town of Sheldon's Webster Cemetery, is inscribed "Charity Manley" (with the "e"); another, "Cornelia Manly" (without the "e"). (Doris Sleath's genealogical record is in the Death Valley National Park Library, Death Valley, California.)

3. Manly's mother, Phoebe (1796–1869), and father, Ebenezer (1794–1859), were married on August 17, 1818, in the Town of Sheldon, Vermont, about nine miles northeast of St. Albans.

4. Whortleberry is another name for huckleberry (genus *Vaccinium*).

5. There are two major domesticated strains of flax *(Linum usitatissimum):* one for fiber production, from which linen is spun, and the other for seed production, from which linseed oil is made. Flax was introduced into Canada from its native Europe in 1617 and soon found its way to the American colonies, where it was cultivated for home fiber production.

6. The bark of eastern hemlock *(Tsuga canadensis)* contains 8 to 10 percent catechol, a chemical used in the tanning industry. To supply the tremendous needs of the industry, vast quantities of hemlock were felled.

7. A work shed, not a privy.

8. Cheese refers to the thick, marmalade-like pulp of the apples.

Chapter II

1. A crossroads.
2. Warren Colburn (1793–1833), American mathematician, published his *First Lessons in Intellectual Arithmetic* in 1821. His simple and concise treatise was used widely in the United States and was translated into many foreign languages.
3. Michigan Territory was created on January 11, 1805. In 1834 Congress enlarged the territory, which at one point included all of today's Michigan, Wisconsin, Iowa, and Minnesota, and about half of North and South Dakota. Michigan became the twenty-sixth state on January 26, 1837.

Chapter III

1. Ypsilanti, Michigan, is about eight miles southeast of Ann Arbor.
2. Mary E. (Polly) was born July 27, 1818, at St. Albans, Vermont.
3. To encourage settlement of land northwest of the Ohio River, Congress passed the Northwest Ordinance of 1787, which provided for the establishment of territorial governments and spelled out procedures for achieving statehood. Later, the General Preemption Act of September 4, 1841, provided for the sale of surveyed government land. This act was unofficially called the Squatter's Rights Act. Settlers were permitted to buy 160 acres for $1.25 per acre. Prior to passage of the act, the eastern states vehemently opposed it. They felt promoting emigration to unsettled territories would drain their labor pools. In 1841, U.S. Senator Henry Clay negotiated a compromise wherein 10 percent of the net proceeds of the land sales would be distributed to the states based on their populations. This placated the eastern states and the act passed.
   Jackson County, Michigan, records show that the United States conveyed ten acres of land to Ebenezer Manley on April 1, 1837 (we have been unable to locate the records for the remaining acres).
4. Ague is a malaria-like malady that has three stages: chills, fever, and sweating. Bilious fever is a liver disorder that causes constipation, headaches, loss of appetite, and vomiting.
5. Calomel is mercurous chloride, a white, tasteless powder used as a cathartic. Jalap—named for Jalapa, Mexico—is the dried tuberous root of *Exogonium purga*. As its Latin name implies, it was used as a purgative. Quinine is a chemical extracted from the bark of the cinchona tree (genus *Cinchona*), which is native to South America and has been used since the mid-1600s as a cure for malaria.

Chapter IV

1. A cradle scythe has fingerlike rods attached to it to catch the wheat stalks.
2. On February 1, 1836, Governor Stevens T. Mason made an appeal to the territorial legislature for a penal system. He stated, "To such an extent has evil grown, that ends of justice are entirely defeated, by want of the necessary and proper buildings for the confinement of criminals." On March 22, 1837, two months after

Michigan entered the Union, the prison was approved; on January 12, 1839, the first prisoner was interned. Until about 1895, the prisoners were not allowed to talk to each other—the "silent system" was strictly enforced.

CHAPTER V

1. Nathan Daboll (1715–1818) wrote a 240-page textbook, *Daboll's Schoolmaster's Assistant: Improved and Enlarged. Being a Plain Practical System of Arithmetic: Adapted to the United States,* first published about 1812. It remained in print for almost thirty years.
2. Calvin Flavil (1823–1905); Chester Rice (1833–1915); Allen Clark (1837–1919).
3. The solid rock was probably gypsum, which often caps salt domes. If they hit a salt dome after drilling through this gypsum layer, pure salt could be extracted from the brine. Salt was extremely important for both household and industrial uses.
4. Southport is now Kenosha, Wisconsin, on the western shore of Lake Michigan, six miles north of the Illinois-Wisconsin state line.
5. Hamilton's Diggings, Wisconsin, nineteen miles southeast of Mineral Point, was founded by William S. Hamilton, son of Alexander Hamilton (signer of the Declaration of Independence). William staked the first claim there in 1828. Others flocked to the mineral-rich area, and Hamilton's Diggings was born. Hamilton later renamed the settlement Wiota.
6. Mineral Point, Wisconsin, owes its beginning to lead mining. Numerous strikes were made about 1827, and a permanent settlement sprang up there.
7. Polecat is a common name applied to weasels and skunks. Since skunk odor is never mild, it is more likely that weasels had taken up residence in the building.
8. The Act of April 20, 1836 created Wisconsin Territory out of the western side of Michigan Territory. On May 29, 1848, Wisconsin gained statehood.
9. Burr oak *(Quercus macrocarpa)* grows from Nova Scotia to Wyoming and down through Texas. It has the widest distribution of any oak in North America.
10. In matters of fact, Manly was not prone to hyperbole. Assuming a twelve-hour walking day and a pace of five miles per hour, traveling sixty miles is a credible claim for a young man (without a pack) who has spent his life tramping.
11. Mackinaw City is the northernmost town on Michigan's Lower Peninsula. In about 1715, the French built Fort Michilimackinac here. Then, in 1761, the British took command of the fort after defeating the French in the French and Indian War. They renamed it Fort Mackinac but abandoned it in 1781, when they moved the fort to Mackinac Island.
12. Lake St. Clair is between Lake Huron and Lake Erie. Some authorities consider it one of the Great Lakes.

CHAPTER VI

1. Port Huron, Michigan, is on the St. Clair River, which connects Lake Huron with Lake St. Clair.

2. Prairie du Chien, Wisconsin, is at the confluence of the Wisconsin and Mississippi Rivers and is the second oldest city in the state (Green Bay was the first). The French established a fur trading post here in 1685. It was once a Fox Indians' settlement. Their clan name meant "dog"; thus, the French commemorated the settlement with "du Chien."

3. The brook's water would have been at freezing or even below and would have preserved their meat very well. Had they stored it by hanging it in a tree, Indians would have been able to find and eat it.

4. Early trappers and mountain men relied on many Indian herbal medicines. In this case, the cure was probably worse than the illness.

5. A poll is the broad end of a hammer's head.

6. At its base, the pine must have been two to three feet in diameter. Hacking a canoe out of a butt log would have been a laborious task. Later, on the Green River, Manly would again use his north-woods skills to carve canoes.

7. In the early to mid-1800s, a shingle weaver was someone who sawed and split cedar shingles. (Later the term applied to workers who packaged shingles into bundles.) Sawing was a dangerous occupation due to the lack of guards on the circular saws; it was said a shingle weaver could be recognized by his missing fingers. Constantly breathing cedar dust caused a lung disease called cedar asthma, which was often fatal. Shingle weavers undoubtedly high-graded the northern white cedar *(Thuja occidentalis);* the wood is very rot resistant, which made it ideal for shingles, fence posts, and canoes.

8. Even a starving bear would have a skin weighing more than five pounds. Since the weight of the skin was remarkable, it could have weighed fifty pounds.

9. Public land for $1.25 per acre is, by current standards, ridiculously low. However, in the 1800s, many squatters and settlers could not afford this price, and when Manly returned to Mineral Point in 1850 he said, "I could not now sell it for what it cost me." The area had become economically depressed, since many, like Manly, had moved on to mine gold in California. Manly may have let the property go for taxes.

CHAPTER VII

1. In December 1845, the United States annexed Texas, which set in motion a series of events that culminated with a declaration of war. On May 13, 1846, President Polk signed An Act Providing for the Prosecution of the Existing War between the United States and the Republic of Mexico. United States military forces then seized New Mexico and Alta California.

On February 2, 1848, in the city of Guadalupe Hidalgo, the Treaty of Peace, Friendship, Limits, and Settlement with the Republic of Mexico—commonly called the Treaty of Guadalupe Hidalgo—was signed by plenipotentiaries of both countries. On March 10, 1848, the U.S. Senate ratified the treaty, and on March 16th the president signed it, formally ending the war.

In the treaty, Mexico ceded what became California, Nevada, Utah, and parts of Colorado, Arizona, and New Mexico. Also, Mexico recognized the Rio Grande

River as the boundary between the two countries. The United States in turn paid Mexico $15 million and assumed up to $3.25 million in claims against Mexico.

2. On January 24, 1848, nine days before the Treaty of Guadalupe Hidalgo was signed, James Marshall discovered gold at Sutter's Mill. The mill site, at Coloma on the American River, is now a state park.

3. Prairie La Crosse (now called La Crosse, Wisconsin) is on the Mississippi River, about eighty miles north of Prairie du Chien. La Crosse was named by eighteenth-century French fur traders who witnessed the Winnebago, Sioux, and Dakota Indians playing a ball game on the prairie similar to lacrosse. In 1842 Nathan Myrick—then only eighteen years old—built a cabin at the site and established himself as a fur trader. By 1844 over twenty families had settled in the area.

4. A "pill" is detonating powder mixed with a binder and rolled into small balls waterproofed with wax, varnish, or foil. The pill was placed in a small depression next to the rifle's torch hole, and when the hammer struck it, the pill would ignite and detonate the powder in the barrel. The pill-lock firing mechanism replaced a flint lock in Manly's gun.

5. The Bad Axe River empties into the Mississippi River about forty miles north of Prairie du Chien. The Battle at Bad Axe River—also called Massacre at Bad Axe or Black Hawk War—was the last battle between the U.S. Army and Indians to be fought east of the Mississippi River. Chief Black Hawk (1767–1838), a 65-year-old Sauk war chief, had made a futile attempt to maintain his people's land rights in Illinois and they had retreated northward into Winnebago territory. About a hundred of his men and fifty women and children were killed on August 1st and 2nd, 1832. U.S. forces had only one casualty. Many of the women and children were shot as they attempted to swim across the Mississippi River to safety.

General Greenville M. Dodge (1831–1916), a civil engineer, was a colonel when he commanded the Michigan [Territory] Mounted Volunteers during the Black Hawk War; not becoming a general until the Civil War. After he resigned his military commission in 1866, he became the chief engineer for the Union Pacific Railroad Company and played a key role in designing and engineering the transcontinental railroad, which was completed at Promontory Point, Utah, on May 10, 1869.

6. The fox, goose, and corn conundrum involves a farmer who has to transport a fox, a goose, and some corn across a river in a boat that can carry only the farmer and one other item. If he takes the fox across first, the goose will eat the corn, and if he takes the corn across first, the fox will eat the goose. This story was used in grade schools as an exercise in logic.

Basswood *(Tilia americana)* has stringy bark; the Iroquois Indians perfected a way to make rope from it, a technique woodsmen adopted.

7. St Joseph, Missouri, on the Missouri River.

8. Manly saw the auction in Missouri, which had become the twenty-fourth state on August 10, 1821. As part of the Missouri Compromise, Maine had entered the Union on March 15, 1821, as a slave-free state, and Missouri had then entered as a slave state. This maintained the balance of power between the slave and free states in Congress.

9. This is also spelled Robidoux, most likely the correct spelling. (In diaries and reminiscences, there are at least twenty variations of this name.) Joseph E. Robidoux

(1826–1868) was employed with the American Fur Company. He established a trading post at the Blacksnake Hills (near the site of present-day St. Joseph, Missouri). Joseph then had plans drawn for a city near the trading post and, on July 26, 1843, filed the plans in St. Louis. He soon began selling lots: corner lots for $250; interior lots for $100. In three years the population of St. Jo had reached eight hundred. After John Marshall discovered gold in California in January 1848, St. Joseph became a major staging area for the gold rush and grew rapidly. Thousands of emigrants arrived by wagon trains and countless others by riverboats. St. Joseph is also notable as the eastern terminus of the Pony Express.

10. The new Fort Kearny, Nebraska, stood on high ground one mile south of the Platte River. It had been established in September 1848 (as Fort Childs), but in December 1848 it had been renamed Fort Kearny to honor General Stephen Watts Kearny. This was the first military post established along the Oregon-California Trail; it was abandoned in 1871.

 The old Fort Kearny had stood near Nebraska City, about two hundred miles to the east, on the Missouri River until May 1848.

11. Fort Laramie, Wyoming, was founded in 1849 as the second fort along the Oregon-California Trail. Soldiers stationed here patrolled the trail to provide security against Indian attacks. The fort was abandoned in March 1890.

12. The rampant slaughter of the buffalo—American bison—brought the species to the brink of extinction by the late 1800s. Estimates of total population in the early nineteenth century range from twenty-seven million to one hundred million animals—the latter a gross exaggeration.

13. Courthouse Rock, Nebraska, and its smaller neighbor, Jail Rock, were prominent landmarks on the Oregon-California Trail. These sedimentary rock and volcanic ash monoliths rise about four hundred feet above the North Platte River. Many of the diarists mentioned them in their journals.

14. Cholera is an acute bacterial infection of the bowel characterized by extreme diarrhea and vomiting that cause dehydration. Many emigrants showing signs of the disease in the morning were dead the next day. Cholera killed at least fifteen hundred emigrants along the trail during the peak of the gold rush. Poor sanitation permitted flies to spread the disease.

15. Chimney Rock, Nebraska, a solitary spire twelve miles west of Courthouse Rock, was sketched and mentioned by numerous diarists. It rises 470 feet above the North Platte River. From the base to the tip is 325 feet, and the terminal spire is 120 feet. Many emigrants carved their names in the sandstone base but they are difficult to read because the soft stone has eroded.

16. Scotts Bluff, Nebraska, is now a national monument. This wagon train traversed the bluffs via Robidoux Pass, named for Joseph E. Robidoux [see also note 9], who had a trading post and blacksmith shop there. In subsequent years, the Oregon-California Trail went over Mitchell Pass—an easier and more direct route over the bluffs—about six miles east of Robidoux Pass.

17. These travois were most likely made from the slender trunks of Rocky Mountain lodgepole pines *(Pinus contorta* ssp. *latifolia).*

18. Fort Laramie, Wyoming, is located at the confluence of Laramie Creek and the North Platte River. In 1834, fur trader William Sublette established a trading post on the site and dubbed it Fort William. His main purpose was to trade with the

Indians (the Oregon Trail had not yet been established). He sold his business to the American Fur Company, and in 1849 the U.S. Army bought the site and established Fort Laramie—commonly referred to as the gateway to the Rockies. In the 1850s the Army's main task was to provide security to the emigrants destined for Oregon or California. Toward the end of the 1880s there was little need for the fort and it was decommissioned in March 1890.

The Oregon Trail came into existence in 1841, and by the end of 1848 almost 12,900 emigrants had passed over the trail to settle Oregon Country before it became part of the United States. The United States took possession of Oregon Country—today's Washington, Oregon, and Idaho, and parts of Montana and Wyoming in 1846. In 1848, Oregon Country became a territory, and in 1859 Oregon became the thirty-third state, with its present boundaries.

19. Nathaniel Jarvis Wyeth built the original Fort Hall, Idaho, in 1834. In 1837 he sold it to the Hudson's Bay Company, and they abandoned the fort in 1855. After the Oregon Trail came into existence in 1841, the fort became an important rest and supply stop.

20. Black Hills of Wyoming, west of Fort Laramie.

21. The confluence of Deer Creek and the North Platte River became the future site of Deer Creek Station, an important mail and stage station on the Oregon-California Trail and later a Pony Express station.

22. The coal deposits were first commercially mined in 1883, and by the late 1900s annual production reached 4.2 million tons. Today this area is Glenrock, Wyoming.

23. Independence Rock, Wyoming, is known as the Great Register of the Desert because so many emigrants carved their names on the granite outcrop. This landmark was considered the halfway point of their journey.

24. The South Pass (7,412 feet) is a low pass over the Continental Divide. It is so gentle that many emigrants found it hard to believe they had traversed the Rocky Mountains.

25. Manly's reference here to the summit of the mountains is clearly to the summit of South Pass. In the 1800s, "summit" was used to designate either the summit of a pass or the summit of a mountain.

26. Pacific Springs is about three miles west of and three hundred feet lower than South Pass. It is so named because its water flows westward toward the Pacific Ocean.

27. Manly made a 100-percent profit on his investment, having paid only $30.

CHAPTER VIII

1. The Oregon-California Trail crossed Hams Fork River one mile upstream from where it entered the Green River. Near the crossing, about thirty-two miles northeast of Fort Bridger, the legendary mountain men held their 1834 rendezvous.

2. The map was undoubtedly Frémont's 1848 *Map of Oregon and Upper California* that accompanied his *Geographical Memoir upon Upper California in Illustration of his Map of Oregon and California*. This map covers today's western United States, west of the 104th meridian, which includes Utah and Nevada. The upper half of the map

shows Oregon and Missouri Territories and the southern half shows Upper California and New Mexico—both United States possessions as a result of the Mexican-American war. This map has a mythical east-west mountain range that forms the southern edge of Frémont's Great Basin.

3. The year must have read 1825, not 1824. William H. Ashley (1778–1838) left a diary of his trip down the Green River, but he made no mention of this inscription. On June 2, 1869, Major John Wesley Powell (1834–1902) saw the same inscription when he explored the Green River; by then, the "2" had washed away. Ashley had a varied career: he served as a brigadier general in the War of 1812, manufactured saltpeter, was a merchant, became a surveyor, explored the Missouri and Green Rivers, trapped beaver, traded goods to the Indians for furs, founded an organization in 1830 that evolved into the Rocky Mountain Fur Company, became the first lieutenant governor of Missouri, and served in the U.S. Congress as a representative.

4. Manly meant antlers, not horns. Each winter, elk shed their antlers, growing new ones the following spring; Manly would have seen a set at their maximum size. See Epilogue for more information on John Rogers.

5. Chief Wakara (ca. 1808–1855), the renowned Ute Indian, was known as Napoleon of the Desert. Whites called him Walker. He became famous for his daring horse raids in California. In October 1845, he and his band stole over a thousand horses from the San Bernardino region and drove them eastward. They were pursued to the Mojave River, but the posse was no match for the heavily armed Indians. The Mormons attempted to build alliances with local Indians, treating them with respect and, when possible, placating them with food and supplies rather than fighting them. Even so, they encountered resistance to their takeover of Indian lands. Wakara and his band were friends with the Mormons. Manly and his companions professed to be Mormons; had they not, it is possible they would have been killed.

6. Commonly called the Old Spanish Trail, it ran from Santa Fe to Los Angeles.

7. This was the Gruwell-Derr wagon train. Manly was mistaken, though, when he said they paid their guide $10 per wagon: they did not have (or were not willing to pay) the $10 fee Jefferson Hunt charged. They therefore hired a Mexican guide (for an undisclosed amount). The twenty-three wagons in this train were the first to traverse the Salt Lake–Los Angeles Trail from north to south—one wagon having come up the trail in 1848.

8. The town of Hobble Creek took its name from the creek, which flows into Utah Lake. Mormons settled this fertile area in 1849. The town's name was later changed to Springville to commemorate the excellent freshwater springs in the area. These white settlers had evicted the Indians from lands they had lived on for centuries, hence the need for a fort.

9. Kanesville is now Council Bluffs, Iowa. This was the beginning of the Mormon Trail, which paralleled the Platte River on the north side. The Oregon-California Trail, on the south side of the river, began at Independence, Missouri, and a fork of that trail began at St. Joseph, Missouri.

10. Alexander Pope (1688–1744) was responsible for the moniker Lo that has been applied to North American Indians. In his philosophical poem *Essay on Man,* he

wrote: "Lo! The poor Indian, whose untutor'd mind/Sees God in clouds, or hears him in the wind…"

11. Captain Jefferson Hunt (1803–1879) first arrived in California in January 1847, as a captain in the Mormon Battalion during the Mexican War. There he learned that Isaac Williams was willing to sell his Rancho Santa Ana del Chino (22,234 acres) for $200,000. Discharged from the Army in July 1847, Hunt returned to Salt Lake City in October via the Humboldt Trail. He and other battalion veterans convinced Brigham Young that the Mormon Church should establish a community at the rancho in southern California, but to do so, the Mormons needed to purchase a Spanish land grant, which they did in 1851.

Captain Hunt traversed the Salt Lake–Los Angeles Trail twice. On November 16, 1847, he and eighteen others left Salt Lake for southern California to buy seed grain, cattle, and fruit cuttings. They arrived at Rancho del Chino on December 24th, suffering greatly along the trail and having been forced to slaughter and eat three of their horses. They purchased supplies and two hundred cows (at six dollars per head) and started back to Salt Lake on February 15, 1848. Forty bulls and one hundred cows died (some having been shot by Indians) before the party reached Salt Lake three months later. In March 1848, the second contingent of the caravan followed with a wagon load of seed grain and fruit cuttings. This is reputed to have been the first of wagons to traverse the Salt Lake–Los Angeles Trail. Captain Hunt emigrated to California in 1851 and helped establish San Bernardino. There he served as a California assemblyman for the 2nd District from 1853 to 1854 and for the 1st District from 1854 to 1858.

12. In 1849 the Mormons had not yet purchased a Spanish land grant in southern California. Brigham Young did not consent to the Church's purchase of the rancho, but he gave permission to individual Mormons to do so. They had intended to buy Rancho Santa Ana del Chino from Isaac Williams, but when they brought him the down payment, he refused to sell. Thus, they bought the 35,509-acre Rancho San Bernardino Lugo from José del Carmen Lugo in September 1851 for $77,500 (at $2.18 per acre). On this ranch, the Mormons established the city of San Bernardino. (The reference in the text to San Bernardino is in retrospect.)

13. The destroying angels were reputed to be, in today's parlance, hit men for the Mormon Church. Although much has been written about their ruthless activities, there are conflicting suppositions about the validity of these claims.

14. Some have speculated the Sand Walking Company is a corruption of the San Joaquin Company, but there is no evidence supporting this contention.

CHAPTER IX

1. Little Salt Lake, a salty playa sometimes covered with water, is eighteen miles northeast of Cedar City, Utah. This is near where the Salt Lake–Los Angeles Trail joined the Old Spanish Trail. The party's delay here caused some in the wagon train to doubt Captain Hunt's guiding abilities, and threats were made against his life. However, he had the train's concurrence before attempting this ostensible shortcut down the Beaver River.

2. Captain Orson K. Smith (ca. 1829–1871) was leading a company of twenty packers, probably over Walker Pass, near the southern end of the Sierra Nevada. He had a map drawn by a Barney Ward—though Manly says Williams—who lived in Salt Lake City. Ward had purportedly traversed the Great Basin three times.

3. This "Williams…a mountaineer" may have been Old Bill Williams, a famous mountain man, but it is not likely. Old Bill had died several months before the Jayhawkers arrived at Salt Lake and was not known to have left any maps.

4. Because Reverend Brier was a strong proponent of this route, he later became a scapegoat when the going got rough.

5. "The Smith trail" refers to the trail the Smith pack train followed west. It started near Enterprise, Utah; went up Shoal Creek; dropped into Headwaters Wash, Nevada; and then headed down Beaver Dam Wash. The trail was also called Walker's Cutoff. (It is not clear whether "Walker's" refers to mountain man Joseph Reddeford Walker (1798–1872), or to the Ute Chief Wakara (called Chief Walker by whites), or to Walker Pass. But because the Smith trail was supposed to traverse the Sierra Nevada via Walker Pass, "Walker's Cutoff" most likely refers to the pass.

6. This division occurred November 3, 1849, near today's Enterprise, Utah, where the Smith trail left the Old Spanish Trail. William B. Lorton, a member of the wagon train, recorded in his diary (housed in The Bancroft Library) on November 3, "We [will be] going over a rout[e] never explored by white man, before us all dark & gloomy, to enter mountains of great h[e]ight subject to dre[a]dful snows & frosts." The wagon Lorton was in was one of a hundred wagons that seceded from the Sand Walking Company and ended up in a high area the emigrants named Mt. Misery because of the miserable time they had here trying to find passage accessible for wagons. Eventually a route was found, but only twenty-seven of the wagons chose to continue west; the remainder retreated to the Old Spanish Trail and eventually caught up with Captain Hunt. Here at Mt. Misery, Lorton joined some of the packers and started on foot to California, following Smith's trail. Smith's and Lorton's parties then aborted this venture and headed south to intercept the Old Spanish Trail, which they followed to California.

7. Mormons planned and executed this atrocity, and attempted to blame all of it on Indians. Over one hundred and twenty men, women, and older children of the Fancher wagon train were murdered at the meadows in September 1857. Only one of the "Mormon generals," John D. Lee (ca. 1812–1877), was tried and convicted for the crime. An Army firing squad executed him at Mountain Meadows on March 23, 1877.

8. Utah juniper *(Juniperus osteosperma)* was often incorrectly called a cedar in emigrant diaries. The elevated ground was Mt. Misery, northeast of Beaver Dam Wash, between Pine Park Canyon to the south and Headwaters Wash to the west and north, near the Nevada-Utah state line.

9. Lorton recorded in his diary on November 9th that "poor Naylor died." He added there had been a "quar[r]el over his body for his property. I reprove[d] them have a trial I am witness sell anything for 6 bits. Throw away shirt & give other things away bury him on the mountain."

10. Lorton recorded that snow fell on November 3, 1849. On the 5th, before reaching Mt. Misery, he tells us there was "snow laying still on the ground, which made it bad going for teams"—a compelling reason for turning back.

11. Manly consistently spelled Arcane phonetically, with a final "e," although the family name was spelled without it. Also, in the next chapter only one Earhart son is mentioned, which seems correct.
12. The wagons paralleled Clover Creek, Nevada, but could not continue down the canyon when it narrowed. Now the Union Pacific Railroad traverses this canyon. The wagons exited between Acoma and Barclay sidings and headed northwest toward Panaca, Nevada.
13. These sand pillars are erosional features characteristic of the Panaca Formation. The pillars are sand and volcanic ash deposited in an ancient lake. Based on mammalian fossils, the deposits are dated middle Pliocene, about three million years old. These strange formations occur both north and southeast of Panaca, Nevada. The wagon train passed near the southern formations.
14. Pine burr is an archaic name for pine cone. Seeds from the single leaf pinyon (*Pinus monophylla*) were an important part of the Great Basin Indians' diet. One way they collected the seeds was to pick unopened cones, heap them in piles or in a shallow trench, and lightly parch them with a sagebrush fire. The cones would then open naturally and the seeds would become easy to remove. These Indians also stored green unopened cones, not extracting the seeds until winter.
15. The Jayhawkers had continued north in White River Valley before aborting their northern journey. They then turned south down Coal Valley and caught up with the Bennett-Arcane wagon train, which had crossed the northern end of the Seaman Range via Timber Mountain Pass and turned south in Coal Valley.
16. John Charles Frémont's 1848 report, *Geographical Memoir upon Upper California, in Illustration of his Map of Oregon and California,* was one of those rare federal government reports that become a best-seller. Congress printed 40,100 copies of the report and 30,100 of the map. Late in 1848, a private company also published the report, but without the map, selling it for twenty-five cents a copy.
17. The high peak was Telescope Peak (11,049 feet) in the Panamint Range, just west of Death Valley, California. Manly's description of the hundreds of miles traveled first west, then south, in Nevada is too sketchy for the route to be identified with certainty. The area is now within Nellis Air Force Range, a top-secret government research facility (commonly called Area 51) accessible only to military personnel. There is only limited access to the neighboring Atomic Energy Commission's Nevada [Atomic Bomb] Test Site.

   The high peaks in the other mountains in the area—Inyo Range, Last Chance Range, Grapevine Mountains, and Cottonwood Mountains—would all have had snow on them as well.
18. This means to outmaneuver.
19. Mount Stirling (8,217 feet), in the Spring Mountains, is probably the mountain referred to.
20. The "variegated candy" was fossilized pack-rat urine, called amberat. Pack rats (genus *Neotoma*) build middens in dry caves or sheltered rock crevices and, over centuries, they add plant material to their middens. They also urinate and defecate on the middens, and over time the dried urine builds up and resembles amber. Some middens are at least forty thousand years old.

   Amberat is water soluble, allowing scientists to dissolve it and extract the plant material. They can then carbon-14 date the plant remains. This gives them an excellent history of shifts in vegetation that they can correlate to climate changes. The Indians knew that amberat was inedible.

21. Most historians have concluded this was Cane Spring, nestled between the northern bases of Skull Mountain and Mount Salyer on the Nevada Test Site. Its water is not warm; however, when Manly was here the air temperature was near freezing, so the water may have felt warm in comparison.

22. This is Devils Hole, Nevada, where a rare species of pupfish *(Cryrinodon diabolis)* lives. Their camp was at Collins Spring, three-quarters of a mile south of this unusual water source.

23. In this section of the Amargosa River, water flows only after rainstorms or in very wet winters. One can usually drink small amounts without ill effect. The Jayhawkers entered the Amargosa Desert from the north and missed the numerous freshwater springs in Ash Meadows.

24. This unmapped seep is in Furnace Creek Wash, the eastern gateway to Death Valley National Park. Called "Clay Bowl Spring," the seep is one-quarter mile west of Navel Spring and 8.5 miles east of Travertine Springs.

25. The three Brier sons were Christopher, eight; John, six; and Kirke, four.

26. These were Travertine Springs and Furnace Creek. In the 1800s, the copious creek ran a considerable distance—more than two miles. Describing the creek as flowing only "a few yards" is conjecture on the editor's part. In the February 1888 issue of "From Vermont to California," Manly had described the stream thusly: "The little springs came all together and ran down the canyon some distance and sank in the sand." Today most of the water is captured for domestic use, so the stream no longer exists.

27. Owens Lake was sixty miles due west.

28. Telescope Peak (11,049 feet), the lofty, snowcapped peak, was twenty-four miles southwest of him, but would have looked much closer.

29. The water in Jayhawker Well is still brackish but potable. On old maps, the site is labeled Lost Wagon.

30. Here at Jayhawker Well, near today's McClean Spring, there were numerous mesquite trees, but the Jayhawkers knew that their oak and hickory wagon planks, now tinder dry, would make excellent charcoal for drying meat.

31. See Genesis 19:26.

32. Furnace Creek was christened earlier. The name was already in use in 1861, when Aaron Van Dorn wrote his report about a California Boundary Commission reconnaissance party that entered Death Valley via Furnace Creek Wash with three camels and a string of worn-out mules.

CHAPTER X

1. The party crossed the valley a little north of the location of the present gravel road. This road was initially built by Chinese laborers, who used sledgehammers to pulverize the salt evaporites that characterize Devils Golf Course.

2. They had spent the first night at Tule Spring and the second night at Eagle Borax Spring.

3. Some thought the Panamint Range was the Sierra Nevada and that there would be a prominent trail somewhere to the south of their camp, leading to Walker Pass.

4. The high peaks in the Panamint Range—Porter, Sentinel, and Telescope—all had snow on them.

5. Six Springs Canyon. A prominent Indian trail ascended the alluvial fan and entered this canyon. However, it was obvious from the valley floor that taking wagons up and over the range via this canyon was impossible.

6. The well was Mesquite Well, now completely dried up. This water source, shown on old maps, was about twelve miles south of Eagle Borax Spring, their former camp.

7. Warm Spring Canyon. A prominent Indian trail went from Mesquite Well south a couple of miles and angled into the canyon. A fork of the trail went up Anvil Canyon. The smooth Pleistocene fan made an inviting wagon route into and over the mountain range. Some thought this was the entrance to Walker Pass.

8. Manly had rushed ahead and scouted up Anvil Canyon far enough to determine that the wagons would not be able to traverse the range via this canyon.

9. After hearing the bad news, they had retreated to Mesquite Well.

10. The good spring was Eagle Borax Spring. The water there was potable and there was considerable grass for the oxen.

11. Mr. Bennett's children were George, born in 1842 (seven years old); Melissa, born October 9, 1845 (four years old); and Martha, born January 21, 1848 (two years old). Mr. Arcane's child was Charlie, born May 1, 1848 (under two years old).

12. The Wades had four children with them: Harry George, fifteen; Charles, eleven; Almira, nine; and Richard, five. Manly probably did not consider Harry George a child any longer (but he does not mention a grown son either).

13. Arrastre Spring is named for the crude, gold-ore milling structure immediately above the spring. An arrastre is an eight to twelve-foot circular depression in the ground, lined with large, flat rock. Ore was placed in the ring and a mule or donkey dragged a large millstone around and around until the ore was ground fine. "Fines" were then panned or treated with mercury to extract the gold. There are several arrastres scattered throughout Death Valley National Park, typically near water sources. Manly and Rogers could see the summit of Sentinel Peak, which blocked the view of Telescope Peak.

14. "The summit" refers to the summit of a pass, not a mountain. The pass, unofficially called Rogers Pass (7,160 feet), is at the headwaters of Pleasant Canyon. The Indian trail from Arrastre Spring crossed it. Manly and Rogers ascended a hill a quarter-mile southwest of the pass. From there they saw the Sierra Nevada seventy miles to the west and realized they could not return in the time allotted.

15. They had crossed the Rocky Mountains via the gentle grade over South Pass and had not been impressed with the Rockies. The stunning view of the Sierra Nevada was an awesome sight from this vantage point, where they could see the Mt. Whitney massif (14,495 feet), the highest mountain in the lower forty-eight states.

   Throughout this section of the book, cardinal directions are askew and have been replaced by correct directions in brackets. The book's original editor undoubtedly would have used Manly's map—now in the Palmer Collection of the Huntington Library, San Marino, California—to orient herself. However, Manly had drawn the map to fit the size and shape of his paper, without regard to correct orientation.

16. The San Gabriel Mountains, labeled the Coast Range on Frémont's 1848 map, were far to the south.

17. From their vantage point, the logical route was to drop into Middle Park and thence down Middle Park Canyon. They had no way of knowing that Middle Park Canyon curves northwest and emerges into Panamint Valley, 1.5 miles south of Ballarat.

18. As they descended Middle Park Canyon, they found rainwater in a rock depression. The two ranges are the Slate and Argus Ranges.

19. They had an excellent view northward up Panamint Valley, and as they continued down the alluvial fan, the view opened to the south. From this vantage point the only logical route westward was over the Slate Range via a low gap now called Manly Pass.

20. This stream is still there and is still extremely salty.

21. Manly and Rogers had started up a ridge on the eastern flank of the Slate Range, immediately south of Fish Canyon. The tracks they found when they dropped into Fish Canyon were the Brier party's tracks, not the Jayhawkers'. The Brier party had dug holes in the bottom of a small box canyon where Reverend Brier had found damp sand at the base of a dry, vertical fall. He called this spot "a Silent Sepulchre."

    During the Pleistocene, copious water and gravel excavated a basin in the bedrock at the base of the fall. This tank–*tinaja*–then filled with sand, and rainwater accumulated under the sand. The water could not percolate downward because of the solid-rock basin, and it was slow to evaporate because the sand above provided a dry mulch. The men waited for water to drain into their holes, then scooped it out. In this slow, laborious way they depleted all the water in the *tinaja*. Only another storm could recharge the tank. Water can still be found here after digging down a foot or so.

22. Had they stayed on the Indian trail that headed due west across Searles Valley, they would have found water in Great Falls Basin, but they headed south here.

23. Elsewhere Manly wrote, "We believed we could see trees [south of the lake]; and, if so, the lake must be fresh" (in the April 1888 issue of "From Vermont to California"). However, the trees were the Trona Pinnacles, a moonscape where many movies and television shows have been filmed. The wine color is caused by halophytic bacteria, found in salty and brackish lakes throughout the world. When Manly and Rogers tasted the water they were, needless to say, bitterly disappointed.

24. Manly and Rogers decided not to follow the Brier party's tracks, which would have taken them to Indian Joe Canyon, but instead headed directly west into the Argus Range via east Burro Canyon, where they hoped to find water.

25. From the western side of the Argus Range they could see the Sierra Nevada, which was twenty miles to the west. The plain is Indian Wells Valley.

26. They descended the western flank of the Argus Range via west Burro Canyon.

27. This snow mountain was the Sierra Nevada, and the wash was from the Coso Range.

28. Had they immediately veered north a couple of hundred yards after exiting west Burro Canyon they would have found Paxton Lake, a small, brackish pond with

barely potable water on the eastern edge of Indian Wells Valley. Instead they followed the south-trending outwash from the canyon, and a small rise to the north blocked their view of Paxton Lake. The nearest snow was northward—either Volcano Butte (5,882 feet) or Louisiana Butte (6,876 feet).

29. Similar thin sheets of ice can still be found here. A few days before Manly and Rogers found their ice, it rained heavily in Indian Wells Valley. Water accumulated in various shallow depressions, the surface freezing at night. The water below the ice percolated into the ground, leaving thin sheets of ice high and dry, so to speak.

30. This bluff is the toe of Black Mountain, twenty-two miles to the southwest.

31. Indian Wells Spring is on a bench where the water is impounded in a cave dug into the hillside. (Today the spring supplies water for the residences at Homestead on Highway 395.)

32. Manly and Rogers did not see Isham (also spelled Ischam) because they had deliberately departed from the route of the Brier party to increase their probability of finding water.

33. This camp was in a side canyon feeding into Last Chance Canyon in the El Paso Mountains. It is on the route of Indian Horse Thief Trail.

34. One of the forks mentioned here is close to the junction of Highways 14 and 178, the latter crossing Walker Pass—the goal of the fabled Walker's Cutoff. The Georgia-Mississippi boys (whom Sheldon Young called the Bug-smashers) had left Jayhawker Well in Death Valley on December 29, 1849, and had crossed Walker Pass before a storm closed it. Sheldon Young, one of the Jayhawkers, kept a daily diary, a typescript of which is in the Huntington Library. It is difficult to identify the individual members of the Bug-smashers because, like a covey of quail, they periodically scattered in different directions, came together again, formed new alliances, and scattered again. We know the advance party that followed the trail over Walker Pass made it to the goldfields, because George W. B. Evans, a prospector who lived at Agua Fria (six miles west of Mariposa) recorded in his diary on January 29, 1850, that twelve of them arrived at the Mariposa Mines, and on February 9 that ten more arrived. The pass itself is named for Joseph Reddeford Walker (1798–1872), who traversed it in 1834 with 52 men, 315 horses, 47 beef, and 30 dogs—the latter destined for the cooking pot.

35. Desert Spring—commonly called the Willow Corral—is now on private property eleven miles north of California City. The willows have been choked out by tamarisk, an exotic tree that has invaded many desert water holes and streams. Water no longer flows here: the water table dropped because farmers mined the aquifer to water their crops.

36. A sure sign they were on the Indian Horse Thief Trail.

37. Manly elsewhere described this ground as "very soft and light as snuff" (in the April 1888 issue of "From Vermont to California").

38. This spur is the El Paso Mountains, parallel to the Garlock Fault.

39. These were the San Gabriel and San Bernardino Mountains.

40. The last two sentences refer to the Sierra Nevada.

41. Wilson's Peak might have been an early name for Mt. Wilson (5,710 feet), now the site of the Mount Wilson Observatory, seven miles northeast of Pasadena. However, Mt. Wilson was not visible from Manly's vantage point because higher mountains blocked the view. (It is possible that Manly's editor inserted Wilson's

Peak; the name does not appear in the February issue of "From Vermont to California.")

42. They were heading due south toward the San Gabriel Mountains.

43. Joshua tree *(Yucca brevifolia)* is found throughout the Mojave Desert and grows to a height of thirty-five feet. It is a member of the lily family.

44. The Old Spanish and Salt Lake–Los Angeles Trails joined in southwestern Utah, and the combined trail crossed Cajon Pass to terminate at Pueblo de Los Angeles.

45. This was Barrel Springs, four miles southeast of Palmdale, on the San Andreas Fault. Recent archeological evidence shows that the springs supported human habitation as long as seven thousand years ago. It was also a major camp along the Horse Thief Trail.

46. California juniper *(Juniperus californica)* is able to survive and thrive in the desert mountain environment.

47. This brook is within the Thousand Trails–Soledad Canyon Recreational Park, two miles south of Acton.

48. On March 9, 1842, Don Francisco Lopez and two friends had found gold in nearby Placerita Canyon (near Newhall). This discovery triggered California's first gold rush, localized in southern California. But unlike John Marshall's 1848 discovery, Don Francisco Lopez's 1842 discovery was not widely publicized. (Had it been, California might still be under Mexican rule.) Between 1842 and 1862, the placer deposits in southern California yielded about five million dollars in gold. Nine days after Marshall's discovery, the Mexican-American War ended with the signing of the Treaty of Guadalupe Hidalgo, and Alta California became an American possession.

49. Instead of continuing down the bed of the Santa Clara River around this spur, Manly and Rogers followed an Indian trail over it that led to a spring just west of the pass. The trail continued northwest toward today's Saugus.

50. It was January 25th, ten days after they had left the party in Death Valley.

51. This adobe building was built in 1804 as an *asistencia* (boardinghouse) for the San Fernando Mission and was later part of the Rancho San Francisco. The structure was about 105 feet long and 17 feet wide and was located about a half-mile south of Castaic Junction. Manly and some of the other Death Valley forty-niners refer to this place as Rancho San Francisquito, the name of a rancho in the Los Angeles basin. Confusion also exists because a canyon nearby is called San Francisquito Canyon.

52. By this time they had used twelve of the allotted fifteen days.

53. They had crossed the notoriously steep San Fernando Pass (2.5 miles south of Newhall). The trail was so steep that in 1852 Henry C. Wiley built a windlass system to haul wagons up the grade. In 1854 Phineas Banning made a thirty-foot-deep cut through the mountain, thus eliminating the need for the windlass, and this cut became known as Newhall Pass. Wagons now had a relatively easy way to cross the mountain. In 1863 General Edward F. Beale deepened Banning's Cut (Newhall Pass) to ninety feet. (Interstate 5 now bypasses this historic spot.) The original road continued north up San Francisquito Canyon, past Elizabeth Lake, thence west to Fort Tejon and into the San Joaquin Valley.

54. Mission San Fernando Rey de España is 1.5 miles west of the city of San Fernando. The site was selected because abundant water came from four nearby

springs. The herd, numbering twenty-one thousand in 1819, was noted for its quality. The mission's major product was hides, used for shoes, saddles, and door coverings, and also, because nails were scarce, for rawhide thongs used to lash timbers and boards together. During the Mexican War, Colonel Frémont and his men briefly occupied the mission.

55. Dr. Erasmus Darwin French (1822–1902), a physician, came to California in 1846 with General Stephen Watts Kearny's Army of the West to tend the wounded. After the Mexican-American War, he deserted and took up cattle ranching at the Tejon Ranch. Later, during chance encounters with survivors of the Death Valley party, he learned about the fabulous mountain of silver that became known as the Lost Gunsight or the Gunsight Lead, so named because one of the argonauts had found a silver float in Emigrant Wash or Emigrant Canyon. (At the mines the argonaut had a gunsmith carve a sight from the float for him.) In the summer of 1850 and again in 1860, French made futile attempts to find the legendary mountain of silver. In the end he took nothing from the Death Valley region, but he did leave his name behind. Darwin Canyon, Darwin Falls, and the mining town of Darwin are all named for him.

56. Three women would have included Mrs. Wade, as well as Mrs. Bennett and Mrs. Arcane. However, later (as well as earlier, in the July 1888 issue of "From Vermont to California"), Manly mentioned only two women with four children stranded in the desert. He must have known the Wades would not await his return.

57. The number of children is correct for Mrs. Bennett and Mrs. Arcane.

58. Chief Wakara's camp on the Green River.

59. They returned via San Francisquito Canyon.

60. In 1861 Manly would take the stage from San Francisco to Los Angeles, passing by Elizabeth Lake. He commented that when "we reached Elizabeth Lake, the beautiful sheet of freshwater where Rogers and I took a big draught of this sweet fluid," he had been reminded of "the sad '49 days."

61. San Francisquito Canyon is several canyons west of Soledad Canyon, the canyon that Manly and Rogers, the Jayhawkers, and the Brier group all descended.

62. Desert Spring.

63. Indian Wells Spring.

64. Paxton Lake.

65. Deadman Canyon.

66. East Wilson Canyon.

67. The rocky ravine was Indian Joe Canyon, four miles north of Trona. Indian Joe Spring is a mile from the mouth of the canyon. The water's terminus, named Providence Spring by Mrs. Brier, varies from year to year. This canyon contains classic examples of an upside-down stream: in places the water flows beneath the gravel but periodically surfaces when it encounters a solid rock barrier.

68. Searles Valley and Searles Lake.

69. Redlands Canyon was visible from Manly Pass. (They could not see Goler Wash, a canyon some people think Manly and Rogers ascended, six miles south of Redlands Canyon.)

70. Until recently, a clearly visible Indian trail ascended the steep rampart into the canyon; it skirted to the north of Manly Fall, a ninety-five-foot vertical dry fall.

The trail and the fall are now both obliterated by an open-pit gold mine at the mouth of the canyon.

71. This barrier, now called Ox-Jump Fall, is just below Redlands Spring.

72. Although Ox-Jump Fall was only ten feet tall, a vertical drop from the central part of the ledge where it ascends the canyon wall was much greater.

73. Redlands Spring is a permanent spring with excellent water. Later its water was piped to the mouth of the canyon, where prospector and miner Harry Briggs lived for many years.

74. From the summit of the pass at the headwater of Redlands Canyon, they could see the general area where they had found water—Arrastre Spring—but they could not see the spring itself because a ridge blocked their view.

75. Mesquite Well.

76. They found Captain Culverwell on February 9, 1850. He had returned to Eagle Borax Spring with the others but left with the Earharts to follow the Wades south. Apparently he was unable to catch up or keep up with the Earharts and decided to return to Eagle Borax Spring only to die on the way back, probably a few days before Manly and Rogers discovered his corpse.

77. Accounting for all the wagons is difficult because there is not enough data. The parties had remained at Eagle Borax Spring for an unknown length of time. Then some or all had moved south to Bennetts Well. There are two likely reasons for the move: the oxen would have eaten all the grass around Eagle Borax Spring and the water would have been markedly better at the well later named for Asabel Bennett. Archeological evidence confirms Indians occupied this latter site, collecting mesquite beans, and dug the well long before the arrival of forty-niners.

78. The date was February 10, 1850.

79. These are the Black Mountains, also called the Coffin Mountains. North of Furnace Creek Wash this range is called the Funeral Mountains.

80. There are now many mesquite trees around Bennetts Well, but the lack of shade then does not mean mesquite trees were absent in 1850; mesquite, a deciduous tree, is leafless in the winter.

81. The rise from the valley floor to the summit of Telescope Peak is one of the greatest sustained elevational gains on Earth. No wonder many of the lost emigrants thought they must be at the base of the formidable Sierra Nevada.

82. Mrs. Arcane was five months pregnant, but probably only her husband and Mrs. Bennett would have known this. Julia was carried to term but died nineteen days later. Had she been born prematurely, she probably would not have survived as long.

83. The nearer route was via Galena Canyon or the south fork (the dogleg fork) of Six Springs Canyon.

84. The party could not have gone from the valley floor to Arrastre Spring in one day, particularly driving oxen and caring for sick children. The distance is over sixteen miles with a vertical rise of 5,790 feet. There must have been an additional camp not mentioned.

85. The vantage point was two miles from Arrastre Spring. In the September 1888 issue of "From Vermont to California," Manly said it was about "a quarter of a mile to the summit" (likely meaning 1,320 vertical feet) when he and Rogers first

viewed the Sierra Nevada. Manly's editor inadvertently converted a vertical distance to a horizontal one.

86. The Panamint Crest—Telescope Peak, Sentinel Peak, and Porter Peak.

87. They are the Black Mountains now.

88. History does not tell us who uttered these words. Had either Bennett or Arcane uttered this phrase, Manly would have given appropriate credit. Some writers think that Mrs. Bennett gave Death Valley its name, others that Mrs. Brier did, but there is no evidence to support these views. Manly is quoted (in the *Pioneer* on April 28, 1877) as having exclaimed, when his group exited the valley, "There lies Death Valley." The name first appeared in print on March 16, 1861, in the *Los Angeles Star.* Despite the name, only one of the emigrants died in Death Valley proper—Captain Culverwell.

CHAPTER XI

1. They followed an Indian trail that contours south from Arrastre Spring to Redlands Canyon. The trail is on the uphill (northwest) side of Striped Butte.

2. The bottom of Ox-Jump Fall is now filled with rocks from a ramp built in 1860 by Bennett and his companions (see Epilogue) and improved in 1867 by the U.S. Army to get their horses up the dry fall. Most of the ramp is now gone because gullywashers periodically plummet down Redlands Canyon.

3. They entered the Slate Range via Fish Canyon and camped at or above Reverend Brier's "Silent Sepulchre," not on today's Manly Pass.

4. They had camped above the mouth of Indian Joe Canyon; the lake is Searles Lake.

5. Their camp in the Argus Range was at 4,300 feet in a basin at the headwater of west Wilson Canyon where the dry gulch called Sweetwater Creek emerges.

6. Deadman Canyon.

7. The water in Paxton Lake is potable, but barely so.

8. Middle of Indian Wells Valley.

9. Indian Wells Spring is at Homestead, at the base of the Sierra Nevada, five miles north of Freeman Junction.

10. This unusual rock formation is called Robbers Roost. Later, on February 25, 1874, Tiburcio Vasquez would use these rhyolite monoliths as his rendezvous site for a raid on the stage station at Freeman Junction.

11. They crossed the El Paso Mountains through Last Chance Canyon.

12. They camped on a small playa in the hills two miles southwest of the mouth of Last Chance Canyon. The lake he mentions is Koehn Dry Lake, which is usually dry but has extremely salty water in wet years. They did not traverse the mountains through today's Red Rock Canyon; instead they followed the Horse Thief Trail in Last Chance Canyon.

13. Desert Spring, also called the Willow Corral. This is the western edge of the Great Basin, but they still had to cross the Mojave Desert, which stretched fifty-five miles to the south.

14. In his diary, Lorton dates the defection from Captain Hunt's leadership as November 3rd. Some of the wagons did proceed westward on the 4th.

15. Located near California City.

16. They camped at Barrel Springs on the San Andreas Fault, four miles southeast of Palmdale.

17. Telescope Peak is visible from here on clear days, which are now rare.

18. Manly's editor for the book made significant changes to the original text found in the September through December 1888 issues of "From Vermont to California," sometimes adding sentences, with the apparent goal of making the story more colorful. For instance, in the November issue of his original text, Manly simply said, "We kept on down to the little brook where Rogers and I tried the experiment of 'eating crow,' and made camp." The following passage is an embellishment by the editor.

19. They had taken the path over the "point of hill" and were resting at the meadow (and spring) on the west side of it.

20. The mission *asistencia,* one-half mile south of Castaic Junction, was then being used as the residence for the family of Don José Salazar.

21. This is Rancho San Francisco, not San Francisquito.

22. They were crossing the notoriously steep San Fernando Pass, 2.5 miles south of Newhall.

23. These two families had gone to Mt. Misery but had turned back and followed Captain Hunt down the Old Spanish Trail.

24. A saddletree is the wooden frame of a packsaddle; in this case nothing more than two X-frames joined by slats like those currently used to lash loads on the backs of burros.

CHAPTER XII

1. It appears this account is unedited by Manly or his editor. McMahon eventually studied medicine and became a doctor.

2. Fort Bridger, on the Black Fork River in southwestern Wyoming, is on the Oregon–California Trail. Jim Bridger and Louis Vasquez started constructing this fort in late 1842 and completed it in 1843. The fort had several crude buildings and served as a trading post for emigrants and Indians and became an important destination point along the trail. Bridger's first fort was on the Green River and his second and third forts were on the same site on the Black Fork River.

3. If a horse is ridden hard or has been without water for some time and then drinks copious amounts of cold water and is not made to exercise, it can get a crippling inflammation in the hooves. This happens because the hooves are not flexible and cannot expand.

4. The fort, on the Uinta River, was first built in winter 1832–1833 by Kit Carson near a Ute village (near today's Whiterocks, seventeen miles west of Vernal, Utah). Then, in 1837 or early 1838, Antoine Robidoux built another fort nearby. Fort Uinta was strategically located on an important trade route between Taos, New Mexico, and Utah.

5. The Uinta Range is sixty miles east of Salt Lake City. These east-west trending mountains include the highest mountain in the state—Kings Peak (13,528 feet).

6. According to the Mormon Church, the Danites were a secretive group of Mormons organized in 1838 by Sampson Avard, who was attempting to use the

Church to gain personal power. Members took oaths of secrecy, and their avowed purpose was to defend the Church against mob persecution. Avard tried to manipulate the Danites to carry out violent retribution. The organization, according to the Church, disbanded the same year it organized. The literature is replete with claims that the Danites were sanctioned by the Church and operated in secrecy to carry out acts of revenge, but the Church denied this. Danites are often equated to the feared destroying angels.

7. Scotts River, Siskiyou County, where gold was discovered in 1850. One nugget found here weighed 141 ounces.

8. In 1863 Dr. McMahon was to apply for a Solano County medical position to care for sick indigents. The annual salary was $925; he did not get the job.

CHAPTER XIII

1. This chapter is a major rewrite of Manly's text in the January, February, and March 1889 issues of "From Vermont to California." Much of the route these emigrants traveled is within Nellis Air Force Range's Area 51 and the Nevada Test Site west of Area 51, and therefore inaccessible for historical fieldwork.

2. Knoxville and Galesburg are near the western edge of Illinois.

3. In winter 1848–1849 members of John Frémont's Fourth Expedition resorted to cannibalism, as did members of the Donner party the winter before. These tragedies were known to the emigrants, and they were eager to take steps to prevent becoming snowbound.

4. Old Bill Williams died March 14, 1849, several months before the Jayhawkers arrived at Salt Lake, so it must have been another Williams who drew their map.

5. At least one member of the group had a copy of Frémont's 1848 *Map of Oregon and Upper California* depicting an east-west mountain range as the southern border of his Great Basin. Even though Frémont had noted "these mountains are not explored" and had also labeled the region through which the cutoff route supposedly went as "unexplored," some evidently thought they would find water flowing south from the canyons of Frémont's mythical mountain range.

6. The man consulted and hired was Captain Jefferson Hunt (not John Hunt, his son). Captain Hunt had traversed the Salt Lake–Los Angeles Trail two times prior to guiding the wagon train. He had gone to southern California in December 1847 to buy supplies, and in May 1848 members of his company had arrived back at Salt Lake with a wagon. His was the first wagon reputed to traverse the Salt Lake–Los Angeles Trail.

7. Hobble Creek, where they gathered, is sixty-one miles south of Salt Lake City.

8. Captain Orson K. Smith was leading a company of packers destined for the California goldfields via Walker Pass.

9. An Indian trail descended into Headwaters Wash and followed the stream that drains into Beaver Dam Wash. Near the trail, on the south side of Headwaters Wash, Henry W. Bigler carved his initials and the date November 3, 1849. The initials are still visible, but the date has completely eroded away. A branch of the main trail leaves the wash one-half mile west of Tunnel Springs and ascends a side draw,

where William Thomas Osborn carved "OSbORN 49" on a rock wall during a scouting trip to find a feasible route for the wagons—he found none.

10. Mt. Misery is, as mentioned earlier, northeast of Beaver Dam Wash between Pine Park Canyon and Headwaters Wash near the Nevada–Utah state line.

11. Mr. Naylor died November 9, 1849, of tuberculosis (consumption).

12. That is, from almost every elevation where a good sighting could be obtained.

13. Only in wet years or after rainstorms are these playas covered with water. The water is usually only an inch or two deep, but it may cover hundreds of acres, sometimes vanishing within days. This camp was probably on the western edge of Groom Lake in Area 51.

14. When Manly and other scouts climbed high peaks along the trail, they saw snow-covered mountains far to the west. These included the Panamint Range and several other mountain ranges north of the Panamints.

15. Jim Martin was one of the Georgia–Mississippi boys (Bug-smashers). Martin's Pass is thought to be Towne Pass, nineteen miles north-northeast of Telescope Peak in the Panamint Range.

16. Spring Mountains, Nevada.

17. Glauber's salt (hydrated sodium sulfate) was used as a mild laxative. Johann Rudolph Glauber (1604–1668), a Bavarian alchemist, discovered it.

18. The Jayhawkers paralleled the Amargosa River southward, and Sheldon Young records they camped from December 13 through December 18, 1849, at one spot along the river. There they shod their oxen and sent out scouts to explore what Young called "damn hard looking country." Most of the time the Amargosa River is dry; during parts of the year, it is an upside-down river where water flows underground just below the sand. The scouts discovered a low pass through the mountains west of today's Death Valley Junction. The wagons reached the pass via a gentle grade and rolled over the mountains where Furnace Creek Wash funneled them into Death Valley.

19. This ephemeral lake forms in wet years.

20. Manly's version of this encounter in the February 1888 issue of "From Vermont to California" described the old man thusly: "He was entirely blind and so crippled that he moved around about on all fours"; it did not include comparison to a beast.

21. This camp was at Jayhawker Well near McClean Spring, the headwaters of Salt Creek. The water from the spring is still too salty for humans or livestock. Two hundred feet east of the spring, though, they discovered potable water in a shallow well that had been dug by Indians. The potable (barely so) water is within two feet of the surface. Today, birds and animals rely on this well for their water.

22. See Genesis 19:26.

23. They used the wagon wood because it was tinder dry; they may also have constructed a crude smokehouse with the planks.

24. This sentence does not appear in the January 1889 issue of "From Vermont to California," and it appears that Manly's editor was overly influenced by the hyperbole in Edward Coker's reminiscences (see Chapter XIV). The Jayhawkers per se were not "almost skeletons," nor were they despondent as implied here, although two older men—Mr. Fish and Mr. Isham—who traveled with the Brier group after leaving Death Valley were rapidly fading and would die about a week later.

25. Some of the emigrants thought the Panamint Range was the Sierra Nevada, which is actually eighty miles to the west. Others thought the Panamints were the "Coast Mountains" depicted on Frémont's 1848 map. From Jayhawker Well the Martin party (also called the Georgia-Mississippi boys or the Bug-smashers) followed the well-trodden Indian trail that led them toward Martin's Pass (probably today's Towne Pass).

26. From Jayhawker Well, the emigrants would not have been able to see Towne Pass, but a prominent Indian trail did go westward from the well, skirted the toe of Tucki Mountain, and headed for Emigrant Canyon and Towne Pass. Another trail continued north to an unnamed spring we call Juliet Spring in honor of Juliet Brier, and on to Triangle Spring. (Juliet Spring is unofficially called Palm Tree Spring in reference to a nonnative tree growing there.) This northern trail is the one the Brier party and Sheldon Young's group followed. When they reached Juliet Spring, they saw that the only reasonable pass through the mountain range was the low gap now called Towne Pass and headed for it. Sheldon Young tells us they had a dry camp this night, which means they did not stop to camp at the spring.

27. The beeline course from Juliet Spring to Towne Pass went through the northern edge of the sand dunes.

28. There is not sufficient data to identify this lone camper. "The summit" refers to the summit of the pass—Towne Pass—and not the summit of a mountain—Pinto Peak.

29. They would now have been in the northern part of Panamint Valley, about where Highway 190 crosses the valley.

30. This Indian camp was also called Horse Bones Camp because John and Juliet Brier mentioned seeing horse bones here. It is now called Warm Sulphur Springs and is five miles north of Ballarat. The good water could refer to the flow from Hall Canyon, which in wet years reaches the valley floor. However, the water at Warm Sulphur Spring is also potable, and historical evidence shows this area was used as an Indian village.

31. Manly and Rogers came upon the holes the Brier party had dug in upper Fish Canyon, but Manly and Rogers found no water in them and assumed that those who went before had likewise failed to find any. But the Brier party did find water in the damp sand at the base of a dry, vertical fall, an area Reverend Brier named "A Silent Sepulchre." They used the limited amount of water, so none was left when Manly and Rogers arrived there. This was not near the summit of the range, although it was in the upper part of the canyon. Manly also assumed this was the Jayhawker party, but such was not the case. A number of men had joined Brier: Carter, Isham, Fish, Grosscup, Vance, and Gould.

The Jayhawkers entered the north end of Searles Valley via an Indian trail that crosses the Slate Range where it joins the Argus Range. This pass is 1.3 miles northwest of where the Trona-Wildrose Road crosses the Slate Range. Sheldon Young recorded their passage in his log on January 11, 1850: "This day [we] went over a range of mountains [Slate Range], very steep and difficult....In this valley is a lake [Searles Lake]." Young was among those who, on January 12th, found that the lake "proves to be salt." Other Jayhawkers stayed on the Indian trail on the west side of the valley and found freshwater in Great Falls Basin, two miles north of Indian Joe Canyon—the site of Providence Spring.

32. Searles Lake in Searles Valley. The brine from this lake is currently being mined; over two billion dollars' worth of chemicals have been extracted from the lake. The Briers mention, in letters and articles, that they exited from a canyon (Isham Canyon, Slate Range) and went to the lake thinking it contained fresh water. The Jayhawkers, on the other hand, crossed the northern end of the Slate Range. Some came straight down Searles Valley and met the Brier party at the edge of Searles Lake. Mrs. Brier went to pray in the shade at Point of Rocks while several men went into the Argus Range looking for water. About five miles north, Deacon Richards found water in Indian Joe Canyon, and Mrs. Brier named this water source Providence Spring.
33. Isham traveled with the Brier party, not the Jayhawkers. When those at Providence Spring heard he had not come into camp, some went back with water.
34. The Brier party did not cross Searles Valley but went directly south to the lake, as is clear in "From Vermont to California." (The Indian trails they unfortunately departed from led straight across the valley to water in Great Falls Basin and Indian Joe Spring, both year-round water sources. They evidently forgot the truism that Indian trails lead from water to water.)
35. Some trail buffs and historians have incorrectly assumed Providence Spring was the little stream found by those "who bore farthest to the right." Not so. Providence Spring flows out of Indian Joe Canyon, which also has large granite boulders. Those who bore farthest to the right, who crossed Young Pass and kept on an Indian trail, found a little stream in Great Falls Basin, which has piles of tremendous rocks.
36. The Sierra Nevada is not visible from Searles Valley. They knew the Sierra Nevada was before them because they saw the massif after they crossed Towne Pass.
37. They had entered the Argus Range via east Wilson Canyon, again following a prominent Indian trail. From the pass into this elevated basin there would have been a clear view of the Sierra Nevada.
38. "This valley" is Indian Wells Valley. They descended the western flank of the Argus Range via boulder-strewn Deadman Canyon. The editor next refers to this valley as "the plain," but they are the same place.
39. Paxton Lake, a small brackish lake, near the mouth of Deadman Canyon. The water is potable but barely so.
40. John Rogers found the thin sheets of ice in this area.
41. Indian Wells Spring.
42. Indian Horse Thief Trail.
43. This harsh criticism was not totally justified. Reverend Brier suffered from diabetes and wasted away from 175 to 75 pounds during this trip. His wife had no choice but to step forward and assume leadership so her family would survive. Because Reverend Brier was a vocal proponent of the cutoff, he became the scapegoat when conditions were bad, but the decision to take the cutoff was a group decision.
44. This paragraph is not in "From Vermont to California," and later in this chapter there are touching examples of sharing water.
45. Captain Asa Haines's contingent was a day ahead. Manly and Rogers caught up with them in Last Chance Canyon.

46. It is five miles from Indian Wells Spring to Freeman Junction, where the trail divided and one branch went to Walker Pass.
47. They had traversed the El Paso Mountains via Last Chance Canyon.
48. This oasis is commonly called the Willow Corral, but its official name is Desert Spring.
49. The San Gabriel Mountains.
50. They were in the Mojave Desert, north of Edwards Air Base.
51. This accusation may not be justified, as a kit fox or a coyote could have stolen it.
52. William Robinson died at or near Barrel Springs on January 28, 1850. There are conflicting accounts documenting his death (see "The Trunk is Bunk" by LeRoy Johnson in "Proceedings, Fifth Death Valley Conference on History and Prehistory, March 4-7, 1999").
53. Captain Doty was one who kept his rifle. His family donated it to the National Park Service, and it is on display in the Death Valley Visitor Center.
54. Soledad Pass (5,179 feet) is where they crossed the San Gabriel Mountains.
55. Manly already mentioned five who died: Naylor at Mt. Misery, Utah; Captain Culverwell in Death Valley; Father Fish in the Slate Range; William Isham in Searles Valley; and William Robinson near or at Barrel Spring, Antelope Valley. (He did not count Naylor as one who died on the desert.) Nine members of the the Pinney-Savage party died (all but Pinney and Savage), but where they died is unknown. Fortunately William B. Lorton at least recorded the names of the eleven in his diary: "[November] 18th a party of 10 [11] have concluded to go still westward. Chas. McDermet, Jno. [sic] Adams, Savage, Webster, Pinney, 2 Wares, Baker, Semore, Allen," later adding in "Willey" between the lines. Only one of the thirteen who died in the desert died in Death Valley proper.
56. This is the Rancho San Francisco, not the Rancho San Francisquito, which is in the Los Angeles basin.
57. Mission San Buenaventura is in the city of Ventura.
58. In California, oxen were in demand for pulling heavy wagons.
59. They were a little over four hundred miles from San Francisco.
60. The Wade family was not associated with the Jayhawkers (Manly knew this, but his editor did not). The Wades were first allied with the Bennett–Arcane wagon train but usually traveled a day behind them. Mr. Wade drove south out of Death Valley before Manly and Rogers returned to the families.
61. Mission San Luis Rey de Francia is forty miles north of San Diego and five miles east of Oceanside.
62. In the original edition, Manly met with Goller and ventured into the desert in 1862. This error is due to faulty memory or typesetting; we know from contemporaneous newspaper accounts and other sources that these events occurred in 1860.
    Goller's companion found these gold nuggets in the El Paso Mountains, possibly in Last Chance Canyon or one of the gulches that drain into it. This find became known as the "Lost Goller," and many prospectors, including Goller and Manly, searched for it in vain. It is conceivable that a cloudburst created a gullywasher that covered the gold nuggets Goller's partner found.
    In 1893 hundreds of prospectors converged on these mountains, where they extracted small quantities of gold. In 1930 another influx of miners arrived, and records show they staked at least thirteen placer gold claims in Last Chance

Canyon, the canyon the forty-niners went down, and Bonanza Gulch, which drains into the canyon. None of these claims was rich. It is possible the Lost Goller was found and exploited in 1893 or 1930.

Manly's search for the Lost Goller was incidental to a search-and-rescue mission to the Panamint Mountains looking for Charles Alvord, who had been abandoned there by his prospecting companions (see Epilogue).

CHAPTER XIV

1. We do not know if the editor reviewed Erkson's reminiscences with Manly.
2. The Mormon Church started a coinage system in late 1849, which Brigham Young personally supervised. They minted $2.50, $5.00, $10.00, and $20.00 gold coins. In 1851 the U.S. Mint assayed the $10.00 coin; it had only $8.52 worth of gold. Soon bankers and merchants discounted the Mormon coins 20 to 25 percent. Today, Mormon coins rated "rare fine" and "extra fine" are valued up to $90,000.
3. Captain Hunt had not become confused. This episode took place south of Beaver River, not Mountain Meadows, which is one hundred miles to the south. We know from Addison Pratt's diary and other firsthand accounts that Captain Hunt had the concurrence of the wagon train to attempt a shortcut he had heard about that started down the Beaver River. After paralleling the river for twelve miles, they camped. The next day they turned south, away from the river, and traveled another twelve miles, where they had a dry camp while Hunt scouted ahead. While Hunt was scouting, about forty wagons turned around and returned to the river. When Hunt returned two days later, he and his horse were almost dead from lack of water. All the wagons then returned to the main trail and proceeded south. This aborted shortcut caused considerable dissension, and some in the train were so distressed they threatened to kill Captain Hunt.
4. About 1997, Jerry Freeman found an inscription on top of a rock outcrop along the Shoal Creek road. In addition to the date, the inscription has Erkson's initials and part of his name pecked in the rock. It is not likely to be authentic, however.
5. Charles Rollin (1661–1741), French humanist and rector at the University of Paris, wrote the twelve-volume *Histoire Ancienne,* a well-known treatise on ancient history that was translated into many languages. Some of the translations were condensed into fewer volumes.
6. St. George, in southwestern Utah, is at the confluence of these two rivers. The Virgin River, in turn, emptied into the Colorado River, at a location now under Lake Mead.
7. The Muddy River begins at Muddy Spring, six miles northwest of Moapa, Nevada, and flows into the Overton Arm of Lake Mead. The water picks up fine clay in the riverbed, which accounts for the river's name.
8. Before departing on the southern route, William Philipps (Manly spelled it Philips) and his brother John, of Mineral Point, sold about a hundred pounds of flour, some bacon, and other victuals to Manly, who paid for them and gave them to his destitute friends. Now that he was short of food, Mr. Philipps must have rued the day he sold those supplies.

9. This may have been Resting Spring, east of Tecopa, in California.

10. The Gruwell-Derr wagon train—the first train to traverse the Salt Lake–Los Angeles Trail—left Utah Lake a day ahead of the Hunt wagon train. They had hired a Mexican guide who had apparently traversed the trail.

11. Erkson's party was now headed north to the mines. The "long, tedious hill" was the notorious San Fernando Pass. There were five ranchos in California called San Francisquito, but this was not one of them. This was the Rancho San Francisco that the Death Valley parties incorrectly called Rancho San Francisquito.

12. Edward Coker traveled with the Georgia-Mississippi boys (Bug-smashers), but he probably did not start west with them, since he hailed from New York City. This account is filled with hearsay and garbled reminiscences and should be read and interpreted accordingly.

13. Manly mentions that a Mr. Gould accompanied Fish in Death Valley, and Isham may have been with these men.

14. This paragraph is a garbled conglomeration, virtually impossible to unscramble, of information Coker learned years later and wove into a fabulous story.

15. He left the Brier family—not families—at Jayhawker Well in Death Valley.

16. It is very possible Isham did look like a "living skeleton" when Coker last saw him at Jayhawker Well. However, Isham lived several more days before he succumbed to thirst in Searles Valley.

17. They were not at Owens Lake but at Owens Little Lake, twenty-eight miles south of Owens Lake. In the March 1889 issue of "From Vermont to California," Manly relates that the Martin party, of which Coker was a member, "came through by Little Owen's Lake and across Walker's Pass."

18. Owens Lake is several miles across—too wide to ford; Owens Little Lake is only a few hundred feet wide.

19. The "big trail" was the Indian Horse Thief Trail that both Joseph Reddeford Walker and John Frémont had traversed. Walker's Pass was shown, but not labeled, on Frémont's 1848 map.

20. The junction of the two rivers is now inundated by Lake Isabella.

21. They traversed the Greenhorn Mountains (the southern part of the Sierra Nevada) over an Indian trail. Five hundred Indians is a huge exaggeration, of course. Also, this was not December 1849, but mid-January 1850.

22. Porterville in Tulare County, first a stage depot, became a town in 1864; it was named for Royal Porter Putnam.

23. Millerton in Fresno County, also called Rootville, is now submerged by Millerton Lake.

24. Agua Fria, on Agua Fria Creek in Mariposa County, is six miles west of Mariposa. Its gravels showed great promise at first, but they were soon worked out. George W. B. Evans recorded in his diary that twelve men arrived at Agua Fria on January 29, 1850, and ten more arrived on February 9—a total of twenty-two men.

   Evans traveled overland via a route through Mexico and arrived at Agua Fria on October 29, 1849. He never struck it rich, and because of declining health he abandoned gold grubbing. He died December 16, 1850, only 31 years old, in Sacramento. Fortunately, his diary survived.

CHAPTER XV

1. Mission San Buenaventura stands in the city of Ventura. For an in-depth history of each of the California missions, see *The California Missions, A Pictorial History,* edited by Paul C. Johnson (Menlo Park, Calif.: Lane Book Co, 1964).
2. Mission Santa Barbara is in Santa Barbara.
3. Mission Santa Inés is near the town of Solvang, and Mission San Luis Obispo de Tolosa is located in downtown San Luis Obispo.
4. Mission San Miguel Arcángel is in the small town of San Miguel on the east side of Highway 101, nine miles north of Paso Robles. Mission Nuestra Señora de la Soledad is located one mile west of Highway 101, three miles south of Soledad.
5. Mission San Juan Bautista is in San Juan Bautista, about seventeen miles north of Soledad.
6. Pueblo de San José de Guadalupe, founded November 29, 1777, was the first Spanish pueblo established in California. San Jose is the oldest and now one of the largest cities in the state.
7. The women's performance in the tragic Donner Party tragedy of 1846–1847 is a similar example of heroic exploits by women at that time.
8. For a list of the thirteen dead, see endnote 55, Chapter XIII.
9. The coast redwood *(Sequoia sempervirens).*
10. Mission San José de Guadalupe, located fifteen miles north of San Jose near Fremont, was probably California's most prosperous mission. It was a popular resting spot for argonauts venturing from San Francisco to the goldfields.
11. Merced City was a short-lived settlement north of the confluence of the Merced and San Joaquin Rivers. Today's Merced is about twenty-four miles east of the rivers' juncture.
12. *Piojo* literally translated means louse (a small, flat, wingless, bloodsucking insect). Probably these were wood ticks.
13. Big Oak Flat, Tuolumne County, is two and a half miles southwest of Groveland on Highway 120. It was first prospected by James D. Savage, who had worked for John Sutter.
14. A male donkey is called a jackass, often contracted to jack.
15. Garrote, Tuolumne County, was settled by Mexicans in 1850. *Garrote* is the Spanish word for execution by strangulation. In 1850 a murderer was hung in the mining camp; hence the name. In 1875 the town changed its name to Groveland.
16. In the Garrote area, reportedly $25 million in gold was extracted (about 107,139 avoirdupois pounds of gold, at $16 per troy ounce—the value of gold in 1850; one troy ounce equals 0.9115 avoirdupois ounces).
17. Hangtown, now Placerville, was first called Dry Diggings. There are contradictory stories behind the nickname of Hangtown, but reliable sources do document a triple hanging there on January 22, 1849. On April 9, 1850, the town's post office was established and Dry Diggings became Placerville.
18. Gold Lake did not exist. It is not known who created the hoax, but many prospectors were taken in by the fabulous story and untold numbers flocked to the Feather River area.

19. John Marshall discovered gold in a millrace on January 24, 1848, at Coloma, where he was building a sawmill for John Sutter. This discovery started the California gold rush of 1849.

20. Georgetown is about fifteen miles north of Placerville on the divide between the Middle and South Forks of the American River. The first strike here yielded about twenty thousand dollars' worth of gold in six weeks.

21. Georgetown is in El Dorado County, the county immediately south of Placer County.

22. Greenwood, El Dorado County, was apparently named for John Greenwood, a noted trapper and hunter. He established a trading post in Long Valley in 1848 that was called Lewisville in 1850. The name was changed to Greenwood when a post office came to town.

23. Salmon Falls (now inundated by Folsom Lake), was on the South Fork of the American River a few miles upstream from the junction with the Middle Fork. Here the Indians harvested salmon during the fall runs.

24. A vara is a Spanish yard—2.781 feet. This was probably a square lot, 50 varas on each side, making it 19,335 square feet, or 0.44 acres. Today this lot would be worth several million dollars.

25. Yellow fever is an acute, infectious viral disease spread by mosquitoes. Early stages include sudden fever, pain in the head and extremities, and sometimes chills. Later the skin turns yellow and the patient repeatedly vomits. There is no treatment other than absolute rest, keeping cool, and drinking liquids. Today it is considered a "grave" disease; in the 1800s it was even more so.

26. The road from Panama to Las Cruces, on the Chagres River, was used by the Spanish in the sixteenth and seventeenth centuries and paved with cobbles. Spanish galleons unloaded their Peruvian plunder at Panama and hauled it over this road to Portobelo (also Porto Bello and Puerto Bello) on the Caribbean Sea, where it was again loaded on galleons and then taken to Spain. Another trail used by the argonauts to reach the Chagres River went from Panama to Gorgona. The Las Cruces trail had the advantage of being a few miles shorter and readily passable in the rainy season. Both of these important transfer points are now under Gatun Lake, part of the Panama Canal waterway.

27. Their trip down the Chagres River was about forty miles.

28. "Malaria" was used to mean bad air, as well as the disease spread by mosquitoes. The foul air in and around the port city of Chagres was notorious. Hubert H. Bancroft said the town was "surrounded by heaps of filthy offal…[and] greasy, stagnant pools."

29. The fortress was actually San Lorenzo Castle, a fort overlooking the port at the entrance of the Chagres River. (San Juan de Ulloa is an island fort in the Gulf of Mexico and was built to protect Veracruz.)

30. The federal mint at New Orleans, Louisiana, opened in 1838; it closed in 1909.

31. The price of gold was set by Congress in 1850 at $20.67. A hundred years later, without federal controls, it rose to $40.25. In 1980 it reached an all-time high of $594.90; by 2000 it had dropped to $272.65.

32. Lake Pontchartrain, six hundred square miles, lies between New Orleans and the Mississippi River.

33. Peoria is on the Illinois River; the wagon trip to Galena, in the northwestern corner of Illinois, was 270 miles.
34. Foolscap paper is large-sized paper, measuring thirteen by sixteen inches.
35. The first issue of "From Vermont to California" was published in *The Santa Clara Valley*, a horticulture and viticulture magazine, in June 1887, and the final issue appeared in July 1890. For annotated versions of the issues dealing with the rescue of the Bennett-Arcane party, see *Escape from Death Valley* by LeRoy and Jean Johnson. The editors have located 34 of the 38 issues: still missing are January 1888, April 1889, December 1889, and July 1890.

Chapter XVI

1. Work on the Panama Railroad began on May 2, 1850; the first train crossed the isthmus on January 28, 1855.
2. Chagres, on the Caribbean Sea, is the city port where travelers started their sixty-mile journey across the Isthmus of Panama to the Pacific Ocean. From here they took a forty-mile boat trip up the Chagres River and then hired mules and horses, or walked, to Panama on the Pacific Ocean, where they boarded ships for California. Prior to January 1849, trans-isthmus travelers were transported up the river in *bungos,* small boats and canoes that were paddled, poled, and towed up the river. Their destination was either Gorgona or Las Cruces. It took three days to cover the forty miles to Gorgona and slightly longer to go the additional four miles to Las Cruces. By summer 1850, steamers had replaced the *bungos,* but the paddle-wheelers' draft stopped them a couple miles short of Gorgona.
3. Spain founded Panama in 1519 as a port for gold-laden galleons from Peru to unload their cargoes. The gold was then packed over the Isthmus of Panama and reloaded onto galleons for transport to Spain. Destroyed by English buccaneer Henry Morgan in 1671, Panama was rebuilt three years later.
4. Offing is a nautical term with several meanings. In this case, it means they were sufficiently offshore and did not have to be concerned about shallow water.
5. Prior to the Revolutionary War, Britain had transported fifty thousand criminals to the American colonies. After the war, British prisons were again overflowing, and in May 1787, eleven ships left Britain loaded with criminals and settlers for New South Wales, now part of Australia. They arrived in Sydney Cove in January 1788, establishing a settlement and a prison. In 1849 the last shipment of prisoners arrived, and that same year, freed and escaped convicts began emigrating to California. Creating some criminal alliances, Sydney (or Sidney) Ducks allegedly used arson as a means of extortion, setting fires in one section of San Francisco while looting other sections. The city lacked effective law enforcement, and private citizens organized the city's first Vigilance Committee in 1851. They arrested ninety-one men, hanged four (one was from Sydney), and deported fourteen others to Australia.
6. Marysville is on the Yuba River near its confluence with the Feather River. First settled in 1842 as a ranch, the present city was laid out in the winter of 1849–1850. The city was named in honor of one of the survivors of the Donner tragedy: Mary Murphy Covillaud.

7. Downieville was in fact named for Major William Downie, not John Downie. By 1851 it reportedly had a population of five thousand. Around $15 million in gold was mined in the immediate area. One sixty-foot-square claim yielded $12,900 in eleven days.

Goodyears Bar, Sierra County, on the North Fork of the Yuba River, is named for Miles and Andrew Goodyear; it is located about five miles west of Downieville.

Nigger Tent was in Sierra County. There were several place names throughout California with pejorative names. Most, if not all, have been changed. This way station was about five miles below Goodyears Bar. On some early maps and reports the way station is called Negro Tent.

Parks Bar, Yuba County, where Highway 20 crosses the Yuba River, was first named for Dr. John Marsh, who discovered the bar in May 1848, opened a store there, and mined the gravel. In September 1848 David Parks also opened a store there, and his name prevailed. This bar was one of the richest in California: in 1850 five men washed 525 pounds of gold from the bar in a few days. In the late 1860s the town was covered with debris from the extremely destructive hydraulic mining upstream.

8. Wisconsin Flat and Hill, Placer County, are between the North and Middle Forks of the American River, twenty miles northeast of Auburn. A Tertiary-period river channel held the gold, which yielded $600 in only one day to three men. By 1855 the population was fifteen hundred, but after that it dwindled rapidly.

9. Drifting generally applies to hard-rock mining when the miner follows a vein. Here Manly is digging a horizontal shaft parallel to the bedrock, the overburden being an ancient riverbed. It was at the interface of the two strata that rich deposits of gold were found.

10. In 1851 the federal government created the U.S. Assay Office of Gold that allowed California to mint and issue gold ingots and coins until a federal mint could be established out West. This was the first and only time a state was allowed to do this. There were three denominations issued: $10, $20, and $50. Only the $50 coins were called "slugs." The total production of these coins is not known, but it is estimated that in the first three months of 1851, twelve thousand slugs— $600,000 worth—were minted. When the San Francisco Mint opened its doors on December 4, 1853, the Assay Office of Gold ceased production. Today a high-quality slug sells for around $35,000.

11. Undoubtedly Juanita was pregnant. Pregnancy is rarely mentioned in pioneer writing; Manly used a euphemism—condition—to describe her state.

12. John B. Weller (1812–1875) served as a federal representative from Ohio before he emigrated to California, where he served as a U.S. senator from 1852 to 1857.

13. Minnesota, Sierra County, was between the middle fork of the Yuba River and Kanaka Creek.

14. A Long Tom was a wooden trough about twelve feet long with baffles, or ridges, in the bottom board. The tom was set up at a slight angle and gold-bearing gravel was shoveled into the upper end while water cascaded down the trough. The heavy gold sank to the bottom of the slurry and was caught in the bottom ridges. Nuggets and large flakes were manually removed and the fine gold dust could be retrieved with mercury.

15. Nevada City was first called Deer Creek after the site where the first strikes were found in 1849. By the fall of 1850 the population had swelled to six thousand. In September of that year, one fortunate miner found a nugget weighing almost four hundred pounds.

16. In 1851 or 1852 three prospectors discovered placer gold in a small stream in Nevada County. One, on a trip to Nevada City for supplies, boasted about the discovery and when he returned the next day about a hundred prospectors followed him to the claim. The horde did not find gold, so they named the creek "Humbug," and the name eventually stuck to the town that sprang up when hydraulic mining began there. When the town got a post office in 1857, it was renamed North Bloomfield.

17. Bloody Run, Nevada County, earned its name because of the numerous murders committed there.

18. Old-growth sugar pine *(Pinus lambertiana)* was prized for construction because of its straight grain and easy workability.

19. Snow Tent, Nevada County, is two miles southeast of Moores Flat.

20. The fact that Manly and his partners split these boards from logs twelve and sixteen feet long attests to this wood's straight grain. Vast numbers of these trees were logged for shake shingles because the wood was easy to split and produced high-quality shingles.

21. Moores Flat is in Nevada County.

22. French Corral, Nevada County, near the South Fork of Yuba River, was hydraulically mined.

23. Captain Hunt emigrated to San Bernardino and served in the state legislature from 1853 to 1858.

24. "Hall of Corruption" probably referred to city hall and was an ironic name for this saloon, since Californians held San Francisco's city government in low esteem. This was made clear by the two Vigilance Committees that formed in San Francisco in 1851 and 1856. (The 1852 San Francisco city directory does not list this establishment under "Drinking Saloons" and the San Francisco History Center, San Francisco Public Library, has no record of a saloon by this name.) "Soiled dove" is a euphemism for prostitute.

25. The pines were most likely Monterey pine *(Pinus radiata).* It is not now considered a timber species in the area, but in New Zealand, where it was introduced in the 1800s, it is one of the major commercial species. Bishop pine *(Pinus muricata),* a close relative of Monterey pine, also occurs at Monterey but is rare. Both species are indigenous to California.

26. Goats were introduced on Catalina Island in the 1820s to provide meat for ships' crews. The current owners of the island had hoped to remove all the goats and other exotic animals from the island. In the late 1990s the goat population was down to about two hundred; many of these were captured and removed by goat lovers. The peak goat population had been forty thousand.

27. A Spanish league is 2.6 miles.

28. In the 1852 presidential election, General Winfield Scott, a Whig candidate, ran against and lost to Franklin Pierce.

29. Henry Dalton (1803–1843) bought the 45,000-acre Santa Anita Ranch in 1847 for $2,700 and sold it seven years later for $40,000. In 1874 Elias J. (Lucky)

Baldwin bought the ranch for $200,000. Henry Dalton bought the 19,975-acre Rancho Azusa for $1,000 in December 1844. Both ranches were sometimes managed by his brother George.

30. French Camp in Calaveras County, two miles west of Murphys, was a short-lived mining camp.

31. On February 23, 1855, a financial panic forced Page, Bacon & Co. and Adams & Co.—two of the largest banks in California—to close their doors, never to open again. Wells Fargo & Co. survived this "Black Friday." Thousands of depositors lost the hopes and dreams embodied in the gold they had extracted from the riverbeds of California and deposited in these banks.

32. On December 14, 1858, Manly sold his business to Mr. and Mrs. Samuel Covington for $2,000. The sale included his 94-by-100-foot lot, the buildings, and business.

33. Bennett remarried; this is a reference to his second wife (see Epilogue).

34. Manly married Mary Jane Woods, of Lodi, California, on July 10, 1862. Apparently they had no children. They are buried in Woodbridge Cemetery.

CHAPTER XVII

1. These three mining camps—all in Nevada County—are near the Middle Fork of the Yuba River, four to five miles northeast of North Bloomfield. Major hydraulic mining occurred throughout this area.

2. Chip's Flat, Sierra County, was between the North and Middle Forks of the Yuba River.

3. Quicksilver is another name for mercury, a highly toxic liquid metallic element.

4. Amalgam is an alloy of mercury and another metal—in this case gold. Mercury boils at 357°C and gold boils at 2808°C; thus, heating the amalgam above mercury's boiling point drives off the mercury and leaves behind the gold. Prospectors tried to recycle the mercury because of its high cost, but considerable quantities of it escaped during the recovery process. Small quantities of amalgam could be separated by squeezing the alloy in a suede leather bag. The mercury flowed through the leather, leaving the gold in the bag; a small amount of mercury was retained with the gold, and this was burned off.

5. Australia and Van Diemen's Land (now Tasmania) served as penal colonies for the British Isles. Van Diemen's Land had a prison for serious offenders, and from 1834 to 1849 the island had a prison for boys. In the mid-1800s Britain stopped transporting their criminals to these remote outposts.

6. The Sydney (or Sidney) Ducks were criminals who had emigrated to San Francisco from Sydney, Australia. Some formed criminal gangs that prompted public-spirited citizens to organize the city's first Vigilance Committee in 1851; the vigilantes effectively dealt with the Sydney Ducks by lynching and deporting some of their leaders.

7. James P. Casey and Charles Cora were hung by the second (1856) Vigilance Committee on May 22, 1856. Casey, a member of the San Francisco Board of Supervisors, had murdered James King of William for printing an editorial critical of him. Cora murdered U.S. Marshal William Richardson. Casey and Cora were

being held in jail when the vigilantes seized them and took them to Fort Gunny-bags (see note 8). There they were tried, convicted, and sentenced to death.

8. The 1856 Vigilance Committee built Fort Gunny-bags. Two hundred of the committee's strongest men filled gunnysacks with sand; these were used to fortify an existing building. The barrier, five feet high (some say ten feet), thirty feet wide, and two hundred feet long, had portholes through which the vigilantes could fire cannons.

9. Manly wrote these words in 1889, in one of the serialized chapters in "From Vermont to California," which explains the apparent error. Forty-four years had passed from 1850 to 1894, when Manly published this book.

10. Railroad sleeping cars were initially called rolling palace cars.

11. Since this brief section on the Jayhawkers refers to Manly in the third person, it was most likely written by his editor.

12. A mite is a small contribution, or small work.

13. The original edition of this book had his birthdate as the 20th, which is incorrect, and spelled his name "Manley."

Edwards, E. I. *The Valley Whose Name Is Death*. Pasadena, Calif.: San Pasqual Press, 1940.

Evans, George W. B. *Mexican Gold Trail, The Journal of a Forty-Niner,* edited by Glenn S. Dumke. San Marino, Calif.: The Huntington Library, 1945.

Hafen, LeRoy R., and Ann W. Hafen. *Old Spanish Trail, Santa Fe to Los Angeles,* vol. 1 of *The Far West and The Rockies Historical Series*. Glendale, Calif.: Arthur H. Clark Co., 1954.

————, eds. *Journals of Forty-Niners, Salt Lake to Los Angeles,* vol. 2 of *The Far West and The Rockies Historical Series*. Glendale, Calif.: Arthur H. Clark Co., 1954.

Johnson, LeRoy and Jean, eds. *Escape from Death Valley, as Told by William Lewis Manly and Other '49ers*. Reno: Univ. of Nevada Press, 1987. (John Rogers' account and several of Reverend Brier's are in this book.)

Latta, Frank F. *Death Valley '49ers*. Salt Lake City, Utah: Publishers Press, 1979.

Lingenfelter, Richard E. *Death Valley & the Amargosa*. Berkeley: Univ. of California Press, 1986.

Long, Margaret. *The Shadow of the Arrow*. Rev. ed. Caldwell, Id.: Caxton Press, 1950. (Sheldon Young's account is Appendix A in the revised edition.)

Wheat, Carl I. "Trailing the Forty-Niners Through Death Valley." *Sierra Club Bulletin* 24 (June 1939):74–108.

Woodward, Arthur, ed. *The Jayhawkers' Oath and other Sketches*. Los Angeles: Warren F. Lewis, 1949.

Some subentries dealing with narratives are arranged chronologically. End-notes are referenced by page and note number [346 n3], and where necessary, chapter numbers are included [346 (II)n3]. Some place-name entries refer to passages in which Manly describes or refers to specific locations but does not refer to them by name.

Cabbage trees. *See* Joshua trees
California trail. *See* Oregon-
   California Trail
Californios, 109, 114-115, 167-168,
   175, 232, 243, 246, 269, 303
Cane Spring, NV, 344 n21
Carr, Fredrick William, 241
"Carr," Joseph P., negro servant, 241
Cattle. *See* oxen
Chagres (town), 276, 287, 362 n2
Chagres River, 271, 275, 361 n27
Children. *See by* family name
Chimney Rock, NE, 39, 338 n15
Cholera, 39, 63, 209, 338 n14
Churchill, W. W., 297
Cider mill, 3
Clay Bowl Spring (Furnace Creek
   Wash), 84, 344 n24
Cleveland, OH, 6
Clothing, 2, 3, 94, 176
Coal, 40, 339 n22
Coffin's Mountains. *See* Black
   Mountains
Coker, Edward, 243, 354 n24;
   account, 241-243, 359 n12 and 14
Colburn, Warren, 6, 334 (II)n2
Collins Spring (Ash Meadows),
   344 n22
Coloma, CA, 257
Clark, James, 308
Clark, Jerry, 313
Cornish, Nelson, 22, 26
Corral, Willow. *See* Desert Spring
Courthouse Rock, NE, 38, 338 n13
Craycroft, John, 450
Crow, 105
Crucez. *See* Las Cruces
Cuff (dog), 28, 158, 161, 168, 258

Culverwell, Richard I., 76, 82, 94,
   95, 124, 126, 134, 241, 286,
   350 n76, 351 n88
Crump, Old. *See* Oxen
Canoe. *See* Boats
Daboll, Nathan, 15, 335 (V)n1
Dallas, Charles, 35, 36, 37, 40, 44,
   299
Dalton, Henry, 304, 364 n29
Danites, 202, 352 n6
Deadman Canyon (Argus Range),
   118, 146
Death Valley, 86-90, 216-217,
   344 n1; description, 86, 87;
   named, 138, 350 n88
Death Valley wagon crossing, 89-91,
   344 n1-6
Deaths, 357 n55
Desert Spring (Fremont Valley),
   102, 117, 151, 223, 347 n35,
   349 n62, 351 n13, 357 n48
Devils Hole (Ash Meadows), 82,
   344 n22
Dilley, D. J., 27, 306, 309
Doty, Capt. Edward or Edwin, 86,
   100, 147, 207, 214, 218, 221, 224,
   230, 233, 357 n53
Downie, John, 290
Downieville, CA, 290, 292, 293
Eagle Borax Spring (Death Valley).
   See Bennett's long camp
Earhart (Earhard, Ehrhardt, Ahart)
   brothers, 69, 82, 95
East Wilson Canyon. See Wilson
   Canyon
El Paso Mountains, CA, 101,150,
   151, 222, 347 n38, 251 n11,
   357 n47